VISITORS TO THE COUNTRY HOUSE IN IRELAND AND BRITAIN

Visitors to the country house in Ireland and Britain

Welcome and unwelcome

Terence Dooley and Christopher Ridgway

EDITORS

FOUR COURTS PRESS

Typeset in 10.5 pt on 12.5 pt Ehrhardt by
Carrigboy Typesetting Services for
FOUR COURTS PRESS LTD
7 Malpas Street, Dublin 8, Ireland
www.fourcourtspress.ie
and in North America for
FOUR COURTS PRESS
c/o IPG, 814 N. Franklin St, Chicago, IL 60610

© The various contributors and Four Courts Press 2023

A catalogue record for this title is available from the British Library.

ISBN 978-1-80151-027-1

All rights reserved. No part of this publication may be reproduced, stored in or introduced into a retrieval system, or transmitted, in any form or by any means (electronic, mechanical, photocopying, recording, or otherwise), without the prior written permission of both the copyright owner and publisher of this book.

Printed in England
by CPI Antony Rowe, Chippenham, Wilts.

Contents

	LIST OF ABBREVIATIONS	7
	INTRODUCTION	9
1	Visitations: foes *Christopher Ridgway*	15
2	'I feel more like Cinderella, than anyone else you can imagine': Elizabeth Gaskell's visit to Chatsworth *Fran Baker*	52
3	Misplaced hospitality and practical implications: the northern tour of Thomas Sandby and Theodosius Forrest, August 1774 *Kerry Bristol*	75
4	Soup kitchens at English country houses, 1795–1914: a new perspective on elite landscapes *Philip J. Carstairs*	96
5	Knole and its visitors: from medieval episcopal palace to country seat, antiquarian curiosity and treasure house *John Coleman*	116
6	Gloomy inhospitality: limiting access to houses and country estates, 1719–1838 *Peter Collinge*	137
7	'By far the greatest & most perpetual source of happiness in my life has been, & is, seeing': Christopher Hussey's visits to country houses, 1920–70 *Oliver Cox*	157
8	'There seem to be many more people here than I thought we'd asked': building collections of visitors in the Irish country house *Ian d'Alton*	176
9	'An antient seat of a gentleman of Wales': the place of the *plas* in Thomas Pennant's *Tour in Wales* (1778–83) *Shaun Evans*	196

10	Visitors and visiting: a Kerry country house, 1912–39 *John Knightly*	220
11	Visitations: friendlies *Christopher Ridgway*	247
NOTES ON CONTRIBUTORS		265
INDEX		267

Abbreviations

BL	British Library
BM	British Museum
CHA	Castle Howard Archives
CSHIHE	Centre for the Study of Historic Irish Houses and Estates
DIB	*Dictionary of Irish biography*, ed. James McGuire and James Quinn, 9 vols (Dublin and Cambridge, 2010), online version, http://dib.cambridge.org
IHT	Irish Heritage Trust
NAI	National Archives of Ireland
ODNB	*Oxford dictionary of national biography*, ed. H.C.G. Matthew and B.H. Harrison, 60 vols (Oxford, 2004), with supplements and online revisions, https://www.oxforddnb.com
OPW	Office of Public Works
SAGB	Society of Artists of Great Britain
V&A	Victoria & Albert Museum, London

Introduction

No man is an island, entire of itself,
every man is a piece of the continent, a part of the main
John Donne

By substituting 'house' for 'man', John Donne's celebrated dictum about the inter-connectedness of human life conveniently opens up fresh ways of perceiving the country house. Often held to be isolated bastions of elite privilege, socially and economically remote from the population at large, and frequently shielded by walls, gates, lodges and long drives, to the point of near invisibility, the country house was believed to exist apart from mainstream society. Protected and exclusive, concerned with admitting a select few and excluding everyone else, these houses have stood alone in the landscape, and in society, their rural setting at a remove from centres of population.

In fact these places have never been the examples of splendid isolation that such a stereotypical vision might suggest. Their boundaries have always been permeable. Aside from narrow coteries of friends and family, they have continually admitted newcomers, outsiders, staff, neighbours, contractors, officials, suppliers, tourists, as well as a host of other figures. Depending on their intent, benign or hostile, such figures have either been welcomed or variously tolerated, feared, despised, resisted, loathed. Houses have witnessed more abstract visitations too, not always identifiable with human agency, in the form of death, disease, accident or fire.

It is clear that country houses have always been open places, any cordon sanitaire largely an illusory one; the impediments to entry and access breached as much as observed. To a degree families would tacitly accept this, recognizing that their homes had to be staffed, supplied and repaired, that their social life depended upon influxes of guests, and their financial welfare was rooted in a wider economic framework by way of tenants and rents, as well as entrepreneurial endeavour; and in recent times opening their doors to the public has become a financial lifeline. Inward and outbound traffic has been a fact of life. Only a small number were completely reclusive, shunning all contact with the world. The strength of any bridgehead between private house and public sphere would vary from generation to generation, and be influenced by a variety of factors, not least of all the personalities of the occupants.

The familiar record of sociable gatherings, guestbooks, house parties and civilized bonhomie is more than balanced by instances of unwelcome intrusion, through events and incursions that threatened or undermined the household. The country house might be an object of unfavourable scrutiny, entered or occupied by people with few or no links to the owner family, let alone sympathy towards its residents and lifestyle, or simply visited by people with poor manners. Country houses, long after they came to replace the fortified strongholds of the medieval world, were challenged by a range of forces that questioned their existence, and dispelled any illusion that as privileged domains they were insulated from the outside world. Country houses have always had visitors whether welcome or unwelcome.

This book is the latest in the series of volumes drawn from the Annual Historic Houses Conference held at the Centre for the Study of Historic Irish Houses and Estates at the Department of History, Maynooth University.

The essays in this volume cover a spectrum of visitors across the centuries. Fran Baker examines the visit Elizabeth Gaskell made to Chatsworth in 1857, where the renowned authoress unexpectedly found herself invited to meet another celebrity, the duke of Devonshire, and asked to stay overnight; she recorded this as a 'fairy-tale transition' for the personal invitation lifted her from the mass of other excursionists who were also visiting that day. Gaskell was taking a break after a trying period at home and the publication of the *Life of Charlotte Brontë* earlier in the year, a book that did much to promote the Brontës' village of Haworth in Yorkshire as a tourist attraction – a destination the duke of Devonshire had visited only a few weeks earlier.

Kerry Bristol chronicles the northern tour of Thomas Sandby, Theodosius Forrest and friends in 1774. Sandby recorded what he saw for the benefit of others who could read his words and view his watercolours and thereby 'be a partaker in this Excursion'. The itinerary took in many of the grand houses of the day, from Kedleston to Thoresby, Wentworth Woodhouse and elsewhere, and each of these houses elicited varying responses within the group: admiration or dislike was by no means universal.

Philip Carstairs provides a glimpse into a little-known set of arrivals to country houses, the poor and indigent who journeyed to the back door in search of charity in the form of soup kitchens established by philanthropic owners. Against a backdrop of rural distress owners such as the duke of Buckingham at Stowe provided real help, but as Carstairs observes, this ritual was also a form of entertainment for polite families and their elite guests who could observe from the other end of the social spectrum. Charity also served to cement social divisions between the haves and the have-nots, those who could give and those who had no option but to receive.

John Coleman narrates the long and chequered history of Knole in Kent, reputedly the largest private house in England. Home of the Sackville family, it has a long pedigree of visitors, from Horace Walpole and Fanny Burney, to nineteenth-century excursion trains and today's National Trust visitors. The house and its collections have been rescued and revived at various moments, most recently with a major Heritage Lottery Fund award.

Introduction

Peter Collinge discusses how admittance or refusal of entry in the eighteenth century were sometimes arbitrary, and that the right social credentials did not always guarantee access to houses where walls, gates and lodges could send out signals of 'gloomy inhospitality'. There was a 'double identity' to such places: on the one hand travellers would want to visit and explore them, on the other not every owner felt obliged to admit visitors. The appeal of a destination might be determined by reputation or architectural style, with differences in taste between 'olden'-style buildings and newer Palladian and neoclassical architecture. Expectations were not always met, and information was often unreliable in an age of rudimentary travel infrastructure.

Oliver Cox has mined the Scotney Castle Archives to present a picture of *Country Life* writer Christopher Hussey, author of countless articles on country houses as well as invited guest into these homes. He left a very special record in the form of his own visiting books, filled with photographs, watercolour sketches and signatures that counterbalance those of his hosts; from his privileged position, Hussey was instrumental in shaping the country house aesthetic of the twentieth century.

Ian d'Alton examines how country house families had packed social itineraries, and calendars filled with guests and reciprocal visitors. Houses were not only full of things they were also filled with people who, unlike inanimate objects, could display unwelcome characteristics and make unreasonable demands. The unpredictability of human behaviour might easily undo the most meticulously planned gathering, and d'Alton considers the role of the host or hostess, and how they might 'curate' their guests at house parties, whether family, friends and neighbours or celebrities, politicians and royalty. The idea of a collection of guests is ephemeral yet visitors' books record these events, and the volume itself often becomes a prized element in the country house archive.

Shaun Evans addresses an overlooked element in Thomas Pennant's *Tour in Wales* – the place of country houses. Like other travellers in this volume Pennant came from a gentry background, his visits to country seats were as much social as fact-finding expeditions. Evans records how Pennant defined the significance of houses in terms of *plas* and family lineage, their length of occupancy, architectural style and designed landscape – all of which contributed towards a growing sense of national consciousness in Wales.

John Knightley chronicles the social life of Callinafercy House, County Kerry, home of the Leeson Marshall family. Basing his findings on family correspondence, diaries and visitor books from 1913 to 1939, he charts the social rhythms of gentry society. Life consisted of hosting visitors throughout the year, an average of 170 days per year at Callinafercy, added to which were numerous excursions and journeys to other houses as guests, all facilitated by the railway, and then increasingly the motor car. This genteel milieu was interrupted by the First World War and subsequently was then threatened by the War of

Independence and the Civil War, which saw raids on numerous houses by the IRA and by pro- or anti-treaty forces. A stark sign of the changing times is found in the entry for 1922 in the Marshall visitors' book, which notes the arrival of '22 armed men in threes or fours'.

Christopher Ridgway narrates two stories of foes and friends and their impact upon country houses in times of turbulence and peace, arguing that the boundaries separating country houses from the wider world have been in many respects illusory and symbolic. Such houses have variously received, welcomed, endured or resisted all manner of arrivals; these cycles of visitations occur time after time, differing only in degree, and what remains constant, in most cases, is the house itself.

It is to be hoped that this volume will open up further avenues of research beyond that of guests arriving at country houses. For example, pests and vermin were ever present in houses, necessitating regular visits from rat catchers, as can be found in numerous estate accounts; they were matched outdoors by mole catchers paid for eradicating that unwelcome despoiler of carefully tended lawns. The conditions of a building could also determine other kinds of presence: lack of ventilation and damp interiors would lead to the deterioration of fabrics or outbreaks of mould, and encourage pests such as silverfish who can wreak havoc on books. Seasonal fluctuations, warmer weather, and high humidity might encourage the hatching of larvae, resulting in a plague of moths. Beetles, woodworm, flies, wasps, fleas, and termites are all examples of creatures easily able of to find an accommodating habitat in big, old houses. None of them is welcome; they cause damage, lead to a need for expensive repairs, and require extermination. The English Heritage guide to pests illustrates an alarming galaxy of creatures found in country houses; despite improved household regimes and specialist cleaning products owners must always be on the lookout for these intruders. They are the animal kingdom equivalent of house guests who turn into house pests, tiresome presences that infect the building and irritate the household.

Pollution of varying kinds has been an additional incursion: sulphur fumes from coal fires were notorious for degrading leather bindings, and smoke would cause discolouration and scorching. Poor sanitation would result in noxious smells that had no respect for differences between downstairs and upstairs areas, assailing the whole household. A lack of understanding about hygiene might lead to outbreaks of illness, from simple gastric ailments to more serious waterborne diseases such as typhoid and cholera; thus, houses were prey to miasmic and microscopic invaders.

Across many estates the elements would frequently cause havoc: heavy rainfall, storms and high winds were common inflictions, responsible for flooding, fallen trees, and structural damage. Today global trade connections mean that new diseases are affecting estate landscapes, from Dutch elm disease

Introduction

in the 1970s, to phytophthora, ash die-back and acute oak decline, as well as many other arrivals travelling as stowaways, spores, or by wing. The language of defence and vigilance is thus shared by household staff alert to bugs and pests, as well as by gardeners and estate teams whose work is partly defined by combatting such dangers.

A more insidious form of encroachment on houses and estates has been urban sprawl, a modern equivalent of the wartime siege, as development begins to impinge upon and even enclose a house; thus residences that were once surrounded by green acres are reduced to tiny oases in a built-up zone. The growth of Celbridge in County Kildare, for example, has seen a steady diminution of the Castletown demesne since the eighteenth century. The consequence of this is that many country houses are no longer in the country, they have become urban or suburban residences. Each of these topics would merit more detailed investigation that would surely confirm how houses are far from being insular.

Nor can a volume on this topic fail to mention the experience of Covid, that most unwelcome of arrivals from 2020, which led to the cancellation of the Annual Historic Houses Conference – especially ironic given its focus on visiting country houses. Although denied an opportunity to gather in person, during the pandemic people across the world found ways of congregating online to listen to presentations and meet in a virtual format – proof of the adage that adversity is the mother of invention. The digital genie was let out of the bottle as never before, and enormous numbers of people became conversant and comfortable with Zoom and other platforms. Houses and heritage sites responded to this challenge with online programmes that answered demands from their existing visitors, and which also reached far beyond their usual audiences.

With the roll-out of vaccines much of the world has returned to something like the status quo ante, although the pandemic has left medical and economic legacies that will take years to pass, and new macro-economic and political pressures have emerged. Tourism has begun to recover, albeit not quite to the same levels as 2019, but by opening their doors once more country houses hope to remain commercially viable, as the visits of many help to secure their futures. Arguably, more people than ever can now visit country houses, and a binary model is set to exist: the homes of the few continue to open their doors to the many, but real footfall is now vastly augmented through digital platforms that enable access for many more visitors without them necessarily crossing any physical threshold. Houses can be experienced in a prima facie or surrogate manner; moreover, these modes of visiting are complementary and full of dynamic possibilities.

* * *

The editors wish to express their gratitude to a number of supporters and friends of the Centre: to Carmel Naughton who, through the Stackallan donation, made possible this publication, and several other important educational projects; to the Office of Public Works, and most especially Mary Heffernan and Rosemary Collier; this is a long-established relationship that has jointly nurtured talent, scholarship and fresh ways in which to understand and interpret the country house. We are grateful to colleagues in the Department of History at Maynooth University; and to our wider associates for their support, including the Attingham Trust, Historic Houses (UK), Historic Houses of Ireland, Institute for the Study of Welsh Estates (Bangor Universtiy), the Paul Mellon Centre and the Yorkshire Country House Partnership. Our special thanks to Veronica Barry for her tireless administrative work, and to Den Stubbs of Stubbs Design for designing all the literature around the conference.

Finally, we are grateful to the authors for their contributions. Traditionally the conference attracts speakers and delegates from across a broad spectrum, and younger scholars especially are encouraged to attend and participate in the proceedings; we have endeavoured to maintain this custom and we are, as ever, extremely grateful to all the team at Four Courts Press for helping the CSHIHE to disseminate new knowledge to a much wider and ever expanding audience.

Visitations: foes

CHRISTOPHER RIDGWAY

A useful place to begin any survey of unfriendly arrivals is with the dissolution of the monastic houses in Tudor England: here the knock on the door from Thomas Cromwell's commissioners signalled not only an audit of the household and its goods but also an investigation into the conduct of its residents. The commissioners were soon followed by the 'visitors', a group of officials who implemented the surrender of the monastic establishments to the crown; and from here saw the redistribution of these houses among a circle of Tudor courtiers. At each site the monastic buildings were torn down, modified, enlarged or turned into secular households occupied by nobility and gentry, many of whom established dynasties in these country seats.[1] Among the more energetic officials were John Tregonwell, who acquired Milton Abbey in Dorset, Richard Rich, who came to own Leez Priory, Essex; and Thomas Legh, who occupied Nostell Priory.[2]

Later in the century many Tudor households received Elizabeth I on her various progresses through the land, an obligation that incurred months of planning, exorbitant expenditure and hectic days if not weeks of a congested household. In 1602 Sir Thomas Egerton spent over £2,000 entertaining the queen at Harefield, Middlesex; the earl of Lincoln on the other hand absented himself upon learning that the queen was coming to stay; the Paulet family of Basing House, Hampshire, received Elizabeth three times.[3] This level of privilege was double-edged: it may have signalled royal favour but such hospitality often meant ruinous expense. Welcomed and feared in equal measure, the honour was offset not only by cost but by diplomatic delicacies too, an almost

---

1 James G. Clark, *The dissolution of the monasteries, a new history* (New Haven and London, 2021), especially chapters 5 and 7.   2 For the transfer of properties see Jane Whitaker, *Raised from the ruins: monastic houses after the dissolution* (London, 2021), pp 7–21. For each of these figures see their entries in Whitaker, ibid., pp 229–37, 271–7, and also the *ODNB*, where, for example, Rich is described as showing a 'particular relish and acquisitiveness', and Legh as exhibiting an 'abrasive personality'. For Nostell Priory see Christopher Hussey, 'Nostell Priory, Yorkshire', *Country Life*, 111 (16 May 1952), pp 1492–5.   3 Jean Wilson, 'The Harefield entertainment and the cult of Elizabeth I', *Antiquaries Journal*, 66 (1986), pp 315–29; see also Adrian Tinniswood, *Behind the throne: a domestic history of the royal household* (London, 2018), p. 18. The complexity of hospitality is discussed in Felicity Heal, 'Giving and receiving on royal progress' in Jayne Elisabeth Archer et al. (eds), *The progresses, pageants and entertainments of Queen Elizabeth I* (Oxford, 2007), pp 46–61; see also Jean Wilson, *Entertainments for Elizabeth I* (Woodbridge, 1980), pp 52–7. For Basing House, see John Nichols, *The progresses and public processions of Queen Elizabeth I*, 2 vols (London, 1788), i, pp 56, 119; ii, pp 2, 6, 7, 18.

1.1 Milton Abbey, Dorset, which came into the possession of Richard Tregonwell in 1540 after the dissolution of the monastic household (Mary Evans Picture Library).

pathological anxiety not to fall short, displease or offend, along with a constant need to impress and entertain. Royal demands were impossible to refuse, which made the monarch the most exacting of guests, with a vast retinue of important courtiers as well as troupes of hangers-on. While it would be wrong to describe royal visits as universally unwelcome they were very burdensome. The monarch's departure would likely trigger relief as well as an audit of extensive wear and tear from the lengthy revelry; while not exactly despoiled, the house was quite likely missing certain items, and the host's coffers depleted.

Hosting pageantry and spectacle in peacetime was one thing but during the turbulent 1640s visitations were of a wholly different magnitude; the English Civil War was a throwback to the warring era of the Plantagenets, with large buildings targeted by opposing Royalist and Parliamentarian forces. Basing House, home to John Paulet, fifth marquess of Winchester, was the site of one of the most famous sieges. His political allegiance to the king was very clear, and he was said to have incised the family motto, '*Aimez Loyaute*', on the window panes of the house. Basing House stood at a vantage point on the road between London and Portsmouth, and was used as a base from which to organize raids into the neighbouring countryside, either to harass Parliamentarian forces, or to forage for supplies. It was also a refuge for Royalist sympathizers and refugees. It was besieged from 1643 to 1645, repulsing a number of assaults; more than once the

Visitations: foes

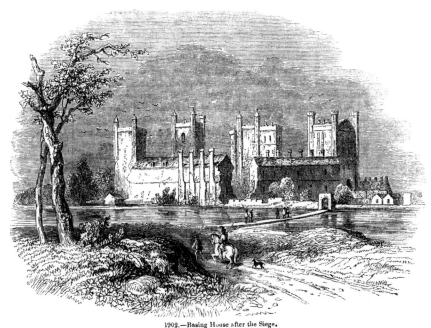

1.2 Basing House, Hampshire, after the siege in 1645 (private collection).

marquess was offered the chance to surrender but on each occasion he refused. The house was periodically relieved by Royalist forces, but in adverse times the lead from the roof was melted down and cast into bullets. In the autumn of 1645 Oliver Cromwell's forces arrived at Basing, having taken the town of Winchester, and unleashed a ferocious bombardment of the complex – Basing was in fact two houses, an old one and a new one standing in extensive grounds. His troops then stormed the house, slaughtering many of the defenders; as was customary, no quarter was given once surrender had been refused. The house had been deemed 'a nest of idolatry', and many of the Catholics were put to the sword. The massacre might have been greater had not the attacking soldiers been diverted by the prospect of plunder. Contrary to all reports, the house was not on the verge of starvation, it was filled with provisions, and opulently furnished – pictures, textiles, books and silver were looted; Cromwell's men swiftly exchanging this plunder with the local population for cash. During the final assault the house caught fire and was reduced to a near ruin. For Cromwell, who had knelt in prayer the night before the assault, the fall of Basing was a significant military triumph, both locally, and strategically in that Basing had symbolized Royalist obduracy; it was for him a victory divinely countenanced. Spared by the intercession of his former prisoner at Basing, the parliamentary Colonel Hammond, the marquess of Winchester was incarcerated in the Tower of London, charged with treason, but released a few years later.

Cromwell ordered the ruins to be 'totally slighted or demolished'. This was partly a tactical decision – he considered Basing too difficult to maintain as a garrison – but also a punitive measure, and the government order stated that 'whosoever will fetch away any stone, brick or other materials ... shall have the same for his or their pains'. This action presaged the twentieth-century fate of many houses across Europe.[4] Basing is often cited as the most notorious instance of the fate of Royalist houses during the Civil War, reduced to ruins by bombardment, assault and demolition. Today only the earthworks remain. But not every house suffered the same outcome. Leaving the wreckage of Basing, Cromwell marched westward, passing Longford Castle, home of the earl of Coleraine. Here he demanded surrender from the commander, Lieutenant General Pell. Mindful of the fate of Basing just forty-eight hours earlier, Pell yielded, and 'fair and equal conditions' were speedily agreed upon. The defenders delivered up all their arms and ammunition; gentlemen were permitted to carry their swords, and officers were allowed to leave with a wagonload of personal property. The house was plundered but left standing, despite Cromwell nearly being shot by one of the defenders.[5]

Further north, in Lancashire, a similar story played out at Lathom Hall, the fifteenth-century fortified home of the earl of Derby. Lathom was left in the capable hands of Charlotte de la Tremouille, countess of Derby, after her husband, James Stanley, was ordered to garrison the Isle of Man. Parliamentary general Sir Thomas Fairfax requested her surrender in February 1644 but the countess refused to yield; three months later Lathom was relieved by Royalist forces and Charlotte departed to join her husband, leaving behind Colonel Rawthorne as commander. The following summer Parliament decided to subdue Lathom and a second siege was raised. By December, recognizing how desperate their plight was with supplies nearly exhausted and no prospect of relief, Rawthorne offered his surrender. Once more the terms permitted officers to retain their swords, and ninety men were given safe conduct to the Royalist garrison at Conwy Castle. Lathom had yielded without bloodshed but this did not prevent the castle being looted and the fortifications torn down.[6]

Such examples were repeated throughout the 1640s, with country houses fortified, fought over, burnt out or razed. For attackers or defenders they were variously sites of resistance or assault; they were strategic objectives or defensive strongholds; their populations of soldiers, refugees and civilians were either allies

---

4 For Basing, see, most recently, Jesse Childs, *The siege of Loyalty House: a civil war story* (London, 2022), but also Wilf Emberton, *Love loyalty: the close and perilous siege of Basing House, 1643–5* (Basing, 1972); for the motto incised on the window, see John Leyland, 'Cromwell at Basing House', *Country Life Illustrated* (20 May 1899), pp 618–20.   5 Tony MacLachlan, *The Civil War in Hampshire* (Landford, 2000), pp 387–9; Colin Pilkington, *To play the man: Countess Derby and the siege of Lathom House* (Preston, 1991).   6 Stephen Bull, *The civil wars in Lancashire, 1640–1660* (Lancaster, 2009), pp 179–211, 268–78; Colin Pilkington, *To play the man: the story of Lady Derby and the siege of Lathom House, 1643–45*

Visitations: foes

1.3 Charles I taken into custody by Cornet Joyce at Holdenby House, engraving by Nicholas Gabriel Depuis, after Peter Angelis, 1728 (private collection).

or enemies.[7] Notwithstanding the attritional nature of siege warfare, when many of these houses fell they were also sources of plenty, such as Menabilly in Cornwall, which was plundered by Parliamentarians in 1644.[8] However, the pattern was by no means one-sided, with Royalist defenders and Parliamentarian attackers. In 1645 the campaign in the East Midlands around the town of Newark witnessed the torching by Royalist forces of the Jermyn family's fortified Elizabethan mansion, Torksey in Lincolnshire; all that survived was a fragment of the west front.[9] In the same year Campden House in Gloucestershire, the Jacobean home belonging to Sir Baptist Hicks, was burnt by Royalist forces in order to prevent it falling into Parliamentary hands.[10]

Some country houses were put to other uses during this period. Holdenby House in Northamptonshire, one of the largest Elizabethan prodigy houses, built

(Preston, 1991). **7** Ronald Hutton and Wylie Reeves, 'Sieges and fortifications' in John Kenyon and Jane Ohlmeyer (eds), *The civil wars: a military history of England, Scotland and Ireland, 1638–1660* (Oxford, 1998), pp 200–1. **8** Mary Coate, *Cornwall in the great Civil War and Interregnum, 1642–1660* (Oxford, 1933), pp 153–4. **9** Alfred Wood, *Nottinghamshire in the Civil War* (Oxford, 1937), p. 95. **10** H. Avray Tipping, 'Campden House and Chipping Campden village, Gloucestershire', *Country Life*, 40 (18 Nov. 1916), pp 602–8; see also the Chipping Campden Historical Society website and article by Mary Fielding, 'The history of Campden House', www.chippingcampdenhistory.org.uk, accessed 26 Feb. 2023.

by Sir Christopher Hatton in the 1580s, had passed into royal ownership in 1607; it was here that Scottish forces delivered a royal 'guest' in 1647 to be handed over to Parliament. Such were the relaxed conditions of Charles I's captivity that while he was at Holdenby he was able to visit the nearby houses of Lord Vaux and the earl of Sunderland, but in July of that year he was removed by Cornet Joyce and his soldiers and taken to Sir Thomas Fairfax's headquarters in Newmarket. In 1650 Holdenby was bought by a Parliamentary officer, Captain Adam Baynes, who began to demolish the house in order to sell off the stone, while keeping the kitchen wing for his own dwelling.[11]

As always to the victor the spoils, and with the triumph of the Parliamentary forces Royalist families and their estates were targeted in the Sequestration Ordinance of 1643; opponents of the new regime were labelled delinquents and faced imprisonment or confiscation of their estates. This was a ruling that applied to royal and church lands as well. In order to recover their lands owners were required to compound, to pay a fine proportional to the value of their estate. The aim of this legislation was principally to replenish the state coffers emptied by years of war, but for many this was perceived as a punitive measure. In addition to paying a fine Royalist owners and soldiers were required to issue an apology and take an oath to obey Parliament. The debate in the House of Commons on Christmas Day 1656 made it clear that the process of confiscation and composition was intended as a restorative measure, aiming to stabilize society. Major General Disbrowe argued of Parliament's opponents: 'It is their reformation, not their ruin, is desired. If they become our friends, let them benefit by their change.'[12] Those on the receiving end of these measures would struggle to agree.

The fines were large but there were ways to mitigate their impacts. Parliament respected estates that had been put into trust before the war; one-fifth of the estate's income was held back to support the family; and it was possible to pay some of the fine not in cash but in kind by transferring leases or annuities. Some owners, such as the second earl of Thanet at Bodiam Castle, Sussex, Sir Richard Leveson of Lilleshall, Shropshire, and Sir George Sondes at Lees Court, Kent, faced fines of up to £20,000 but these were nothing compared to the cost of damage suffered by estates during the war: partial or complete destruction of the house; loss of crops and livestock; felling of timber; and spoliation of parkland. In many cases these owners were able to meet their fines. Often the simplest method was to borrow money from friends and family, or from the London money market, to re-purchase the estate (in effect a compulsory re-mortgage).

11 Mark Girouard, 'Elizabethan Holdenby', *Country Life*, 166 (18 and 25 Oct. 1979), pp 1286–9, 1398–1401; for the king's time at Holdenby see John Matsulak, *The prisoner king: Charles I in captivity* (Stroud, 2017), pp 80–8. For Baynes see his entry in the *ODNB*, and also G. Isham, 'Adam Baynes of Leeds and Holdenby', *Northamptonshire Past and Present*, 2 (1954–9), pp 138–46.   12 John Towill Rutt (ed.), *Diary of Thomas Burton 1656*, 4 vols (London, 1828), i, pp 236–7.

In all but the die-hard cases Parliament was not interested in the identity of the purchaser – it was the proceeds of sequestration that mattered most. While this meant that many estates survived it could entail long-term indebtedness to the detriment of the improvement of the land.[13]

Periods of destruction are invariably followed by periods of rebuilding. For Captain Baynes at Holdenby, watching Christopher Hatton's enormous pile reduce in size was a formula for quick wealth – he was the seventeenth-century equivalent of a demolition contractor. For the inhabitants around Basing House as well as other sites of sieges and assaults, ruin offered them a chance to repair, rebuild, or enhance their own domestic dwellings, or even speculate in the building-materials trade. The rhythms of conflict have always included reconstruction – physical as well as societal and economic.

Later in the century the bloodless revolution of 1688 almost signalled the end of internecine warfare in Britain. However, there were two further spasms of violence, with the Jacobite risings of 1715 and 1745. The failure in the north-east in 1715 was one of the reasons the Young Pretender, Charles Edward Stuart, chose to invade England along a north-west route in 1745.[14] His march south to Derby became an increasingly pointless expedition that gave way to retreat: nowhere was held by Jacobite forces for more than a few days. The campaign was conducted, to begin with at least, in civilized terms, and Charles presented his action as a lawful reclaiming of the crown and not as a rebellion. He adopted the trappings of the monarch, appointing lord lieutenants and clergy, ordering his army to behave well and even paying for his lodging at the houses where he stayed. He was determined to act as an honourable guest, respecting both the law of the land and, almost as importantly, the custom of receiving hospitality.[15]

Throughout the country his reception was mixed. His supporters declared themselves vocally and offered men and provisions; others dissembled or made themselves absent. As Christopher Duffy has remarked: 'If Prince Charles turned up on your doorstep in person, you could, without compromising yourself, arrange to be away.' Thus Sir Robert Menzies vacated Castle Menzies, Perthshire, Sir Nathaniel Curzon left Kedleston in Derbyshire, and at Dumfries Richard Lowthian made himself conveniently invisible by getting extremely drunk.[16] The conduct of the Scottish and English aristocracy and gentry was often ambivalent, bearing in mind that more Scots were under arms against Prince Charles than were fighting for him, and the actions of Cosmo Gordon,

---

13 Christopher Clay (ed.), *Rural society: landowners, peasants and labourers, 1500–1750*, (Cambridge, 1990), pp 246–80; see also H.J. Habbakuk, 'Landowners and the Civil War', *Economic History Review*, new series, 18:1, 'Essays in economic history presented to Professor M.M. Postan' (1965), pp 130–51.   14 For a detailed account of the march south through England, see Christopher Duffy, *The '45: Bonnie Prince Charlie and the untold story of the Jacobite rising* (London, 2003), chapters 8–12; what follows is drawn extensively from this volume.   15 Duffy, *The '45*, pp 186, 291, 411.   16 Ibid., pp 49–50, 292, 297; William McDowall, *History of the burgh of Dumfries*, (2nd ed., Edinburgh, 1873), p. 541.

1.4 Castle Menzies, from John Preston Neale's *Views of the seats of noblemen and gentlemen of England, Wales, Scotland and Ireland*, second series, vol. 2, 1825 (private collection).

third duke of Gordon, were not untypical. Although the Gordons were powerful magnates and champions of Catholicism the duke himself was a Protestant Whig. This did not stop him from turning a blind eye to his factor, Gordon of Glenbucket, supplying arms and horses to Charles. But in March 1746 the duke fled Gordon Castle, abandoning his pregnant wife to the advancing Jacobite forces. Charles interrupted his retreat to Inverness to visit the castle and admire the terraces, fountains and statues, although these had been defaced by the rebels using them for target practice.[17]

The march south may have been foremost a military expedition but in many ways it was no different from a typical royal progress, stopping at houses belonging to the aristocracy and gentry. At these halts Charles would lodge with the owner while his forces would rest and re-provision; however some sites were raided. In October 1745 Aeneas Glengarry led a party into Berwickshire to requisition horses. Arriving at Redbraes, the home of the earl of Marchmont, who was absent, Glengarry was received by the earl's sister, Lady Nimmo, who had hidden the horses. His troops waited outside Glengarry and his officers were entertained indoors but departed empty-handed.[18] When Charles stayed at

[17] Duffy, *The '45*, pp 86, 486; for families whose allegiances were split in 1745 see Ian Grimble, 'Houses divided' in Lesley Scott-Moncrieff (ed.), *The '45: to gather an image whole* (Edinburgh, 1988), pp 113–22. [18] Duffy, *The '45*, p. 205.

Warwick Hall in Cumbria in November he was entertained by two sympathizers, Mrs Warwick and Mrs Howard of nearby Corby Castle. The prince declared the two ladies to be the first civilized company he had encountered since crossing the border on his southward progress; what his hostesses made of the felling of trees in the parkland to make siege ladders is not recorded.[19] As the Jacobite column moved through Cumberland supplies of hay and oats were demanded from Greystoke, Dailmain and Hutton Hall; at Lowther Castle, when no supplies were forthcoming, the house was occupied.[20] When Lord Elcho's column reached Hoghton Tower in Lancashire, home of the anti-Catholic Sir Henry Hoghton, the owner and his wife had fled for Yorkshire; the disgruntled troops plundered the wine cellars and were only prevented from firing the house by one of their leaders.[21] This pattern was repeated as Charles travelled southward with requisitioning parties sent out at each new locality, but as the futility of the march grew ever more apparent the mood among the Jacobites soured, and gentlemanly conduct began to evaporate. Okeover Hall, Derbyshire, was looted several times, although nearby Ashbourne Hall, where the prince and his commanders overnighted, was spared.[22] On their retreat northwards the Jacobite forces visited Lowther Castle, plundering it for a second time. At Drumlanrig, home of the second duke of Queensberry, known as 'the Union Duke' for his part in the 1707 Act of Union between England and Scotland, Charles refused to pay for his lodging, and his forces roasted cattle in the forecourt, rode horses up and down the staircase, and slashed a portrait of William III.[23]

As the action returned to Scotland so the levels of violence and destruction increased on both sides. Blair Castle was home to the Murray brothers, who had divided their loyalties, George raising a force for Charles, while James, the second duke of Atholl, who had inherited the estate following the attainder of his brother after 1715, supported the Hanoverian cause. In September 1745 Charles and his forces arrived at Blair to find the castle empty, but he was entertained by Charlotte Robertson, a Murray cousin and widow from nearby Lude House; she instructed him in the art of bowls, and hosted a ball for the prince and his officers. A year later, in March 1746, retreating from the duke of Cumberland's advancing forces, the Jacobites returned to Blair, which was now garrisoned by Hanoverian forces. The castle was besieged and Charlotte Robertson, whose home at Lude had been plundered by the garrison, fired the first shot in the bombardment of the castle.[24]

When the duke of Cumberland reached Cullen House in Banff, home of the earl of Findlater, his men found it sacked by retreating Jacobites, and

19 Ibid., p. 229; J.A. Wheatley, *Bonnie Prince Charlie in Cumberland* (Carlisle, 1903), pp 23–4. 20 Duffy, *The '45*, p. 244. 21 Ibid., p. 250. 22 Ibid., p. 315; for Okeover see Arthur Oswald, 'Okeover Hall, Staffordshire', *Country Life*, 135 (30 Jan. 1964), p. 224. 23 Duffy, *The '45*, pp 211, 253, 327, 331, 397. 24 Ibid., pp 84–7, 472–6; for Lady Lude see Maggie Craig, *Damn rebel bitches: the women of the '45* (Edinburgh, 1997), pp 10, 21–3, 31–2.

Cumberland was shown the wrecked furniture and 'marks of violence and destruction' throughout the house.[25] After his victory at Culloden Cumberland embarked on a punitive campaign throughout the Highlands and Islands. His visitations were marked by extreme violence: Beaufort Castle, home of Lord Lovatt, was burned, and his cattle confiscated; Lochiel of Cameron's residence at Achnacarry was torched and his gardens despoiled; and several Macdonald residences were destroyed.[26]

The pacification of the Highlands and the confiscation of Scottish estates ensured that Jacobitism was utterly defeated. The forfeiture acts of 1715 and 1745 were not dissimilar to the sequestration orders of the 1640s, but these were aimed primarily at suppressing Scottish dissent and less at raising revenue through fines. For those who proved cooperative, rehabilitation and re-occupation could come quite swiftly. Many of the houses damaged or destroyed would be repaired or constructed anew; the Lovatt lands were returned to his son in 1774 and a new house built on the site of Beaufort Castle. In 1802 Donald Cameron built a new house at Achnacarry beside the ruins of the old castle.[27]

Beyond Britain similar patterns are to be found during periods of revolution and war, with cycles of welcome or unwelcome visitors. The French Revolution has long been seen as an epoch that saw the destruction of the French nobility. This was true in part, with the decree of 1789 abolishing titles of rank and many feudal privileges, and which was followed by acts of forfeiture. But what distinguished the French Revolution was the nature of its ideological assault on the nobility. Monarchy, the church and the elite were all targeted as enemies; among the more strident utterances in his 1791 *The rights of man*, Thomas Paine issued a call 'to exterminate the monster Aristocracy', and lauded how the French had 'destroyed the law of primogeniture'.[28] As mobs began to target noble houses those who chose not to flee began a desperate bid for anonymity, painting out armorial signs on their carriages, or removing them from the facades of their buildings in the hope that concealment would afford a degree of protection.[29]

In the countryside violent anarchy was unleashed with the slogan 'War on the castles, peace to the cottages', and drew in part on the tradition of *jacquerie*, named after the peasants' uprising of the fourteenth century.[30] Buildings were burned, houses looted and collections vandalized: a very specific form of

---

25 Duffy, *The '45*, p. 492; see also William Cramond, *The plundering of Cullen House by the rebels* (n.p., 1887). 26 Duffy, *The '45*, pp 529–32. 27 Annette M. Smith, *Jacobite estates of the forty-five* (Edinburgh, 1982), p. 103; Mary Miers, 'Achnacarry, Inverness-shire', *Country Life*, 198:34 (19 Aug. 2004), pp 46–51; for Beaufort Castle see the Canmore entry on the Historic Environment Scotland website. 28 Thomas Paine, *Rights of man, common sense and other political writings*, ed. Mark Philip (Oxford, 1995), pp 131–5. 29 William Doyle, *Aristocracy and its enemies in the age of revolution* (Oxford, 2009), p 247; John Markoff, *The abolition of feudalism: peasants, lords, and legislators in the French Revolution* (University Park, PA, 1996), pp 220, 226, 504. 30 Doyle, *Aristocracy*, p. 280; Peter McPhee, *Liberty or death: the French Revolution* (New Haven and London, 2016), pp 59, 75–6, 151, 247; Timothy Tackett, *The coming of the terror in the French Revolution* (Cambridge, MA, 2015), pp 59, 82.

Visitations: foes 25

1.5 Chateau Sceaux, Paris (© Antiquarian Images/Mary Evans).

destruction was for mobs to ransack libraries and destroy documents of ownership or patents and proofs of nobility. Physical destruction was compounded by archival eradication, for without proofs of status, ownership and feudal dues, the legal basis for rank became unsubstantiated.[31] Nobles were referred to as '*ci-devants*', translating literally as 'from before', denoting a previous status; it was an uncanny foreshadowing of the Soviet term for the elites swept away after 1917, who became known as 'former people'.[32]

Houses not sacked were confiscated by the state as national assets. As the revolution convulsed Paris the comte de Cheverny retired to his estates at Blois in the Loire valley. But in 1794 he was imprisoned and the chateau was vandalized; on his release he found his parks and gardens desecrated, with the loss of many trees; his library had been ransacked and all title deeds, decrees and

[31] Doyle, *Aristocracy and its enemies*, pp 283–4, 296; Simon Schama, *Citizens: a chronicle of the French Revolution* (London, 2004), pp 404–6; Markoff, *Abolition of feudalism*, p. 226. Interestingly there is one instance of this happening in the English Civil War, at Leighton Hall in Lancashire, a house which was also sacked in 1715, Bull, *Civil wars in Lancashire*, p. 55.
[32] Doyle, *Aristocracy and its enemies*, p. 242; Schama *Citizens*, p. 420; Douglas Smith, *Former people: the last days of the Russian aristocracy* (London, 2012), pp 7, 13.

1.6 Hubert Robert, Demolition of the Chateau of Meudon in 1803 (J. Paul Getty Museum).

coats of arms had been destroyed.[33] Chateau d'Amboise, also in the Loire valley, and home to the duc de Choiseul, was badly damaged and parts were demolished. The fact that it had acted as a jail and incarcerated such enemies of the *ancien régime* as Nicholas Fouquet and the duc de Lauzun did not save it.[34] Sceaux, on the outskirts of Paris, like other royal chateaux, was preserved for the benefit of the people; the formal terraces laid out by Andre Le Notre in the 1680s were made over to cultivation, and the site turned into an agricultural college. In 1798 the building was bought by a wealthy Breton merchant, Jean-Francois Hippolyte, who, in an echo of Captain Baynes at Holdenby a century before, began demolishing the main building, selling off the materials.[35]

Chateau de Meudon, a royal hunting lodge south-west of Paris, suffered a similar fate. Its contents were confiscated and sold, and it was turned into a factory for making aerial balloons; following a disastrous fire it was demolished in 1802, a process recorded in a remarkable painting by the artist Hubert Robert.[36] At Chateau Vizille near Grenoble, an entrepreneurial intervention transformed the identity of the building when Swiss banker Claude Perier purchased the estate from the Lesdiguieres family in the 1780s, not with a view

[33] Doyle, *Aristocracy and its enemies*, pp 297–8.   [34] Jacques Levron, *Le Chateau d'Amboise* (Grenoble, 1949), pp 12–13.   [35] Francois Souchal, *Le vandalisme de la Revolution* (Paris, 1993), pp 159–60; Marianne de Meyenbourg, *Le domaine de Sceaux* (Paris, 2000), p. 23.

to making it a residence, but to turn it into a factory for the family textile-making business, converting the interiors to accommodate looms. In 1788 when the Estates General of the Dauphine were forbidden from assembling in Grenoble, Citoyen Perier offered them the use of the tennis court at Vizille; subsequently the chateau was spared destruction during the revolution.[37]

Attack and persecution may have led to confiscation, destruction and imprisonment among the French aristocracy, but many nobles simply fled, abandoning their houses to the mob, the state, or to new proprietors. Consequently a flood of emigrés fetched up across Europe as desperate guests seeking shelter. Among those finding refuge in England was a small colony at Juniper Hall at Mickleham in Surrey, which included Madame de Stael, Charles de Talleyrand and the marquis de Narbonne; the house was made available to them by wealthy owner David Jenkinson. Despite their elite credentials these exiles were not entirely welcome in the neighbourhood, where their politics and morals were viewed with suspicion.[38]

In France the impact of the revolution was clear to see, with instances of destruction, recovery and, later, restoration and even restitution. Sometimes buildings survived, intact or as ruins, inhabited by original families or not. But in terms of family occupancy it would be more accurate to say that the most significant impact of the French Revolution was not the cycle of death and destruction during the Terror of the early 1790s; of the 16,000 people condemned to death only about 1,100 were nobles.[39] Of far greater significance was the legislative revolution, which saw the establishment in 1804 of the Code Napoleon, and in particular its articles dealing with inheritance. While succession and inheritance had by no means been singular during the *ancien régime*, the Code Napoleon enshrined the principle of partible inheritance, a reform begun during the revolution: all children had equal claim on parental property. This was the opposite of the English model of primogeniture, so envied by French aristocrats. Thus began the practice of dividing estates into ever-smaller portions over the generations. This legislative change would have by far the greatest impact on the French country house.[40] Here was a visitation of a legal kind that changed the status of estates and ownership forever, with consequences more far-reaching than any attacking mob.

Crossing the Atlantic to the American Civil War of 1861–5 provides further examples of hostile or benign arrival especially for plantation owners. While the north viewed the secession of the southern states as an act of rebellion, the south

36 Souchal, *Le vandalisme*, pp 215–16; for the Robert painting see Margaret Morgan Grasselli and Yuriko Jackall, *Hubert Robert* (London, 2016), pp 194, 257–8.   37 Severin Batfroi, *Vizille: un chateau et une revolution* (Grenoble, 2002), pp 20–5. Today Vizille houses a museum of the revolution.   38 Margery Weiner, *The French exiles, 1789–1815* (London, 1960); for Juniper Hall, see Linda Kelly, *Juniper Hall: an English refuge from the French Revolution* (London, 2009).   39 Doyle, *Aristocracy and its enemies*, p. 289.   40 Ibid., pp 318, 328–9; Robert B. Holtman, *The Napoleonic revolution* (Baton Rouge, LA, 1981), pp 92–3.

cast their actions as a noble cause. The cotton, sugar and tobacco economy was crippled as owners and sons went to fight, women were left behind to manage plantations and many enslaved people felt emboldened to escape. Both sides adopted scorched-earth policies: plantation owners burning their crops to prevent them falling into enemy hands, and Union forces pursuing a campaign of destruction and punishment, most famously with William Sherman's march through Georgia, and the destruction he meted out to South Carolina, seen as the seat of the rebellion.[41] Here was another example of armed conflict prompting visitations of an extreme kind conditioned by military necessity as well as political motivation. What is interesting to note is that during the march through Georgia houses that had been abandoned by their owners were more likely to be burned than those still occupied; in these instances it paid to be present when troops arrived, no matter how unwelcome and terrifying that prospect might be, for appeals for restraint could be heeded, as they were in many cases. In Sherman's eyes those who abandoned their houses displayed no affection for them, and they deserved their fate.[42]

Typically there was a see-saw movement of civilized and vindictive conduct. Millwood Plantation outside Columbia in South Carolina, the seat of Confederate General Wade Hampton, was targeted as a bastion of secessionist wealth and dissidence. The family was permitted to salvage a few items of silver and porcelain and a handful of paintings, wrapped up in curtains they had torn down, before Union troopers set fire to the house. A few items survive on display in the Hampton town residence in Columbia today, while the plantation mansion itself remains a ruined hulk.[43]

Confederate General Robert E. Lee's home, Arlington, on the outskirts of Washington DC, was abandoned by his wife Mary in May 1861, and occupied by federal forces. This was both a military necessity, as the house was on high ground overlooking the capital, and also a symbolic move to deprive the commander of the southern forces of his home. Union officers respected family pleas not to damage the building, but troops were billeted in the house and grounds. A year later the property was subject to an insurrection tax, and on non-payment by the Lee family, who could not pay in person, the house was confiscated. It was subsequently sold in 1864, and purchased by the government to create what would become the National Cemetery. After the war the family appealed against the seizure, with the Supreme Court finding in favour of Lee's eldest son, and the family was awarded compensation.[44]

One of the more extraordinary episodes from the war belongs to Clifton, the Surget residence on the heights above Natchez in Mississippi, a town made

[41] For a clear-headed analysis of this chapter of the war see Mark Grimsley, *The hard hand of war: Union policy toward southern civilians, 1861–65* (Cambridge, MA, 1995).   [42] Ibid., p. 196; Brian Holden Reid, *The scourge of war: the life of William Tecumseh Sherman* (Oxford, 2020), p. 380.   [43] Marc R. Matrana, *Lost plantations of the South* (Jackson, MS, 2009), pp 57–9.
[44] Allen C. Guelzo, *Robert E. Lee: a life* (New York, 2021), pp 202–3, 310–11, 419–20.

Visitations: foes

1.7 Arlington House with Union soldiers on the steps, 1864 (Mary Evans/Everett Collection).

wealthy by cotton but which also claimed the highest population of freed slaves in the country. In 1862 the town surrendered to northern forces, and many homeowners who had opposed secession continued with their social lives, extending their invitations to Union officers. Unfortunately the Surgets managed to offend one officer by failing to include him in an invitation; he reacted to this snub by decreeing that the bluffs above the river required extra fortification, and that the most appropriate spot was Clifton. The Surget family was given twenty-four hours to evacuate their belongings before the house was dynamited, to be replaced by Fort McPherson. The Surgets, like other families, had endeavoured to receive friend or foe on the same footing, little realizing that ruin lay not in any political or military misalliance but in a breach of etiquette.[45]

On the other hand northern commander Ulysses Grant behaved with more courtesy when he arrived in Natchez; he requisitioned the Rosalie mansion but ensured that the Little family's possessions were put under guard.[46] When

---

[45] Matrana, *Lost plantations*, pp 10–12; Samuel Wilson, 'Clifton: an ill-fated Natchez mansion', *Journal of Mississippi History*, 46 (1984), pp 179–89; *Mid-Continent Magazine*, 6 (1895), p. 41. I am grateful to Carter Burns of the Historic Natchez Foundation for information on this bizarre episode.   [46] Randolph Delehanty and Van Jones Martin, *Classic Natchez: history, homes and gardens* (Savannah, 1996), pp 86–7.

Sherman reached Savannah he was invited to stay in the house of British-born banker Charles Green. Opinion was divided over this action, some believing Green selflessly volunteered his house to save his fellow citizens the ignominy of hosting the enemy commander; on the other hand Green claimed he welcomed Sherman less on the grounds of hospitality but more in order to ensure his own property would be protected from vandalism. Earlier in his campaign Sherman had stayed at the home of the Revd Heidt by the Ogeechee river, where his men discovered a cache of ammunition hidden in a hen coop; when challenged Heidt protested that they had been planted by Union soldiers, until Sherman's aide-de-camp pointed out they had been manufactured in a southern arsenal. Normally this would have sealed the fate of Heidt's residence, but Sherman left it unscathed. These examples reveal owners who were either powerless to prevent incursion or who managed to appeal to peacetime norms of polite behaviour, relying upon a veneer of civility in time of conflict that was sometimes respected by occupiers.[47]

Unwelcome intrusion in time of conflict is thus a perennial feature of country house history: the examples drawn from the English Civil war, the Jacobite rebellion, the French Revolution, and the American Civil War record for the most part episodes of dispossession and destruction, but it was also possible for houses to escape this fate, endeavouring to accommodate guests no matter how unwelcome. It is also important to bear in mind that well in advance of any arrival by enemy forces houses, and communities, would inevitably be gripped by waves of panic and fear: rumour swept across the north of England in 1745 (as it had in the earlier rising of 1715); and fear coursed through of France in 1789.[48] In 1864, Sherman's march through Georgia generated rumour after rumour as attested in numerous diaries and journals of southern owners. In the cases of Cornelia Jones Pond and Mary Chesnut imaginary fears were soon succeeded by military arrival, and both women watched on as their homes were ransacked, although spared the torch.[49] The classic study of this phenomenon in the French Revolution by Georges Lefebvre shows how this psychological visitation was driven by news, exaggerated or real, false alarm and untrammelled speculation; word of mouth, hastily compiled reports that filled a vacuum of information, coupled with the contagious nature of panic meant that these houses and communities were subject to deeply unwelcome periods of uncertainty long in advance of any hostile arrival.[50]

---

47 Reid, *Scourge of war*, p. 376; Noah Andre Trudeau, *Southern storm: Sherman's march to the sea* (New York, 2009), p. 505. Nancy Alderman notes that after the war Sherman visited Green at his home; Nancy Alderman, 'A biography of Charles Green', pp 15–16, Savannah Biographies, Georgia Southern University, digitalcommons.georgiasouthern.edu/sav-bios-lane/78, accessed 18 Dec. 2022. **48** Duffy, *The '45*, p. 295; Doyle, *Enemies*, p. 206; Schama, *Citizens*, p. 367. **49** Cornelia Jones Pond, *Recollections of a southern daughter*, ed. Lucinda H. MacKethan (Athens, GA, 1998), pp 71–7; C. Vann Woodward (ed.), *Mary Chesnut's civil war* (New Haven, 1981), pp 780, 803–3. **50** Georges Lefebvre and John Albert White, *The great*

1.8 Baroness La Grange and General Sir William Pulteney at Chateau de la Motte au Bois, 1915 (private collection).

Moving from these examples of civil war to international conflict the pattern remains the same, especially during the world wars of the twentieth century, with the main difference being the extent of such destructive visitations, particularly across Europe. The outbreak of war in 1914 had a profound impact upon various landed families in both the western and eastern theatres, with many instances of either a polite or a rude knock at the door. Baroness de la Grange's home, Chateau de la Motte au Bois, located a few miles to the south-west of Ypres, was in an area that might be considered the epicentre of destruction: a corner of north-eastern France and Flanders that had been a corridor for invading armies for centuries, with a long tradition of unwelcome arrivals.

In her memoir, *Open house in Flanders*, published in 1929, Baroness La Grange recounted how she offered the use of the chateau to the French Army in September 1914. She was determined not to abandon her home, believing that it was important she personally supervise her staff and take care of the house, as well as set an example to the local population. After this sector of the front came under British command she played hostess to a succession of British and Commonwealth staff officers, and among her house guests were generals

fear of 1789: rural panic in revolutionary France (Princeton, 1973). On how hearsay stokes fear, see Hans-Joachim Neubauer, *The rumour: a cultural history* (London, 1999), p. 88.

Allenby, Byng and Pulteney. The chateau was separated between her personal quarters and those occupied by the military, but at 5 p.m. she would open the dividing door and offer tea to the staff. Her hospitality and pronounced Anglophilia earned her the nickname the 'Mother of the British Army'.

On the whole the British forces were considerate occupiers; she described Allenby as 'extremely thoughtful and tactful'.[51] However she refused to blow up a bridge in her park, and was irked to discover mirrors attached to the trees as an early experiment in trench periscopes.[52] She hosted a visit from George V in December 1914, but reminders of the war were never far away; just four days later a German plane flew over the chateau. Although only twenty miles from the front she was able to describe August 1916 as a month of 'absolute peace'. This placid existence took on an exotic character when the chateau hosted Anzac staff at Christmas that year and there was an entertainment of Maori dancing.[53]

But this calm was deceptive. On visiting nearby Hazebrouck in 1917 she experienced shellfire, in the spring of 1918 she witnessed the long-range bombardment of Paris and the surprise German offensive in March meant that enemy forces came within two miles of La Motte. The chateau was bombarded and the baroness was particularly distressed not to be able to oversee the salvage of her belongings. The British posted a guard on the house to prevent any pillaging and supervised the evacuation of her furniture. When she was finally able to reach La Motte it was nearly empty and badly damaged.[54] Reflecting on these years of hardship and destruction, the baroness recognized that she could have enrolled as a nurse at the beginning of the war but believed her role as chatelaine was more important, both in ensuring the wellbeing of her home but also playing hostess to a succession of members of the British forces who were both guests and protectors, as well as friends, and for whom she was only too willing to offer such civilities as afternoon tea.[55]

Across Britain houses and estates were pressed into many new wartime uses. The park at Belton House in Lincolnshire was given over to the newly formed Machine Guns Corps in 1915, practice trenches were dug, and a huge garrison grew up in the nearby town of Grantham, with a railway supply line installed.[56] Almost immediately after war began Donington Hall, Leicestershire, was requisitioned as a POW camp for German officers. Surrounded by barbed wire and electric fences, the regime at Donington was a relaxed one, with officers playing sport, and attended by their personal servants. This was the only British camp from which a German successfully escaped, an exceptional example of a 'guest' choosing to abscond from the enforced hospitality on offer. The comforts

[51] Baroness Ernest de la Grange, *Open house in Flanders 1914–18, Chateau de la Motte au Bois*, trans. Melanie Lind (London, 1929), pp 60, 64; the epithet 'Mother of the British Army' was used by Field Marshall Allanby in his introduction to the volume, p. 5. [52] La Grange, *Open house in Flanders*, p. 172. [53] Ibid., pp 65, 70, 224, 237. [54] Ibid., pp 286, 311, 317–27. [55] Ibid., pp 331–2, 358–9. [56] Simon Greaves, *The country house at war: fighting the Great War at home and in the trenches* (London, 2014), pp 32–3.

1.9 German officers playing football at Donington Hall prisoner of war camp (private collection).

at Donington – silver service and wine served at meals – led to comments in Parliament and indignant articles in the press. The camp was finally closed in 1918.[57]

Many houses were turned into hospitals and convalescent homes, among them Dunham Massey, Cheshire, under the supervision of Lady Stamford treating nearly 300 men; and also Clandon Park, Surrey, under Lady Onslow. There was an improvisatory quality to these buildings, with operating theatres situated as close to running water as possible: at Dunham Massey this was beside a toilet at the bottom of the main stairs; at Clandon it was in Lord Onslow's dressing room.[58] Escrick Park, just south of York, was turned into an officers' convalescent home from 1917 to 1919 under the supervision of Irene Lawley, daughter of Lord Wenlock. A precious memento of this time survives in the form of an album filled with photographs, sketches, and limericks recording the pastimes of the patients, which included sports, amateur dramatics, and practical jokes. Clearly Escrick had a relaxed regime and the album is redolent of public

[57] Anon., *German prisoners in Great Britain* (Boston and London, c.1920), pp 5–12; 85–6, 105–7; Norman Nicol, *Captured Germans: British prisoner of war camps in the First World War* (Barnsley, 2017), pp 75–7; Gunther Pluschow, *My escape from Donington Hall* (Barnsley, 2015), pp 106–19. [58] Greaves, *Country house at war*, pp 37–40, 47–8; *National Trust Magazine* (Spring 2014), pp 37–43.

1.10 Page with signatures and photographs from the Escrick Park convalescent home album (by kind permission the Forbes-Adam Collection).

school fun and camaraderie as well as being a throwback to typical pre-war house parties; such a regime was most likely cultivated on purpose as a respite from the horrors of the front.[59]

Such were the affinities within aristocratic society in Europe, and the real links between sections of British and German society, that some families could find themselves facing conflicting loyalties with the outbreak of war. Born in 1873, Mary Cornwallis West came from an impoverished family at Ruthin Castle, north Wales; better known as Daisy, she married Hans Heinrich Hochberg, the prince of Pless, in 1891. This was a fabulously advantageous match, and Daisy left England to live in the official family residence, Pless Castle in Silesia. The outbreak of war left Daisy in an acutely difficult position, with divided feelings towards her country of birth and her adopted land. In her memoir she recorded how she prioritized her three main responsibilities: loyalty to country, husband and family; the duty to nurse the German sick and wounded; and to help British prisoners of war.[60] In 1914 the German High Command had based its eastern headquarters at Pless, and on her arrival Daisy

---

59 The Escrick album remains in the ownership of the Forbes Adam family. 60 *Daisy Princess of Pless by herself* (London, 1928), pp 283, 320.

found it odd that her role as hostess had been usurped by the master of the kaiser's household. Nevertheless the kaiser continued to treat this Englishwoman politely, and on departing wrote to express his thanks at how well looked after he had been.[61] While she may not have been mistress of the household when it accommodated the military high command, social protocol dictated that she was thanked as such.

Castles and houses on the Eastern Front, just as on the Western Front, experienced the see-saw nature of enemy occupation and retreat. Lancut, the home of the Potocki family, was located about 100 miles east of Cracow in what was then the province of Galicia in the Austro-Hungarian empire, and today it is part of Poland. The castle was requisitioned by Austrian troops in the summer of 1914; they quickly retreated from advancing Russian forces only to regain the chateau, and then relinquish it once more later in the year. On reaching the family home in November 1914 the young Alfred Potocki discovered that more damage had been done by Austrian forces than the Russians; the former were suspicious that this ethnically Polish family had somehow colluded with the Russians to prevent too much damage. Potocki endured hostility from Austrian officers, and his case was not helped by the fact that his cousin was on the Russian staff who had been billeted at Lancut. When he reached the castle in November he found the place a shambles.[62] For a region sandwiched between the German, Austrian and Russian empires, it was difficult to decide who presented the greatest danger or offered the surest security, especially as the old order began to fall apart after 1917.

Houses and estates located in contested land would always suffer the most. Across Belgium mansions were occupied and plundered, families expelled or interned.[63] In many cases these spacious residences with their extensive grounds, became ideal quarters for the high command, for staff officers or regiments. The scale of German occupation of chateaux in Belgium during the war was extensive, and with occupancy came all manner of peril. Throughout the country some sixty properties were destroyed and not rebuilt. Around Ypres alone thirty-four chateaux suffered, with sixteen completely destroyed. The forms of occupation varied, and so too did the extent of damage and destruction.

Chateau d'Ingelmunster became a German headquarters for the duration of the war, and the Comte de Montblanc and his family were expelled. At Chateau Gerimont the owner, Monsieur Warnaffe, was arrested and accused of supplying arms to the local population; sentenced to be shot, he claimed that German casualties were a result of enemy fire and not fire from Belgian civilians, or *francs tireurs*. An autopsy proved him correct and he was reprieved. At Chateau de Durbay the sixteen-year-old Comte d'Ursel was deported to Germany; his

61 Ibid., pp 347–53, 361–4, 412, 430.   62 Count Alfred Potocki, *Master of Lancut* (London, 1959), pp 62–5.   63 Details on the following chateaux are drawn from Francois-Emmanuel de Wasseige, 'Les chateaux Belges et la Grande Guerre', *Demeures Historiques & Jardins*, 183 (Sept. 2014), pp 4–33.

1.11 The high towers of Chateau de Zellaer made it an ideal observation post for German forces in 1914 (private collection).

compatriot, the Comte de Beauffort at Chateau de Mielmont, was imprisoned when it was discovered he was treating wounded French soldiers; ironically, after the war Mielmont was turned into a sanatorium for deportees returning from Germany. Other chateaux were more ecumenical in their medical regimes: Countess van Steen and Baroness Rosée treated French and German wounded alike at Chateau Chevetogne and Chateau de la For; at Chateau de Tillier Germans and Belgians were nursed; Chateau Nerom was used as an ambulance station but this did not prevent it from being torched by retreating German forces.[64] German demands at Chateau du Boussu included the installation of electricity and upgraded bathrooms as part of its transformation into an officers' home. But in 1916 more sinister alterations were made, as the ground floor was turned into prisoners' quarters, with interrogations held against the incongruous backdrop of fine historic interiors. Outdoors the park was trashed, and in 1918 the house was substantially damaged when a nearby munitions train exploded.[65]

The military value of chateaux was apparent when in 1914 General von Moltke used the high tower at Chateau de Zellaer as an observation post for the German assault on Walem outside Antwerp. Elsewhere chateaux became objectives in themselves. Chateau Gheluvelt was the headquarters for the British

64 Ibid., pp 4, 7, 14, 16. 65 Ibid., p. 7.

Visitations: foes

1.12 Chateau Hooghe before and after bombardment, a pair of views from a postwar postcard (private collection).

Le Château de la Hooghe lez Ypres,
avant et après le Bombardement.
Hooghe lez Ypres castle before and after the Shelling.

Visé Paris N° '315

21st infantry brigade in October 1914, but a month later it was overrun by German forces and completely destroyed. There are countless instances of the gradual and violent degradation of these kinds of properties in extreme circumstances. Chateau Hooghe, home of the Vincks family, could be said to be a typical example. The family fled in the face of invading forces, and the chateau was used as a German ambulance station; it was recaptured by French forces a month later, and Lieutenant Maurice Laurentin, an architect in civilian life, left a record of the damage from bombardment by both sides. Continual shellfire further damaged the roof and in January 1915 troops billeted in the building lit open fires indoors to keep themselves warm. Unsurprisingly the building went up in smoke, leaving just a derelict shell. In April 1915 English troops occupied the ruins, which then came under intense artillery fire until nothing remained but a cratered landscape. What had begun the war as a desirable set of quarters had been progressively targeted until nothing remained, but even that didn't stop the location being of tactical advantage in the ferocious world of trench combat, and the rubble-strewn landscape was the scene of bitter fighting. After the war the Vincks family returned and built a modest villa close to the site of the chateau.[66]

The reality was that buildings suffered at the hands of both Allied and German forces, especially if they were of military significance, whether located in important positions, or because it was necessary to deny opposing forces the advantages the buildings offered. Thus Chateau de Pierpont was dynamited by the Belgian Army, who also sacked Chateau de Bist. Houses that survived were frequently plundered: Chateau Neville was ransacked on the pretext that the owner was in secret communication with Belgian forces; at Chateau d'Acoz two thousand bottles of wine were liberated from the cellars on the pretence that they were destined for Red Cross use; and at Chateau Franc the Weret family concealed as many treasures as possible, but by the time German forces departed in September 1914, everything had been discovered and looted.[67]

On the English side the vision of generals spending an idle and comfortable war in the safety of chateaux far away from the front line has become a national cliché. Field Marshal Haig established his headquarters at Chateau Beaurepaire at Montreuil sur Mer, some sixty miles from Ypres. From here the British campaign was planned and executed with Haig making frequent journeys to advance headquarters nearer the front line. In 1931 an equestrian statue of Hague was erected in the town conferring on him the status of visitor in perpetuity as well as permanent friend of France.[68]

Among other occupants of Belgian chateaux was flying ace Manfred von Richthofen, whose squadron operated from an airfield beside Chateau Roucourt in 1917. Later that year the Red Baron commandeered Chateau Marke near Courtois; this had been occupied by German forces more or less continuously since 1914, with the Bethune family forced to move into a handful of upstairs rooms. For all their chivalry in the skies the baron and his fellow pilots proved to be not only unwelcome but also light-fingered guests at Marke. On their departure in 1917 they took away over two hundred items belonging to the family.[69]

---

66 Ibid., pp 4, 5, 16; for Hooghe see also Nigel Cave, *Sanctuary Wood and Hooge* (Barnsley, 1993), pp 39–41, 77–9, and *Ypres and the battles of Ypres* (Clermont-Ferand, 1919), pp 105–6. 67 Wasseige, 'Les chateaux Belges', pp 6, 7, 9, 11, 12. 68 Gary Sheffield, *The chief: Douglas Haig and the British Army* (London, 2011), p. 141. The statue was toppled by German forces in 1940 only to be replaced in 1950; in 2009 the town produced a brochure, *Montreuil sur Mer au coeur de la Grande Guerre*, haigstatuemontreuil-sur-mer.org/the-story-behind-the-statue, accessed 30 Oct. 2022. 69 Wasseige, 'Les chateaux Belges', pp 8–9; Mike O'Connor and Norman Francis, *In the footsteps of the Red Baron* (Barnsley, 2004), pp 26–30, 76.

When the scholar and public intellectual, Gilbert Murray, toured the Western Front in 1916 to compile a series of articles, he decided to offer a picture of the devastation he had witnessed and chose the fictional name of 'Chateaumort' for the area he was visiting; this was a generic scene to conceal the real location and satisfy the military censor. His choice of name was significant. Given the familiar suffixes for the word '*chateau*' in French, Chateau Neuf (Newcastle), or Chateau Vieux (Oldcastle), Murray's choice was only too apt, Chateaumort (Deadcastle), given that all he could see around him was a visitation of immense carnage and destruction.[70]

For many houses Murray's phrase became a terrible reality. Chateau de Rosendal, south of Ypres, was set in grounds with woodlands, a moat and a lake. Pre-war images show a building that might best be described as a stylish late nineteenth-century villa. Originally home to Gustav de Stuer, it was occupied in 1914 by French troops, but a year later this sector of the line was transferred to British command. Over the following three years it was used as a brigade headquarters, a field hospital and a burial site, and the chateau was rechristened Bedford House by the men of the Bedfordshire Regiment who were stationed there. Since it was situated in close proximity to the front, it inevitably was targeted by enemy artillery. Although fierce fighting took place all over the vicinity it was never captured by the Germans, but by 1917 the main house had been virtually destroyed, save for the deep cellars, which were used as a dressing station. The surrounding terrain was increasingly pressed into service as a series of small cemeteries, which were enlarged after the Armistice and added to with graves transferred from other burial sites. By 1919 Bedford House had become an official Commonwealth Graves Commission Cemetery, and come the end of the war Chateau Rosendal had quite simply ceased to exist; there was neither home nor estate for the family to reclaim, and the name of the house has been erased too. In this extreme example, the house hosted family and guests prior to 1914, was visited by fighting troops, injured soldiers and medical orderlies during the war, not to mention enemy artillery and today is the resting place for more than five thousand headstones, less than half of which are identified burials. Chateau Rosendal or Bedford House is thus renowned for being visited by the dead and the unknown. Sites like these would become standard places to visit for Western Front tourists after the war, and by 1919 Michelin was publishing illustrated guides to the major battlefields.[71]

Chateau Fraineuse was one of several chateaux used by the German high command, whose headquarters were based at nearby Spa, but in July 1920 it

[70] Gilbert Murray, 'Somewhere in France', *Westminster Gazette*, 5 June 1916.   [71] The chateau has multiple spellings Rosedaal, Rosendal, Rozendaal; it was also known as Kerskenhoove Castle, and later christened Woodcote House by British troops, in addition to becoming known as Bedford House. Jon Cooksey and Jerry Murland, *Ypres: Nieuwpoort to Ploegsteert* (Barnsley, 2012), pp 138–9. See also, Brian Murphy, 'Dark tourism and the Michelin World War I battlefield guides', *Journal of Franco-Irish Studies*, 4:1 (2015), pp 1–9.

1.13 Huis Doorn today with a bust of Kaiser Wilhelm II on the front lawn (private collection).

played host to the Spa conference at which the Supreme War Council of the Allies met with representatives from the Weimar Republic to discuss war reparations and German disarmament.[72] Fraineuse was also the last residence of the kaiser before he abdicated in November 1918 as revolutionary unrest erupted in Germany. He hurriedly crossed the border into Holland, never to set foot on German soil again; Queen Wilhelmina, shocked at his unexpected arrival, granted him asylum, but the Dutch authorities were faced with the problem of where to house the exiled emperor. However, Count Aldenburg-Bentinck agreed to make his moated castle at Amerongen outside of Utrecht available. For the next eighteen months the kaiser was effectively under house arrest there; his mail and telephone calls were censored, and he was not permitted to leave the grounds without a Dutch escort. His household was reduced and he lived in fear of assassination, or kidnap by the Allies to put him on trial for war crimes. In 1920, with his affairs settled in Germany, and in receipt of large sums of money, he purchased Huis Doorn from Baroness van Heemstra and settled there until his death in 1941. As a visitor attraction today Huis Doorn is still known for its last arrival-cum-resident, who was one among many of a long European tradition of noble fugitives.[73]

[72] Wasseige, 'Les chateaux Belges', p. 23. [73] John C.G. Rohl, *Wilhelm II: into the abyss of war and exile, 1900–1941* (Cambridge, 2014), pp 1188–1204.

The appeal of country houses to armies was varied. While not the only type of target – towns, villages, hilltops and other features in the terrain were also bitterly contested – they often represented significant vantage points in terms of location or topography and thus became targets. Despite their exclusive status shielded by woods and parkland, they were prominent structures. The closer they were to the fighting the more likely it was that they would face damage and destruction, and contested land would mean there was a priority to possess or dispossess. Topographical command was synonymous with military advantage. But it is also clear that big houses were attractive to the high command for they offered comfort, spaciousness, and a degree of seclusion. Their occupation by officer classes would echo a peacetime social structure: military hierarchy being just another form of class distinction, albeit in uniform, as NCOs, ordinary soldiers, batmen, cooks and drivers would perform the equivalent of servants' roles for the top brass. The social hierarchy indoors is also a reminder that on their own buildings cannot perform the roles of hospitality, shelter, comfort or entertainment; whether in peacetime or war they require staff or personnel to make them function.

The story of the Second World War was almost an exact replica of the 1914–18 years in terms of occupation and destruction. In Britain ever more houses were requisitioned for a variety of uses: Bletchley Park, Buckinghamshire, used as a code-breaking centre, is the most famous example; but Hatfield House, Hertfordshire, and Eaton Hall, Cheshire, became hospitals; Egginton Hall, Derbyshire, was taken over by Bomber Command, while Bentley Priory, Middlesex, was used by Fighter Command; schools occupied Blenheim and Castle Howard; the grounds of Lowther Castle were used for tank training; Trent Park, Middlesex, housed German prisoners of war and the building was wired in order to eavesdrop on their conversations; Mentmore Towers, Buckinghamshire, and Penryhn Castle, Caernarvonshire, both housed artworks evacuated from London; and Achnacarry Castle, rebuilt after the tumult of 1745, was used as a commando training centre.[74] Across Europe houses that were spared annihilation found themselves requisitioned. In the east Red Army destruction and occupation during 1944–5 was followed by decades of Soviet appropriation with a wide range of new occupants and uses. These comprised state institutions, such as agricultural colleges, hospitals or quarters for the communist elite, a transformation driven by ideological animus.[75]

---

[74] John Martin Robinson, *Requisitioned: the British country house in the Second World War* (London, 2014); Julie Summers, *Our uninvited guests: the secret lives of the British country house 1939–45* (London, 2018), where the introduction is tellingly entitled 'The invasion of privacy'; Marcus Binney, *Country houses and secret agents: Sir John Soane's Museum lecture* (London, 2002); Helen Fry, *The M room: secret listeners who bugged the Nazis in World War Two* (n.p., 2012). [75] Max Egremont, *Forgotten land: journeys among the ghosts of east Prussia* (London, 2011), pp 116–21, 126–32; Marcus Binney et al., *Silesia: the land of dying country houses* (London, 2009), lists many houses and castles abandoned or re-purposed, for example, Chrostnik, Dobrocin, Kunow, Piotrowek, Wisniowa, pp 67, 69, 81, 95, 111.

Both conflicts also witnessed an enormous increase in long-range attack, which meant that destruction could be visited upon houses by an unseen enemy from far away. In the seventeenth and eighteenth centuries limitations in range meant that canon and field pieces were in close proximity to their targets, more or less visible to the opposing side. By the First World War shelling might be directed at targets many miles away, although batteries would depend on intelligence fed back to them by forward observers. Those under attack would have little idea of the whereabouts of their adversaries, or indeed who they might be. The rise of aerial warfare added another dimension to conflict, and even Britain, protected from invasion by the Channel, could not escape early Zeppelin raids. In May 1915 bombs were dropped in the grounds of Craig Castle in Aberdeenshire; British warships in the nearby Cromarty Firth were the likely targets of this raid along the Scottish coast, but the arbitrary nature of aerial bombardment presented a new and disturbing threat to country houses with indiscriminate attack from above. It was sufficiently known as a hazard for the agent at Castle Howard to make enquiries on the outbreak of war in 1914 if the house could be insured against such attack.[76] A quarter of a century later the concerted attacks of the Luftwaffe would account for several country house casualties, most notably Holland House on the outskirts of London in 1940, as well as others, mainly in the south of England.[77]

It is important to understand that this chronicle of hostile visitations extends well beyond wartime or revolution. The view of an estate as a microcosm might suggest that it was an enclosed world, but in fact it was subject to exactly the same forces as the wider world. Political and civil protest could lead to attacks on houses, as for example, during the reform bill riots of 1831, when the homes of noted anti-Reformers were targeted: these included Nottingham Castle, the residence of the duke of Newcastle, and Colwick Hall, home to John Musters; according to press reports Musters was 'no meddler in politics' and his home may well have been attacked because as a magistrate he had presided over convictions of poachers. The animus of the crowd was entirely directed at his property, as the house was stormed and its contents destroyed or looted. The ladies of the house, sheltering in one room, were left alone, and the servants were assured by the mob that they would not be hurt.[78]

---

[76] *Aberdeen Evening Express*, 4 May 1915; military censorship meant that the report was necessarily vague describing the bombs as landing 'on the policies of a mansion'; more details can be found at iancastlezeppelin.co.uk/2/3-may-1916 and aberdeenvoice.com/2013/05/zeppelin-over-insch/, accessed 26 Feb. 2023. For the insurance enquiry see estate correspondence, Charles Luckhurst to ninth countess of Carlisle, 19 Aug. 1915 (Castle Howard Archives (hereafter CHA), F8/3/63, No.539).   [77] Derek Hudson, *Holland House in Kensington* (London, 1967), pp 125–7; see also the entry in James Lees Milne's diary, for 28 Apr. 1942, Lees Milne, *Ancestral voices* (London, 1975), pp 52–3. He also recorded damage to Mount Edgcumbe, Plymouth, Friday 9 Oct. 1942, ibid., p. 108; Beeston Hall, Norfolk, 5 Feb. 1944, Knole Park, Kent, 22 Feb. 1944 and 27 Oct. 1944, Lees Milne, *Prophesying peace* (London, 1977), pp 18, 26, 126.   [78] *Leeds Intelligencer*, 20 Oct. 1831, p. 3; *Morning Post*,

Visitations: foes 43

1.14 Clayton Grange, Lancashire, set on fire by rioters in 1878, as depicted in the *Illustrated London News* (private collection).

Similarly, industrial unrest would also lead to house attacks. For example, during a dispute with cotton workers in Blackburn in 1878, mill owner Colonel Jackson's house, Clayton Grange, was sacked by a mob and burnt.[79] One of the most graphic accounts of a politically motivated attack on a country house is to be found in Disraeli's novel *Sybil*. Set against the backdrop of Chartist agitation, the story climaxes with a mob sacking Mowbray Castle; entwined with this story is a romantic plot that involves the humble heroine's claim to the Mowbray estates, which is only proved when documents of proof are secured during the attack on the castle.[80]

Beyond the big house itself in the wider countryside poachers were frequent intruders on estates, often precipitating pitched battles with gamekeepers in what was likened to a state of war in the 1890s, with armed clashes at Longnor Hall, Shropshire, on the marquess of Zetland's grouse moors in Cleveland, and Eaton Hall, Cheshire. Estates as widespread as Temple Newsam, Yorkshire, Newham Paddock, Warwickshire and Heaton Park, Lancashire, all experienced

15 Oct. 1831, p. 3; *The Times*, 14 Jan. 1832; *Derby Mercury*, 26 Oct. 1831. See also the *Report of the proceedings against parties charged with burning Nottingham Castle … and sacking Colwick Hall, Nottingham assizes, 4–14 Jan. 1832* (Nottingham, 1832).   **79** *Burnley Advertiser*, 16 May 1878.   **80** Benjamin Disraeli, *Sybil, or the two nations* (London, 1845); the attack takes place in book vi, chapter 12.

fierce confrontations with poaching gangs. In 1845 the earl of Carlisle ordered night-watching on the Castle Howard estate to stop because of the 'hazard to human life'.[81]

Rural unrest might be sparked by prices and food shortages, and incendiarism was the favoured tactic, with the burning of barns and hay ricks, where the targets were not so much farmers as their landlords, as, for example, on Lord Darnley's estate at Cobham Hall, Kent, and Caister Hall Farm, Norfolk, both in 1830.[82] Another kind of unlawful incursion onto private land can be found with instances of trespass: individuals might be poachers, vandals or protesters, such as those who participated in the mass trespass at Kinder Scout in Derbyshire in 1932 to challenge the structure of landownership in the UK; or they might be the constitutionally nosey, such as the young John Harris, whose career as a distinguished architectural historian began with various episodes of illicit entry, thereby proving there are virtues in transgression.[83]

There are other examples of hostile intrusion in the form of burglary and robbery, such as the theft of Old Master paintings from Charlton Park, home of the earl of Suffolk, in 1856. In 1907 there was the trial of a gang of robbers nicknamed 'The Aristocrats' because they targeted the houses of the nobility such as the earl of Sheffield and Lord Sefton; in 1938 a Reynolds portrait valued at £10,000 was cut from its frame at Shillinglee, Surrey, home of Earl Winterton.[84] More recently Floors Castle, seat of the duke of Roxburghe, saw the theft of valuables worth £275,000 after a burglar rowed across the river Tweed in a dinghy to enter the castle. In 2008 members of the notorious Johnston gang, responsible for thefts from country houses across the country, with an estimated value of between £30 and £80 million, were jailed for twenty years.[85] Violent encounters included the activities of the Coggeshall gang in Essex in the 1840s, convicted of robbery and setting fire to Coggeshall House, and in 1894 an armed thief was apprehended as he exited Stinsford House, Dorset, home to Captain Perry.[86] More recently, in 2016, at Goodwood House, Sussex, Lord and Lady March were tied up in a raid when jewellery worth £700,000 was stolen.[87]

---

81 Harry Hopkins, *The long affray: the poaching wars in Britain* (London, 1985), pp 184, 204, 207, 229, 226, 238, 265–6, 276–7. Sixth countess of Carlisle to John Henderson, 28 Feb. 1845 (CHA, F5/3 Bundle 1).   82 E.J. Hobsbawm and George Rudé, *Captain Swing* (London, 1993), pp 101, 223, 229; Barry Reay, *The last rising of the agricultural labourers: rural protest in nineteenth-century England* (London, 1990), pp 61–5; John E. Archer, *Social unrest and popular protest in England, 1780–1840* (Cambridge, 2000), pp 17, 21. *Newcastle Courant*, 4 Dec. 1830. 83 Nick Hayes, *The book of trespass: crossing lines that divide us* (London, 2020), pp 1–3, 19–21; Guy Shrubsole, *Who owns England?* (London, 2019), pp 250–2; John Harris, *No voice from the hall: early memories of a country house snooper* (London, 1998), pp 42–4, 55–7, 109–13. 84 *Derby Mercury*, 22 Oct. 1856; *Bridlington Free Press*, 27 Dec. 1907; *The Scotsman*, 12 Aug. 1938.   85 *Daily Mirror*, 14 May 1994, p. 9; *The Times*, 7 Aug. 2008.   86 *Essex Standard*, 2 Feb. 1849; *Essex Herald*, 13 Mar. 1849; Karen Bowman, *Essex boys* (Stroud, 2015), pp 93–9; *Post and Gazette*, 23 Feb. 1894.   87 *The Times*, 16 Jan. 2016.

1.15 Arthur Orton, who claimed to be Sir Roger Tichborne, in Newgate prison after his conviction in 1872 (Mary Evans Picture Library).

Other lawbreaking intruders, menacing in a different way, might take the form of 'pretenders', most famously in the episode of the Tichborne claimant, a cause célèbre that captivated Victorian England, as Arthur Orton claimed to be the heir to the Tichborne baronetcy in 1866. Not only were a title and wealth at stake here, so too was Tichborne Park in Hampshire; had Orton succeeded, he would have dispossessed other members of the family of their home. Instead, he was found guilty of perjury and the claim repudiated; as a result, this suspect cuckoo in the Tichborne nest spent ten years as a guest of her majesty in various prisons.[88]

Although unwelcome, pretenders might be classed as fictional visitors, imposters who turn out to be not who they say they are; they may have attempted entry under false pretences but could be expelled once the fraud has been exposed. In that sense they are not real, for all the litigation and distress they might cause. However, there is another class of unreal visitor to country houses,

---

88 See Rohan McWilliam, *The Tichborne claimant: a Victorian sensation* (London, 2007), and Robyn Annear, *The man who lost himself: the unbelievable story of the Tichborne claimant* (London, 2002). For John Dow's claim in 1835 he was Viscount Lascelles, see Kirsten McKenzie, *Swindler's progress: nobles and convicts in the age of liberty* (Cambridge, MA, 2010).

spectral presences: ghosts, which for some people are intensely real, whereas for others they amount to little more than folklore. Ghosts have a literary pedigree stretching back to the Gothic novels of the eighteenth century and earlier, but they are also the mainstay of the late Victorian stories of M.R. James. In fiction the most successful stories exploit the tension between real apparitions and figments of the imagination, most notably in Henry James' *Turn of the screw* (1898), and more recently Sarah Waters' *The little stranger* (2009). Countless houses claim spectral ancestors or troubled spirits that continue to visit them as a reminder of misfortunes or terrible deeds in the past, and their influence might range from the malign to a protective guardianship. These phantom visitors also have a role to play in promoting houses as attractions to the public, thus, today Chillingham Castle, Northumberland, advertises itself as Britain's most haunted historic castle. The popularity of ghost trails is testimony to how this kind of apparently unwelcome guest can benefit a house.[89]

War, occupation, revolution, riot, theft and fraud are all characterized by human action (as well as haunting to some degree); their causes and effects are defined by individuals or groups of people who target houses with specific intents in mind. There are other agencies responsible for unpleasant and damaging visitations to country houses, the most common and destructive of which is fire. Since 1700 there have been more than two thousand recorded episodes in country houses; overwhelmingly, these have been instances of accidental fire, although there have been some episodes of arson.[90] The causes have been many: candles, oil lamps, poorly built or badly maintained chimneys, kitchen stoves, electricity, gas, storage of flammable materials, as well as carelessness on the part of servants, such as in 1826 when the marquess of Sligo's library was destroyed after a servant left a candle burning in the room.[91]

In 1871 Warwick Castle was partially destroyed in a fire that began in the early hours in apartments where decorators and plumbers had been at work, thereby signalling one of the most common causes of fire – the presence of contractors. At Belvoir Castle in Rutland in 1816, the blaze began in the carpenter's room in the west wing while refurbishment was ongoing. Such examples could be repeated countless times – plumbers, painters, decorators, roofers etc. were all welcome presences when improving and refurbishing a house but not viewed so favourably if they acted carelessly.[92] New technologies also presented a different

---

[89] The literature on ghosts and haunted country houses is vast; see, for example, J. Wentworth Day, 'The ghosts of Athelhampton', *Country Life*, 140 (1 Dec. 1966), pp 1442–3; 'The ghost of Raynham Hall, an astonishing photograph', *Country Life*, 80 (26 Dec. 1936), pp 673–4; 'Ten haunted Historic Houses Association houses', *Historic Houses Magazine*, 41:3 (Autumn, 2017), pp 35–8. Websites abound, such as, nationaltrust.org.uk/lists/our-most-haunted-places. [90] The following is drawn from the author's work in progress towards a history of fire in country houses, with accounts drawn from newspaper reports, house archives and published memoirs. [91] *Public Ledger and Daily Advertiser*, 25 Jan. 1826. [92] Warwick Castle, *The Daily News*, 4 Dec. 1871, p. 3; Belvoir, *Morning Post*, 29 Oct. 1816, p. 2; *Derby Mercury*, 31 Oct. 1816, Postscript, pp 2–3; 'Examination taken on oath before Thomas Norris,

range of risks: oil lamps had a habit of exploding, showering the vicinity with flaming fuel as at Aldborough Hall, Yorkshire, in 1901, and Powderham Castle in Devon a year later. Among the most bizarre causes is the suspicion that the fire at Bellister Castle, Northumberland, in 1900 was caused by mice nibbling matches in a cupboard – a hitherto unheard of danger presented by verminous visitors.[93] These examples point to a curious mix of agencies – human action, or inaction by way of neglect and carelessness, and the roots of these accidental outbreaks lie somewhere along this spectrum. Time and time again commentators remarked on the lack of preparedness and preventative measures in households. In an editorial in *The Field* magazine in 1910, after a fire at Castle Freke, County Cork, house owners were castigated for their passive attitude towards the dangers of fire, the author at a loss to understand how 'in some strange way they look upon fire as a visitation', deeming such calamity as almost inevitable, little more than a social inconvenience that would happen one day. An owner could absent themself or pretend to be away as a safeguard against troublesome guests coming down the driveway, but very few doors could resist the entry of smoke and flames.[94] What is interesting to note is how myriad press reports described the blaze in terms that personalized the fire, likening it to a malignant and marauding invader, a living creature, or 'devouring element'; and in 1893, surveying the ruins of Highfield House in Yorkshire after a fire, the local reporter remarked how a 'devastating fury had evidently knocked fiercely at the door'.[95]

Salvage and rescue also became an essential part of this story. Frequently, local people rushed to the scene to assist the household and fire brigade in saving objects from the blazing building. While very welcome, the enthusiasm of these volunteers often led to items being damaged; at Belvoir Castle in 1816 'great injury' was done to furniture that was thrown out of the windows by over-eager helpers; the vigorous efforts of locals at Baginton Hall, Warwickshire, in 1889, and Culdees Castle, Perthshire, in the same year, are just two more instances of many when damage was caused by the well-intentioned efforts of those who had arrived to assist.[96] At Naworth Castle in 1844 many of the locals turned out not to rescue household items but to help themselves to the contents of the cellar, and became drunk.[97] Helping hands would also be followed by crowds of onlookers curious to witness the destruction; following in their footsteps would

---

clerk to one of his majesty's justices of the peace' (Belvoir Castle Archives, MS 128). I am grateful to the present duke of Rutland for permission to consult the Belvoir Archives. **93** *East Riding Telegraph*, 2 Feb. 1901, p. 7; *Devon and Exeter Gazette*, 6 Feb. 1902; *Sunderland Daily Echo*, 7 Feb. 1900, p. 4. **94** *The Field*, 19 Mar. 1910. **95** For example, the fire at Charleton House, *Montrose, Arbroath and Brechin Review*, 4 Mar. 1892; Aqualate Hall, *Shrewsbury Chronicle*, 2 Dec. 1910, p. 4; Ballyheigue Castle, *Wexford Conservative*, 25 Nov. 1840; Abbotsbury, *The Western Gazette*, 14 Feb. 1913; Highfield, *Hull Daily Mail*, 1 Feb. 1893. **96** *Northampton Mercury*, 2 Nov. 1816, p. 2; Baginton, *Leamington Spa Courier*, 12 Oct. 1889; Culdees, *Dundee Advertiser*, Monday 8 July 1889, p. 7. **97** *Illustrated London News*, 25 May 1844; in his journal the seventh earl of Carlisle described the people behaving like 'wild beasts', 22 May 1844 (CHA, J19/8/1).

1.16 Naworth Castle, Cumbria, on fire in May 1844; local inhabitants have arrived to help rescue items from the house, as depicted in the *Illustrated London News* (private collection).

be family members, neighbours, insurance agents and, eventually, builders or demolition men.[98] In many instances guard had to be mounted over the contents piled high on the lawns, but police presence didn't always prevent individuals taking the opportunity to profit from the chaos and confusion.[99]

One of the starkest consequences of fire was homelessness, although many families had secondary residences, town houses or relatives they could stay with. After being burned out at Uffington House on 20 December 1904, Lord and Lady Lindsey initially sought refuge in their steward's house on the estate, before neighbours Lord and Lady Exeter, at Burghley House, invited the couple to stay for Christmas.[100]

Instances of incendiarism are rare among this long list. For example, in 1926 butler Ronald Cowl appeared in court accused of setting fire to Howsham Hall in Yorkshire.[101] But there was one intense period during the years 1912–14 when houses were targeted by suffragettes: these extreme visitations came to Penshurst

[98] For example at Blenheim, *The Era*, 10 Feb. 1861; Brocklesby, *Hull Daily Mail*, 26 Mar. 1898; Cantonteign House, *Western Times*, 21 Oct. 1912; Cortachy Castle, *Dundee Courier*, 2 Apr. 1934. [99] For examples of police guards, see: Carton House, *Freeman's Journal*, 22 Dec. 1855; Cressingham House, *Reading Mercury*, 8 Dec. 1883; Maidwell Hall, *Northampton Mercury*, 22 Feb. 1895. For theft, see: Bush House, *Potter's Electric News*, 17 Jan. 1866; Charleton House, *Montrose, Arbroath and Brechin Review*, 4 Mar. 1892 and *Dundee Evening Telegraph*, 4 Mar. 1892; Burrough Court, *Leicester Evening Mail*, 9 Feb. 1944. [100] *Sheffield Daily Telegraph*, 23 Dec. 1904, p. 4. [101] For Howsham, see *The Times*, 25 Aug. 1926.

Place, Kent; Orlands and Abbeylands, County Antrim; Begbrook House, Bristol; and Aberuchill Castle, Perthshire, which was earmarked with two other houses in the vicinity in February 1914 as part of a concerted attack. At each site suffragette literature was discovered as well as petrol tins, and evidence that windows had been deliberately left open to accelerate the spread of the fire.[102] This outburst of incendiarism is virtually unique in the history of fires on mainland Britain, but has a contemporary counterpart in Ireland with the series of burnings during the War of Independence and the Civil War, a chronicle expertly told by Terence Dooley. The significant difference between these two campaigns is that for the suffragettes, arson was a form of violent protest; the parties who attacked elite houses in Ireland, meanwhile, had a variety of motivations, from punishing and dispossessing an enemy to reprisals for killings and burnings elsewhere, to an opportunity to grab land, or to settle local scores behind a political fig leaf. These extreme actions were sometimes executed ruthlessly, but in other instances raiders evinced a deferential or even apologetic attitude, as if embarrassed at the inconvenience they were causing the occupants, who had perhaps done them no personal harm, as was the case at Palmerston House, Lismullin and Moydrum.[103]

The consequences of fire, whether deliberate or accidental, are many and grave: homelessness, loss of employment, harm to the local economy, not to mention instances of death. Clandon Park, Surrey, gutted by fire in April 2015, was no longer able to function as a visitor attraction in the aftermath, adversely affecting the livelihoods of numerous people. At the time of the fire, many bookings and deposits for weddings had been made; these had to be cancelled and the money returned, depleting its coffers, not to mention leaving many couples disappointed, as well as suppliers and contractors. Clandon was a dismal re-run of an earlier National Trust disaster at Uppark House, Sussex, in 1988, which faced a similar array of problems in the aftermath of the blaze. However Uppark underwent an enormous restoration programme, returning the house to the condition it was in on the day of the fire in 1988, and it subsequently reopened its doors to popular acclaim.[104] At Clandon debate has ranged back and forth as to the fate of the building, and in the summer of 2022 the Trust announced plans not to undertake a complete rebuild but to preserve the shell as a ruin and use this as an opportunity to re-imagine the house, confident that the

---

102 Penshurst, *Manchester Courier*, 18 Sept. 1913; Orlands, *Daily Express*, Friday 10 Apr. 1914; Abbeylands, *Newcastle Daily Journal*, 28 Mar. 1914; Begbrook, *The Suffragette*, 21 Nov. 1913; Aberuchill, *Dundee Courier*, 5 Feb. 1914. See also Simon Webb, *The Suffragette bombers: Britain's forgotten terrorists* (Barnsley, 2021).   103 Terence Dooley, *Burning the big house: the story of the Irish country house in revolution, 1920–23* [exh. cat.] (Maynooth, 2022), p. 40; see also his comprehensive *Burning the big house, the story of the Irish country house in a time of war and revolution* (New Haven and London, 2022), which situates burnings in a longer history of agrarian protest.   104 Christopher Rowell and John Martin Robinson, *Uppark restored* (London, 1990).

1.17 The shell of the burnt out mansion at Clandon Park, Surrey (copyright National Trust Images/James Dobson).

'broken raw beauty' of the building will enable a different range of stories to be told.[105] In due course it is hoped visitor numbers will recover and the site will resume its role in the local economy; in 2019 visitors to gardens and house numbered 20,000, compared to pre-fire figures of 50,000. Clandon is set to join the ranks of other great ruined houses such as Lowther Castle, Cumbria; Witley Court, Worcestershire; Powerscourt, County Wicklow; and Seaton Delaval, Northumberland. These apparently inhospitable interiors, partially open to the skies, attract visitors who are absorbed by the spectacle of ruins.

This chapter has illustrated how open, exposed and vulnerable, country houses have been, on the receiving end of unwelcome, unfriendly, inconvenient or destructive visitations, whether physical, social, legislative, financial or otherwise. However it is important to conclude with two key observations. Firstly, for all the inimical character of these incursions, many houses survived these encounters, and their families have, mostly, endured too. Granted, some

[105] 'New plans for Clandon Park', youtube.com/watch?v=blvHFJM1AjE&t=28s, accessed, 18 Dec. 2022.

houses did not survive these destructive episodes, but a good number were repaired or rebuilt, the families in question able to refashion their lives. Even in instances of loss there is usually a testamentary record of some sort that can chronicle the trials and tribulations of unwelcome arrival as well as triumphs over adversity.

Second, few visitations are permanent, visitors – whether welcome or unwelcome – come and, on the whole, do go, even if they leave behind them a trail of devastation. Country houses are highly resilient, able to withstand extraordinary levels of shock and damage; they are also immensely adaptable structures able to be put to differing uses by a multitude of occupants: family home, social venue, armed garrison, military headquarters, interrogation centre, prison, hospital, target and so on. However, no matter how beleaguered they appear, beset with enemies real or abstract, they also have no shortage of friends in the form of families, guests, visitors and various supporters and stakeholders, as will be discussed in a later chapter.[106]

---

[106] See Chapter 11.

'I feel more like Cinderella, than anyone else you can imagine': Elizabeth Gaskell's visit to Chatsworth

FRAN BAKER

On Saturday 12 September 1857 the writer Elizabeth Gaskell (1810–65) and her daughter Meta arrived at Chatsworth House in Derbyshire, equipped with their 'green card', which entitled them to a tour of the house by the housekeeper.[1] Gaskell's visit – memorably described in one of her most entertaining letters – was to take a different shape from the one she had envisaged, and has interesting things to tell us about her status as an author, the relationship between writers and aristocratic patrons in the Victorian period, the rise of literary tourism as a leisure pursuit alongside country-house visiting, and middle-class social mobility in the mid-nineteenth century. However, Gaskell began the day simply as one of twenty individual tourists and five parties who signed the Chatsworth visitors' book that Saturday in September.

To set her visit in context: in the mid-nineteenth century Chatsworth was one of the largest and best-known stately homes in England, owned by the Cavendish family, dukes of Devonshire. The original sixteenth-century house, built by family ancestor Bess of Hardwick, had been replaced in the late seventeenth century by a magnificent baroque mansion, built by Bess' descendant William Cavendish, first duke of Devonshire. William Spencer Cavendish (1790–1858), who became sixth duke in 1811, embarked on a series of significant alterations to his ancestral seat with the architect Sir Jeffry Wyattville, including the substantial new North Wing.

Gaskell was visiting eight years after the railway station had opened at nearby Rowsley; widely advertised as the station for Chatsworth, it brought tens of thousands of visitors to the house each year, the last part of their journey facilitated by coaches and carriages.[2] The house itself was open six days a week; admission was free, and, as Peter Mandler points out, it was 'the most visited country house in the land throughout the nineteenth century.'[3] Weekdays saw many organized trips, including summer excursion trains arranged by the entrepreneur Thomas Cook, as well as visits by societies and other groups; six days before Gaskell's visit, a 'very large party' of workmen formerly employed

---

1 J.A.V. Chapple and Arthur Pollard (eds), *The letters of Mrs Gaskell* (2nd ed., Manchester, 1997), p. 471. 2 Adrian Tinniswood, *A history of country house visiting* (Oxford, 1989), p. 144.
3 Peter Mandler, *The fall and rise of the stately home* (New Haven and London, 1997), p. 62.

2.1 *Carte de visite* photograph of Elizabeth Gaskell by Alexander McGlashon, 1860–5 (courtesy of the University of Manchester).

2.2 Photographic portrait of the sixth duke of Devonshire, Brighton Talbotype Gallery, c.1852 (© The Devonshire Collections, Chatsworth, reproduced by permission of Chatsworth Settlement Trustees).

at Tapton Colliery was due to make an excursion to Chatsworth.[4] While not all visitors would have toured the house itself, many of them did. In a letter of April 1858, Sarah Paxton (wife of Joseph, the sixth duke of Devonshire's agent) wrote wearily that there had been 1,000–1,500 people 'tramping through' the house that day.[5] Excursion trips did not run at weekends, but the casual tourist trade alone could boost visitor numbers to around 2,000 a day.[6]

4 The *Derbyshire Times* and *Chesterfield Herald* announced in their issue of Saturday 5 Sept. 1857, that the visit was due to take place on Monday.   5 The Devonshire Collections, Chatsworth (hereafter DC), P/1354.   6 Mandler, *Fall and rise*, p. 93.

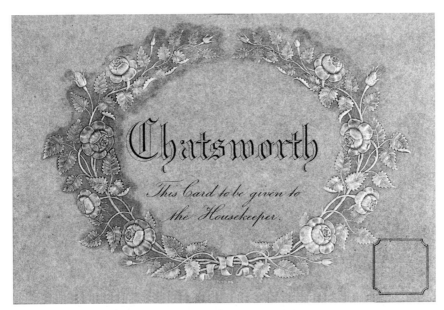

2.3 An example of a green visitor's ticket like the one Gaskell used to gain entry to Chatsworth (© The Devonshire Collections, Chatsworth, reproduced by permission of Chatsworth Settlement Trustees).

There is some uncertainty around exactly who signed the visitors' books that survive in the Devonshire Collection Archives. For example, the number of signatures on the day of Gaskell's visit must represent only a small proportion of the overall number of visitors. It seems that 'excursionists' did not sign – groups like the Tapton colliers certainly have no presence in the book. This suggests that those who signed were more likely to have been well-to-do independent visitors and their families or parties.

It was the sixth duke who introduced entry to Chatsworth via tickets or cards that had to be obtained in advance of a visit. The archives hold a selection of these tickets – some unused and others with names inscribed on them, or corners torn off, suggesting that they were collected from visitors on entry.[7] Most of the surviving examples date from the 1840s, suggesting this is an innovation which dates from that decade and reflects an increase in visitor numbers: the earliest surviving visitors' book covers a substantial period (1828–33), but from 1841 onwards each year had a dedicated volume. Entry by ticket would also have been in keeping with general trends of the time.[8] Many of the cards have handwritten notes on them identifying the party to be admitted, and a proportion of these are in the duke's own handwriting; in a number of cases he added special permissions, for example, that the ticket holder should be shown the Emperor

---

7 DC, DF4/3/1/1/2. 8 Tinniswood notes that by mid-century 'entry by ticket was becoming increasingly common'; Tinniswood, *A history*, p. 142.

2.4 William Cowen, 'View of Chatsworth from the west', 1828. This watercolour of Chatsworth in its parkland shows the long North Wing added to the original baroque house by the sixth duke, terminated to the north by the Belvedere Tower (© The Devonshire Collections, Chatsworth, reproduced by permission of Chatsworth Settlement Trustees).

Fountain. Tickets came in orange, green and blue. There is no written evidence to indicate what these colours denoted – perhaps different levels of access or the level of attendance provided – but surviving used tickets reveal that both blue and green tickets were issued to notable visitors, ranging from historian and archivist Sir Francis Palgrave to American actress Charlotte Cushman.

Motivations for visiting were varied, but Chatsworth had something for most visitors. With its seventeenth-century state rooms and spectacular wall and ceiling paintings by Laguerre and Verrio, it also represented 'the very height of modern aristocratic luxury'.[9] The sixth duke's opulent new North Wing had only been fully completed in the 1840s, and the gardens boasted a range of spectacular new features like the Rock Garden, Emperor Fountain and – most extravagant of all – the Great Conservatory; these were all creations of head gardener Joseph Paxton, who had been knighted in 1851 for designing the Crystal Palace, and by 1857 he was also the duke's agent. For many visitors,

9 Mandler, *Fall and rise*, p. 62.

viewing the duke himself – even from a distance – was a highlight of their visit. His liberality in permitting such extensive access to his estate was widely praised, and by the 1850s he had achieved great popularity and become a 'national figure': he was one of the celebrities of his day.[10]

Most of what we know about Elizabeth Gaskell's visit in September 1857 is graphically described in a long letter she wrote to her daughter Marianne. She was a prolific letter writer – despite the known destruction of much family correspondence, over a thousand of her letters survive today, and her Chatsworth letter has been identified by the editors of her correspondence as one of the two most interesting that she wrote about her travels.[11]

Writing at Chatsworth on the morning after her visit on Sunday 13 September, Gaskell delighted in the 'delicious pen' she had at her disposal, and regretted she only had a letter to write rather than a book.[12] She told her daughter:

> I feel more like Cinderella, than any one else you can imagine. I am writing before breakfast; waiting for Meta, who I heartily wish was ready; for I do not ... know what room we are to breakfast in or how to find it out in this wilderness of a palace of a house.

She went on to describe their journey to Rowsley from Manchester on a very wet Friday, seated on the outside of the coach; after a night in a hotel at Rowsley, they made their way to Chatsworth with their entry card. At an early point in their visit, they received a message from the duke, who was not yet up – 'he is paralytic, & unable to move except in a bath chair, but quite clear in his mind &c'. As they were being shown around by the housekeeper, the 'duke's gentleman' came to tell them that luncheon was at 2 p.m. and that rooms had been prepared for them as they had been invited to stay. Gaskell and her daughter were disconcerted by this: they lacked appropriate clothing and had not been aware that there were other visitors staying at the time; they discovered that these included members of the Cavendish family – 'Mr & Lady Louisa Cavendish' (Richard, brother of Lord Burlington, who would succeed the sixth duke, and his wife), 'the two Miss Cavendishes' (presumably their young daughters Alice and Susan) and 'Mrs [Caroline] Norton', a well-known writer and law reform campaigner. However, they decided that the opportunity to become the duke's private guests and mix in such company was too good to miss for the sake of an inadequate wardrobe, 'so we bravely consented to stay'; a maid was sent back to Rowsley to retrieve what clothes they had, and Meta jokingly suggested dressing themselves for dinner in the thick satin curtains from her

---

[10] James Lees-Milne, *The bachelor duke: a life of William Spencer Cavendish, sixth duke of Devonshire* (London, 1991), p. 203. [11] Chapple and Pollard, *Letters*, p. xviii. [12] This and all subsequent quotes from Gaskell's letter are taken from the edited version in Chapple and Pollard, *Letters*, pp 470–3. The original is part of the Gaskell Family Collection.

2.5 A nineteenth-century photograph of Paxton's Great Conservatory, which Gaskell enjoyed being driven through in a carriage. The people give an idea of its vast scale (© The Devonshire Collections, Chatsworth, reproduced by permission of Chatsworth Settlement Trustees).

mother's bed. The duke himself came to see them before they were conducted to the Sketch Gallery, which Gaskell emphasized was 'not usually shown'. Two new galleries were added to the second floor of the house by the sixth duke, and used to display the outstanding collection of Old Master drawings put together by the second duke of Devonshire in the early eighteenth century; a guide to Chatsworth published in 1872 called this 'the most choice and extensive collection of original drawings by the Old Masters in any private collection'.[13] To have been granted a private view of these artworks was a privilege indeed for Gaskell and her daughter.

After luncheon Joseph Paxton took events in hand ('he is quite the master of the place as it were') and arranged drives for the afternoon. Gaskell and Meta travelled in a 'little low pony carriage, and four lovely (circus-like) ponies, postillions &c'. She emphasized the fairy-tale quality of their experience in her letter by reiterating that they 'felt like Cinderella'. She recounted how they were driven through the grounds, 'seeing views and improvements, & all the fountains

13 Llewellynn Jewitt, *Chatsworth* (Buxton, 1872), p. 29.

playing, and all the waterworks going, and ending by driving *through* the conservatory home, to *dress* for dinner' (Meta in a gown borrowed from the accommodating Caroline Norton). On descending to the library in the evening, they found 'half the clergy in the County of Derby with their wives, Oh! so fine; and the County Member & his wife'. Joseph Paxton and his wife Sarah were both present, 'he almost like the host'. After dinner the duke's new sculpture gallery and orangery were lit up and they were treated to a programme of music from the duke's private band; this provided an opportunity for Gaskell to speak to the duke, who was better able to hear while music was playing; she sat next to him throughout the concert and commented that 'he talked pretty incessantly.' They stayed up until midnight, and in the morning breakfasted at 9.15 (Gaskell having been terrified of oversleeping as guests were expected to have their own servants in attendance to rouse them); they then attended church – presumably St Peter's in the estate village of Edensor – although the duke was not present. She subsequently added a postscript to her letter written from Rowsley at lunchtime the next day, reporting that they had travelled there to meet the coach. Unfortunately no account of their second night at Chatsworth survives.

However, the Gaskells' fairy tale transition from tourists to honoured guests is reflected in the archive: as well as Gaskell's signature in the visitors' book, she and Meta are listed in the duke's private guestbook for that day.

When she initially obtained her visitors' ticket, Gaskell could not have anticipated quite what an opportunity it would present: part of her motivation for visiting Chatsworth was simply her love of travel and a need for escape. However, the timing of her visit is highly significant, as discussed below, and it is clear that Gaskell fully intended to maximize every benefit her visit afforded.

The mid-nineteenth century was 'the first great age of country-house visiting',[14] and Gaskell loved travel, new experiences and meeting people. She had an interest in historic houses; one of her first pieces of published writing was a description of Clopton Hall that appeared in William Howitt's influential book *Visits to remarkable places* (1840). She also enjoyed using every new place she visited as inspiration for her fiction, and there are echoes of her Chatsworth letter in the young Molly Gibson's experience at Cumnor Towers in Gaskell's final novel, *Wives and daughters*, serialized from 1864 to 1866; Molly is dazzled by the mirrors, velvet curtains and pictures in gilded frames, but concludes that she could never be a lady: 'I should lose myself every time I had to fetch my bonnet, or else get tired of long passages and great staircases long before I could go out walking.'[15]

Gaskell was also ready for some recreational time away from home: she had just spent several rather stressful months at her family home in Manchester hosting an endless stream of visitors who were visiting the city for the Art

---

[14] Mandler, *Fall and rise*, p. 4. [15] Elizabeth Gaskell, *Wives and daughters*, ed. Angus Easson (Oxford, 1987), p. 25.

Treasures Exhibition;[16] in addition, she was anxious over her daughter Meta's engagement to an army officer, Captain Charles Hill, and his sudden recall to India after the outbreak of the rebellion in May 1857. Most significantly, she had faced a barrage of criticism over her book *The life of Charlotte Brontë*, published in March that year. The biography of her friend and fellow writer Brontë (1816–55) was widely praised on publication, with favourable reviews appearing in leading newspapers and journals such as *The Times*, the *Athenaeum*, the *Spectator* and others. It is now recognized as one of 'the greatest of English biographies',[17] as well as the first full-length biography of one female writer by another. However, only two months after publication, all unsold copies of the rapidly issued second edition were recalled and a letter of retraction issued following a threat of legal action from the solicitors of Lady Scott (formerly Mrs Lydia Robinson). Without revealing her name, Gaskell had depicted her as the seducer of Branwell Brontë, tutor to her son, and hence the indirect cause of much suffering for his sister Charlotte. This was just the first in a series of complaints from individuals about their depiction in the biography, and was followed by a second threat of legal action. In mid-August she wrote to her publisher, George Smith: 'Every one writes to me, whose name has been named I think; or whose grandmother's great uncle once removed has been alluded to.'[18] She spent the whole summer of 1857 hard at work on producing a third, revised, edition which was being advertised as 'just ready' on 5 September.[19]

Gaskell's biography had another major impact which was already being felt by summer 1857: through the book, she 'largely invented Haworth as a tourist destination'.[20] The concept of visiting sites associated with authors was not new – particularly in Europe; however, 'in the nineteenth century this itinerary expanded both socially and geographically, as highbrow and middlebrow readers embarked on pilgrimages to literary destinations within Britain'.[21] The development of Shakespeare's birthplace in Stratford, Burns' birthplace in Alloway, Walter Scott's house Abbotsford and Brontë enthusiasts making the pilgrimage to Haworth are all cited as instrumental in this trend.[22] The rise of literary tourism is generally viewed as part of the wider growth of cultural nationalism in the nineteenth century, which was also reflected in the opening up of the country house to a much wider range of tourists. Abbotsford was consciously designed by Scott himself during his lifetime as a place of pilgrimage; in contrast, the parsonage at Haworth was a private, domestic space, which attracted increasing fascination as a result both of Charlotte's writings and (far more influentially) Gaskell's posthumous biography. Gaskell's emphasis on

16 'We are worn out with hospitality', she wrote to a correspondent in late August; Chapple and Pollard, *Letters*, p. 470.   17 Alan Shelston, 'Introduction' in Elizabeth Gaskell, *The life of Charlotte Brontë*, ed. Alan Shelston (Middlesex, 1987), p. 9.   18 Chapple and Pollard, *Letters*, p. 465.   19 *Examiner*, 5 Sept. 1857.   20 Nicola J. Watson, *The literary tourist* (Basingstoke, 2006), p. 111.   21 Nicola J. Watson, 'Introduction' in Nicola J. Watson (ed.), *Literary tourism and nineteenth-century culture* (Basingstoke, 2009), p. 3.   22 Ibid., p. 2.

Brontë's domestic life reflects the problematic role of women as published writers at that time.

Gaskell's depiction of Haworth as a remote, windswept and desolate village was at odds with the reality of the town; Christine Alexander points out that it was a large and busy manufacturing community important to the district's wool trade.[23] However, the memorable first chapter of Gaskell's biography, in which the reader is taken on a journey from Keighley to Haworth ('crowned with wild, bleak moors' both grand and oppressive), to the parsonage and the family memorials in the church, embodies the 'Brontë myth', which her book largely created.[24]

Souvenirs were already on sale in Haworth by summer 1857, and following the publication of Gaskell's biography the earlier trickle of tourists making their way to the town 'now became a flood' — with many people attempting to gain entry to the parsonage, meet Patrick Brontë (who outlived all his children) and see the house where the famous sisters had composed their works.[25]

Among the earliest of these literary tourists was the sixth duke of Devonshire. Although he had stopped keeping a diary by 1857, the brief 'date book' he continued to maintain, together with newspaper reports, make it possible to trace some of his activities that summer. On 8 August, he left London for Chatsworth, from where he travelled to Bolton Abbey in north Yorkshire, another of his estates, arriving there on 11 August. On Monday 24 August, he made the journey from Bolton Abbey to Haworth, some fourteen miles away, where he was one of the privileged few visitors who were granted an interview with Patrick Brontë in the parsonage. It was widely reported in regional newspapers that the duke paid a visit to the Revd Brontë 'as a proof of his Grace's high estimation of the venerable incumbent, and of departed worth and genius'.[26] According to Juliet Barker, the duke also invited both Patrick and Arthur Nichols (Charlotte's widower) to visit him at Bolton Abbey in September.[27] This return visit never happened, but Patrick clearly felt it was important to inform Gaskell of his meeting with the duke: on 24 August — the day of the visit — he wrote to Gaskell, reassuring her of his support for the biography despite the 'mix'd cup' that both of them had experienced as a result of it, and mentioning '[w]e have ... many

---

23 Christine Alexander, 'Myth and memory: reading the Brontë parsonage' in Harald Hendrix (ed.), *Writers' houses and the making of memory* (New York and Abingdon, 2008), p. 96. 24 Elizabeth Gaskell, *The life of Charlotte Brontë*, ed. Alan Shelston (Middlesex, 1987), p. 55. 25 Sarah Tetley and Bill Bramwell note that photographs of the Revd Patrick Brontë, his church and the parsonage were available to purchase from the chemist's shop on Main Street: 'Tourists and the cultural construction of Haworth's literary landscape', in Hans-Christian Anderson and Mike Robinson (eds), *Literature and tourism: reading and writing tourism texts* (London and New York: 2002), p. 158; Juliet Barker, *The Brontës* (London, 1994), p. 810. 26 Quote taken from the *Newcastle Journal*, 29 Aug. 1857; also widely quoted in other newspapers. 27 Barker's evidence for this is inferred from a scrap of paper dated Bolton Abbey, 27 Aug. 1857 with the ducal coronet and part of a note; Barker cites this as being in an unidentified private collection.

Visiters [sic] weekly. – Amongst the rest the duke of Devonshire has call'd and stopped with us about an hour'.[28]

Given the publicity – and controversy – surrounding Gaskell's biography of Charlotte Brontë, it seems very likely that the duke was prompted to make his visit as a result of reading accounts of it (whether positive or otherwise). There is no evidence that he purchased copies of the Brontës' works on publication – no copies of first editions survive in the Library at Chatsworth – or indeed any evidence that he had read Gaskell's biography by this date. However, there is a copy of the 1855, fifth edition of *Jane Eyre* at Chatsworth. This bears a cipher used by the seventh duke of Devonshire, but it seems that some of the books acquired towards the very end of the sixth duke's life (he died in January 1858) were either bound or stamped by the seventh duke. The fifth edition, appearing eight years after first publication, was the main edition available in 1857; a cheap reprint had also been issued, but this is unlikely to have been considered appropriate for the ducal shelves. This points to the possibility that the sixth duke purchased a copy of *Jane Eyre* around this time – potentially because of the publicity surrounding Gaskell's biography or even as a result of his visit to Haworth.

Patrick Brontë's letter to Gaskell meant that she was fully aware of the duke's recent visit to Haworth and his interest in Charlotte Brontë, and this could well have influenced her choice of Chatsworth as a holiday destination in September. At this stage in her career, Gaskell's profile was higher than ever; the Brontë biography was achieving high sales, and was the first book she published with her name publicly attached as author; she had also moved to a new, more prestigious, publishing house – that of Smith, Elder, publishers of Charlotte Brontë's works, who also published novelists such as William Thackeray, George Eliot and Thomas Hardy. On learning of the duke's interest in the Brontë family, and by extension her own biography of Brontë, she may have seen the visit as an exciting opportunity for an introduction to the duke and the chance to make an influential new social contact, as well as discussing the work of Charlotte Brontë, and promoting her own work.

Usually, discussions of Gaskell's letter describing her Chatsworth adventure emphasize her astonishment at being told rooms had been prepared for them. However, closer scrutiny of her letter reveals that while she did not necessarily anticipate being invited to stay at Chatsworth as a guest, she certainly expected to be summoned to meet the duke. He was closely involved with the issuing of visitors' tickets, so would have been aware that Gaskell and her daughter were planning to look around Chatsworth on that date, and in her letter Gaskell describes how on arrival, '*as I expected* I had soon a message from the duke, who was not yet up' (author's italics).

---

[28] Dudley Green (ed.), *The letters of the Reverend Patrick Brontë* (Stroud, 2005), p. 261.

Elizabeth Gaskell's visit to Chatsworth

2.6 Undated note from the sixth duke of Devonshire [to Elizabeth Gaskell], probably handed to her on the day of her visit to Chatsworth (courtesy of the University of Manchester).

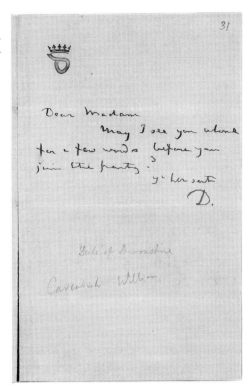

Among Gaskell's own papers at the John Rylands Research Institute and Library in Manchester is a small note that has been overlooked until now. Described in the collection's finding aid as addressed to an 'unidentified female', signed 'D', and with a later annotation indicating that this was the duke of Devonshire, it is undated and its place of origin not indicated. The notepaper, bearing the Duke's cipher and ducal coronet, and the handwriting (which by this stage of his life had deteriorated significantly as the result of a stroke several years earlier) make it clear that this was indeed written by the sixth duke of Devonshire. It reads:

> Dear Madam,
> May I see you alone for a few words before you join the party?
> Y[ou]r H[umb]le serv[an]t
> D

It is very likely that this note was intended for Gaskell herself, and would have been handed to her by a servant at some point during her day at Chatsworth. It may well have been the note she referred to receiving on arrival; her letter indicates that the duke was wheeled in his bath chair to meet her and Meta before they viewed the sketch gallery and joined the other guests at luncheon, so this may have been the private meeting the duke had requested.

Gaskell does not reveal in her letter what was discussed at that meeting, or indeed what she and the duke spoke about during the concert in the evening. However, in light of the duke's recent visit to Patrick Brontë, the publicity surrounding Gaskell's biography and the very recent publication of the third, revised, edition, it is likely that this was a major topic of their conversation. Despite Gaskell's depiction of Patrick Brontë in her biography of his daughter as 'eccentric and strange ... almost misanthropical',[29] he was always highly supportive of Gaskell's work and may well have expressed this during his interview with the duke that August. In her thank-you letter to the duke for his hospitality, Gaskell expressed her gratitude for his 'sympathising words',[30] which also suggests he had some insight into the problems she had faced on publication of the biography.

The duke's respectful closing of his note with what certainly looks like 'humble servant' is also striking in a note written by an aristocrat to a middle-class female writer (he did not commonly use this form of words in his valedictions): it perhaps says something both about the duke's own attitude to literature, the status of literature at this point in the mid-nineteenth century, and indeed Gaskell's own status as a professional author.

The duke was well-known as a patron of art – his new sculpture gallery was designed to display modern sculpture, much of which he commissioned, and he donated money to causes connected with sculpture. However, he also acted as a literary patron: he gave money to the impecunious writer Leigh Hunt; befriended many writers, to whom he granted favours; and acted as patron of the Guild of Literature and Art, established by Charles Dickens and Edward Bulwer Lytton (discussed in more detail below). His patronage was hailed by contemporaries such as Stephen Glover, whose *Peak guide* describes how 'His Grace has devoted his princely revenues to the patronage of the fine arts, to the encouragement of literature, and to that splendid yet judicious style of living that renders the luxuries and embellishments of society the channels of public benefit.'[31]

Beyond patronage and on a more personal level, the duke was also an enthusiastic consumer of the literature of his day. Well known as a bibliophile, his book collecting resulted in one of the finest private libraries, containing incunables, Shakespeare quartos and folios, medieval manuscripts and more. However, it also included contemporary novels – many of which are still present in the library today. These are not all finely bound three-volume sets: in a number of cases it is clear that the duke was purchasing novels by writers like

---

29 Gaskell, *Life*, p. 90.   **30** John Chapple and Alan Shelston (eds), *Further letters of Mrs Gaskell* (Manchester, 2003), p. 172; original in DC, CS2/346/0.   **31** Stephen Glover, *The Peak guide* (Derby, 1830), p. 50.

2.7 A watercolour of *c.* 1827 by W.H. Hunt showing the sixth duke's library – converted from the first duke's gallery. This shows the library following the first phase of work; further changes took place at a later date, including the addition of a gallery, a parquet floor and a richly coloured carpet – all of which Gaskell would have seen on the evening of her visit (© The Devonshire Collections, Chatsworth, reproduced by permission of Chatsworth Settlement Trustees).

Dickens and Thackeray as they were issued in monthly parts, and the survival of some individual wrappers indicates that he was having these bound into volumes once the serialization was complete. Comments he made also indicate his literary enthusiasms; on Dickens, he commented: 'I never missed reading a number of his beginning with *Pickwick*, and told him I could pass examination on all his histories.'[32] When Thackeray's *Vanity fair* was being serialized in 1847–8, he wrote to the author requesting a portrait of the novel's protagonist Becky Sharp,

32 Quoted in Michael Slater, *Charles Dickens* (New Haven and London, 2011), p. 325.

which the writer happily supplied, along with a humorous outline of how the novel would conclude.[33] More relevant to this context, he also possessed a first edition of Gaskell's first novel, *Mary Barton* (1848), and the first volume edition of *North and south* (1855) – both 'condition of England' novels – so he would have been aware of her work (and the debates it prompted) before 1857.[34]

The duke also had a talent for writing himself, although his only major publication, privately printed for friends and acquaintances, was *The handbook of Chatsworth and Hardwick* that appeared in 1845. The duke lent a copy to Charles Dickens when the latter visited Chatsworth, and Dickens read it on the train home from Chesterfield to London, writing to its author, 'I could mention some things in it which it would require a very nice art to do as well in fiction. The little suggestive indications of the old servants, and old rooms – and the childish associations – are perfect little pieces of truth.'[35]

His acquaintance with Dickens arose from what was probably the duke's most significant act of literary patronage, which placed him at the centre of the debate over the 'dignity of literature' and the professionalism of authorship that was playing out in lectures, periodicals, and books during the late 1840s and 1850s. While many authors agreed that '[l]iterature has become a profession',[36] there was a disagreement between those (like the philosopher, writer and partner of George Eliot, G.H. Lewes) who placed authorship on a par with the 'traditional' professions like law or the church, and those (like Thackeray) who were happier to associate literature with commerce, and position writers as wage labourers.[37] Dickens was largely in the former camp. He acknowledged the writer's reliance on the buying public, but sought to lend dignity to the occupation through an ideal of 'professional labour'.[38] With friend and fellow writer Edward Bulwer-Lytton, he proposed the establishment of a Guild of Literature and Art – a professional membership institution for writers that would provide annuities and pensions for authors who required financial assistance. He believed this would free writers from an outdated culture of aristocratic patronage and ad hoc charitable handouts.

The duke of Devonshire's love of the theatre was well known, and Dickens was already associated with the duke's agent, Joseph Paxton, through a newspaper venture. This connection prompted the novelist to write directly to the duke on 4 March 1851 asking whether he would allow Dickens and his

---

33 DC, CS2/324/0a.   34 'The condition of England' was a phrase coined by Thomas Carlyle in his essay *Chartism* (1839) about the 'condition and disposition' of working people. The term was subsequently applied to a group of mid-nineteenth-century novels that addressed the condition of the industrial working classes at a time of social unrest – highlighting the growing gulf between rich and poor in England, and pointing to the need for reform.   35 DC, CS2/342/3.   36 G.H. Lewes, quoted in Linda H. Peterson, *Becoming a woman of letters: myths of authorship and facts of the Victorian market* (Princeton, 2009), p. 34.   37 The debate is covered in detail in Richard Salmon, *The formation of the Victorian literary profession* (Cambridge, 2013).   38 Ibid., p. 118.

colleagues to stage Bulwer-Lytton's play, *Not so bad as we seem*, at the duke's London residence, Devonshire House, in the presence of Queen Victoria, with the aim of raising funds for the new guild. In a typically flattering tone, he stated that 'there is no other [gentleman in this land] on whose generous attachment to Letters and Art, I so implicitly rely'.[39] A similarly fulsome letter was sent to the duke by Bulwer-Lytton to accompany the proposed dedication to the duke that would preface the play.[40]

The duke was only too happy to oblige and immediately contacted Buckingham Palace to secure the royal presence; the play successfully premiered at Devonshire House on 16 May 1851 before the queen, Prince Albert, and an audience of carefully selected guests, whose ticket costs would fund the venture and who, it was hoped, would also voluntarily subscribe. The duke – an enthusiastic scrapbooker – kept an album devoted to the event, into which he pasted all of the relevant correspondence, guest lists, programmes, audience lists, cuttings of reviews and other papers.[41]

The irony of the duke acting as aristocratic patron to an organization that aimed to liberate authors from aristocratic patronage appears to have been lost on the parties concerned, but perhaps reflects that this was a transitional time for writers. As well as gaining professional status, authors were becoming celebrities in their own right, rivalling aristocratic celebrities like the duke of Devonshire himself. In fact in his novel *Ranthorpe* (1847), G.H. Lewes posited the idea of an 'aristocracy of the intellect' – a select cultural body that would supplant the traditional aristocracy of birth and wealth, and prompt people to make pilgrimages to authors' houses to see the contexts in which they wrote.[42] Writers increasingly found themselves being 'lionized': this was largely couched as a social pastime in which society hostesses would compete to secure the presence of male literary stars (known as 'lions') at their parties.[43] However, this was not as gender restricted as traditionally supposed, as Elizabeth Gaskell herself discovered. In 1849, on her first visit to London after the publication of her first novel, she wrote to thank a correspondent (probably her publisher Edward Chapman) for his 'friendly warning against being "lionized".'[44]

While never a celebrity to rival Dickens, whose novels, journalism and lecture tours made him a household name and brought him considerable wealth, Gaskell nevertheless became a successful and well-known writer, and Dickens invited her to contribute to the very first issue of his magazine *Household Words* in 1850. She was not afraid of tackling controversial issues in her fiction: *Mary Barton* drew attention to the plight of Manchester factory workers and was strongly criticized by members of the city's industrial elite; and in *Ruth* (1853) she addressed the topic of unmarried motherhood and the 'fallen woman'. Initially she made the

---

39 DC, DF4/3/2/12.   40 Ibid.   41 Ibid.   42 Salmon, *Literary profession*, p. 73.   43 Tom Mole, 'Introduction' in Tom Mole (ed.), *Romanticism and celebrity culture, 1750–1850* (Cambridge, 2009), p. 6.   44 Chapple and Pollard, *Letters*, p. 71.

decision to hide behind anonymity, aware of the controversy her work might cause and not wishing to draw attention to herself as a female writer. Anonymity and use of pseudonyms were strategies often used by women authors, for whom professional status and celebrity were more complex issues to navigate than for their male counterparts; thus the Brontë sisters appeared in print as authors Currer, Ellis and Acton Bell respectively, and George Eliot was the nom de plume for Mary Ann Evans. The 'dignity of literature debate'[45] largely excluded women. Although writing was one of the few areas of work at that time which offered women the opportunity to work on an equal status with men, the cost of this was often to be cast as 'unfeminine': a middle-class woman's primary duties were considered to be the home and her role as wife and mother.

Gaskell struggled with the tension between 'home duties' and her own desire to write and publish.[46] While she was still reluctant to affix her name to her work, her letters reveal that by the 1850s she was highly professional and confident in the value of her writing: she negotiated with different publishers to secure the best payment; she published her short stories both in journals (usually those of Charles Dickens) and in collected editions, which enabled her to make money from the same story twice over; and as she had an understanding husband, she had control over her own earnings.

Life was very different for Caroline Norton, one of Gaskell's fellow guests at Chatsworth on 12 September 1857. Norton was the granddaughter of Richard Brinsley Sheridan, who had moved in the same circles as the sixth duke's mother, Duchess Georgiana, and so was an old friend of the Cavendish family. The sixth duke was godfather to her eldest son, Fletcher, who was also given Cavendish as one of his middle names; in some of her letters to the duke, she addressed him as 'uncle'.[47] She was a prolific writer of poetry who also published novels, edited and contributed to magazines and 'saw herself as what would now be termed a professional writer'.[48] However, her earnings went to her husband, George Chapple Norton. He subjected his wife to both mental and physical abuse, and following their separation in 1836, he refused her access to her children. As a married woman she had no legal existence of her own, and was essentially the property of her husband. She campaigned to change the law, publishing several influential pamphlets and lobbying political contacts. Her work played a large part in the passing of the Infant Custody Act in 1839. This, 'the first piece of feminist legislation in Britain', gave separated or divorced wives custody of their children up to the age of seven, and access rights thereafter.[49] More significantly, given the date of her first meeting with Gaskell at Chatsworth on 28 August 1857

---

45 Outlined on p. 66.   **46** Chapple and Pollard, *Letters*, p. 106.   **47** DC, DF4/1/5: 54 letters from Caroline Norton; these have not been used by either of Norton's twenty-first-century biographers.   **48** Antonia Fraser, *The case of the married woman: Caroline Norton* (London, 2021), p. 28.   **49** Diane Atkinson, *The criminal conversation of Mrs Norton* (Chicago, 2013), p. 274.

(just over a fortnight earlier), the Matrimonial Causes Act was passed – legislation influenced in part by Norton's *English laws for women in the nineteenth century* (1854). The act gave separated wives existence in the eyes of the law and enabled them to sign contracts and deeds without guarantors. It also meant that married women could control the earnings they made through their own publications.[50]

Elizabeth Gaskell was familiar with Norton's work and used an extract from her poem 'The child of the islands' (1845) as one of the chapter epigraphs in her novel *Mary Barton*. It is unclear whether the women had met prior to 1857. In a letter from Gaskell to her daughter Marianne dated September 1854, she sent regards to Ann Norton and Mrs Norton;[51] the editors of her correspondence suggest that Mrs Norton is Caroline, but the identity of Ann is unclear – and there are no other references to an earlier meeting between the women. However, they certainly corresponded *after* their meeting at Chatsworth – there are two surviving letters from Norton dating from 1859 among Gaskell's papers in Manchester.

Significantly, Gaskell also carefully preserved her note from the duke of Devonshire among her papers, and stored it not with her correspondence, but with the letters identified as forming her autograph collection.[52] She was an enthusiastic autograph hunter, and was discerning about whose letters or signatures she collected: in 1854 she wrote to a correspondent, 'I don't much care for statesmen and have a handsome quantity of unknown peers at your disposal … only I like having people I really *do* care for; I myself personally, either in the way of like or dislike, – and not people I am perfectly indifferent to.'[53] This suggests the value she placed on the duke's note, but also hints at the way she felt it reflected on her own reputation: Gaskell was adamant that no biography should be written of her, but Pamela Corpron Parker has suggested that she used her autograph album as an 'oblique form of autobiography', through which she displayed 'her professional alliances with the leading cultural figures of the day'.[54] Clearly the duke was one peer whose opinion she did value, and his note – with its 'humble servant' sign-off – provided evidence of her upwardly mobile trajectory at this point in her career.

Four days after leaving Chatsworth, Gaskell sat down to write a thank-you note to the duke for his generosity in allowing them to stay and 'for the opportunity of a leisurely inspection of so many of the rare treasures in your possession'. With the letter she sent an enclosure: 'I have the greatest pleasure

---

50 Norton's campaigning and the ultimate passage of the Matrimonial Causes Act are discussed in Fraser, *Married woman*, pp 181–95 and Atkinson, *Criminal conversation*, pp 375–95.   **51** Chapple and Pollard, *Letters*, p. 304.   **52** Elizabeth Gaskell Manuscript Collection (University of Manchester Library, Eng. MS 732/31).   **53** Chapple and Shelston, *Further letters*, p. 108.   **54** Pamela Corpron Parker, 'Woman of letters: Elizabeth Gaskell's autograph collection and Victorian celebrity' in Maureen Daly Goggin and Beth Fowkes Tobin (eds), *Material women, 1750–1950: consuming desires and collecting practices* (London and New York, 2009), p. 267.

2.8 Elizabeth Gaskell's thank-you letter to the duke, 17 Sept. 1857 (© The Devonshire Collections, Chatsworth, reproduced by permission of Chatsworth Settlement Trustees).

in the world in sending you the enclosed letter from Charlotte Brontë to me, which I have chosen out as being, in my opinion, the most interesting I ever received from her, and consequently the one I like best to offer to your Grace.'[55]

The enclosed letter is indeed interesting, and would have had great significance to Gaskell; in June she had written to someone begging for a sample of Brontë's handwriting that 'all I have it is of importance to keep, otherwise I should have had great pleasure in sending you some'.[56] The letter appears to have been carefully selected by Gaskell to send to the duke: it both reinforces her depiction of Brontë in the biography, and touches on the issue of women's role in society, which is central to the biography and to debates around authorship during this period.

---

55 Chapple and Shelston, *Further letters*, p. 172. The original letter is in DC, CS2/346/0.
56 Chapple and Pollard, *Letters*, p. 457.

The letter was the first that Brontë wrote to Gaskell after their initial meeting at the holiday residence of Sir James Kay-Shuttleworth near Windermere in August 1850. By this date, Brontë had lost all her siblings and was living with her father in Haworth; her letter opens: 'Papa and I have just had tea; he is sitting quietly in his room, and I in mine; "storms of rain" are sweeping over the garden and churchyard; as to the moors – they are hidden in thick fog.'[57] This reinforces Gaskell's depiction of the solitary life led by Brontë amid the wildness of the north Yorkshire moors. Gaskell had not visited Haworth at this point, but had already formed strong opinions of it and its influence on Brontë's creative imagination. It also reflects one of the challenges she faced with her biography: Brontë and her sisters had been accused in reviews of 'coarseness' in their writing, and the author of *Jane Eyre* had been accused of being unfeminine. The emphasis on the wildness and remoteness of their home was an attempt to justify some of the more extreme elements of Brontë's fiction – pointing up the difference between life in remote Yorkshire and life in the civilized metropolis. The letter also emphasizes Charlotte's domestic duty as a daughter who remained in her childhood home caring for her father – something Gaskell felt it was important to stress in the biography.

However, the same letter shows Brontë to be very much a part of wider cultural life: she commented on Tennyson's *In memoriam*, which she found 'beautiful ... mournful [and] monotonous', and noted that she was sending Gaskell a copy of Wordsworth's *Prelude* which she hoped would amuse her while she was incapacitated by an injured ankle. Significantly she also touched on the role of women in contemporary society. Referring to a recent article in the *Westminster Review* (a review of Sarah Lewis' book, *Woman's mission*), she acknowledged that 'Men begin to regard the position of Women in another light than they used to do ... They say – however – and to a certain extent – truly – that the amelioration of our condition depends on ourselves. Certainly there are evils which our own efforts will best reach – but as certainly there are other evils – deep rooted in the foundations of the Social system – which no efforts of ours can touch – of which we cannot complain – of which it is advisable not too often to think.' This reflects some of the more rebellious opinions of her fictional heroine Jane Eyre, who lamented the lack of options open to single women with no independent income.

This was something Gaskell struggled with in her presentation of Brontë. She wanted to defend the reputation of her friend against accusations of coarseness by emphasizing her duties to her family, but found this difficult to reconcile with Brontë's career as a professional writer. The result was what Linda H. Peterson has dubbed the 'Parallel Currents' model of female authorship, which Gaskell

[57] All quotes taken from edited letter in Margaret Smith (ed.), *Selected letters of Charlotte Brontë* (Oxford, 2007), p. 173. The original letter remains, with its covering letter from Gaskell, in the Devonshire Collections.

conceived as a solution to this paradox – so named because at the point of publication of *Jane Eyre*, Gaskell stated, '[h]enceforward Charlotte Brontë's existence becomes divided into two parallel currents – her life as Currer Bell [the pseudonym Brontë published under], the author; her life as Charlotte Brontë the woman. There were separate duties belonging to each character – not opposing each other; not impossible, but difficult to be reconciled.'[58] This was a convenient way of addressing the problem and enabled Gaskell to balance – albeit uneasily – the roles of domestic exemplar and talented author. Both of these separate 'lives' can be observed in the letter from Brontë that Gaskell presented to the duke as a gift.

In her thank-you letter to the duke, Gaskell also mentioned that she was arranging to have a copy of the revised edition of the biography sent to Chatsworth. This volume still exists in the library today: the spine bears the seventh duke's cipher, but as a late acquisition of the sixth duke's it seems likely that the binding or the stamping occurred posthumously, as with the fifth edition of *Jane Eyre*.

There must have been at least one further letter from Gaskell to the sixth duke, which apparently does not survive. A letter from Gaskell stored among the seventh duke's papers only came to light recently and was first published in 2020.[59] Although it was catalogued as having been sent to the duke himself, the mode of address ('My Dear Sir') suggests it is far more likely that the addressee was Joseph Paxton, the master of ceremonies who Gaskell had met during her Chatsworth visit. Dated 4 March [1858], Gaskell wrote: 'In January last I forwarded the late duke of Devonshire two letters of Mr Brontë's to me, (expression[s] of thorough satisfaction with his daughter's Memoirs,) which his grace had asked to see, and promised to return.' The duke died on 18 January, so he may never have had the opportunity to look at these letters, transcripts of which she helpfully enclosed. They are further endorsements of Gaskell's work from Patrick Brontë: in the first, dated 2 April 1857, he wrote admiringly of Gaskell's biography, the first edition of which he had just received, and reiterated that she had been the first choice of biographer for his daughter. The second, dated 9 September 1857, was his response to the revised third edition; Patrick felt it had 'arrived at a degree of perfection, which was scarcely attainable, in a first, and second Edition' and he hoped it would go down 'to the latest posterity'.[60]

If Paxton responded to Gaskell's letter, his response does not survive among her own papers, but he clearly arranged for the return of the two letters from

---

[58] Elizabeth Gaskell, *The life of Charlotte Brontë*, ed. Alan Shelston (Middlesex, 1987), p. 334.
[59] Fran Baker, 'This wilderness of a palace of a house', *Gaskell Society Newsletter*, 69 (Spring 2020), pp 5–12. [60] The transcripts and Gaskell's covering letter to Paxton are in DC, DF5/3/4/8.

Patrick Brontë that Gaskell had sent: these are now housed among others at the John Rylands Research Institute and Library in Manchester.

Thus ended Gaskell's short acquaintance with the sixth duke of Devonshire, but her visit to Chatsworth reflects a general movement during this later stage of her career 'into the company both of influential professionals and of country house society'.[61] The editors of her letters suggest that in the last fifteen or so years of her life, many of her correspondents 'are titled or have acquired titles in some way ... The new contacts ... register movement into a different sphere – not deliberately sought after, but perhaps an inevitable consequence of her talent for what we would now call networking, and an index too of the fluidity of English middle and upper class society at this particular moment in the mid-nineteenth century.'[62]

The party at Chatsworth was interesting in terms of its social make-up: two professional women writers (both of whom had aroused controversy in very different ways) mixing with members of the 'traditional' male middle-class professions ('half the clergy in the County of Derby') along with one of the wealthiest aristocrats in the nation, and members of his extended family, all at a party where Paxton, the son of a farm labourer who had been knighted, and his wife were acting as hosts.

Lauren Butler has examined relationships among the Chatsworth estate community in light of Pierre Bourdieu's concepts of capital – both cultural capital (the social assets of an individual, such as their education and style of language, which can promote social mobility), and social capital (essentially the status gained through advantageous social connections). She demonstrates how non-elites were able to accrue both types of capital through their association with Chatsworth.[63] In considering the trust he placed in the Paxtons, Butler also suggests that by using his wealth and power to enfranchise and invest in individuals like Joseph Paxton, the sixth duke carved out a role for himself in a rapidly changing society, as a patron of middle-class talent.[64]

The same might be said of the support he gave to the newly professionalized middle-class community of writers – not just financial support, but through associating his name with endeavours like the Guild of Literature and Art, acting as an enthusiastic commercial consumer of their literary outputs, through word-of-mouth recommendations, and by developing friendships or partnerships with prominent writers like Dickens who represented the new 'celebrities' of the age.

Elizabeth Gaskell loved turning life into stories, and compared herself twice to Cinderella in her letter describing the Chatsworth visit. However, this is disingenuous; there was certainly no fiction – or magic – involved in her

---

61 Chapple and Shelston, *Further letters*, p. xvii.   62 Ibid., p. xviii.   63 Lauren Butler, 'Power at the power house: agency and authority on the Chatsworth estate, 1811–1877' (PhD, University of Sheffield, 2019), p. 43.   64 Ibid., p. 92.

transition from day visitor to house guest. She knew that it was her reputation as a writer which afforded her the opportunity to move in such circles. At this point in her career, she was no longer hiding behind anonymity: *The life of Charlotte Brontë* was the first book she published openly under her own name. She was aware of her status and marketability as a professional writer, and she was a member of the 'aristocracy of the intellect', whose work had made an obvious impact on a duke. When the opportunity arose, she chose to use her status both to increase her cultural capital, securing privileged access to the 'treasures' in the duke's collection that were 'not usually shown' to visitors; and to build on her social capital by extending her already impressive social network.

Misplaced hospitality and practical implications: the northern tour of Thomas Sandby and Theodosius Forrest, August 1774

KERRY BRISTOL

As the present volume amply demonstrates, country houses have attracted a wide range of publics for nearly as long as they have been in existence. However, the seeds of our modern heritage industry were sown in the eighteenth century, and recent scholarship has been increasingly concerned to tie the rise of domestic tourism to phenomena as wide-ranging as the upsurge in the number of country houses being built or rebuilt and illustrated in publications, improved road networks, new technologies in carriage design, an increase in infrastructure such as inns and guide and travel books, and to the social shift that turned informed knowledge of the arts into a marker of 'politeness' and 'taste' for both aristocracy and aspirant middle classes.

This rise in domestic tourism was accompanied by a corresponding rise in travel accounts. Some of these were published but many manuscript accounts survive today in libraries and archives. Each account is as unique as its author; thus the well-known surveys of the economic or agricultural health of the nation by Daniel Defoe and Arthur Young have a different agenda from Thomas Pennant's interests in natural history, or the descriptions of sites visited by elite travellers such as Philip Yorke, Caroline Lybbe Powys or Sophia Newdigate en route to stay with friends and family. Cumulatively these many accounts testify to a fascination with the history, built environment and landscape of Britain and Ireland that only increased as the century progressed.

One such account was written and illustrated by the Nottingham-born architect Thomas Sandby (1721–98), who had begun his career in the office of a local land surveyor before he and his brother, the landscape painter Paul Sandby, relocated to London and took up posts as draughtsmen to the Board of Ordnance.[1] A connection with William Augustus, duke of Cumberland, resulted in Thomas's appointment as deputy ranger of Windsor Great Park, where he executed works that included the formation of Virginia Water, a bridge, grottoes and artificial ruins.[2] As Howard Colvin noted, Thomas was also 'an accomplished topographical artist, whose watercolour drawings cannot easily be distinguished from those of his brother'.[3]

1 Luke Herrmann, *Paul and Thomas Sandby* (London, 1986), p. 12. 2 Jane Roberts, *Royal landscape: the gardens and parks of Windsor* (London, 1997), pp 31–76. 3 H.M. Colvin, *A biographical dictionary of British architects, 1600–1840* (London, 2008), p. 897.

3.1 Thomas Sandby, 'Wentworth Woodhouse', 1774, pen, grey ink and grey wash, with watercolour, over graphite on paper, 19.6 x 34.6cm. British Museum, no. 1904,0819.413, asset no. 1289443001.

Sandby's original account of his tour in the Midlands was last seen in the 1980s and its present whereabouts is unknown,[4] but a single sheet combining some text and a view of the 'Devil's Hole' in the Peak District, and several watercolour drawings of country houses on separate sheets, survive in the British Museum,[5] while the British Library also holds a complete copy of the manuscript bound between two other travel accounts in a volume entitled *Forrest's tours*.[6] The British Library volume contains a tour through northern France and the Low Countries in 1769 whose author remains unknown, a version of Sandby's 'A tour into Derbyshire' of 1774, and a third account inscribed 'A journey to Paris, by Theo: Forrest. August 1777'. Theodosius Forrest was a solicitor, artist and composer, who appeared in Nathaniel Hone's satirical print of 1772, 'Monachum non facit cucullus' ('The robe does not make the monk') alongside the antiquarian Francis Grose.[7] Forrest, Hone and Grose were all

---

[4] Sigrid de Jong, 'The picturesque prospect of architecture: Thomas Sandby's Royal Academy lectures', *Architectural History*, 61 (2018), pp 73–104 at p. 77, 101 n. 12. It may be the volume sold at Christie's in November 1994. See Ann Sumner, 'The Chippendale firm at Harewood: early visitors' experiences', *Furniture History*, 54 (2018), pp 227–42 at p. 240 n. 33.   [5] BM, 1904,0819.423, Thomas Sandby, 'The Devil's or Peak Cave, Castleton, Derbyshire, a leaf from the artist's illustrated tour'; BM, 1904,0819.406–13.   [6] BL, Add. MS 42,232, *Forrest's tours*.
[7] G.B. Smith, revised by Philip Carter, 'Theodosius Forrest', *ODNB*; William Hauptman, 'Francis Grose (1731–91), the "Antiquarian Falstaff". A slender biographical entertainment',

intimates of the Sandbys, Forrest having studied with the two brothers in 1753.[8] The Sandbys' influence pervades Forrest's surviving works.[9] This complicates any attribution of the watercolours in 'A tour into Derbyshire', especially as the handwriting of all three accounts in *Forrest's tours* appears to be identical to that in the British Museum's single sheet, attributed to Sandby. Differences in detail between the British Museum's views and their counterparts in the British Library's version of 'A tour into Derbyshire' suggest that the latter is not merely a copy of the former; however, until the original manuscript resurfaces one can only be sure of the fact that Sandby was its author, while Forrest may have been the transcriber and illustrator. This uncertainty renders 'A tour into Derbyshire' more than the sum of its parts as the account performed several roles for its creator(s).

In what was already a time-honoured tradition, Sandby stated that the 'Tour' had been written so others could share the journey vicariously, and that the sketches would allow the reader to 'in some measure, be a partaker in this Excursion'.[10] But this particular account, written by an architect and (possibly) transcribed by an artist, also functioned as a memento of a tour made in the company of like-minded and long-standing friends: the sculptor-architect William Tyler, the miniaturist Samuel Cotes and a Capt. Robert Elves. In the 1760s Sandby, Forrest, Cotes and Tyler had exhibited with the Society of Artists of Great Britain (SAGB) and, after Sandby and Tyler became founder members of the Royal Academy in 1768, Forrest and Cotes joined them as exhibitors.[11] The manuscript thus reflects *their* experiences, conversations and opinions, although Sandby's architectural interests predominates.

The time allotted for the excursion north was finite and the itinerary planned carefully. No doubt because the tour was founded on a long-standing belief that travel should be useful,[12] recently built country houses were a dominant part of their itinerary, although the party was also drawn to Gothic churches, public buildings, industrial sites and medieval ruins; there are also numerous comments

---

British Art Journal, 20:3 (Winter 2019/20), pp 68–84 at pp 70–1. I am grateful to Brendan Rooney for sharing his research on Hone and Forrest.   **8** Martin Postle, 'The Sandbys and the Royal Academy' in John Bonehill and Stephen Daniels (eds), *Paul Sandby: picturing Britain* (London, 2009), pp 29–37 at p. 30.   **9** For example, www.metmuseum.org/art/collection/search/421656 or www.mutualart.com/Artwork/Windsor-Castle-from-Home-Park/808240C9F8AC9DEC, accessed 24 Oct. 2021.   **10** BL, Add. MS 42,232, ff 28–9. On the communal nature of middle-class travel journals, see Kirsty McHugh, 'Yorkshire tourists: the beginnings of middle-class travel in Georgian Britain', *Yorkshire Archaeological Journal*, 90:1 (2018), pp 111–27 at p. 114.   **11** Algernon Graves, *The Royal Academy of Arts: a complete dictionary of contributors and their work from its foundation in 1769 to 1904*, 4 vols (London, 1905–6), i, pp 175–6; Algernon Graves, *The Society of Artists of Great Britain, 1760–1791; the Free Society of Artists, 1761–1783* (London, 1907), pp 65–6, 94, 262; Colvin, *Biographical dictionary*, p. 1063; Matthew Hargraves, *Candidates for fame* (London, 2005), pp 80–1; Ingrid Roscoe et al., *A biographical dictionary of sculptors in Britain, 1660–1851* (London, 2009), p. 1293; Smith and Carter, 'Theodosius Forrest'.   **12** Ian Ousby, *The Englishman's England* (Cambridge, 1990), p. 9; Nicholas T. Parsons, *Worth the detour: a history of the guidebook*

on the ornamental use of water and 'picturesque' landscapes, something of interest to Sandby whose assessment of the impact of architecture on the senses was expounded in his Royal Academy lectures delivered 1770–96.[13] Notwithstanding Sandby's thoughts on the emotional responses a building and its landscape could invoke, the concern of this essay is with the processes and itineraries of country house visiting because the 'Tour' was first and foremost a travel diary, written in the moment, privileging eye-witness descriptions over academic theory. The physical experience of walking or riding contributed to the enjoyment (or lack thereof) at particular sites,[14] and buildings were depicted as they appeared when approached by carriage or on foot rather than as orthographic projections, which was the customary format familiar in contemporary architectural treatises, for example, in the two volumes of *Vitruvius Britannicus* (1767, 1771), to which Sandby subscribed. This publication had been co-edited by James Gandon, a friend who had also exhibited alongside the brothers at the SAGB.[15] Key houses visited on 'A tour into Derbyshire' were illustrated in *Vitruvius Britannicus*, and the volumes may have helped shape their itinerary.

The journey was partly dictated by the routes available to their modes of transport (stagecoach and post-chaise) and partly by a socially conditioned understanding of what was worth seeing.[16] Plans were predicated on an expectation that the exterior of a house and its garden would be available to view, even if visiting the interior was restricted to specific times and days. Carole Fabricant has suggested that allowing access to grounds and/or a house was an aristocratic means of coercing the middle classes into accepting increasingly exclusive power structures by 'fostering the illusion of shared property and ownership', and encouraging appropriate tourist behaviour,[17] but Sandby's manuscript suggests far greater class autonomy and independence. He and his friends often engaged in 'inside answerable to the outside' theory.[18] If the exterior did not live up to expectations, no attempt was made to cross the threshold, even if the house was open. Once indoors, however, their route was dictated by the presence/absence of the family, but it was not reliant on a servant's understanding of the objects tourists might wish to see; nor was their experience influenced by individual country house guidebooks (although they

(Stroud, 2007), p. 114.   13 de Jong, 'The picturesque prospect of architecture', pp 77–88, who identifies the influence of Lord Kames and Edmund Burke, in particular.   14 Jon Stobart, 'From magnificent houses to disagreeable country: Lady Sophia Newdigate's tour of southern England and Derbyshire, 1748' in Amanda L. Capern et al., *Women and the land, 1500–1900* (Woodbridge, 2019), pp 127–48 at p. 146.   15 James Gandon and Thomas Mulvany, *The life of James Gandon* (Dublin, 1847; repr. 1969), pp 17, 23, 35–6, 39, 40, 171, 186–90.   16 Carole Fabricant, 'The literature of domestic tourism and the public consumption of private property' in Felicity Nussbaum and Laura Brown (eds), *The new 18th century: theory, politics, English literature* (London, 1987), p. 256.   17 Fabricant, 'The literature of domestic tourism', p. 259.   18 Cynthia Wall, 'A geography of Georgian narrative space' in Miles Ogborn and Charles W.J. Withers (eds), *Georgian geographies* (Manchester, 2004), p. 119.

may have carried a county guide[19]). This gave them more freedom to respond individually to a site.[20]

The tour began when the five friends met at Tyler's home in Vine Street, Piccadilly; they then boarded the Nottingham Stage Coach at Islington.[21] The party was typical of the prosperous middle classes who had the leisure and disposable income to travel, but the stage coach was not an elite means of travel, and pretensions to social status were necessary if the traveller was to avoid inedible food and dirty bed linen.[22] The party self-consciously asserted their superior status on several occasions, but never to any effect.[23] Stoically reminding themselves that 'we went out to Feast the Eye more than the Belly',[24] after a night in transit the friends were rewarded with an approach to Northampton 'interspersed with Gentlemen's Seats and Beautifull Landscapes'.[25]

In Northampton, Sandby noted that All Saints Church, rebuilt after a fire devastated much of the town in 1675, 'has a pretty effect, which it owes more to the form of the Portico, than to the Goodness of the Architecture which is of Ionic construction',[26] a marketplace let down by buildings not 'good enough to Merit any further Description' and 'the County Hall which is a handsome Stone Edifice, and if not Designed by Sir Christopher Wren, is very much in His Style'.[27] The latter building, actually the sessions house, may be the work of Henry Bell, who was also responsible for the design of All Saints.[28] Taking a direct route north, the party passed through Market Harborough, where 'one handsome Church with a lofty Spire ... is the only thing we could observe worth our Notice',[29] and Loughborough, 'where there is a large Gothic Church, with an ample square Tower'.[30]

As these comments attest, Sandby remarked on churches nearly everywhere the party stopped, and frequently when they were simply passing through a

19 BL, Add. MS 42,232, f. 48.   20 Jocelyn Anderson, *Touring and publicizing England's country houses in the long eighteenth century* (London, 2018), pp 46, 51.   21 BL, Add. MS 42,232, f. 22.   22 Jon Stobart, 'Magnificent and mundane: transporting people and goods to the country house, *c.*1730–1800' in Jon Stobart (ed.), *Travel and the British country house* (Manchester, 2017), p. 172.   23 See, for example, BL, Add. MS 42,232, ff 23–4: 'We arrived [at Nottingham] a little before Sun set and put up at the White Lion, our accommodation here was not much to the Credit of Mr Percey the Landlord of that once Noted Inn, whom we found ... too great a Man to wait on us himself nor did he use his Authority in making his Servants give proper attendance for We were Obliged to ring the Bell half a Dozen times before any one made his appearance to receive our Commands, which were then given in a peremptory manner, that they might think us somewhat better than common Travellers in a Stage Coach are found to be. Of which the ample Supper we bespoke, might give them some room to imagine: Yet the Chamber Maid dirty in herself, might think, as we were only Passengers in one of those Vehicles, that We shou'd be properly Accomodated if We Slept in Sheets that were laid in before, and so She lodged us in Dirty Linnen ...'.   24 Ibid., f. 22.   25 Ibid.   26 Ibid., ff 22–3.   27 Ibid., f. 23. Sandby admired Wren's buildings but did not agree with his methodological position as set out in *Tracts*, first published in 1750, a copy of which was in Sandby's library. de Jong, 'The picturesque prospect of architecture', pp 92, 95.   28 Colvin, *Biographical dictionary*, p. 116.   29 BL, Add. MS 42,232, f. 23.   30 Ibid.

locality. He may have equated the state of a church with the religious health of the nation and was certainly religious enough to forego drawing on the sabbath.[31] He was drawn to genuine Gothic architecture, but not to the same degree as Francis Grose whose interest in the subject had not rubbed off on him.[32]

Loughborough was followed by the village of Bunny, where the party alighted. Here, 'the late Sir Thos Parkins Built a very whimsical Seat on one side of a pretty Park, which He also surrounded with a brick Wall'.[33] However, what drew their attention more than Bunny Hall was the monument to Parkyns (1664–1741) in St Mary's Church. The left panel depicts Parkyns in the stance of a wrestler (he was a patron of wrestling), while in the right he lies supine in defeat overlooked by Father Time. It is a monument preposterous enough to elicit comment,[34] but Sandby confined himself to recording a translation of the inscription:

> Here thrown by Time, Old Parkins laid.
> The first fair fall He ever had;
> Nor Time without the aid of Death
> All else He threw, and will those twain,
> As soon as He gets up again.[35]

It was not unusual for travellers to blend their experiences with published accounts, and since there is no evidence that Sandby could read Latin or Greek, he may have turned to a printed source, but the origin of this translation remains elusive.[36]

From Bunny, the party travelled to Nottingham, where they stayed at the White Lion since the location afforded an opportunity to explore the famous vaults cut into the rock beneath.[37] With local pride, Sandby recorded that Nottingham's marketplace was 'the handsomest and largest in the Kingdom' and

31 Ibid., f. 53.   32 Grose believed that medieval monuments were worthy of study in their own right because they were the 'foundations of the history of the nation'; Hauptman, 'Francis Grose', p. 75. Later in the manuscript (f. 51), the medieval steeple of All Saints, Derby, is described as 'bold, well designed and not Crowded in the capricious and injudicious Manner we frequently see in Buildings of this sort, for here no part is too predominant for the other', suggesting he found it an exception to the rule. His descriptions of monastic ruins are also not those of a melancholic proto-Romantic nor were they written by someone looking for vital indicators of past lives and events. He was frequently disappointed by heaps of medieval masonry. See BL, Add. MS 42,232, ff 32, 53.   33 Ibid., f. 23.   34 In the entry for Bunny, Pevsner recorded that 'Thanks to the church and its Wrestling Baronet, [Bunny is] one of the most rewarding villages in south Notts.' Quoting John Throsby's suggestion that the monument was 'wrought out of a fine piece of marble by his chaplain in a barn', he could not resist a droll aside: 'in the r. bay a little figure of a man laid out on a straw mat, and a ridiculous Father Time by his side, which look as if they were carved by the chaplain'. Nikolaus Pevsner and Elizabeth Williamson, *The buildings of England: Nottinghamshire* (London, 1997), p. 85.   35 Ibid.   36 Charles L. Batten, *Pleasurable instruction: form and convention in eighteenth-century travel literature* (London, 1978), p. ix.   37 BL, Add. MS 42,232, f. 24.

The northern tour of Thomas Sandby and Theodosius Forrest, August 1774 81

that two large caverns on the outskirts of the town made 'an exceeding Romantic and awfull appearance'.[38] An attempt was made to visit coal mines owned by Lord Middleton, but 'it being Sunday they were not Worked';[39] fortunately Middleton's seat, Wollaton Hall, was accessible. The house, designed by Robert Smythson in the 1580s, was considered by some to be 'the noblest building in this county',[40] and would have been known to Sandby in his youth. The building and its environs prompted a description that reveals the typical traveller's trope of measuring 'the unfamiliar by reference to the familiar':[41]

> This is an Ancient & Magnificent Pile of Buildings with the Doric, Ionic, & Corinthian Orders one above another, Set on a Basement Story, The Hall which is large & placed in the center of the House includes three Storeys, receiving its Light from the upper one. It has another lofty Room over it of the same Length & Breadth. On the four Angles of this, on the outside are circular Turrets something like Centry Boxes on the Angles of Bastions in fortified Places. This part of the Building rises above the rest, much in the same manner the Egyptian Hall does at the Mansion House in London, with this difference that You can walk all round it on the Leads of the other part of the House. The whole Building has a very Noble & Picturesque appearance ... much enriched with Ornaments, such as were in fashion towards the end of the fifth [*sic*] Century, But are Superior to any thing of the kind I have yet seen.[42]

This is the first appearance of the word 'picturesque' in the manuscript but, much like Sandby's use of 'beautiful' and 'romantic' elsewhere, its theoretical underpinning as something pleasing to both eye and emotions is inexact. As Jocelyn Anderson has noted, 'many tourists' reflections on country houses as buildings were dominated by their enjoyment of houses' 'visual force and consideration of situation'.[43] Sandby was equally drawn to Smythson's use of the classical orders on Wollaton; something that was not unusual as even the first edition of Defoe's *Tour* (1724–6) made mention of 'the four Pavillions of the Dorick order on the top'.[44]

Another local building deemed worthy of notice was the castle, a seat of the duke of Newcastle, which merited two watercolours and a description of comparable length to that of Wollaton, although its baroque style and 'Grotesque Ornaments' were received less favourably than the drama of its setting, which commanded from its 'most Noble Terrass ... a View over a Country not much unlike, or inferior to that from Windsor Castle'.[45]

38 Ibid.   39 Ibid.   40 P. Russell and Owen Price, *England displayed*, 2 vols (London, 1769), i, p. 390.   41 Ousby, *The Englishman's England*, p. 2.   42 BL, Add. MS 42,232, f. 25.
43 Anderson, *Touring and publicizing England's country houses*, p. 68.   44 Daniel Defoe, *A tour through the whole island of Great Britain*, eds P.N. Furbank et al. (London, 1724–6; 1991), p. 232.   45 BL, Add. MS 42,232, f. 25.

The view from Nottingham Castle afforded sightings of Belvoir Castle, Clifton Hall and Wollaton, and also the streets of Nottingham, set into the hills so that 'the fronts of many handsome Houses are distinctly seen, as well as its Churches and some other public Buildings'.[46] Chief among the latter was

> the County Hall built a few years ago by Mr Gandon, who made two Designs for it, the plainest and least expensive of which was adopted. In the Center it has four three Quarter Doric Columns Supporting their Entablature, and an Attic over them; But the whole is in too plain a Style of Architecture to Merit any encomiums, but this was not his fault, the few Embellishments he proposed to have introduced in the elevation, from parsimonious Views were Obliged to be Omitted, & not even a sham Window or Nich allowed to enliven the Blank spaces on each side the Center. As a Lover of Architecture I cannot help wishing the other Design had been carried into Execution, it would have been an Ornament to the place, and done some Honor to the Artist as well as to the County ...[47]

Sandby was almost certainly drawn here for personal reasons and his measured assessment of the building reflects that connection. Gandon had been one of five men approached for designs for a new county hall in 1768 after he had been introduced by the Sandbys' acquaintance William Mason to Sir George Savile and 'other influential gentlemen'.[48] His initial designs, illustrated in *Vitruvius Britannicus* (1771), were accepted but, as Gandon's recent biographer has remarked: 'The prudent public servant is inclined to confuse money with value',[49] and simpler designs were requested. The result is unimpressive. Nonetheless, Sandby's desire to see it is a reminder that he was loyal to old friends.

After allowing himself a final remark that the town of his birth 'would puzzle a person well acquainted with most others in England to Name its equal',[50] Sandby's time in Nottingham came to an end. Departing in post-chaises, the party passed Nuthall Temple, 'an elegant Seat', and Rufford Abbey, which elicited more praise for Sir Charles Saville's attempt to reforest the landscape than for the house itself,[51] and into the Dukeries, that part of the county famous for its number of ducal seats. Their initial stop was the duke of Kingston's Thoresby Hall, designed by John Carr, who had supplied Woolfe and Gandon with the drawings engraved for *Vitruvius Britannicus*.[52] This was the first of the houses Sandby's party visited that was illustrated in *Vitruvius Britannicus*, and perhaps for that reason it was not one he sketched. Aside from its size (small enough to qualify as a 'villa') and the disproportionate nature of the service wing

---

46 Ibid., f. 28.   47 Ibid.   48 Gandon and Mulvany, *The life of James Gandon*, p. 25.
49 Hugo Duffy, *James Gandon and his times* (Kinsale, 1999), p. 58.   50 BL, Add. MS 42,232, f. 28.   51 Ibid.   52 John Woolfe and James Gandon, *Vitruvius Britannicus* (London, 1771),

that blocked views of the lake, it had little impact.[53] The ornamental use of water, on the other hand, caught Sandby's professional attention. Like most tourists, he was aware of 'the changing taste in garden design and the crucial role of buildings within … landscaped gardens',[54] but he was also interested in the mechanics of the garden, remarking on the route of waste water into a river that flowed behind the house and out towards 'a handsome Brick Building … composed in an elegant and simple Gothic style; this is built for an Object to adorn the River and at the same time serves for a Water Mill'.[55]

From Thoresby, the party travelled to Clumber, another seat of the duke of Newcastle, where Sandby scoffed at the duke's pretensions and puffed his own superior taste:

> His Grace must have very great Ideas, if He calls this enclosure a small one, or the House a Cottage; It is a neat elegant looking Building, of a Delicate whitish coloured Stones to which it chiefly owes its Beauty, the Architecture not being in a great or Masterly Style, nevertheless it is what will please many People from its singularity and lightness. On the front to the River it has a very handsome Arcade, supported by double Columns something like that at Gloucester Lodge [Windsor, which Sandby remodelled for Maria, Countess Waldegrave, *c*.1771].[56]

The next stop was Welbeck Abbey, belonging to the duke of Portland, 'But the outside of His Mansion did not invite us to see what was within, as it had no ways an appearance suitable to the Dignity of its owner,'[57] making explicit his expectation that an unimpressive exterior could only lead to an equally underwhelming interior and, in so doing, fail to reflect the superior social status of the owner.

Worksop Priory was visited the following morning before the party walked to the duke of Norfolk's Worksop Manor, designed by James Paine with input from the duchess. Sandby devoted one of his longest descriptions to this seat, beginning with praise for the 'truly Picturesque' nestling of the lawns within a chain of hills.[58] Approaching what was intended to be the north wing of a vast quadrangle, he recorded: 'We came to the Garden Front of this Magnificent House, which, being much greater than some of our party had conceived fill'd them with exclamations of Astonishment and great Surprize.'[59] Akin to Philip Yorke's assessment of the house as 'a vast pile of building', and Richard Sulivan's that it was a 'prodigious pile of unfinished building', the size impressed.[60] While his companions marvelled, Sandby sketched.

pls 11–13.   **53** BL, Add. MS 42,232, ff 28–9.   **54** Stobart, 'From magnificent houses to disagreeable country', p. 137.   **55** BL, Add. MS 42,232, f. 29.   **56** BL, Add. MS 42,232, f. 29; Colvin, *Biographical dictionary*, p. 897.   **57** BL, Add. MS 42,232, f. 29.   **58** Ibid.   **59** Ibid. **60** Joyce Godber, 'The travel journal of Philip Yorke, 1748–63', *Bedfordshire Historical Record*

3.2 Theodosius Forrest after Thomas Sandby, 'Worksop Manor', British Library, Add. MS 42,232, f. 30r.

Some fifteen minutes later, they determined to 'see if the internal parts afford equal Satisfaction to the External'.[61] In an era when admission procedures were tightening up – in 1768 Arthur Young had required a letter of introduction because Worksop 'was not shewn'[62] – their access appears accidental: their 'old friend' Francis Hayman, then employed restoring paintings in the ducal collection, had heard of their presence, and obtained a master key to let them in.[63]

> The long range of Rooms exhibited at on View are neatly, but not highly finished, having no inriched Ceilings in them; the great Stair Case is Painted in Chiaro Oscuro by _____ a Pupil of _____ if the Drawing of the figures had been equal to their effect they would have pleas'd the Conniseur as much as they Charm the unskilled, or Ordinary Spectators, who imagine it to be Sculpture rather than Painting, the Deception is so well managed. There are two small Peices done by the Master of this Artist, that does Him great Honor, for they are so well Drawn, and so

Society, 47 (1968), pp 125–63 at pp 127–8; Richard Sulivan, *A tour through parts of England, Scotland, and Wales, in 1778*, 2 vols (2nd ed.; London, 1785), ii, p. 259. 61 BL, Add. MS 42,232, f. 29. 62 Arthur Young, *A six months tour through the north of England*, 4 vols (London, 1770), i, p. 366. 63 BL, Add. MS 42,232, f. 31. Hayman exhibited with the SAGB and was a founding member of the Royal Academy. Brian Allen, *Francis Hayman* (London, 1987), p. 9. For Hayman and Pugh, where it is asserted that this Hayman cannot be Francis Hayman, see npg.org.uk/research/programmes/directory-of-british-picture-restorers/british-picture-restorers-1600–1950-h, accessed 29 Sept. 2021. Herbert Pugh exhibited with the SAGB 1760–76, including 'A view of the Old Abbey gate-house at Redford, near Worksop' in 1775. Graves, *The Society of Artists of Great Britain, 1760–1791*, p. 205.

exquisitely well Painted, that they cannot fail giving Pleasure to the most curious Observer, I think them the best Deception of this sort I ever saw.[64]

While a valuable record of a house demolished in 1843, Sandby's description is redolent of disappointment; however, as the unexecuted south wing was the intended site of the state rooms, he saw only the family's apartments and staircase. Blank spaces in the manuscript indicate that the name of the artist responsible for the stairhall decoration was to be added later, although Hayman should have been able to identify him for Sandby as Theodore de Bruyn, who had become a student at the Royal Academy in 1773.[65]

Given that art collections were a key tourist attraction, and that the 'decades following 1770 saw a rapid increase in the publication of country house guidebooks, many of which discussed art collections in great detail', Sandby's account of the collections is also low key.[66] According to William Bray, there was no catalogue for Worksop Manor,[67] but a Royal Academician being guided through an art collection by a fellow Academician might be expected to comment on Holbein's *Christina of Denmark* or van Dyck's *Madagascar portrait*. Instead, only two paintings, possibly by Jacques Parmentier,[68] and the drawing room tapestries caught his eye.

Their visit at an end, the friends returned to their hired carriages for the short drive to Sandbeck Park, newly remodelled by James Paine for Lord Scarborough, although again the architect's name is conspicuously absent from the account.[69] This is surprising because Sandby named architects when he knew them and Worksop and Sandbeck are both illustrated in Paine's *Plans, elevations and sections, of noblemen and gentlemen's houses* (1767), to which Sandby subscribed. Tyler had also worked with Paine at Bagshot Park, Surrey.[70] The reluctance to identify him must be residual bad blood dating from the formation of the Royal Academy by a group seceding from the SAGB in 1768. In an internal power struggle concerning the constitution of the SAGB's directorship, the hanging committee of the annual exhibitions and the construction of a new exhibition space, Paine had been pitted against Sir William Chambers when the latter was appointed the society's treasurer. After a particularly rancorous

64 BL, Add. MS 42,232, ff 29, 31.   65 Bray described the stairhall painted with figures 'so relieved, that they perfectly stand out from the wall. It is the performance of one *Bruyn*, a *Fleming*', *Sketch of a tour into Derbyshire and Yorkshire* (2nd ed.; London, 1783), p. 334. De Bruyn exhibited with the Free Society and SAGB, including 'Sculpture; in chiaro-oscuro', and 'Painting; do. Representing two of the large pictures done by him for His Grace the Duke of Norfolk at Worksop Manor' in 1770. Graves, *The Society of Artists of Great Britain, 1760–1791*, p. 73; Edward Croft-Murray, *Decorative painting in England 1537–1837*, 2 vols (Feltham, 1970), ii, pp 177–8.   66 Jocelyn Anderson, '"Worth viewing by travellers": Arthur Young and country house picture collections in the late eighteenth century' in Jon Stobart (ed.), *Travel and the British country house* (Manchester, 2017), p. 140.   67 Bray, *Sketch of a tour into Derbyshire and Yorkshire*, p. 334.   68 Croft-Murray, *Decorative painting in England*, i, pp 256–7.   69 Peter Leach, *James Paine* (London, 1988), p. 208.   70 Ibid., p. 173.

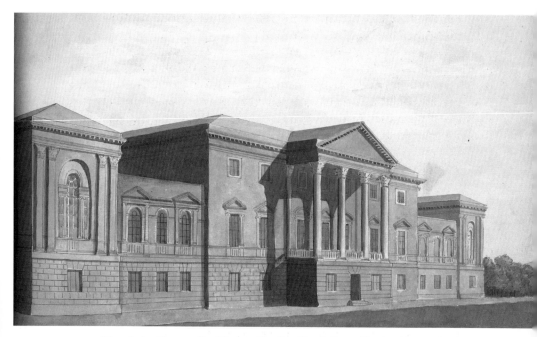

3.3 Theodosius Forrest after Thomas Sandby, 'South Front Harwood House', British Library, Add. MS 42,232, f. 36r.

meeting in November 1768, Paul Sandby resigned his directorship at the same time as Chambers and joined him as a founder member of the new Royal Academy that Chambers had been working behind the scenes to establish.[71] In Sandby's assessment Sandbeck and its architect were wanting, so the group decided not to venture in:

> The repetition of so many Pediments in the front of this House, however well that form may please the Artist, has certainly a bad effect and betrays a Poverty of invention. I cou'd therefore Wish for his own sake he had suppressed the two on the extremities on each Front, where they never can be introduced with any degree of Propriety, especially when there is one in the Center ... As we were told the inside of the House would give us but little Satisfaction, We entered not therein ...[72]

Instead, the men directed their attention to Roche Abbey, which had featured frequently in Paul Sandby's work since 1763.[73] Locating such sites was not always easy – in this case the abbey was on the edge of the park at Sandbeck and had not yet been encompassed in its 'Capability' Brown landscape.[74] Sandby's

71 Hargraves, *Candidates for fame*, pp 63–109, esp. p. 85. 72 BL, Add. MS 42,232, ff 31–2.
73 Bonehill and Daniels, *Paul Sandby*, p. 184. 74 Jane Brown, *The omnipotent magician*

party separated and they were not reunited for another ninety minutes, at which point the ruins 'fell short of our Expectations'.[75]

The next stop was Rotherham, before the party arrived at Wakefield. After touring the town the following morning, they departed for Leeds and the real reason for venturing north: Harewood House, newly constructed seat of Edwin Lascelles. Most unusually, Sandby's account begins within the house, and it was Thomas Chippendale's furniture that first elicited his approbation rather than Robert Adam and John Carr's exteriors:

> This Gentleman's Noble Mansion is not intirely compleated within, but it only wants the Furniture to two of the principal Rooms. This was of little Consequence to Us, as we had sufficient examples of the great Elegance and propriety in what is already Furnished, which seems to be well considered, having great affinity with the Stucco and Carved Ornaments in each apartment ... no Building I have yet seen pleases me so much.
>
> It stands on the Declivity of a Gentle rising Ground, The North Front to which You first approach, The entrance being on that side, is on the highest part. You Ascend the Principal Story by a Broad flight of Nine Steps which leads You into a regular and well finished Hall, Thirty one feet Broad, Forty one in length and about Sixteen Feet high, as are all the rest of the Rooms on this Story, and of suitable Dimensions to accompany the Hall; a thing that should always be attended to in Buildings of this sort, For when You enter a Magnificent Hall, including two Stories You seldom meet with other Rooms of equal Grandeur, and are generally Disappointed in Your expectations, by the impression made on Viewing the largest Room first, which too frequently is a useless one, here it is not so, and the Number of handsome Rooms, so Varied both in their Shape and Dimensions excited very pleasing Ideas, having fully answer'd those we had Conceived of them from the Accounts of such as had Visited this Place before us.[76]

This is Sandby's first detailed commentary on interiors and, in this context, it is noteworthy that a drawing attributed to him in the British Museum of the principal floor plan of Harewood derives from *Vitruvius Britannicus* rather than Adam's Office for it shows the South Dining Room with the concave corners that were omitted when the house was built.[77] Sandby's comments suggest he had prepared carefully beforehand, and they reflect his interest in the visual impact of architectural ornament, and a preference for an incremental build-up of grandeur as one progressed through interiors.

(London, 2011), pp 284–7. 75 BL, Add. MS 42,232, f. 32. 76 Ibid., ff 32–3. 77 BM, 1904,0819.409, Thomas Sandby, 'Ground plan of Harewood House, near Leeds'; Woolfe and Gandon, *Vitruvius Britannicus* (1771), pl. 24. Eileen Harris, *The genius of Robert Adam*

In his analysis of the entrance façade, Sandby decided the visual effect would have been greater, and the balance between vertical and horizontal improved, had the full elevation been visible, although he recognized that this was impossible to achieve because the house was set into a hill that necessitated placing most of the ground floor in a well on the north side; 'notwithstanding this, it is very elegant', he concluded.[78] His comments on the south façade were more critical as he found that Adam's contravention of a hierarchy of ornament resulted in too much emphasis on the two-storey 'links' between the main block of the house and higher wings.

> This will sometimes be the Consequence when an Architect does not follow one uniform Idea, and who not having resources within himself, must have recourse to the invention of others, and introduce and mix their Ideas with his own. This has certainly been the Case, here, for the three circular headed Windows I am speaking of, on each side, are exactly copied from part of Dioclesians Baths at Rome, and are ... in a different Style from the rest, altho these by some People may be thought to give Variety to the Elevation, it destroys that Simplicity and Uniformity which ought to prevail in every Building that aims to stand the Test of Criticism.[79]

Sandby's solution was to omit the pediments and reduce the window size. His reference to 'variety' reveals a familiarity with Adam's definition of 'movement', which had appeared in print a year earlier in the first instalment of *The works in architecture of Robert and James Adam* (1773).[80] Adam was not a close friend, but the Sandbys had been acquainted with him from at least 1758, and Paul had contributed figures to plates in Adam's *Ruins of the palace of the Emperor Diocletian at Spalatro* (1764).[81] However, much like his fellow Academician Joshua Reynolds and friend Gandon, Thomas Sandby believed it was the synthesis of exemplars that produced the best, most original, work.[82] Harewood was too various and the influence of the Baths of Diocletian too undigested for his tastes.

Having ventured as far north as they had planned, the journey south followed a different route, from Wakefield to Barnsley. The artificial ruins erected at nearby Wentworth Castle proved an aesthetic stumbling block: they seemed 'too trifling' and 'unnatural' to allow the 'imagination to trace the Connection

---

(London, 2001), p. 144, suggests that Carr gave Woolfe and Gandon drawings for publication. 78 BL, Add. MS 42,232, f. 33.   79 Ibid., ff 33–4.   80 Robert Adam, *The works in architecture of Robert and James Adam*, ed. Robert Oresko (London, 1773; 1975), p. 46, n. A.   81 Robert Adam to James Adam, 11 Dec. 1758 (Scottish Record Office, Edinburgh, Clerk of Penicuik Muniments, GD18 4854); Robert Harding, 'Robert Adam, *Spalatro*' in Robin Simon and Maryanne Stevens (eds), *The Royal Academy of Arts: history and collections* (London, 2018), p. 548.   82 Edward McParland, *James Gandon: Vitruvius Hibernicus* (London, 1985), pp 182–4.

The northern tour of Thomas Sandby and Theodosius Forrest, August 1774

3.4 Theodosius Forrest after Thomas Sandby, 'Wentworth Woodhouse', a near identical view to that by Sandby, but lacking the two figures in the doorway on the right, British Library, Add. MS 42,232, f. 40r.

between the parts, that there may appear a probability that such, or such a Building had existed on the spot',[83] and it was with difficulty that Sandby persuaded his friends to visit the house, accompanied by Carr, then employed on the stables at the neighbouring estate of Wentworth Woodhouse. Negative opinions were soon swept away by the beauty of the landscape and a house Sandby described as being 'in the Venetian Taste of Architecture'.[84] The façade that captured his imagination, attributed to the Prussian court architect Johann von Bodt, had been erected c.1710–20 for Lord Strafford.[85] It 'soon Obliterated the Impression his Artificial Castle had made on my fellow Travellers' minds, as well as my Own' and its 'Simplicity and Uniformity' filled Sandby's mind 'with pleasing Sensations', especially the uniformity of the windows with their gilded sashes that gave him 'the greatest Satisfaction, as it exemplifies that Simplicity

83 BL, Add. MS 42,232, f. 37.   84 Ibid., f. 39.   85 Colvin, *Biographical dictionary*, p. 135.

which excites our admiration in the Works of Antiquity'.[86] Even the Palladian windows were 'by much the handsomest of that form I have met with'.[87]

Astonishingly, Sandby and his friends did not enter the house and thus he recorded no comments on the long gallery designed by James Gibbs that had attracted other visitors;[88] but Sandby was no admirer of Gibbs and this may have been enough to dissuade him from seeking access.[89]

Neighbouring Wentworth Woodhouse was not a top tourist destination, but those who braved the poor roads came to see the longest façade of any English country house. Much as they did at Wanstead, long-recognized as the inspiration for the east façade of Wentworth Woodhouse, most tourists admired the portico. In 1770, Arthur Young had described it as 'lightness and elegance itself; the projection is bold, and when viewed aslant from one side, admits the light through the pillars at the ends, which has a most happy effect'.[90] This façade appealed to Sandby's conservative taste and he depicted it from an oblique angle to maximize its visual impact.[91]

While Sandby and his friends were admiring the façade, Lady Rockingham sent a servant to issue an invitation to dine and stay the night so that they might tour the park thoroughly.[92] This upset their plans to progress a stage further on the journey south but, with Carr in their midst, a refusal would have been impolite and impolitic. It was not uncommon for owners or their servants to offer hospitality to visitors, but demonstrations such as this were not always received gladly.[93] Young may have praised the hospitality at Wentworth Castle and referred to 'that unpopular and affected dignity in which some great people think proper to cloud their houses' by restricting access, but for his generation 'hospitality' meant something different than it had for previous generations.[94] By the 1770s, a distinction could be made between 'hospitality' in the sense of allowing visitors access to state rooms and gardens, and the older sense of 'hospitality' associated with the communal great halls of 'Ye olde Englande' where dining took place. The latter may have been seen as an imposition by a class of traveller who had little interest in interacting with the owners of those same attractions.

Sandby's irritation spilled over into his assessment of the landscape at Wentworth Woodhouse, and he found little remarkable beyond the Hoober

---

86 BL, Add. MS 42,232, f. 39.   87 Ibid.   88 Nathaniel Spencer, *The complete English traveller* (London, 1771), pp 505–6; Alexandre de La Rochefoucauld, *To the Highlands in 1786: the inquisitive journey of a young French aristocrat*, ed. Norman Scarfe (Woodbridge, 2001), p. 53.   89 All Saints, Derby, is later described as 'in a Clumsey style, such as are almost all Mr Gibs's Designs'. BL, Add. MS 42,232, f. 51.   90 Young, *A six months tour through the north of England*, 1, p. 278.   91 BL, Add. MS 42,232, ff 39, 41.   92 BL, Add. MS 42,232, f. 41.   93 BL, Add MS 15,776, Journals of travels in different parts of England and Wales, 1735 and 1743, by Revd Jeremiah Milles, f. 25; Richard Pococke, *Travels through England*, ed. James Joel Cartwright, 2 vols (London, 1888), i, p. 55; Caroline Girle Powys, *Passages from the diaries of Mrs Phillip Lybbe Powys of Hardwick House, Oxon*, ed. Emily J. Climenson (London, 1899), p. 11.   94 Young, *A six months tour through the north of England*, 1, p. 148, quoted in

Stand and a reflecting telescope. Even the meal awaiting them in the octagonal summer house came too soon after the lavish spread the marchioness had already provided.[95] Two canals were dismissed as 'of no extraordinary sise' and 'the Lawn ... too much circumscribed, and the Prospect greatly intercepted' by a hill that the marquess was in the process of levelling.[96] This is strikingly at odds with contemporary publications such as Spencer's *The complete English traveller*, for whom 'the gardens contain such a profusion of art blended with nature, that it would require a volume to describe every particular'.[97] Sandby's failure to comment on the political messages conveyed in the gardens at Wentworth Woodhouse and Wentworth Castle, and the family rivalry that had prompted their construction, also suggests that his party was immune to this type of associative garden, although, more prosaically, they may simply have been uninterested in bickering cousins.

The lack of comment on the interiors at Wentworth Woodhouse is more mystifying. Apart from the dimensions and use of scagliola in the Marble Hall, there are no assessments of the sculptures, van Dycks or works by Stubbs including the celebrated *Whistlejacket*.[98] Sandby had spent nearly forty-five minutes chatting with the marchioness in the gallery and traversed 'at least Two Thousand feet to the Room appointed for my repose', yet it is almost as if he had never been inside.[99]

From Wentworth Woodhouse, it was a short journey to Sheffield and then east into the Peak District to Castleton and one of the Wonders of the Peaks, the 'Devil's Hole', which Sandby described as 'a large Subteranious Cavern'.[100] Finding himself more intrepid than his companions, he was the first to take the 'ferry' – a small vessel that he thought resembled a butcher's tray – across what most visitors called the 'river Styx'[101] and progress into the second vault.[102] A further stretch of water was traversed before they descended a few yards to hear 'the Choristers of the place Sing in their customary Strain to such as resort hither'.[103]

This experience was similar to that of most visitors,[104] but Sandby's account once again reveals him as a man not given to flights of fancy. Seemingly dissatisfied, his party declined to penetrate any further and instead returned to their inn to refresh themselves before a visit to the remains of Peveril Castle, 'a very insignificant Building'.[105] For someone supposedly interested in picturesque theory, it should be noted that Sandby and his friends refused to climb Mam Tor, the so-called 'shivering mountain',[106] which Sandby found to be 'only a High rugged Hill on one side of which it is so steep and composed of Loose Earth, mix'd with Gravel, that it is frequently Shivering down ... But I cannot think

Anderson, *Touring and publicizing England's country houses*, p. 43. **95** BL, Add. MS 42,232, f. 41. **96** Ibid., ff 41–2. **97** Spencer, *The complete English traveller*, p. 506. **98** BL, Add. MS 42,232, f. 41. **99** Ibid., f. 42. **100** Ibid., f. 43. **101** Ousby, *The Englishman's England*, p. 137. **102** BL, Add. MS 42,232, f. 46. **103** Ibid. **104** Ousby, *The Englishman's England*, pp 134, 136. **105** BL, Add. MS 42,232, f. 48. **106** Ousby, *The Englishman's England*, p. 132.

this very alarming';[107] Elden Hole proved equally anticlimactic, as 'its amasing Depth only exists in the imagination of the Credulous'.[108] At the end of a long, hot day, the party spent the night at Tideswell, where there was 'nothing worth our notice except the Church'.[109]

The final Wonder that the party visited was Chatsworth, a house long part of the tourist itinerary. Invariably, visitors commented upon the contrast between the rugged landscape of the surrounding area and what Defoe described as 'the most delightful Valley' in which the house was situated,[110] and Sandby was no exception.[111] However, the house itself increasingly fell short as architectural taste moved away from William Talman's baroque style of the 1680s. Visiting Chatsworth in 1719, John Scattergood had found himself so overwhelmed by the beauty of the contents and the abundance of high-quality glazing that he 'got so into an enchanted castle that I know not how to get out'.[112] In contrast, Philip Yorke found the house full of 'useless rooms' in 1763, and in 1789 a dyspeptic John Byng blamed Duchess Georgiana for 'all the foolish glare, uncomfortable rooms, and frippery French furniture of this vile house'.[113] Sandby may not have been misogynistic in his comments but he remained ambivalent. The place was worth seeing but the house, though 'executed in a very expensive manner', lacked elegance and would be liked only by those who had never studied architecture and 'are unacquainted with the Harmony of Chast Design, and the Beauty of just proportion, from whence true Elegance is Derived'.[114] By the end of the century, James Plumptre would dismiss the Palace of the Peaks as 'little worth seeing' and 'formerly one of the wonders of Derbyshire'.[115]

Finding that there was no accommodation to be had at Matlock, the party sought refuge at an alehouse in a nearby village, and the remainder of the afternoon was devoted to walking in the surrounding landscape. Forrest and Sandby both wished to stay longer in the vicinity: 'In places like this a Painter might make many profitable Studies where Nature has been somewhat extravagant in her Various Combinations of Picturesque forms, or Noble Compositions.'[116]

With time pressing, after Derby came Kedleston Hall, one of the most consistently admired houses in England.[117] Here Sandby found 'a most Sumptuous House built ... from a Design of Mr Robert Adam', although the façade he admired for its 'very elegant and Majestic Appearance' was begun to

---

[107] BL, Add. MS 42,232, f. 48. [108] Ibid., f. 49. [109] Ibid. [110] Defoe, *A tour through the whole island of Great Britain*, p. 251. [111] BL, Add. MS 42,232, f. 49. [112] Rosie MacArthur, 'Gentlemen tourists in the early eighteenth century: the travel journals of William Hanbury and John Scattergood' in Jon Stobart (ed.), *Travel and the British country house* (Manchester, 2017), p. 96. [113] 'The travel journal of Philip Yorke', 162; John Byng, 'A tour in the Midlands, 1789', *The Torrington diaries*, ed. C. Bruyn Andrews, 4 vols (London, 1935), ii, p. 37. [114] BL, Add. MS 42,232, f. 49. [115] Ian Ousby (ed.), *James Plumptre's Britain. The journals of a tourist in the 1790s* (London, 1992), p. 72. [116] BL, Add. MS 42,232, f. 50. [117] Anderson, *Touring and publicizing England's country houses*, p. 76.

3.5 Theodosius Forrest after Thomas Sandby, 'Lord Scarsdale's Garden Front' (Kedleston Hall), British Library, Add. MS 42,232, f. 52r.

designs supplied by Paine before he was supplanted by Adam in the owner Nathaniel Curzon's favour.[118] Kedleston was included in Paine's *Plans, elevations and sections* ... , but his tenure had been brief. Sandby's assessment of Adam's more revolutionary south façade – 'very handsome, and in a more Singular Taste, [but] ... inferior to the other' – again reflects his more conservative tastes and his watercolour was composed to disguise the backs of the quadrant corridors exposed by the absence of their counterparts on the garden façade.[119] Unable to tour the house because 'the Hours allotted to shew this Noble Edifice were past', they returned to Derby 'not a little Disgusted at our Landlord, who knew the Hours appointed to see that House'.[120]

The next day, passing through Loughborough, Mountsorrel and Leicester, they dined at Uppingham. A delay of some hours before post horses could be acquired rendered it dark when the party arrived at Stamford. The next morning, a visit to St Mary's Church to see the monument erected to 'The great Cecil Lord Burleigh' allowed Sandby to reflect on an important historical figure before visiting the house he had built. Most visitors reserved their commendations for Antonio Verrio's painted decoration in the state apartment or the picture collections at Burghley, but Sandby's response was rather different.[121] Unexpectedly, he reveals himself to have been a perceptive admirer

118 BL, Add. MS 42,232, f. 51. 119 Ibid. 120 Ibid., f. 53. 121 See, for example, BL, Add. MS 15,776, Journals of travels in different parts of England and Wales, 1735 and 1743, by Revd Jeremiah Milles, f. 78; *Britannica Curiosa*, 6 vols (2nd ed.; London, 1777), iii,

of Elizabethan architecture at a time when few visitors expressed enthusiasm for buildings of this era.[122] Horace Walpole, who could be expected to respond positively to older buildings, had praised the house in 1763 as 'A noble Pile! the Inner Court is beautifull Scenery', but even he was more interested in the collections than the architecture.[123] Even at the end of the century, William Gilpin could assert that sixteenth-century houses like Longleat were 'objects of curiosity ... [with] little beauty and I should suppose less convenience',[124] and the painter Edward Dayes found the value of Haddon Hall to lie in its ability to demonstrate how the economy had improved: 'the poorest person at present possessing apartments, not only more convenient, but at the same time better secured against the severities of the weather'.[125] Sandby's appreciation of the freedom from academic strictures with which Burghley had been designed, and the resulting delight he took in an exterior he saw as little altered since its construction, was surely a worthy precursor of the Elizabethan Revival of the nineteenth century:

> This certainly is one of the most singular Houses in the Kingdom, and though of a mixt Style of Architecture in the taste of the fifth [sic] Century, has great Merit. It has two extensive Fronts, and the ends are not far short of their Dimensions, In the Center is a spacious Quadrangular Court, in a very particular Taste, but much superior in point of Design to any of the Fronts exhibitting a more Beautiful Scene that I ever saw in any House Ancient or Modern, and it wou'd be a difficult task for an Artist tied down to the Rules of Grecian Architecture, to Produce a Building with such various and Picturesque Forms, & cou'd almost make Him wish to forget ... his Rules of Symmetry and proportion to indulge a Luxuriant fancy, such as is displayd in this Sumptuous Structure ... What added much to our Satisfaction in this Place was to see it in such good repair and hav'ing undergone so few alterations, such as Sashing some of the Windows, and Modernising a few of the Rooms. In every other respect it still appears nearly the same as it must have done when first finished, to the great Credit of its Noble Possessor.[126]

pp 316–17. Further examples are discussed in Anderson, *Touring and publicizing England's country houses*, p. 80. **122** Esther Moir, *The discovery of Britain. The English tourists 1540 to 1840* (London, 1964), p. 63; Anderson, *Touring and publicizing England's country houses*, p. 80. **123** Paget Toynbee (ed.), 'Horace Walpole's journals of visits to country seats &c.', *Walpole Society*, 16 (1628), pp 9–80 at p. 58. **124** William Gilpin, *Observations on the western parts of England* (London, 1798), pp 125–8 quoted in Moir, *The discovery of Britain*, p. 64. **125** E.W. Brayley (ed.), *The works of the late Edward Dayes: containing an excursion through the principal parts of Derbyshire and Yorkshire* (London, 1805), p. 12. **126** BL, Add. MS 42,232, f. 55. Sandby did not share the attitude towards the past of his antiquarian friend Grose or contemporaries such as Richard Gough, as discussed in Rosemary Hill, *Time's witness* (London, 2021), but his appreciation of Elizabethan architecture is perhaps akin to that found in publications of a later generation such as C.J. Richardson, *Observations on the architecture*

Travelling by stagecoach via Stilton and Stevenage, the party arrived at Hatfield in Hertfordshire, 'where we slept that Night, and saw the great House there belonging to Lord Salisbury as You went over this Building with me last Year, a Description of it is unnecessary here'.[127] There Sandby closed the account.

Sandby's 'Tour into Derbyshire' is a document that can be read on several levels. The itinerary was orthodox and the party's reactions to many sites similar to those of their contemporaries. Nowhere is this more evident than in the Peak District, where Sandby's account reflects a tourist's response to what he saw as he saw it, as recorded in countless eighteenth-century manuscripts, rather than in the over-blown accounts of picturesque theorists and the professional writers of travel guides. He and his friends had little genuine enthusiasm for rough and rugged terrain, which could be enjoyed at a distance but not when one had to traverse it. They preferred the combination of 'nature' and 'art' evident in many of the estate landscapes they visited. There Sandby revelled in the emotional impact of natural and built environment, loosely invoking vocabulary such as 'picturesque' and 'beautiful' to describe what he saw. Undoubtedly influenced by the thinking of Lord Kames and Edmund Burke, he nevertheless worked from the unfamiliar to the familiar like any other tourist, and one must leave space for him to respond as a man as well as an Academician.

On another level the itinerary was driven by Sandby's professional interests. The desire to see newly built country houses and their collections was common, but the emphasis he placed on analysing their exteriors was not. Exposure to art collections was not the purpose of the journey and at many houses entry was never sought. Time and again he revealed himself as an architectural conservative – not for him the delights of the cutting-edge neoclassicism that he saw at Harewood and Kedleston; he privileged the regularity and repetition of a neo-Palladian taste that was increasingly out-moded by 1774. When confronted with buildings that stood outside the classicizing norm of the new-build, however, he found a different voice. His admiration of Wollaton and Burghley makes one regret even more that he had not visited Hardwick Hall instead of the Palace of the Peaks.

Finally, the bonds of friendship were important. They helped shape the itinerary, facilitated entrance to Worksop Manor, and probably prompted the misplaced hospitality at Wentworth Woodhouse. The existence of 'A tour into Derbyshire' as an original manuscript, a contemporary illustrated copy, and a series of individual watercolours draws us into an eighteenth-century world where the experience of travel was shared with, and enjoyed by, more than one audience.

of England during the reigns of Queen Elizabeth and King James I (London, 1837) and the sensitive alterations made to Charlecote Park, the Elizabethan house, after G.H. Lucy inherited it in 1823, for which see Clive Wainwright, 'Charlecote Park, Warwickshire I-II', *Country Life*, 177 (21–8 Feb. 1985), pp 446–50, 506–10.   127 Ibid., f. 56.

Soup kitchens at English country houses, 1795–1914: a new perspective on elite landscapes

PHILIP J. CARSTAIRS

INTRODUCTION

Fourteen days in prison was the sentence the magistrates handed down to Mary Phillips on 22 October 1841. Her crime was in some ways unremarkable: theft of eight pounds of mutton, some fat, a piece of bread and some cheese, the property of her employer, his Grace, the second duke of Sutherland.[1] The borderline between servants' pilfering and legitimate perquisites was dependent on where one stood in the household hierarchy, and her sentence was lighter than most handed out by magistrates that day. Reported in the *Staffordshire Gazette*, what offended the newspaper's moral sentiment was that the theft was of victuals the duke had provided for feeding the poor at the soup house at Trentham Hall, the Leveson-Gower family's Staffordshire country seat.

The focus of this essay will be one aspect of this tale that the papers found unremarkable and almost passed over: that the duke had a purpose-built soup house at Trentham Hall from which he provided charity to the poor. The poor, for whom the soup house was ostensibly built and the stolen food intended, were not even bystanders in the *Gazette*'s report. Why they were poor and why charity was needed, let alone why there was a soup house at Trentham Hall, were questions that did not cross the journalist's mind. Exploring these issues offers a new perspective on the kinds of social activity in and around country houses, as well as revealing a very specific kind of visitor. Two case studies, Stowe House and Trentham, demonstrate how rural charity was practised. Further examples show that soup charity was not unique to the great landowners or their houses, that it was regular and widespread at the houses of the rural gentry and continued throughout the nineteenth century.

The principal source for research into soup kitchens during the long nineteenth century, with a focus on five counties – Northumberland, Staffordshire, Hertfordshire, Buckinghamshire and Kent – has been local newspapers, not family or estate records. The British Newspaper Archive, where more than 42 million pages of the British Library's collection of historic newspapers have been digitized, has been an invaluable resource. Its word-searchable format makes it easier to trace the topic, and provides a glimpse into a subject which is rarely listed in the index to family papers or estate records.

1 *Staffordshire Gazette*, 28 Oct. 1841.

The data gathered includes significant numbers of newspaper reports about wealthy individuals, particularly country landowners, providing soup to the poor. These reports seem to parallel those of institutional charities ladling out soup in the towns. Until 1851 half the English population was still living in rural not urban areas and so this data on rural charity is significant.

That landowners gave charity to the local poor, including soup, is unsurprising and is occasionally referred to in studies of rural social history.[2] Nineteenth-century cookery books, celebrity chefs and newspapers published recipes for making soup for the poor alongside more exotic fare such as turtle soup and lobster bisque.[3] However, the implications of this charitable action for the country house and its role within the community have not been considered. But one should begin by asking why was charity necessary in the first place?

POVERTY AND THE COUNTRYSIDE

The long nineteenth century saw living standards for rural labourers deteriorating through the effects of enclosure, changes in conditions of employment, increasing under-employment, the introduction of agricultural machinery and rising food prices.[4] By the 1790s labourers could rarely afford anything other than bread and cereals for their families with very occasional small quantities of meat.[5] In industrial and mining areas, farm labourers were somewhat better paid and in Northumberland the persistence of a system of annual hiring meant better security for many. Some farm workers were lucky enough to receive cheap food from their employers and home-grown potatoes also contributed significantly to their diet.[6] However, the balance between comfort and hunger was a fine one.

If people had to turn to the Poor Law for relief, they found local officials who were increasingly hostile to their plight and, after the Poor Law Amendment Act of 1834, they faced a stark choice between destitution or the workhouse. During the 1870s, many aristocratic landowners began further cutting back on the paternalistic benefits they had provided such as pensions or medical assistance.[7] In most rural communities there were relatively few people with wealth and most of these were the landowners. The landed elite not only provided most of the

---

2 G. Mingay, *Rural life in Victorian England* (Stroud, 1990), pp 99, 186.   3 I. Beaton, *Mrs Beeton's book of household management* (London, 1861), p. 84; A. Soyer, *Soyer's charitable cookery: or the poor man's regenerator* (London, 1848), p. 11.   4 K. Snell, *Annals of the labouring poor: social change and agrarian England, 1660–1900* (Cambridge, 1985).   5 D. Davies, *The case of labourers in husbandry: stated and considered, in three parts* (Bath, 1795), p. 8; F. Eden, *The state of the poor* (London, 1797).   6 D. Oddy, 'Food, drink and nutrition' in F. Thompson (ed.), *The Cambridge social history of Britain, 1750–1950* (Cambridge, 1990), pp 251–78 at 255.   7 E. Hurren, *Protesting about pauperism: poverty, politics and poor relief in late Victorian England, 1870–1900* (Woodbridge, 2007), pp 132–3, 150–2.

work either directly or through tenant farmers, they were also important figures in the church and the administration of justice. Thus the obligation to support their community fell on them; in exchange for power and deference from the poor, they had to ensure that people could get the basic necessities to survive, through affordable food, housing and regulation of work, and if necessary the provision of welfare. Their willingness and ability to maintain this traditional moral economy waned during the late eighteenth century and by the early nineteenth century it was apparently moribund.[8] The evidence discussed here suggests that charity in the form of food was one part of the moral economy that remained remarkably resilient in the face of this decline (or perhaps because of it), and much of this charity emanated from the manors and country houses within their parks.

THE COUNTRY HOUSE AND PARK

The established modern view of eighteenth- and nineteenth-century country houses and their parks is that they were 'landscapes of exclusion' from which common people, especially the poor, were barred.[9] Boundary walls, gates and lodges served further to 'isolate the household from the outside world' and create privacy.[10] They were places for pleasure for their owners and guests, as well as expressions of exclusive power. The house and park legitimized the status of its occupants, although this display was primarily aimed at polite society, associates, rivals and the gentry.[11]

As mid-eighteenth-century polite society became wider and less hierarchical, country houses and parks were reshaped to reflect new modes of social interaction. House guests circulated through different activities in different rooms. The symmetry and axial planning of pleasure gardens and parks was superseded by a more natural landscape with a sequence of carefully arranged views enabling the space to perform similar functions to that of the house.[12] Middle-class tourists began to visit the more accessible houses, using guidebooks that described and explained the beauties of the house and gardens.[13]

---

8 E.P. Thompson, *Customs in common* (Pontypool, 1991), pp 36, 200; P. Dunkley, 'Paternalism, the magistracy and poor relief in England 1795–1834', *International Review of Social History* 24:3 (1979), pp 371–97 at p. 379; L. Stone and J. Stone, *An open elite? England, 1540–1880* (abridged edition, Oxford, 1986), p. 179; G. Claeys, *Machinery, money and the millennium: from moral economy to socialism, 1815–1860* (Princeton, 1987), p. 18.   9 T. Williamson, *Polite landscapes: gardens and society in eighteenth-century England* (Stroud, 1995), p. 108.   10 L. Stone, 'The public and the private in the stately homes of England, 1500–1990', *Social Research*, 58:1 (1991), pp 227–51 at p. 231.   11 T. Williamson, 'Gardens, legitimation and resistance', *International Journal of Historical Archaeology*, 3:1 (1999), pp 37–52.   12 T. Williamson, *Polite landscapes*, p. 110.   13 J. Anderson, *Touring and publicizing England's country houses in the long eighteenth century* (New York, 2018).

During the long nineteenth century, shooting became increasingly fashionable as a competitive social activity for the wealthy.[14] Parks became game reserves. Landowners increased security to protect game from the predations of poachers; the criminal law, enforced by the landowners as justices of the peace, became more draconian in its punishment of poaching. The Victorian desire for family privacy also began to exclude uninvited visitors and outsiders. From around 1840, space within houses was subdivided to improve the moral and physical well-being of the household by segregating occupants by class, employment, status and gender.[15] This impression of growing exclusion and differentiation would seem to leave little room for the poor except as labourers or servants. However, it will be argued here that this had more to do with the invisibility of the poor to many modern eyes than with their absence.

SOUP AS CHARITY

Hospitality for guests, neighbours and strangers, and charity for the poor had routinely been provided at the houses of wealthy medieval and Tudor landowners. The sixteenth century saw the beginning of a cultural shift from an absolute religious duty to provide for the poor to a more focussed moral calculation as to the benefits of giving. The performance of charity moved from the lower end of the hall to the gate outside.[16] Later Poor Laws also had the effect of distancing the destitute and needy, locating them further away from the elite house and household.

By the time local newspapers become widely available in the mid-eighteenth century, soup was being distributed regularly from some country houses. The formula 'beef/meat, bread and broth', which first appeared during the severe winter and famine of 1739–49,[17] was repeated in articles during the remainder of the century. So, for example, every week Sir Charles Bunbury of Barton Hall, Great Barton, Suffolk provided beef, broth and rye bread to the poor of the parish.[18] As a standard package of philanthropic relief, it was reminiscent of the more ancient hospitality of 'beef/meat, bread and ale/beer' provided to travellers and the poor at great houses and so represents both a continuation and an adaptation of that tradition.

The final decade of the eighteenth century saw bad weather, poor harvests and rapidly rising cereal and bread prices.[19] When combined with the effect of

14 T. Williamson, *Polite landscapes*, p. 134.   15 M. Girouard, *Life in the English country house: a social and architectural history* (New Haven, 1978), p. 270; M. Girouard, *The Victorian country house* (New Haven, 1979), pp 18, 28.   16 F. Heal, *Hospitality in early modern England* (Oxford, 1990), pp 24, 30, 98–101.   17 C. Corbet, *The open heart and purse: or, British liberality display'd* (London, 1740).   18 *Oxford Journal*, 31 Jan. 1767.   19 W. Stern, 'The bread crisis in Britain, 1795–96', *Economica*, new series, 31 (1964), pp 168–87 at p. 174; R. Wells, *Wretched faces: famine in wartime England, 1793–1801* (Stroud, 1988), p. 40.

national recessions and the Napoleonic Wars, the situation for the poor became dire. Famine ensued. In towns and cities large-scale relief funds operated and soup kitchens opened up. Soup was eagerly promoted as the ideal form of relief by the authorities, inspired by the 'scientific' research of Count Rumford, which seemed to show that a small quantity of soup could sustain a person better than meat or bread.[20] In rural areas, country house owners were increasingly reported to be providing soup to their local poor. The soups were usually made of beef and thickened with peas and barley.

Diarist William Hervey recorded how Lord Grimston was distributing soup to seventy or eighty local poor at Gorhambury House, Hertfordshire in August 1795.[21] Grimston's neighbour, Lady Georgiana Spencer, also provided soup to the local poor, who came to Holywell House, St Albans, from up to seven miles away.[22] One very cold winter, to avoid the poor struggling with the journey over icy roads, she decided to distribute the soup to their homes using a donkey, even though Holywell House was right next to the road on the edge of St Albans. The experiment was unsuccessful: the donkey was scalded by the hot soup and ran amok, as a newspaper claimed some eighty years after the event.[23]

STOWE HOUSE

Hervey was also a frequent visitor at Stowe House, Buckinghamshire, about 55 km north-west of Gorhambury. Here, during the 1795–1801 dearth, John Dayrell, vicar of Stowe, described Richard Temple-Nugent-Brydges-Chandos-Grenville, later the first duke of Buckingham and Chandos, distributing soup to '800 of his poor neighbours' in January 1800.[24] The population of Stowe parish in 1801 was only 311 including staff at Stowe House. The surrounding seven parishes could only muster 1,200 more, so these 800 probably consisted of the entire population of the poor of these parishes and may even have included people from the town of Buckingham. Dayrell's use of the term 'neighbours' suggests this was seen as ancient hospitality and charity, not poor relief.

The numbers fed are indicative of the extent of both the crisis and the duke's charity. This largesse was not a one-off. It was 'the practice at Stowe to provide soup during the winter to the poor' as well as 'beef, bread, plum pudding and

20 F. Redlich, 'Science and charity: Count Rumford and his followers', *International Review of Social History*, 16 (1971), pp 184–216 at p. 192; W. Gratzer, *Terrors of the table: the curious history of nutrition* (Oxford, 2005), p. 62.   21 S. Hervey (ed.), *Journals of the Hon. William Hervey, in North America and Europe, from 1755 to 1814; with order books at Montreal, 1760–1763* (Bury St Edmunds, 1906), p. 411.   22 Countess Dowager Spencer, 'Extract from an account of the manner in which the poor have been supplied with rice and beef at St Albans' in T. Bernard (ed.), *The reports of the Society for Bettering the Condition and Increasing the Comforts of the Poor* (London, 1802), iii, pp 216–20 at p. 218.   23 *Hertfordshire Advertiser*, 1 Feb. 1879.   24 Letter to Revd John Brewster of Durham, from his friend Revd John Langham Dayrell, vicar of Stowe, 23 Jan. 1800 (Centre for Buckinghamshire Studies, D22/25/59).

beer to 540' at Christmas.[25] Elizabeth Wynne (later Betsy Fremantle), as prolific a diarist as Hervey, recorded that 'near 300 poor people dined in [Stowe] house' on 25 December 1797 and on 18 December 1799 '300 poor people dined here on the remains of last night's supper', which had been to celebrate Lady Buckingham's birthday.[26] Hervey reports similar events, for example, on Christmas Day 1802: 'In the hall dined labourers, their wives and children, in all 262'; and a week later, '1803 January 1 Saturday being New Year's Day all the poor of the parish with their families dined here'.[27]

These Yuletide entertainments for the poor took place either in the main hall or in the servants' hall; they straddled the border between traditional hospitality and charity. Providing food to neighbours, tenants and the poor over the twelve days of Christmas had a long tradition when beer, bread and broth secured the fealty of recipients for the following year.[28] It also provided vital sustenance to enable the poor to survive the winter. The tradition was flexibly adapted and interpreted as a cover for providing charity that might otherwise humiliate recipients; it persisted into the twentieth century. Lady Rose hosted annual Christmas celebrations at Rayners, her house in Tylers Green, Buckinghamshire, which were reported in the press between 1894 and 1908; at these gatherings coal, clothing and other useful presents were given to many as well as soup, meat, dumplings and bread to 115 ticket-holders representing over 800 people. The Roses had already built a new parish hall containing a soup kitchen in 1886.[29]

However, at Stowe soup was probably taken away by recipients. In 1846, Martha Foddy, 74, died of apoplexy on the way home from Stowe House where she had gone to *fetch* soup (she was not regaled on the premises as were polite visitors to Stowe).[30] To say that she got soup at Stowe simplifies the story and fails to ask exactly where she got the soup and how she got there.

The increasing grandeur of country houses and their isolated situation in landscaped parks meant the poor had to make long journeys on foot to receive charity. Martha lived in Water Stratford, nearly 4 km away. Her journey was gradually uphill, much of it along one of the straight, tree-lined avenues that led to the north front of the house. She would have passed through several sets of gates, each more elaborate than the last, then past two lodges, before crossing Oxford Water, an ornamental lake, via a bridge decorated with urns and grotesque carved faces. The road continued past the deer park towards the domed cupolas of the Boycott Pavilions, one on each side of the road, each massively bigger than any of the cottages in Water Stratford. The Boycott Pavilions marked the end of the deer park and the beginning of the landscaped gardens. Here the road levelled out, but the north-west wing of Stowe House was still 600 metres further on, and the house itself over 200 metres in length.

25 *Windsor and Eton Express*, 25 Dec. 1824.   26 A. Fremantle (ed.), *The Wynne diaries, 1789–1820* (Oxford, 1952), pp 293, 302.   27 Hervey, *Journals*, p. 418.   28 Heal, *Hospitality*, p. 74.   29 *South Bucks Standard*, 29 Dec. 1899; *Buckinghamshire Herald*, 13 Nov. 1886.   30 *Buckinghamshire Herald*, 7 Feb. 1846.

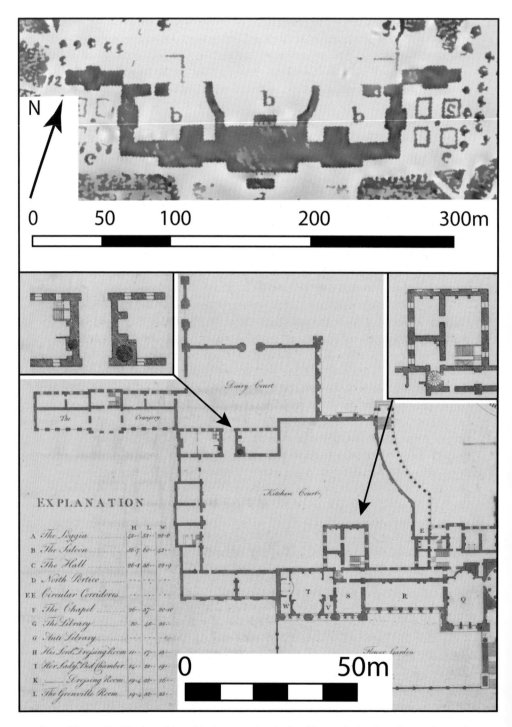

4.1 Stowe House, Buckinghamshire with the west wing in detail beneath, in 1817; the two insets show the Dairy Court and brewery buildings with large stoves (left), and the main kitchen block (right), from J. Seeley, *Stowe: a description of the house and gardens* (Buckingham, 1817).

As Martha approached the north front of Stowe House, she probably turned right through a pedimented arch into the Dairy Court. From here only the park side of the house could be seen; the private garden side remained out of sight. The kitchens (still used by the school that occupies the house today) were just beyond the Dairy Court, through a covered passageway under a building now known as the Carpenters' Block, in the next courtyard, the Kitchen Court. Plans show the block bisected by a carriageway, with a large stove in the corner of one room and a smaller stove in the other; a staircase in one room is evidence of an upper floor.[31] The larger stove may have been for the brewery, which occupied this building,[32] and the smaller stove may be evidence of a laundry. Soup was either made here using one of these stoves or in the kitchens.

It is doubtful whether Martha, or any of the hundreds of others attending from surrounding parishes to get soup, were captivated by the beauties of the house and grounds as many of the vistas, temples and follies and main lake were not visible from her route and the house barely so. However, the scale of the park and house would not have been unnoticed. Each leg of the journey could have taken the 70-year-old nearly an hour. The journey would have been equally arduous from other nearby villages, detouring west around the landscaped gardens. Whichever route the poor took they would not have seen Stowe House until they arrived there. This visual surprise was the same for polite guests who might only have caught a distant glimpse of the house framed in the Corinthian Arch from their carriage. For the pedestrian poor the distance emphasized the power and remoteness of the residents. Their journey crossed several boundaries, from cottage to public highway and then into the park through gates and past lodges and landscaped gardens before reaching the service quarters of Stowe House. Each boundary marked a transition in the landscape from village to fields to estate to park to garden and house, each new zone becoming more ordered and enclosed, finishing in a courtyard overlooked by the house whose principal rooms were on a *piano nobile* above. Movement was predetermined by the strictures of the park, gardens and house. Landscape and architecture exerted their influence not just by imposing a view, but by determining which route people took. Stowe further exercised power by remaining invisible until the last minute and then overwhelming the visiting poor by its scale. Martha's journey was both arduous and intimidating.

The creation of the landscaped park moved the gate where the poor are generally thought to have received charity further away from the house. If the journey for Martha and others was this laborious, particularly in wintertime, and if the park and house were private, why did the duke not simply pay someone to make and distribute soup in each of the surrounding villages? The poor had to

31 J. Seeley, *Stowe: a description of the house and gardens of the most noble and puissant prince, Richard Grenville Nugent Chandos Temple, marquess of Buckingham* (Buckingham, 1817).
32 M. Bevington, *Stowe House* (London, 2002), p. 90.

visit the house, because they had to be seen. It is no coincidence that diarists Wynne and Hervey were guests of the duke's visiting Stowe to enjoy his hospitality but also witness his generosity to others. The regular wintertime visits of the tenants and the poor as dependants were a vital part in the display of the duke's wealth and patronage, emphasizing an aristocratic identity that, while very distant from the poor, could also dispense charity to them. His magnanimity and receipt of gratitude and respect was part of a custom that reached directly back to medieval paternalism.[33] Soup distribution needed to be a public act, not an invisible one, so the ritual took place in the most theatrical of venues, Stowe mansion house, and not at obscure cottage doors in nearby villages. If the poor knew soup was available at the house, so too did everybody else. The act of giving and receiving soup created a mutual recognition of the social and personal identities of giver and receiver, thereby reinforcing an established local hierarchy.[34]

The visits of the poor to Stowe were theatrical and entertaining for polite guests. The attendance of the family and house guests at such events was customary.[35] Elizabeth Wynne described a supper for sixty poor children as being 'a pretty sight' (30 December 1797); as well as labourers planting trees in the garden who 'passed before the house ... forming a ludicrous procession, some with spades, forks or rakes ... the band playing before them' (14 January 1808); and her sister was amused by the 'different mixture of people' at the tenants' ball (19 December 1804).[36] Festivities for the duke's birthday included a thousand poor people from each of twelve neighbouring parishes, headed by their clergyman and a banner, marching into dinner in front of the duke's guests.[37] The poor were not merely spectators or passive recipients of food, they were both actors and part of the audience. Often ill-shod and thinly dressed, the poor entered a stage to perform a script that was not of their making. Unlike tourists for whom an inn had been built just outside the gardens, tucked out of view, they were not there by choice.

Until May 1847 when the Grenville family fortunes collapsed under a mountain of debt run up by the profligate second duke, soup continued to be distributed from Stowe. After 1847 Stowe House was closed to visitors and its contents sold. Stowe House and its gardens remained in possession of the family until 1889, occupied by a skeleton staff. The second duke died bankrupt in 1861, living at a hotel in Paddington, London. The third duke continued to use Stowe House as a residence until his death in 1889, when the house was let to the Comte de Paris.[38] Although no further soup distributions were reported after

---

33 Girouard, *The Victorian country house*, p. 45.   34 E. Goffman, *Relations in public* (Harmondsworth, 1971), pp 194–9.   35 Girouard, *Life in the English country house*, p. 240.   36 Fremantle, *The Wynne diaries*, pp 293, 485, 373.   37 *Oxford University and City Herald*, 13 Jan. 1810.   38 J. Beckett, *The rise and fall of the Grenvilles, dukes of Buckingham and Chandos, 1710–1921* (Manchester, 1994), pp 226, 266–75.

1846, charity almost certainly continued to be distributed from Stowe House, albeit on a reduced scale, as the family retained significant land in the vicinity. The Comte died at Stowe in 1894, leaving an endowment for the deserving poor of Stowe parish, showing that both rural poverty and charity continued.[39]

TRENTHAM

The Leveson-Gower family, the dukes of Sutherland, avoided the financial ruin that overtook the dukes of Buckingham, although their Highland tenants paid a heavy price for modernization that took place in the clearances between 1750 and 1860. At Trentham, just one of many family seats, soup distribution to the poor was first reported during the 1795–1801 famine when the marquess and marchioness of Stafford, parents of the first duke, relieved the poor from parishes for miles around with 'bread, beef and broth'.[40] Distributions continued throughout the nineteenth century: the family were distributing bread and beer at 'the Trentham Gate' in 1816,[41] and estate accounts record regular charitable deliveries of soup, bread and beer from 1818 until 1882.[42]

The accounts include a set of rules delineating who was entitled to what: beer was provided to pensioners, the travelling poor (vagrants and tramps who were allowed only one pint), strangers and the sick poor. The family took an organized approach to local charity. From the 1840s pre-printed ledgers included sections recording soup given to the poor of Trentham and Burton, which was 4 km away.

Soup was still being given away in 1894 when the duchess was present at a distribution of soup, clothing and other goods to about 120 recipients.[43] At the same time she was entertaining a large party of house guests, between eighty and ninety attendees of the Trentham Bible Class, who were treated to a substantial 'knife-and-fork tea' in the gallery, and later about sixty of the old people resident on the estate. Her remarkable display of hospitality, spanning a broad spectrum of visitors to Trentham, was enacted at Trentham Hall in locations chosen to reflect the social standing of each class of visitor.

The references to the soup house and Trentham Gate are to the building known as the Poor's Lodge. Some country houses were located very close to roads and villages, with their parks only on two or three sides; this proximity meant the gateway was a visible link between the house and the outside world; Trentham Hall was such a place. The Lodge was a two-storey classically inspired building with symmetrically placed windows, ornate quoins and a low-pitched

---

39 W. Page (ed.), *A history of the county of Buckingham* (London, 1927), iv, p. 237. **40** *Staffordshire Advertiser*, 20 Feb. 1796. **41** *Morning Post*, 27 Nov. 1816. **42** Records of the Sutherland-Leveson-Gower family, estate monthly general reports and farm, time and pay reports (Staffordshire Record Office, D593/L/6/2/22). **43** *Staffordshire Advertiser*, 29 Dec. 1894.

4.2 The Poor's Lodge, with Trentham Hall behind, 1905–6 postcard (courtesy of The Westlands Collection, Brampton Museum, Newcastle-under-Lyme).

gabled roof. It was situated on the north side of the house, at the gate to the stables and coach yard, north-east of the house, just before the entrance to the churchyard. It was positioned facing the public road that passed by the church, and divided the main house from a further range of service buildings to the north that included a brew house, bake house, poultry yard and kitchen gardens.[44] It was most likely constructed in the early nineteenth century and is probably shown on the 1809 estate map.[45] It was demolished in 1911 along with much of Trentham Hall.

The Poor's Lodge must have contained a stove for cooking the soup, as well as living quarters for the lodge-keeper on the upper storey. An 1826 inventory of the contents of the Poor's Lodge included twenty-one one-quart cans,[46] which would have been used for soup. A quart was generally the amount of soup served at institutional soup kitchens, for which the poor were often expected to pay a penny. The newspaper reports and the accounts show careful discrimination

44 P. Sambrook, *Country house brewing in England, 1500–1900* (London: 1996), p. 202.
45 Records of the Sutherland-Leveson-Gower family, map of the marquess of Stafford's Trentham estate (Staffordshire Record Office, D593/H/3/444 (201/31893)).   46 P. Sambrook *Country house brewing*, p. 213.

between different categories of recipient. The elderly (many of whom may have been former employees) and the religious might be permitted to enter the main house, but the rest were allowed only as far as the gate, where they received portions dependent on their status.

Attending to the needs of the local poor was a landowner's important and ancient obligation and the poor had an absolute moral right to the common decencies of life from their landlord.[47] 'Property has its duties', said the *Kentish Gazette* in 1845, uttering a cliché of the time,[48] while lauding the earl of Winchelsea for his weekly distribution to the poor of Boughton Aluph.[49] However, these duties conflicted with a growing perception of the poor as being less a heaven-sent object upon whom to exercise charity and more a problem of disorder, dirt and disease requiring social distance and reform.[50] Charity might do more harm than good. An article in the *Illustrated London News* condemned the owner of a Gothic house, shown in a picture by George Haydock Dodgson, providing a Christmas dole at the gate of his house, saying, 'the only thing I approve of is that the lower classes are made to keep their distance and are not allowed to come up to the house to annoy their betters'. As far as the writer was concerned, the poor were undeserving charlatans, and it was highly regrettable that such things still happened in 'country districts'.[51] A contemporary Buckinghamshire newspaper editorial criticized the slavish dependence of the 'inhabitants of rustic spots' on some 'little-great man' and for accepting soup and flannel and the landowners' desire for flattery, homage and honour.[52]

The liminal location of the Poor's Lodge demonstrates the Leveson-Gower family's attempts to manage the conflict between traditional charity and hospitality (both of which they were keen to maintain) and keeping the poor in their place. The lodge stood at the border between public and private. It was closer to the stables and farm buildings than to Trentham Hall. Guests were admitted to the hall, but certain groups of visitors needed to be kept at a distance. The building made a public statement, being on the road and next to the entrance to the church, that here was a family still observant of their Christian duty despite growing criticisms of paternalistic charity, but it marked the difference in status that soup recipients now had. They had been removed from the lower end of the hall to the courtyard by the gate to the house and then later to the entrance to the stables.

47 G. Scott, *Remarks on secular & domestic architecture, present & future* (London, 1857), p. 180. **48** D. Roberts, *Paternalism in early Victorian England* (London, 1979), p. 129. **49** *Kentish Gazette*, 21 Jan. **50** L. Lees, *The solidarities of strangers: the English Poor Laws and the people, 1700–1948* (Cambridge, 1998), pp 20, 82, 111; D. Andrew, *Philanthropy and police: London charity in the eighteenth century* (Princeton 1989), p. 135; D. Valenze, 'Charity, custom and humanity: changing attitudes towards the poor in eighteenth-century England' in J. Garnett and C. Matthews (eds), *Revival and religion since 1700: essays for John Walsh* (London, 1993), pp 59–78 at p. 61. 1845. **51** *Illustrated London News*, 20 Dec. 1856. **52** *Bucks Chronicle and Bucks Gazette*, 22 Sept. 1855.

OTHER LANDOWNERS

Lesser landowners than the dukes of Buckingham or Sutherland did similarly, although on a more modest scale. In Northumberland, A.J. Cresswell Baker JP supplied the poor liberally with soup every Wednesday and Friday 'from the front of Cresswell Hall'.[53] The front of the house was approached from the north-east by a long drive that ran past the lodge, through woodland before arriving at a small gatehouse, right in front of the house. This area was immediately adjacent to the service block, where the kitchens were located and was connected to the house by a curving colonnade, typical of this period.[54] The poor came down the road to the house from the north-east, past a lodge along a curving track, the house invisible until they had arrived. The spectacle of the poor arriving for their soup could be seen by those in the house while Cresswell Hall's private south side, with ornamental grounds and uninterrupted views of the sea, remained invisible, protected by woodland and belts of trees.

At Thornton Hall, Buckinghamshire, a Victorian Tudor/Gothic country house, home to the Cavendish family, built around a late medieval or early Tudor courtyard house, the soup kitchen (as it was referred to) used the seventeenth-century laundry block next to the brewery, again to the north-east of the house. The laundry and brewery were accessed through a low doorway from an irregularly shaped courtyard on the north side of the house. The laundry and brewery formed the west side of the courtyard; workshops and a wall formed the north and east sides respectively. The courtyard had a small entrance on the east side and large gate between the brewery and the workshops. The arrangement was similar to Stowe only on a smaller scale. The main house and its ornamental gardens were discreetly shielded from view by walls and trees.

Lady Anglesey distributed soup to twenty-four poor families all winter from Druid's Lodge about 500 metres north of Plas Newydd House, Anglesey.[55] Sir Edward and Lady Dering ran an estate soup kitchen at Surrenden House for Little Chart and Pluckley, Kent, from at least 1862 until Lady Dering's death in 1897.[56] The house sat on the parish boundary and the Derings had significant land holdings in both parishes. In County Durham, C.J. Clavering, esq., and Lady Williamson ran soup kitchens at Axwell Park and Whitburn Hall, respectively, and Richard Foster built a soup kitchen at the White House, Wrekenton.[57] The less wealthy adapted existing outbuildings. Thus, in the later nineteenth century, the Pryor family established a soup kitchen (at which the poor had to contribute a penny to the cost of soup) at Weston Manor,

---

53 *Newcastle Courant*, 18 Feb. 1832.   54 P. Sambrook and P. Brears, *The country house kitchen, 1650–1900* (Stroud, 2010), p. 56.   55 *Staffordshire Advertiser*, 29 Jan. 1842.   56 *South Eastern Gazette*, 14 Jan. 1862, *Whitstable Times and Herne Bay Herald*, 11 Sept. 1897.   57 *Newcastle Courant*, 7 Jan. 1832, *Newcastle Journal*, 15 Dec. 1855, *Newcastle Daily Chronicle*, 16 Dec. 1861.

Soup kitchens at English country houses, 1795–1914

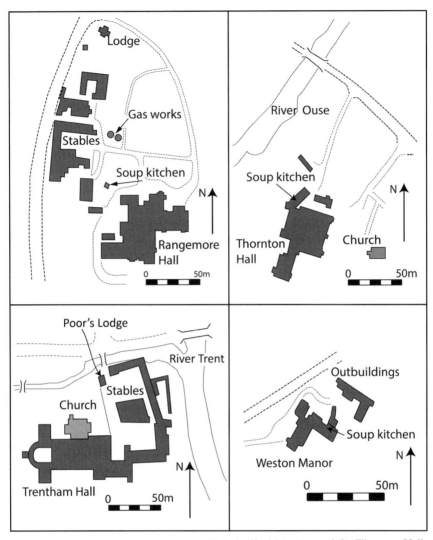

4.3 Soup kitchen locations at Rangemore Hall, Staffordshire (upper left); Thornton Hall, Buckinghamshire (upper right); Trentham Hall, Staffordshire (lower left); and Weston Manor, Hertfordshire (lower right). Trentham is shown in its 1809 configuration, before Charles Barry's remodelling of 1833 (drawing by author).

Hertfordshire. The soup kitchen was probably in a disused early nineteenth-century kitchen at the very back of the manor house; the family also provided soup free from their other house at The Park, Weston (later rebuilt as their private country house).[58]

58 *Hertford Mercury*, 10 Apr. 1886.

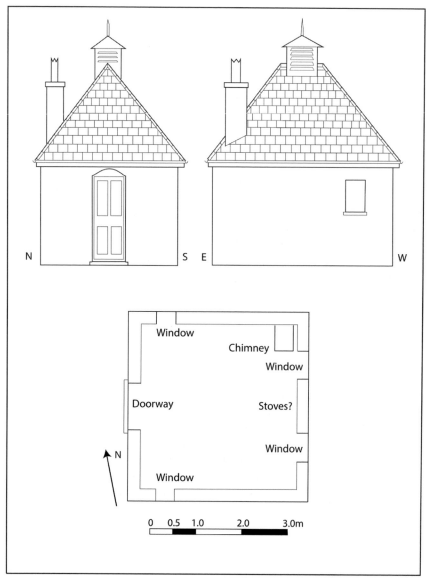

4.4 The soup kitchen at Rangemore Hall; west elevation (top left), north elevation (top right), floor plan (bottom) (drawing by author).

The Bass brewing family of Burton-on-Trent created the Rangemore estate in Staffordshire in the mid-nineteenth century, buying Rangemore House and the surrounding farmland. The family then built a village with a church, school and farm cottages, and enlarged the house to become Rangemore Hall or The

Lawns. Michael Bass was MP for Stafford, created baronet in 1882 and then ennobled as Lord Burton in 1886. He improved and enlarged the house between 1898 and 1901 in anticipation of a visit of King Edward VII in 1902.[59] The soup kitchen is not marked on the 1883 Ordnance Survey map, but first appears on the 1901 edition. The small single-storey building has a hipped, almost pyramidal, roof and a louvred cupola for ventilation. The interior walls are tiled with cream and brown tiles that appear to be original and may have been designed to recall the colours of beer. Its location halfway between the house and the stables on the north (service) side of the house is similar to other country-house soup-making facilities. It could have been accessed from the nearby road via the stable block area, or by turning off the main driveway before reaching the house. Its entrance faces away from the house towards the stables. The soup kitchen was partly screened from the house by densely planted trees to the north and west of the house and it was completely invisible from the gardens and landscaped park on the other side of the house.

It is unclear whether the Rangemore Hall soup kitchen ever saw much soup-making as no documentary evidence for its use is known. Perhaps it was more of a gesture by the newly ennobled businessman and brewer to the concept of what a member of the aristocracy should have on their estate. However, the estate was not far from Burton and in an area likely to see significant numbers of travelling poor, so it may have seen active service.

Not every member of the landed elite provided soup from their country houses to the poor. Others preferred to establish facilities in the villages around their estates. Earl Howe opened four or five soup kitchens in the villages round Gopsall, Leicestershire, and the marquess of Bute at first provided soup from Luton Hoo's kitchens before opening a soup kitchen in Luton.[60] Each of the Buckinghamshire and Hertfordshire branches of the Rothschild family paid for soup kitchens in their neighbouring towns and villages (as well as healthcare facilities, libraries and reading rooms). In part this may have been a desire for privacy, but there was also a strong Jewish tradition of discreet charity rather than a paternalistic desire for homage.

SOUP AND PATERNALISM

Paternalistic charity in the form of gifts of food did not disappear either in the early nineteenth century or after the onset of deep agricultural recession in the late 1870s and early 1880s as has been suggested.[61] Established aristocratic

[59] Historic England List Entry Number 1190947, official listing for The Lawns, Tatenhill, Rangemore, Staffordshire, historicengland.org.uk/listing/the-list/list-entry/1190947, accessed 1 Feb. 2021. [60] *Staffordshire Advertiser*, 27 Feb. 1847; *Hertford Mercury and Reformer*, 9 Jan. 1841. [61] Thompson, *Customs*, p. 36; J. Gerard, 'Lady bountiful: women of

families, the gentry and newcomers to elite society participated. The *nouveaux riches* who had bought country estates eagerly adopted the role of the squire and undertook significant philanthropic projects.[62] Sir Philip Rose, who provided soup, at Tylers Green, was a city lawyer; Lady Lawson provided soup from Hall Barn Manor, Beaconsfield, three years after newspaper proprietor Lord Lawson had been ennobled.[63] Lady Addington's distributions of soup in Gawcott, North Marston and Thornborough (all in north Buckinghamshire) were first reported after her husband, John Hubbard, banker and merchant, became Lord Addington in 1887.[64] Many of these former town dwellers would have subscribed to urban soup kitchens and brought this custom with them to their country houses. They participated in the community just as had their predecessors, with displays of local charity at harvest and Christmas.[65] This charity was modest, still tied to paternalistic authority and often withheld from those not displaying appropriate deference, but there was nothing new in this. Local government reform, the First World War, the beginnings of the welfare state and the disappearance of almsgiving in the early twentieth century contributed to finally bringing an end to a long tradition of providing food to the hungry local poor.[66]

The charity was not, however, simply a continuation of the eighteenth-century moral economy, but a re-creation of it. The poor were not entitled simply because they were poor, they often had to demonstrate their deservingness through seeking work from the landowners. Earl Brownlow provided work to Berkhamsted's unemployed labourers at Ashridge House, Hertfordshire, rewarding them with soup.[67] As well as providing soup in Weston, the Pryors took on unemployed labourers.[68] In Hardwicke-with-Weedon, Buckinghamshire, during a harsh winter, Henry Cazenove doubled the 'usual quantity of soup' and provided work. What further points to a re-invention of paternalistic charity here is that Cazenove was not even a landowner but a retired stockbroker; the only land he owned was the fifty-five acre grounds of the Lillies, his country house.[69]

Soup was a relatively new form of relief that really only became prevalent in the 1790s. By its very nature, it required facilities to make and was inconvenient to transport in bulk. People needed to travel to receive it. Visiting the house perpetuated the face-to-face charity of olden days; the practice served to

---

the landed classes and rural philanthropy', *Victorian Studies*, 30 (1987), pp 183–210 at p. 202.
62 J. Moore, 'The impact of agricultural depression and landownership change on the county of Hertfordshire *c.*1870–1914' (PhD, University of Hertfordshire, 2010), pp 38, 146, 153.
63 *South Bucks Standard*, 15 Mar. 1895.   64 *Buckingham Express* 16 Nov. 1889, 14 Jan. 1893.
65 A. Howkins, *Poor labouring men: rural radicalism in Norfolk, 1870–1923* (London, 1985), pp 3, 15, 35.   66 D. Cannadine, *The decline and fall of the British aristocracy* (London, 2005); B. Harrison, 'Philanthropy and the Victorians', *Victorian Studies* 9:4 (1966), pp 353–74 at p. 353.   67 *Bucks Chronicle and Bucks Gazette*, 8 Feb. 1868.   68 *Hertford Mercury*, 10 Apr. 1886.
69 *Buckinghamshire Herald*, 5 Feb. 1881; Local Government Board, *Return of owners of land, 1873; presented to both houses of Parliament by command of her majesty* (London, 1875).

maintain deferential behaviour in rural areas long after it had waned in cities. The provision of charity also fitted in well with a wider revival in elite moral values which devoted greater resources to local welfare.[70] Providing 'traditional' charity to the local poor legitimized new landowners' social position and showed that they subscribed to the re-invented chivalry that had recently emerged. A chivalrous gentleman took care of his dependants and those less fortunate than him.[71] Mr and Mrs Harcourt's twice-weekly distributions from Ankerwycke maintained 'the real character of the Old English Gentleman and Lady' observed one reporter.[72] Ankerwycke was the site of a Benedictine nunnery from which Henry III had fed a thousand poor, six hundred years previously.[73] The distributions of soup at Alnwick Castle kitchens by the duke and duchess of Northumberland and the Countess Bridgewater's building of a soup kitchen within the ruins of Berkhamsted Castle also echo a re-imagined medieval past in which the lady of the house joined her husband in providing alms to the needy in their community.[74]

Soup was also cheap to make, and did not even require the family's presence to distribute since estate managers, housekeepers or stewards could fulfil the role of almoner. Thus the practice may have been able to survive the constrained circumstances in which many country house owners found themselves during the late nineteenth century. Soup was also sometimes more freely available at country houses than at urban institutional soup kitchens: Mary Phillips' crime was committed in late October in a mild autumn; most urban soup kitchens did not even consider opening until late December. Soup was also free to recipients at country houses (Weston Manor's charge being the exception), whereas at urban soup kitchens the poor routinely had to pay about half of the cost-price.

Charity is proof of inequality, marking a gulf between the haves and the have-nots; as commentators and social scientists were well aware, charity could lead to resentment, envy and discontent.[75] The great nineteenth-century essayist Ralph Waldo Emerson warned that 'The hand that feeds us is in some danger of being bitten' perhaps because the wealthy take too much satisfaction in giving bread to the hungry.[76] Giving alms could turn the recipient into a beggar, a condition that could provoke great fear and anxiety given that begging was a criminal offence in Victorian Britain, and frowned upon by the middle-class artisans and tradesmen.[77] By the late eighteenth century, charity and poor relief were thought

---

[70] Girouard, *Victorian country house*, p. 4.   [71] M. Girouard, *The return to Camelot: chivalry and the English gentleman* (New Haven, 1981), p. 260.   [72] *Buckinghamshire Herald*, 25 Dec. 1841.   [73] S. Dixon-Smith, 'Feeding the poor to commemorate the dead: the *pro anima* almsgiving of Henry III of England, 1227–72' (PhD, University College London, 2003), p. 162.   [74] *Newcastle Courant*, 16 Jan. 1819 and 18 Feb. 1832; *Bucks Gazette*, 5 Apr. 1845; Gerard, *Lady bountiful*, at 188.   [75] M. Mauss, *The gift: the form and reason for exchange in archaic societies* (London, 2002), pp 23, 83.   [76] Ralph Waldo Emerson, *Essays: second series* (Boston, 1844), p. 176.   [77] M. Douglas, 'Standard social uses of food: introduction' in M. Douglas (ed.), *Food in the social order: studies of food and festivities in three American*

to undermine the poor's independence; a view that only grew during the Victorian era.[78] To give was therefore an expression of superiority and to receive was an acknowledgment of inferiority.

The poor had little choice but to pay homage when they were hungry. Measuring the poor's response to the charity they received is partly dependent upon one's theoretical position: optimists choose to see rural harmony bolstered by philanthropy,[79] whereas pessimists see simmering resentment, expressed in poaching, vandalism and attacks on livestock and property, and only thinly veiled by a show of deference.[80] Mrs Pardiggle's fictional visit to the brickmaker's house in Charles Dickens' *Bleak House* saw her proselytizing and inflicting inappropriate charity that is met with muted resistance.

Charity was welcome to the extent it was necessary. It consoled the poor, kept them from starvation, gratified the rich, and delivered a measure of social solidarity.[81] The landed classes knew this: the Leveson-Gowers considered that during the Swing disturbances in 1830–1, the family's hospitality provided their Staffordshire property with some protection from the depredations of disgruntled rural labourers.[82]

Newspaper reports invariably describe the poor as grateful, eager and even enthusiastic recipients of charity, who were willing to walk miles to get soup. One agricultural labourer from near Faversham, Kent, reported appreciatively to an oral history project that before the First World War, 'About once a week, a message would be sent round the village that if he and others went up to the big house at a certain time, they could have some soup. He smacked his lips at the memory, and said "oh it was good, really good"'. Then he added that what the big house did was 'every day they cleared any left-overs on dinner plates into a big vat, and boiled them all up, for distribution once a week.'[83] Despite the appreciation this particular recipient expressed, Consuelo Churchill, chatelaine of Blenheim Place, Oxfordshire, was not impressed by the practice. She claimed to have been the first person to separate the different courses of leftover food destined for the poor into different containers in around 1900 to provide more appetizing food.[84]

---

communities (London, 2003), p. 10; M. Roberts, 'Reshaping the gift relationship: the London Mendicity Society and the suppression of begging in England 1818–1869', *International Review of Social History*, 36:2 (1991), pp 201–31 at p. 224.   78 Andrew, *Police*, p. 143; R. Humphreys, *Sin, organized charity, and the Poor Law in Victorian England* (London, 1995).   79 Mingay, *Rural life*, p. 187.   80 H. Newby, 'The deferential dialectic', *Comparative Studies in Society and History*, 17:2 (1975), pp 139–64 at p. 143; Snell, *Annals*, p. 388.   81 Roberts, *Reshaping the gift*, p. 215.   82 E. Richards, 'Captain Swing in the West Midlands', *International Review of Social History*, 19:1 (1974), pp 86–99 at p. 92.   83 Anthea Jones, personal communication, 5 Feb. 2019.   84 C. Balsan, *The glitter and the gold* (Maidstone, 1973), p. 68.

CONCLUSION

Country houses were neither public nor absolutely private. While the estate might be guarded by lodges, bounded by fences, gates, walls and ha-has, these boundaries were permeable. The poor were not merely tolerated as visitors but welcomed, even if access was carefully managed. Being charitable was essential for maintaining the identity of the landed classes and a justification for their great privilege. The distribution of charity and indeed hospitality seems to have been focussed in wintertime, when it was most needed and when the family was more likely to be at home; a lot more besides soup was regularly given: clothing, coal, meat, wine and money. The practice was also firmly enough established for many landowners to devote special buildings or parts of existing buildings for the purpose. There are still many questions to answer about exactly who received this largesse and what proportion of country house owners took part in the custom, although the practice seems to have been widespread and the recipients numerous among this under-recognized category of country house visitor.

Knole and its visitors: from medieval episcopal palace to country seat, antiquarian curiosity and treasure house

JOHN COLEMAN

Knole in Kent occupies a unique place in the ranks of the most important country houses in Britain due to its combination of antiquity and scale, the grandeur of its exterior and interior embellishments, and its extensive collections, including paintings by Thomas Gainsborough, Joshua Reynolds, Anthony Van Dyck, Peter Lely and many others, as well as an unrivalled collection of seventeenth-century royal furniture from Whitehall and Hampton Court palaces, which have been in the house since 1701. For more than half a millennium numerous visitors have been hosted in its four and a half acres of buildings, set in a twenty-five-acre walled garden, and surrounded by a 1,000-acre medieval deer park.

After acquiring the manor of Knole in 1456, Thomas Bouchier (1404–86), cardinal archbishop of Canterbury, and lord chancellor of England (1455–6), created a palace suitable to accommodate the head of the pre-Reformation church in England, and his entourage and guests. Knole was subsequently enlarged and embellished to impress visitors with the status of members of the Sackville family, who held high office of state and became dukes of Dorset in the early eighteenth century. Over the centuries there have been royal visitors, from Henry VII to Prince Charles, the prince of Wales. The writer and gardener Vita Sackville-West, who was born there, describes a persistent legend that it is the largest private house in England – a calendar house, with seven courtyards, fifty-two staircases and three hundred and sixty-five rooms – though Vita admitted that it is doubtful if anyone had ever counted.[1] From examination of guidebooks from the nineteenth century to the present day, it is evident that members of the public have never been in a position to fully attest to its scale as they have never been admitted to more than about twenty rooms.

Knole has been on the itinerary of the educated tourist since the late eighteenth century, when its ancient splendours meant that it began to achieve iconic status as part of the national patrimony; a guidebook to the portraits, 'with a brief description of the place', was published in 1795, and a 'history and

1 Vita Sackville-West, *Knole and the Sackvilles* (1922; London, 1991), p. 19. The best modern account of Knole is Robert Sackville-West (Lord Sackville), *Inheritance: the story of Knole and the Sackvilles* (London, 2010). 2 H.N. Willis, *Biographical sketches of eminent persons whose portraits form part of the collection of John Frederick, duke of Dorset, and a brief description of the*

Knole and its visitors

5.1 *The Eve of St Agnes* (Keats), 1862–3, by Sir John Everett Millais (1829–96); the artist's wife Effie is depicted in the King's Room at Knole (The Royal Collection).

topographical sketch' was published in 1817.[2] Later, when Knole's future looked precarious, its status as a national treasure was such that, despite the lack of an adequate endowment, it was accepted by the National Trust in 1946; Lord Sackville remains in residence under an arrangement facilitated by legislation passed at the time.[3]

Knole has been frequently depicted in paintings, engravings, lithographs and photographs; these range from the early eighteenth-century bird's-eye views drawn by Leonard Knyff and engraved by Jan Kip for *Britannia illustrata* (1709) to picturesque watercolour views and engravings by Paul Sandby *c.*1775, engravings by John Preston Neale (1780–1847) in his *Views of seats* (1818) and romantic depictions of its interiors by Joseph Nash (1809–78) in his *Mansions of England in the olden times* (1839–49). The king's room also provided the pre-

place (London, 1795). J. Bridgman, *History and topographical sketch of Knole* (London, 1817).
3 The country houses scheme, established under National Trust acts of 1937 and 1939, allows for arrangements whereby donor families and their heirs may be permitted to continue living

Raphaelite painter John Everett Millais with a suitably romantic setting for his subject painting based on John Keats' poem, *The Eve of St Agnes*.

Knole supplied inspiration for Thomas More's *Utopia*, published in 1516; More had served in the household of Cardinal John Morton (1420–1500), archbishop of Canterbury and lord chancellor, and Morton provided the model for More's benevolent prince. The scale of the household described by More is reflected in the vast medieval kitchen and the arrangement of tables in the great hall, which remained in place two hundred years later with a top table for the archbishop, senior officials, and guests, and three lower tables set out for the household; one of the long tables remains in the hall.[4]

Cardinal Morton was one of Henry VII's most trusted advisers and the king stayed frequently at Knole in the 1490s.[5] Later Knole provided a convenient stopping off point for Henry VII's son, Henry VIII, on account of its proximity to Hever Castle, the family home of his second wife, Anne Boleyn. Like so much church property, Knole was appropriated by the king following the Reformation. In 1533 archbishop of Canterbury, Thomas Cranmer (1489–1556), tried to hold onto Knole by deflecting Henry's interest to the nearby episcopal palace at Otford; but the king declared that he 'would have Knole', as he considered Otford to be 'rheumatic'.[6] Having acquired the house Henry seems to have lost interest and the place fell into dilapidation before being resuscitated by Queen Mary I (1516–18), who gifted it as a residence to Archbishop Cardinal Pole (1500–58). Queen Elizabeth I stayed for five days in 1573, and Knole subsequently passed to her lord treasurer and cousin Sir Thomas Sackville, first earl of Dorset (1536–1608). Thomas Sackville was a sophisticated Renaissance man, an author and a politician who travelled on diplomatic missions in the Low Countries, Italy and France. Between 1603 and 1608, serving as lord treasurer under Elizabeth's successor King James I, Thomas spent lavishly on the house, enlarging its size to the current footprint; he further impressed visitors by commissioning a series of grisaille paintings on the great stairs depicting the virtues and the ages of man. However, Thomas was prevented from showing off the full splendour of his house as he died in the year of its completion.

During the sixteenth century, in the time of his grandson Edward (1591–1652), fourth earl of Dorset, lord chamberlain to King Charles I, the house was ransacked by Commonwealth forces and its furnishings removed. Charles Sackville, the sixth earl (1638–1706), was a poet and entertained his friends, including John Dryden (1631–1700), in the room that has become known as Poet's Parlour.

in National Trust properties. This is very often the case. **4** Thomas More, *Utopia* (London, 1974), p. v. **5** *ODNB*, vol. 39, pp 421–5. **6** *DNB*, vol. 14, pp 15–31. Vita Sackville-West cites an account by Cranmer's secretary, Ralph Norice, in the state papers of Henry VIII. Sackville-West, *Knole and the Sackvilles* (1st ed. 1922; London, 1991, p. 23). There is also a collection of documents exchanged between Cranmer and the king about the archbishop's manors, including Knole and Otford, among the Sackville Papers at Kent County Record

5.2 Knole House, Kent, 1809, etching by Letitia Byrne after a drawing by Paul Amsinck, in William Miller's *Tunbridge Wells and its neighbourhood* (1810) (The Roseries Collection/Mary Evans Picture Library).

Influential eighteenth-century visitors included Horace Walpole (1717–97), Fanny Burney (1752–1840) and Edmund Burke (1729–97), who all recorded their impressions. In the twentieth century Knole inspired literary fiction through the works of Eddy Sackville-West, Virginia Woolf and Vita Sackville-West. Diarist James Lees-Milne left an illuminating record of his visits in the early 1940s while negotiating arrangements between the family and the National Trust.[7]

Horace Walpole, influential aesthete and incorrigible gossip, visited twice. In a letter to his friend Richard Bentley on 5 August 1752 he recorded his impressions: the park was 'sweet', he was charmed by the 'beautiful decent simplicity' of 'the outward court'; the rooms were filled with 'loads of portraits', and he was particularly impressed by the 'ancient magnificence' of the furniture throughout the house, particularly remarking on the 'stiff chairs' and

Office, U1590/T1/3. 7 A visit on 27 Oct. 1944 is described in James Lees-Milne, *Prophesying peace* [diaries 1944–5] (London, 1977), p. 125. For further detail about Knole, see Lees-Milne's *People and places: country house donors and the National Trust* (London, 1992),

'embroidered beds, richly worked in silk and gold'. With his characteristic cattiness, Walpole described the countess of Middlesex in Van Dyck's full-length portrait as 'a bouncing kind of lady-mayoress', but he failed to mention one of the artist's finest works, the portrait of Lady Frances Cranfield, the countess' daughter.[8] Walpole was fascinated by all things medieval, which inspired the design of his residence at Strawberry Hill in Twickenham, begun in 1749 and completed by 1790.[9] In a letter of 27 April 1753, Walpole had told Horace Mann that he was intent on 'imprinting the gloomth of abbeys and cathedrals on one's house'.[10] Strawberry Hill has echoes of Knole in the deliberate irregularity of plan, the importance of the long gallery and the quirky main stairs in a confined space with grisaille decoration on the walls and heraldic 'rampant' beasts on the newel posts, reminiscent of the similarly placed Sackville leopards at Knole. The picturesque canopied recesses opposite the windows in the great gallery at Strawberry Hill were based on the tomb at Canterbury of Knole's fifteenth-century occupant Archbishop Bouchier.[11] Walpole's privately printed 1784 *Description of Strawberry Hill* includes detailed lists of furniture, pictures and curiosities, many of which were gifted to him by his friend and fellow collector Lady Elizabeth (Betty) Germain (1680–1789), who had lived at Knole for many years as the guest of the first duke of Dorset.[12]

Walpole recorded in his journals a return visit to Knole a quarter of a century later on 30 August 1780 when he was particularly struck by acquisitions made by the third duke (1749–99), who had spent a year in Italy on his grand tour in 1770–1.[13] These included a representation of a satyr and a woman attributed to Annibale Carracci (1560–1609), as well as a number of portraits commissioned by the third duke from Reynolds.[14] He noted the 'most beautiful' silver furniture but could only say that the pieces were 'very old', when in fact they date from the later seventeenth century, so could hardly have been described as 'very' old in Walpole's time. Neither Walpole's correspondence nor his journals was published until the twentieth century so they cannot have had a direct influence on nineteenth-century visitors. Even his *Description of Strawberry Hill* had limited circulation, only one hundred copies of the 1774 edition were printed and two hundred of the second 1784 edition; however, these were mostly given to his friends who were trend-setters in aesthetic matters. The aesthetic of Strawberry Hill was also imbibed by a wider audience of educated visitors, all of

p. 174.   **8** Walpole to Richard Bentley, 5 Aug. 1752, *Horace Walpole's correspondence*, ed. W.S. Lewis et al., 48 vols (New Haven, 1937–83), xxxv (1973), pp 132–3.   **9** For Strawberry Hill see John Iddon, *Strawberry Hill and Horace Walpole* (London, 2011), and Michael Snodin (ed.), *Horace Walpole's Strawberry Hill* (New Haven, 2009).   **10** Walpole to Horace Mann, 27 Apr. 1753, *Horace Walpole's correspondence* (1960), xx, p. 20.   **11** John Iddon, *Strawbery Hill and Horace Walpole* (London, 2011), p. 18.   **12** *Description of the villa of Mr Horace Walpole* (Strawberry Hill, 1784, facsimile edition, London, 2010).   **13** Horace Walpole, 'Visits to county seats', *The Walpole Society*, 16 (1927–8), pp 9–80 at p. 77.   **14** The picture of a satyr, under the title *Salmacis and Hermaphroditus*, with a new attribution to Ludovico Carracci, was sold by the Knole Trustees at Christie's in London on 6 July 2006 for

which led to widespread appreciation of Knole from the nineteenth century onwards by artists and the wider public.

Fanny Burney, playwright, novelist and sometime live-in companion of Queen Charlotte, visited Knole in 1779. She recorded in her diary that she was impressed by the collection of pictures and the state rooms:

> One of them had been fitted up by an earl of Dorset for the bedchamber of King James I when upon a visit to Knole: it had all the gloomy grandeur and solemn finery of that time. The second state room a later earl had fitted up for James II ... Well, this James II's room was more superb than its predecessor's – flaming with velvet, tissue and tapestry, and what not. But the third state room was magnificence itself: it was fitted out for King William. The bed curtains, tester, quilt and valence were all of gold flowers, worked upon a silver ground; its value even in those days, was £7000.[15]

Burney was mistaken, as James I never visited Knole and none of the state beds had been made or purchased in preparation for a royal visit.[16] The state beds in the King's Room and Venetian Ambassador's Room had been made for King James II and only came to Knole from royal palaces in 1701 after they were acquired by the sixth earl of Dorset (1638–1706), as perquisite of his office as lord chamberlain to King William III and Queen Mary II. Although the three great state beds Burney saw had been at Knole for less than eighty years by the time of her visit in 1779, as with the silver furniture noted by Walpole, facts had given way to the construction of a more attractive myth in a grander narrative of the house and its owners.

Burney's misconceptions were perpetuated in John Brady's 1839 *Guide to Knole*, which described it as a 'deservedly celebrated mansion'; he intended his guide for the public so that 'persons visiting' would have 'an opportunity of carrying away with them some memento of its attractions'. Brady also repeated the belief that the bed in the King's Room (which Burney believed had been acquired for a visit by William III), had been acquired for a visit by James I, and the bed in the Venetian ambassador's bedroom was 'said to have been prepared for the reception of King James II'.[17] Brady further embroidered Burney's narrative by putting a price on the bed 'of gold and silver tissue' in the King's Room – an even more astronomical £8,000.

By the time Burney visited Knole in 1779 it had been for over a decade in the care of John Frederick Sackville (1745–99), third duke of Dorset, who amassed an art collection on his grand tour and, on his return home, became Joshua Reynolds' greatest patron, commissioning twenty works, including portraits of

£7.4 million. **15** Quoted in Olivia Fryman, 'Rich pickings, the royal beds as a perquisite 1660–1670', *Furniture History*, 50 (2014), p. 121. Charlotte Barrett (ed.), *The diary and letters of Madam D'Arblay*, 2 vols (London, 1842), i, p. 258. **16** Olivia Fryman, 'Rich pickings', pp 119–36. **17** John Brady, *Guide to Knole*, 1839, p. 156 and p. 131.

the actress Mrs Abingdon, writer Oliver Goldsmith, actor manager David Garrick and lexicographer Samuel Johnson.[18]

The third duke has been described by Amanda Foreman as a 'debaucher of other men's wives'.[19] From as early as 1769 he exhibited permissive attitudes when he welcomed Lady Sarah Bunbury and her lover Lord William Gordon to Knole, where they took refuge after she had fled from her husband and newborn child – fathered by Gordon.[20] The duke's own elopement with Lady Derby in 1778, when she deserted her husband and children, was a public scandal;[21] it is likely the couple hid away at Knole. Foreman also documents his later relationships with Georgiana, duchess of Devonshire, and Lady Elizabeth Foster, which were conducted at various times in Paris in the following decade while he was British ambassador at the French court 1783–9; and possibly at Knole too.

The duke had wide musical interests and was a noted patron of opera in London. There is a catalogue at Knole of the duke's extensive collection of sheet music of various types, including chamber music ideal for playing by the duke and his visiting friends.[22] The composer Felice Giardini (1716–96) was a frequent visitor and substantial payments to him are recorded in 1785 and 1790; his portrait by Gainsborough (1763) remains in the house. The duke also commissioned Gainsborough's double portrait of the celebrated singer Elizabeth Linley (wife of playwright and politician Richard Brinsley Sheridan) and her precocious composer brother Thomas (the painting is now at the Clark Art Institute, Williamstown, Massachusetts). The duke held concerts in the Cartoon Gallery and a double violin case with his coat of arms remains there as well as a harpsichord of $c.1770$ made by Jacob Kirkman (1710–92).

His affair with Lady Derby having petered out, the duke took up with the opera dancer Giannetta Baccelli, who was given apartments at Knole, and when Burney visited in 1779 she was told that some rooms were out of bounds because Baccelli was in residence. The special place Baccelli occupied in the duke's life is reflected in the fact that he commissioned Gainsborough to paint her portrait, which was exhibited at the Royal Academy in London in 1782 (now in Tate Britain).[23]

By the time the duke returned from revolutionary France to Knole in 1789, Baccelli had taken up with the earl of Pembroke, and the duchess of Devonshire had also ended her affair with him, much to his distress. The following year he married an heiress, Arabella Diana Cope (1767–1825); understandably, the

18 John Coleman, 'Reynolds at Knole', *Apollo (National Trust Annual)* (1996), pp 24–30. 19 Amanda Foreman, *Georgiana, duchess of Devonshire* (London, 1998). 20 Stella Tillyard, *Aristocrats* (London, 1994), pp 269–70. 21 Dorset's relationship with Lady Derby is dealt with in detail Horace Bleackley's biography of her mother – *The story of a beautiful duchess: being an account of the life and times of Elizabeth Gunning* (London, 1907). 22 Wyn K. Ford, 'Music at Knole' in *National Trust Studies 1979* (London, 1979), pp 160–79. 23 Elizabeth Einberg, *Gainsborough's 'Giovanna Baccelli'* (London, 1976).

recumbent figure of Baccelli by sculptor Locatelli was then consigned to the attics, and Gainsborough's portrait of her also stored out of sight.[24]

After his marriage, music continued to be enjoyed at Knole: a manuscript book of short score exercises dated 1793 is inscribed 'della Duchess Dorsset'. The composer Giovanni Paolo Martini (1741–1816), who had been employed at the pre-revolutionary court of Louis XVI, during the duke's time as ambassador, dedicated piano pieces to the duchess. Musical parties were a feature of life between 1790 and 1792, when the duchess settled accounts for hire of harpsichords from John Broadwood, who was also paid for regular visits to tune keyboard instruments.[25] The duchess arranged music and dancing lessons for her children, and in 1807 Francesco Bianchi (1752–1810) wrote pieces for her daughters Mary and Elizabeth – including a duettino. There were also scores in the collection at Knole for duets composed by the castrato Agrippino Rosselli (fl. 1784–1800), a noted performer at the King's Theatre in the Haymarket. After the death of the duchess musical life at Knole continued, such as a grand chorus sung at a concert in June 1853.

In their visits, Walpole and Burney were greeted by lavishly furnished interiors that still characterize visitors' first impressions of Knole today. Seventeenth-century royal furnishings, tapestries, and portraits of historical figures and members of the Sackville family had been carefully arranged to blend into their Jacobean setting. This historical blending was noticed in 1791 by Edmund Burke (1729–97), who wrote approvingly to the third duke:

> I, who am something of a lover of antiquities, must be a great admirer of Knole. I think it is the most interesting thing in England. It is pleasant to have preserved in one place the succession of several tastes of ages; a pleasant habitation for the time, a grand repository of whatever has been pleasant at all times. This is not the sort of place which every banker, contractor or nabob can create at his pleasure. I am astonished to find so many of your rank of so bad a taste as to give up what distinguishes them, and to adopt what so many can do as well or better than they. I would not change Knole if I were the duke of Dorset for all the foppish structures of this Augustan age.[26]

Burke's reaction was partly shaped by his influential *Philosophical enquiry into our ideas of the sublime and beautiful* (1757), which was to inform Romantic sensibilities in art, architecture and landscape design.[27] Rejecting the slavish

---

24 Irish readers will be particularly familiar with a small copy of Gainsborough's portrait that came to the National Gallery of Ireland as part of the Beit Collection from Russborough, County Wicklow.   25 Win K. Ford, *Music at Knole* (1979), p. 175. Broadwood's detailed invoice dated 1791 is among the Sackville Papers at Kent County Record Office (U269/A252/3).   26 Robert Sackville-West, *Inheritance* (2010), p. 127; Vita Sackville-West, *Knole and the Sackvilles* (1991), p. 191.   27 Paul Guyer, 'Introduction' to Edmund Burke's

imitation of idealized classical art and architecture, Burke had recommended how 'pleasure of the imagination ... is much higher than any which is derived from a rectitude of judgment'.[28] He might even have had Knole in mind when he wrote in his *Philosophical enquiry* of a building with 'towers, halls, galleries and other chambers' where 'elegant mouldings and fine festoons, glasses [mirrors] and other mere ornamental furniture, will make the imagination rebel against the reason'.[29] Despite the elaborate Jacobean re-working of Knole and changes in the following centuries, Burke was attracted to the pervading and unifying ancient atmosphere of the place, which had already struck Walpole and Burney.

Burke was more than a casual visitor to Knole, he was a close friend of the duke, and Ozias Humphry's portrait of him remains at Knole. For Burke, country houses and estates such as Knole were not merely places of retreat for the metropolitan elite but rooted their aristocratic owners in landed property, which made them the very foundation on which the state rested. The whig Burke had been horrified by the revolution in France, and in his *Reflections on the revolution* he argued that pre-eminence in government should be given to those who 'by birth' had inherited land and wealth, and that the 'nobility is the graceful ornament of the civil order. It is the Corinthian capital of polished society.'[30]

In accord with Burke's characterization, Knole formed a uniquely authentic and timeless composite of landscape, ancient house and richly decorated interiors crowded with a carefully arranged collection of precious objects. This set the tone for how Knole was to be viewed by the Sackville family and presented to an increasingly wider public audience. Knole was to develop the twin personalities identified by Burke: the private seat of the Sackville family, and a place of pilgrimage for curious members of the public. Proximity to London meant that it increasingly drew the attention of numerous sightseers who chose to spend their leisure time visiting country houses.

In 1793, just two years after Burke wrote his letter to the duke, Knole featured in a tour guidebook to Kent entitled, *The ambulatory: or a pocket companion in a tour around London, within circuit of twenty-five miles*. This was followed in 1795 by the publication of H.N. Willis' dedicated guidebook to portraits in the house, and in 1819 the Knole steward, John Bridgeman, published his *History and topographical guide to Knole*.

Brady's guidebook of 1839 provides details on the seventeen show rooms open to visitors; the majority, on the first floor of the south front overlooking the garden, had become museum-like in their presentation, while others included on

---

A philosophical enquiry into our ideas of the sublime and beautiful (1757; Oxford, 2015) and in the text of Edmund Burke's, *Philosophical enquiry* (2015), p. 6. 28 Burke, *Philosophical enquiry*, p. 24. 29 Ibid., p. 87. 30 Edmund Burke, *Reflections on the revolution in France* (1790; New Haven and London, 2003), pp 44, 117.

Knole and its visitors

5.3 Joseph Nash, 'Children playing games in the long gallery at Knole', from Joseph Nash, *The mansions of England in the olden time* (1839–49) (Mary Evans Picture Library).

the public itinerary also continued to be regularly used by the family. These included the medieval Gothic chapel, the dining parlour, the great hall, the ballroom and the crimson drawing room. Other parts of the house remained entirely in the private domain. Increasing numbers of the public were admitted after a regular direct train service from London to Sevenoaks was introduced in 1862, providing easy opportunity for Londoners of modest means to make the half-hour train journey and pay a day visit to Knole house and park. The romantic antiquarian sensibility, commended by Burke to the third duke, could be more widely shared by members of the public, and would in time come to inform how Knole was perceived as part of a shared national heritage on account of its historical styles, contents and associations.

Artists were attracted to Knole from the late eighteenth century and numerous views of the exteriors were painted and sketched. By the time Paul Sandby painted his view of the west front in the early 1770s, the formal approach to the house and the layout of the gardens shown in Knyff's engravings, earlier in the century, had given way to a fashionable picturesque landscaping.[31] The production and circulation of engraved views increased public awareness,

31 The original Sandby watercolour is in a private collection.

5.4 'A game of croquet during a visit of the prince of Wales on 5 July 1866', *Illustrated London News*, 7 July 1866 (author's collection).

including those after Sandby by Michael Angelo Rooker (1775), and two views drawn by John Preston Neale and engraved for his *Views of seats*.[32] More importantly for promulgating a widespread awareness and appreciation of Knole, there are seven views of Knole's interiors in Joseph Nash's influential *Mansions of England in the olden times* (1839–49) – more than any other house.[33]

The early nineteenth century saw change in the family occupation of the house. The third duke's son had died in a tragic accident at the age of 21, and Knole was left in the care of his mother; on her death Knole passed to her daughter Mary (d. 1864) and subsequently to her younger daughter Elizabeth (1795–1870), who married George West, fifth earl De La Warr (1791–1869); hereafter the family names were conjoined as Sackville-West. Elizabeth and her husband hosted the young prince and princess of Wales at a fete on 5 July 1866, followed by a banquet and dance that evening.[34] The royal party travelled by train and was greeted at Sevenoaks station by a guard of honour of the 33rd Kent Rifles, and a royal salute was delivered in the park. Two days later the *Illustrated London News* depicted the royal party and guests in the garden with the south front in the background. There was an even more important royal visitor the

[32] There is an impression of Michael Angelo Rooker's 1775 engraving after Sandby in the British Museum (1870, 1008, 479); John Preston Neale, *Views of the seats* (London, 1818), i, p. 206.   [33] Joseph Nash, *Mansions of England in the olden times*, second series (London, 1840).
[34] Note by Sevenoaks Preservation Society, batandballstation.com/Royal_Visits_21778.aspx,

following year; on 23 November 1867 the *Illustrated London News* reported that Queen Victoria had travelled by special train in a 'state coach' to Sevenoaks and then by coach to Knole, where she 'remained for luncheon'. This was a more private affair in contrast to the large fete the previous year marking the visit of her heir and his wife.

By 1874, when the house had been inherited by the duchess' son Mortimer, first Lord Sackville, the house and grounds received ten thousand visitors each year. However, in 1884 Mortimer closed the house to the public, complaining that unruly members of the public were damaging the historic furnishings in the show rooms and disturbing the deer in the park.[35] Mortimer's attempt to close off the park resulted in public protests when locals tore down barriers he had put in place to block the entrance gates. Hotels and inns in Sevenoaks had developed a thriving business among trippers, and residents of the town were not pleased with restrictions to the park and house, which they had come to regard as a local amenity. Despite this opposition the house remained closed until after Mortimer's death in 1888. His brother Lionel, who succeeded him, was better disposed to the public and re-opened the house; however, opening times were restricted, and visitor numbers only reached 3,500 in 1890 and 2,000 after 1900.

Lionel, second Lord Sackville (1827–1908), had enjoyed mixed success as a diplomat before inheriting Knole. During his time in the foreign service he had set up home abroad with Pepita, a celebrated Spanish dancer with an international career.[36] After the elderly Lionel succeeded, his vivacious young daughter Victoria (1862–1936) arrived at Knole in 1889 and the house took on new life as a centre of Victorian and Edwardian social life. Three years later in 1892 Victoria married her father's heir, and her first cousin, also named Lionel (1887–1928), who in due course succeeded as 3rd Lord Sackville. However, the consequences of Victoria's father's relationship with the Spanish dancer Pepita came back to haunt the young couple as Victoria's brother Henry claimed that their father and Pepita had married and that he was therefore the rightful heir. Henry was not welcomed when he turned up at Knole on 5 October 1898 and tried to force his way past the servants into the house; he only left after his father called the police.[37] After he engaged in an unsuccessful legal action to prove his title, Henry was entirely ostracized.

In this glamourous era the fashionable world revolved around the prince of Wales and the Marlborough House set.[38] Victoria Sackville first met the prince when she was at Cannes with her father in 1889, and then again later the same year when she attended a garden party at Marlborough House in London with

accessed 15 May 2021.   **35** Philip Mandler, *The fall and rise of the stately home* (London, 1997), pp 200–5.   **36** Vita Sackville-West, *Pepita* (London, 1947). *Pepita* deals extensively with Vita's mother Victoria (Lady Sackville). Robert Sackville-West's *The disinherited* (London, 2014) deals with Victoria and her 'disinherited' siblings.   **37** Susan Mary Alsop, *Lady Sackville* (London, 1998), pp 132–3.   **38** Adrian Tinniswood, *The house party: a short history of leisure, pleasure and the country house weekend* (London, 2019).

her father's sister Lady Derby; she was also invited to join the prince for supper at a ball hosted by the duke of Westminster at his London home, Grosvenor House.[39] On 9 December a package arrived at Knole addressed to Victoria; it had come to Sevenoaks by train from Sandringham, and contained four pheasants, four partridges and two wild ducks.[40] Having been fortified by a strict Catholic education at a convent in Paris (her Spanish mother Pepita had been a Catholic), and realizing that her background left her socially vulnerable, Victoria was not open to seduction by the prince. Holding firm paid off as, in June the following year (1890), she was married at Knole to her cousin, the heir to Knole. The prince of Wales acknowledged her social success by sending her best wishes and a gift of a broach.[41] Victoria was now firmly ensconced in society; she attended the celebrated Devonshire House ball on 2 July 1897 wearing an eighteenth-century dress that had belonged to Arabella, the last duchess to reside at Knole. Thirty years after their first visit to Knole, the prince and the princess of Wales returned on 10 July 1898.[42] Despite the fact that Edward expected to be able to choose the guests, Victoria was able to persuade him not to invite his mistress, Lady Warwick, nor his new friend Mrs Keppel, saying that she preferred to invite the county ladies, particularly as the princess would be present.[43] Victoria bought a large leather-bound visitors' book in which guests on the day placed their signatures and into which she later pasted a photograph of the party in the garden by local photographer, Charles Essenhigh-Corke.

Victoria needed funds to modernize the house to provide the best of comforts to those who came to stay for house parties, which usually ran from Friday to Monday. Electricity was installed throughout (the decorative light switches still survive today) and modern bathrooms were fitted with running hot water. To provide funds, Victoria sold the Gainsborough portrait of Giannetta Baccelli, as well as that of Elizabeth and Thomas Linley (now in the Sterling and Francine Clarke Institute, Williamstown, MA), as well as Hoppner's portrait of the third duke's three children (now in the Metropolitan Museum of Art, New York) and also two pieces by Reynolds: *Mrs Abington* and his *Gypsy Fortune-teller* (now in the Rothschild Collection at Waddesdon); copies of these latter two paintings hang in place of the originals at Knole. The American financier J.P. Morgan, who purchased the Gainsborough portraits of the Linleys, was invited by Victoria to lunch at Knole, and she persuaded him to buy the tapestries from the chapel, which are now in the Boston Museum of Fine Art. So vast was the Knole Collection, formed over hundreds of years, that these sales do not leave noticeable gaps as their places have been filled by pieces from the reserve collections. Nowadays visitors benefit from the acceptance by the government of works of art in lieu of inheritance tax, so that Reynolds' masterpiece *Count*

39 Alsop, *Lady Sackville*, p. 85.   **40** Sackville Papers, Kent County Records Office, U269/C487/11.   **41** Sackville Papers, Kent County Record Office, U269/C487/13.   **42** Alsop, *Lady Sackville*, p. 142.   **43** Ibid.

Ugulino and his children passed into the care of the National Trust a quarter of a century ago and was allowed to remain in situ as part of the settlement.

In her novel, *The Edwardians* (1930), Victoria's daughter Vita Sackville-West describes a country house weekend at Chevron, a fictional representation of Knole. Vita detailed the hierarchy of household servants at Chevron necessary to cater for entertaining large numbers of guests; presided over by the butler, Mr Vigeon, and the housekeeper, Mrs Wickendon, the staff included a bevy of maids, who were supplemented at the weekends with personal ladies' maids and valets who arrived with guests.[44] The dinner described in *The Edwardians* was inspired by Vita's memory of a banquet at Knole in May 1904 captured at the time in a photomontage by Essenhigh-Corke.[45] The character Viola, in the novel, has her hair 'tweaked and frizzed' similar to the style worn by the young Vita in the photomontage of the 1904 banquet.[46] Vita's maid many years later remembered looking into the hall from the minstrel's gallery during the banquet and noticing the precocious young Vita happily chatting to Lord Balfour.[47]

Victoria had a legion of male admirers: she was sculpted by Rodin; Edwin Lutyens designed a house for her in Brighton, and she flirted with William Waldorf Astor. Most important of all was John Murray Scott, who donated the Wallace Collection to the nation. He was a frequent visitor to Knole, bought her a house in Mayfair and bequeathed to her a quarter of a million pounds worth of French eighteenth-century furniture, as well as a cash lump sum to Knole estate.[48]

Vita's father published a beautifully bound guidebook to Knole in 1906, and a second one two years later. These guidebooks feature illustrations by Charles Essenhigh-Corke (1852–1922),[49] who, by the end of the nineteenth century, ran a successful business in Sevenoaks with exclusive rights to photograph of the collections at Knole. Essenhigh-Corke also painted fifty watercolours of Knole, forty-two of which were turned into postcards sold to visitors. These watercolours echo Nash's romantic interpretation, though the interiors are not populated with figures. The postcards undoubtedly helped spread the fame of Knole, especially as a convenient destination within easy reach of London. Peter Mandler suggests that Knole and its park was the most popular destination for outings by those who lived in south London, as Hatfield was for north Londoners – both were easily accessible by train.[50] Ever the opportunist, Essenhigh-Corke photographed the medieval barns when they were ablaze during a devastating fire in 1887, and advertised mounted copies for sale at two shillings each.

Knole is famous for its association with the iconic 'Knole Settee' of *c.*1635–40, which was one of the items of royal furniture that arrived at the house in

---

44 Vita Sackville-West, *The Edwardians* (London, 1930; 1983), p. 23.   **45** Ibid. (1983), p. 41.
46 Ibid., p. 12.   **47** Ibid., p. 41.   **48** Vita Sackville-West, *Pepita* (London, 1937).   **49** Myra Ecker, 'The man who painted Knole', *Country Life* (4 Dec. 1997), p. 152.   **50** Mandler, *The*

1701. It was first selected for special mention in the 1906 guide (it is sometimes referred to as a couch or sofa);[51] and was the focus in a painting, signed with the monogram 'PL' or 'LP' and dated 1854, which was purchased by the National Trust some years ago. The Knole settee had come to represent the typical furniture of 'olden times', and featured in subject paintings, including *Stealing the keys*, exhibited by Marcus Stone at the Royal Academy in 1866 (National Gallery of New South Wales). The settee appealed to American tastes for old English furniture, and in 1895 was the template for the version made by Morant of Bond Street for the home of George Washington Vanderbilt, Biltmore in North Carolina. The 'Knole Settee' continues to spawn countless reproductions and variants found across the world. New versions are invariably marketed as a 'Knole Settee' though purchasers probably have little idea of the origin of the style and its name.

Most important for Knole's literary fame were Vita Sackville-West, novelist, poet and celebrated gardener, and her friend the novelist Virginia Woolf. Vita, an only child, adored Knole from growing up there when she had the run of the place. She never recovered from the sense of loss she experienced when she realized that, as a woman, she could not inherit her ancestral home. In 1922 she published *Knole and the Sackvilles*, a romanticized family history. In 1928 Virginia Woolf was inspired by the story to pen a love letter to her friend in the form of her historical novel *Orlando*, whose eponymous hero/heroine was described by James Lees Milne as 'the handsome and gallant androgenous young duke of their [Virginia's and Vita's] conceptional fancy'.[52] Vita posed as Orlando for photographs in the first edition, along with portraits from Knole. Like Vita, the modern-day Orlando wallows in an aristocratic inheritance, but Woolf provided a sting in the tale; Orlando reflects:

> Am I a snob? The garter in the hall? The leopards? My ancestors? Proud of them? Yes! Greedy, luxurious, vicious? ... Lying in bed of a morning ... fine linen; silver dishes; wine; maids; footmen. Spoilt? Perhaps. Too many things for nothing.[53]

Before the publication of *Orlando*, Knole had already been the model for Vair in the 1926 Gothic novel *The ruin* by Vita's less well-known cousin, Eddy Sackville-West (1901–65), biographer, novelist, and music critic who eventually became fifth Lord Sackville. Echoing the vision of Edmund Burke down the centuries, Vair is described by Eddy as a magical unified work of art where 'the

---

fall and rise of the stately home, pp 200–5.   **51** Geoffrey Beard and John Coleman, 'The Knole settee', *Apollo* (Apr. 1999), pp 24–8 and Christopher Rowell, 'A set of early seventh-century crimson velvet seat furniture at Knole', *Furniture History*, 42 (2006), pp 27–72.   **52** James Lees-Milne, *People and places: country house donors and the National Trust* (London, 1992), p. 181.   **53** Virginia Wolfe, *Orlando* (London, 1928), p. 279.

5.5 The Knole settee in the Leicester Gallery at Knole. Watercolour dated 1854, signed with monogram 'LP' or 'PL' (National Trust).

5.6 The recently restored Knole settee in its new case being installed in the Leicester gallery at Knole (National Trust).

5.7 A visitor in Eddy Sackville-West's music room, featuring a fire screen painted by his friend, the artist Duncan Grant (National Trust).

pictures – the countless pictures – the china, the carvings, the silver, the gold, the furniture – all possessed a composite soul with which to rule their masters'.[54]

On the death of Vita's father in 1928, Eddy's father Major General Sir Charles Sackville-West (d. 1962), inherited the estate and moved into the grand apartments on the south side with his second wife, American, Anne Bigelow, a friend of Wallis Simpson who was first entertained at Knole in the early 1930s, along with her second husband, Ernest Simpson. Though Wallis thought the Sackvilles were 'hopelessly stuffy' in comparison with the prince of Wales and his friends, she was not above accepting further invitations and even returned with the prince.[55] Eddy, as heir presumptive, took up residence in a suite of apartments on the west front, including the outer wicket tower. After decorating his apartments he entertained his artistic friends there including painters Duncan Grant and John Banting, and, of course, Virginia Woolf, and his cousin Vita. Grant and Banting painted decorations on some of the furnishings in Eddy's rooms, as was the wont of the Bloomsbury artists.[56] And in the 1940s John Piper (1903–92) painted two typically brooding wartime exterior views.[57]

54 Emma Slocombe, 'The reluctant heir; Edward Sackville-West at Knole', *National Trust Historic Houses and Collections Annual 2016* (in association with *Apollo*), p. 21.   55 Michael De-la-Noy, *Eddy: the life of Edward Sackville-West* (London, 1988) and Adrian Tinniswood, *The house party* (London, 2019), p. 21.   56 There is a beautifully illustrated chapter on Eddy's rooms at Knole in Nino Strachey, *Rooms of their own* (London, 2018).   57 Nathaniel Hepburn, *John Piper in Kent and Sussex* [exhibition catalogue] (Mascalls Gallery, Tonbridge,

Knole and its visitors 133

5.8 A sense of foreboding pervades the view of Knole from the north by John Piper; one of a pair commissioned by Eddy Sackville-West in 1943 (The Sackville Collection, © the Piper estate, photograph Mascalls Gallery).

By the mid-1930s Knole's future was uncertain, and the possibility was raised of transferring it to the National Trust. The celebrated diarist James Lees-Milne, interlocutor between the National Trust and Eddy's father, left a vivid account of the protracted negotiations that led to Knole passing to the Trust in 1946, and of the early days after the Trust took up its responsibilities.[58] Lees-Milne's task was made easier as he was a friend of Eddy, and of Vita and her husband Harold Nicholson. Knole was a pioneering case of the Trust taking on a major historic house at a time when their survival was in grave doubt. Lees-Milne described the 'charming' Major-General Sir Charles Sackville-West, fourth Baron Sackville, as being preoccupied with the intolerable burden of looking after the vast place when he was reduced to employing 'one maid to keep 250 bedrooms clean'. When Lees-Milne was invited to tea at Knole on one occasion, Lord Sackville appeared 'as exquisitely dressed as ever, in a blue tweed suit and canary-coloured waistcoat which, when his delicate build and abrupt movements were taken into account, brought to mind that domesticated bird'.[59]

Kent, 2011). The Mascalls Gallery has closed and I am grateful to Peter Miall, former curator of Charleston farmhouse in West Sussex, for directing me to Charleston (charleston.org.uk.), where Nathaniel is now curator, and has been most helpful, providing a photograph, and directing me to the trustees of the John Piper estate, who were equally helpful in clearing copyright.   **58** James Lees-Milne, 'Sackville of Knole, Kent' in his *People and places: country house donors and the National Trust* (London 1992), pp 166–83.   **59** Ibid., p 176.

Lees-Milne described the condition of the house and its contents with piles of dust from woodworm beneath the seventeenth-century royal chairs, which were riddled with the pests. Advice was taken from Ralph Edwards, keeper of furniture and woodwork at the Victoria and Albert Museum, while George Wingfield Digby reported on the condition of tapestries and carpets. On the advice of Digby, a retired V&A craftsman, C.W. Fletcher, was engaged 'for preliminary de-worming', and Mrs I. Ray, 'an accredited needlewoman' and former V&A employee, who, conveniently, lived in Sevenoaks, was engaged to repair fabrics on the furniture that were 'irretrievably decayed'. Lees-Milne drove the distinguished Lady Smith-Dorrien of the Royal School of Needlework down to Knole, and this marked the beginning of work by the school on the Venetian Ambassador's Room bed hangings. Over subsequent years the Trust, with significant assistance from public funds, has invested vast sums on repairing the fabric of the buildings.

Lees-Milne recalled that in the early days, the Trust received a great number of 'grumbles' from visitors and he thought these might be prompted by the reception the public received from one of the staff, whom he described as 'the dragoness at the gate' or the 'extraordinary gauleiter figure with the walking stick who frightened him to death'. Lees-Milne reflected that in those early days, as with some other Trust houses where some staff had been employed previously by donor families, 'the pre-Trust inhabitants of Knole still feel and sometimes show, that they are doing the public a great favour in admitting them to My Lord's house at all'. Lees-Milne noted that at the opening over Easter 1947, 1,082 visitors came to Knole, and by the May bank holiday of that year the number had risen to 2,090.[60]

Vita was invited to write the first official National Trust visitor guidebook to the house; Lees-Milne recalled that not a word of her text needed to be queried, 'so accurate was her description of the location of each picture and each stick of furniture', though it was almost twenty years since her last visit before her father's death in 1928.

On his father's death Eddy Sackville-West had shown no interest in taking on responsibility for the house and estate; he said that he found living there 'extremely disagreeable' and, particularly in summer, felt it was like the middle of Hyde Park, being 'all but impossible to walk outside the garden walls without stepping on a prone figure'. He had lived at West Wickham during the war and subsequently shared an old rectory at Long Critchel in Dorset with some like-minded friends; he eventually settled at Coolville, the house he bought outside the village of Clogheen, County Tipperary. Having converted to Roman Catholicism in Ireland, he was buried in the local churchyard.[61] Eddy offered Vita the opportunity to take charge of Knole but Sissinghurst, the home and

60 Ibid., p. 174. 61 See Simon Fenwick, *The Critchel boys: scenes from England's last literary saloon* (London, 2021).

5.9 Visitors in the Venetian Ambassador's Room with a glass screen protecting the newly restored state bed (National Trust).

garden she shared with her husband Harold Nicholson, had become her passion. Instead, cousin Lionel and his family moved into Knole in 1961 and he inherited the title on Eddy's death in 1965.[62] Like Eddy, Lionel harked back to a quieter age, and soon regretted the decision to admit the public to the gardens where the lawn came right up to the windows of his sitting room; he once declared: 'I'll tell you what I call public open days – black Wednesdays.'[63] Today the National Trust welcomes tens of thousands of visitors annually to Knole. While the traditional antiquarian route through the show rooms full of royal relics remains at the centre of a visit, new areas have been opened to visitors in response to changing public interests and expectations.

The Heritage Lottery Fund and the Royal Oak Foundation have supported the £20 million 'Inspired by Knole' project begun in 2010 and completed in 2018.[64] This has dramatically affected how Knole presents itself to the public. The house has always attracted scholars, particularly those studying its furnishings and important paintings; and it has been revisited by generations of *Country Life* writers.[65] A great wave of new scholarship is reflected in the series

[62] Emma Slocombe, 'The reluctant heir; Edward Sackville-West at Knole', *National Trust Historic Houses and Collections Annual 2016* (in association with *Apollo*), pp 19–27 at p. 21. [63] Lionel Sackville-West, sixth Lord Sackville (1913–2004), 'Knole' in Sybilla Jane Fowler (ed.), *Debrett's the stately homes of Britain, personally introduced by their owners* (New York, 1982), pp 44–55 at p. 44. [64] Richard Hill, 'Inspired by Knole' in *National Trust Historic Houses and Collections Annual 2016*, pp 1–2. [65] Robert Sackville-West (later Lord Sackville),

of articles in the 2016 issue of the *National Trust Historic Houses and Collections Annual*, which is entirely devoted to Knole.[66]

Striking the balance between engaging with the spirit of the place and preserving its special qualities has become particularly critical at Knole due to the fragility of the exceptionally important textile hangings on the seventeenth-century royal state beds and upholstered seat furniture. To demonstrate its commitment to the highest conservation standards Knole is now an accredited museum. And while traditionally the Trust has been reluctant to mediate the visitor experience suitable compromises have been made, with, for example, the introduction of glass screens around the state beds in the Venetian Ambassador's Room and the Spangle Bedroom. The Knole Settee is displayed in a transparent box, but importantly it is placed in the Leicester Gallery, where it has stood for centuries.

Public interest in the life of servants and previously hidden spaces has been satisfied by opening of the Retainer's Gallery above the great hall, which has been restored to something closer to what Joseph Nash saw when he was painting his views. Similarly conservation in action can be seen with the recently opened studios in the reconstructed medieval great barn, which itself has a beautifully restored hipped roof, for the first time since the original was destroyed by the fire in 1887.

A particular change to the visitor experience has been the recent opening of rooms that had been occupied by Eddy Sackville-West in the early twentieth century: this was allowed the house to express more of its complex and many faceted histories by displaying, the interiors captured in Nino Strachey's handsome volume on Eddy's rooms at Knole.[67] Graham Sutherland's 1955 portrait of Eddy, bequeathed to the National Trust many years ago, has finally found an appropriate home in the suite of rooms he occupied as a young man. Eddy described the portrait in a letter to Sutherland as 'absolutely masterly ... it is a work of genius, which will be of interest to people long after I have gone'.[68]

In the second decade of the twenty-first century Edmund Burke's vision of a public and private Knole still holds true: the Sackvilles remain in residence in their private domain, and the customary antiquarian route through the house remains the primary public visitor experience, with the addition of Eddy Sackville-West's apartments. It is a house that continues to represent its story to current occupants and transient visitors.

Knole [National Trust guidebook] (1998 and regularly reprinted) has a good short bibliography and a more extensive one is included in his *Inheritance* (2010). **66** *National Trust Historic Houses and Collections Annual 2016* (National Trust in association with *Apollo*). **67** See Nino Strachey, *Rooms of their own* (London, 2018). **68** Slocombe, 'The reluctant heir', p. 25.

Gloomy inhospitality: limiting access to houses and country estates, 1719–1838

PETER COLLINGE

INTRODUCTION

In 1764, Horace Walpole discovered that his servants had refused admission to some visitors to Strawberry Hill, Twickenham.

> A quarter before ten today, I heard the bell ring at the gate ... I inquired who it was? The prince of Mecklenburgh and De Witz had called to know if they could see the house. My [servants] told them I was in bed, but if they would call again in an hour, they might see it. I shuddered at this report, and would it have been the worst part! The Queen [Charlotte] herself was behind, in a coach: I am shocked to death and know not what to do! ... It will certainly be said that I refused to let the Queen see my house.[1]

Initially, Walpole encouraged visitors to see his Gothick creation, but by 1769 was writing: 'I am now so tired of it, that I shudder when my bell rings ... It is as bad as keeping an inn, and I am often tempted to deny its being shown, if it would not be ill-natured to those that come and to my housekeeper.'[2] Making matters worse, regulations designed to admit only one party per day (maximum of four, no children, tickets obtained in advance) tended to be ignored by the public.[3] In 1774, Walpole produced a *Description of the villa* detailing Strawberry Hill's contents for his own use but in 1784 confessed, 'I am so tormented by visitors to my house, that two or three rooms are not shown to abridge their stay ... If the visitors got the [*Description*] into their hands, I should never get them out.'[4] As an owner, Walpole was not alone in facing a dilemma. On the one hand was a sense of duty founded on a tradition of offering hospitality to strangers, combined with granting access as a way of managing and manipulating owners' political, social and economic interests. In addition, granting access enabled retainers to supplement their incomes through visitors' tips.[5] On the

---

1 Walpole to Lord Hertford, 3 Aug. 1764, W.S. Lewis et al. (eds), *Horace Walpole's correspondence* (New Haven, 1937–83), 48 vols (1974), xxxviii, p. 418.   2 Walpole to Revd William Cole, 14 June 1769, *Horace Walpole's correspondence* (1937), i, p. 166.   3 Walpole to Lady Ossory, 19 June 1784, *Horace Walpole's correspondence* (1965), xxxv, p. 435.   4 Quoted in Stephen Clarke, '"Lord God! Jesus! What a house!": describing and visiting Strawberry Hill', *Journal for Eighteenth-Century Studies*, 33:3 (2010), pp 357–80 at p. 359.   5 Dana Arnold, 'The country house: form, function and meaning' in Dana Arnold (ed.), *The Georgian*

other hand lay a desire for privacy at home as observed by the duchess de Nino in 1834, 'English people ... hate to be seen.'[6] As visitor numbers grew, however, tourists came to regard country houses as part of their wider pleasurable engagement with resorts, landscapes and visits to industrial premises, and expected house owners to be more accommodating.[7] Indeed, that committed country house visitor, the Hon. John Byng (1743–1813), later Viscount Torrington, thought that 'no one shou'd suffer his place to be visited, but with the intention to make those visitors happy'.[8]

By examining those occasions when legitimate admittance was either intentionally or accidentally refused or restricted, this essay argues that access depended as much on the attitudes, perspectives and preferences of unexpected visitors and tourists as it did on those of owners and servants.[9] Entry, thus, depended on far more than simply taking the measure of a visitor's appearance.[10] Even for those with the right credentials, the carriage drive to admittance was strewn with potential hazards.

Research into domestic travel and tourism in the long-eighteenth century and beyond is well-established in classic studies by Esther Moir, Ian Ousby and Adrian Tinniswood.[11] Studies of the transformation of houses and estates into visitor attractions have been matched by others focusing on buildings, lifestyles and changing consumption patterns.[12] Specific aspects regarding who went, where, what they saw and their responses, have been analysed by Dana Arnold, Julius Bryant, Stephen Clarke, Rosie MacArthur and Hannecke Ronnes and

country house: architecture, landscape and society (Stroud, 1998), pp 1–19 at p. 16; Dana Arnold, 'The country house and its publics' in Arnold, *The Georgian country house*, pp 20–42 at pp 22–3, 25; Adrian Tinniswood, *The polite tourist: four centuries of country house visiting* (London, 1998), pp 62–3, 92, 94.   **6** Quoted in Tim Mowl and Brian Earnshaw, *Trumpet at a distant gate: the lodge as prelude to the country house* (London, 1985), p. 16.   **7** Hannecke Ronnes and Renske Koster, 'A foreign appreciation of English country houses and castles: Dutch travellers' accounts of proto-museums visited en route, 1683–1855' in Jon Stobart (ed.), *Travel and the British country house: cultures, critiques and consumption in the long eighteenth century* (Manchester, 2017), pp 106–26 at p. 108; Jocelyn Anderson, '"Worth viewing by travellers": Arthur Young and country house picture collections in the late eighteenth century' in Stobart, *Travel and the British country house*, pp 127–44 at p. 127; Tinniswood, *Polite tourist*, pp 113–17; Barrie Trinder, *"The most extraordinary district in the world": Ironbridge and Coalbrookdale* (3rd ed.; Chichester, 2005), p. 1.   **8** John Byng, *The Torrington diaries containing the tours through England and Wales of the Hon. John Byng, 1781–1794*, ed. C. Bruyn Andrews, 4 vols (London, 1934–8), i, p. 48.   **9** Arnold, 'The country house and its publics', p. 29.   **10** Stephen Clarke, 'A fine house richly furnished: Pemberley and the visiting of country houses', *Persuasions*, 22 (2000), pp 199–217 at p. 200.   **11** Esther Moir, *The discovery of Britain; the English tourists* (London, 1964); see also Ousby, *The Englishman's England*; Tinniswood, *Polite tourist*.   **12** Peter Mandler, *The fall and rise of the stately home* (New Haven, 1997); John Cornforth, *The country houses of England, 1948–1998* (London, 1998); Richard Wilson and Alan Mackley, *Creating paradise: the building of the English country house, 1660–1880* (London, 2000); Mark Girouard, *Life in the English country house* (London, 1978); Christopher Christie, *The British country house in the eighteenth century* (Manchester, 2000); Jon Stobart and Mark Rothery, *Consumption and the country house* (Oxford, 2016).

Renske Koster, among others.[13] In a growing field of study, attention has been focused on the visitor experience with an important study by Jocelyn Anderson on touring and publicizing the country house in the long eighteenth century.[14] Within this body of scholarship, it is acknowledged that while 'attracting tourists has always been part' of their function, country houses have simultaneously 'appeared exclusive' and 'deliberately forbidding'.[15] Ousby, in particular, has explored how such places were presented as 'attractions to be entered and viewed' by those whose wealth provided them with the leisure and mobility to do so, while also noting occasions when admittance was not granted.[16] This duality is also noted by Mark Girouard: 'Country houses could project a disconcerting double image – relaxed and delightful to those who had the entrée, arrogant and forbidding to those who had not'.[17] Public access, however, was granted because, as Dana Arnold observes, for a house 'to be effective as a statement of authority and rank it had to be seen'.[18] Furthermore, for collections to be admired beyond the owner's circle, houses had to be 'just sufficiently permeable to admit visitors'.[19]

This double identity is further explored here through correspondence, journals, newspapers, guidebooks and architectural treatises, and draws on the experiences of more than twenty visitors, including John Byng. He, more than most, commented extensively on those occasions in his journals when access to houses was refused, irrespective of the reason. In general, Byng liked 'old' buildings and decried the 'new'; reserving his most damning comments for 'abominable' red-brick houses.[20]

It is widely assumed and promoted, not least by the owners and custodians of houses, that tourists were routinely admitted to properties in the eighteenth century.[21] Mandler, however, has cautioned against assuming that they received vast numbers of tourists.[22] Some, like Strawberry Hill, Middlesex; Blenheim, Oxfordshire; Stowe, Buckinghamshire; and Chatsworth and Kedleston, both in Derbyshire, were well-known for admitting visitors, producing catalogues and/or constructing inns for travellers. Their eighteenth-century owners regarded admission as part of the responsibility that came with their social position, or as an expression of politeness, power, or artistic endeavour. While

---

13 Arnold, 'The country house and its publics', pp 20–42; Julius Bryant, 'Villa views and the uninvited audience' in Dana Arnold (ed.), *The Georgian villa* (Stroud, 1998), pp 11–24; Clarke, 'A fine house richly furnished', pp 199–217; Rosie MacArthur, 'Gentleman tourists in the early eighteenth century: the travel journals of William Hanbury and John Scattergood' in Stobart, *Travel and the British country house*, pp 94–6; Ronnes and Koster, 'A foreign appreciation of English country houses', pp 106–26. 14 Jocelyn Anderson, *Touring and publicising England's country houses in the long eighteenth century* (London, 2018). 15 Ousby, *The Englishman's England*, p. 61. 16 Ibid., p. 65. 17 Girouard, *Life in the English country house*, p. 242. 18 Arnold, 'The country house and its publics', p. 22. 19 Mandler, *Stately home*, p. 2. 20 Byng, *Diaries*, i, pp 340–1. 21 Ousby, *The Englishman's England*, p. 61; Mandler, *Stately home*, p. 10; Moir, *The discovery of Britain*, p. 58. 22 Mandler, *Stately home*,

Stowe's landscape gardens, for example, were seen to exemplify 'an ideal Whig vision of government', Horace Walpole declared that Strawberry Hill was 'built to please my own taste'.[23] For some owners, however, granting access was an extension of tradition which they bore with a degree of resignation: 'The Hospitality my Ancestors exercised for some generations', wrote Lord Deerhurst of Croome Park, Worcestershire, in 1750, 'makes it impossible for me to effect any privacy or retirement there. It has always been an Inn and must remain so'.[24] Deerhurst's perspective encapsulates the essential dichotomy between houses and their publics. From ostensibly 'public' places such as Blenheim to rarely opened or less-visited residences like the Bishop's Palace in Farnham, Surrey, visitors sometimes adopted an air of presumption about access. As Adrian Tinniswood recounts, some sat on ancient furniture, jumped on tables, broke off bits of statuary, scrawled on walls, removed objects and generally poked and prodded about.[25] Disgruntled by unregulated intrusions, some owners responded with forbidding points of access, high walls, steel traps, signs, prosecution notices, elaborate rules, admission policies, tickets and guided tours. Some refused access altogether. Others took more extreme action. In 1753, the Revd Francis Gastrell demolished Shakespeare's New Place, in Stratford-upon-Avon, to stop the influx of tourists.[26] He was not alone; eventually Alexander Pope's villa at Twickenham was sold to the owner of the neighbouring property, Baroness Howe, who demolished it in 1807.[27] Access arrangements could also change with the arrival of new generations, owners or occupiers. Strawberry Hill became more difficult to access when Lady Waldegrave took up residence in 1810.[28] By 1838, the previously accessible grounds of Kenwood House, Hampstead, were 'at no season ... shown to strangers'.[29]

ARCHITECTURAL STYLE

Prior to venturing forth, those who lacked personal knowledge of estates and houses consulted guidebooks, travel accounts and engravings. They sought the advice of friends and acquaintances, and perused maps to locate properties on or near established travel routes. As knowledge and experience accumulated, and

pp 1, 10.   **23** National Trust, *Stowe landscape gardens* (London, 1997), pp 5–6; *A description of the villa of Mr Horace Walpole* (Strawberry Hill, 1784), p. iv.   **24** Lilian Dickins and Mary Stanton (eds), *An eighteenth-century correspondence, being the letters of Deane Swift, Pitt, the Lyttelons and the Grenvilles, Lord Dacre, Robert Nugent, Charles Jenkinson, the earls of Guilford, Coventry, & Hardwick, Sir Edward Turner, Mr Talbot of Lacock, and others to Sanderson Miller, esq., of Radway* (London, 1910), pp 162–3. Katie Feluś, *The secret history of the Georgian garden* (London, 2016), p. 22.   **25** Tinniswood, *Polite tourist*, p. 94.   **26** Ousby, *The Englishman's England*, pp 39–41.   **27** Bryant, 'Villa views and the uninvited audience', p. 15.   **28** Clarke, '"Lord God! Jesus! What a house!"', p. 365.   **29** John Claudius Loudon, *The*

sometimes without these attributes, likes and dislikes emerged. A person might avoid a property due to a dislike of a particular style of architecture or the way it had been interpreted, the feelings evoked or the connotations associated with it. For others, the sense of disappointment that ensued when places failed to live up to expectations created by the prior acquisition of knowledge was sufficient reason not to proceed beyond the lodge. For yet others, limitations on access were accidental, usually resulting from mistimed visits. All of these factors could result in visitors refusing – or being refused – entrance to premises, or curtailing and even abandoning their outings altogether.

In deciding where or where not to visit, it was the subject of architecture that drew the most comment from contemporaries. In their pioneering survey of lodge buildings, Tim Mowl and Brian Earnshaw recount an anecdote by architect John Papworth in his 1818 treatise on rural residences.[30] An 'old nobleman' assessed the characters of estate owners solely from the appearance of buildings at the entrances to their domains. 'If he percieved characteristics objectionable to him in their lodges', the nobleman declined to 'visit those with whom he intended to pass short spaces of time during his tour'.[31] The physical appearance of a lodge, therefore, was integral in promoting or dampening curiosity about what lay beyond. As first impressions of 'repulsiveness or other objectionable features' were 'not easily eradicated', lodges 'should be of the favourable kind'.[32] The sentiments of Papworth's 'old nobleman' are glimpsed elsewhere. The Revd James Plumptre thought: 'A Lodge is at all times but a piece of ostentation, and, unless, it leads to a magnificent house, is certainly out of character.'[33] As seen from the road, Lady Louisa Stuart thought Harewood House, Yorkshire, 'looks very splendid, and is beautifully situated, but I should be tempted to judge a little from what I know of the owners there too'.[34] At Broadlands, Hampshire, John Byng cared for neither the house's architecture, nor, seemingly, the owner (whom he knew) and did not attempt to gain admittance.[35] Even invited guests might limit the length of their visit to a place they had an aversion to. Writing to her sister Lady Louisa Stuart, Lady Carlow declared: 'I am sorry to find you are likely to have Lady M. at Luton [Park], but think you may rely upon her dislike to it hindering her visit from being long.'[36]

suburban gardener and villa companion (London, 1838), p. 673.   **30** Mowl and Earnshaw, *Trumpet at a distant gate*, p. vi.   **31** John B. Papworth, *Rural residences: a series of designs for cottages, decorated cottages, small villas ...* (London, 1818), p. 78; Mowl and Earnshaw, *Trumpet at a distant gate*, p. vi.   **32** Papworth, *Rural residences*, pp 78–9.   **33** James Plumptre, *James Plumptre's Britain; the journals of a tourist in the 1790s*, ed. Ian Ousby (London, 1992), p. 93.   **34** Lady Louisa Stuart to the duchess of Buccleuch, Dec. 1788, in Mrs Godfrey Clarke (ed.), *Gleanings from an old portfolio, containing some correspondence between Lady Louisa and her sister Caroline, countess of Portarlington, and other friends and relations*, 3 vols (Edinburgh, 1895–8), ii, p. 114.   **35** Byng, *Diaries*, i, p. 82.   **36** Lady Carlow to Lady Louisa Stuart, 7 July 1781 in Clarke, *Gleanings*, i, p. 126.

6.1 Wollaton Hall, Nottinghamshire (photograph by the author).

The age of a property ('old, 'new' or 'modern') or its architectural style and the reactions and associations it evoked, if negative, brought forth criticism and the refusal of some to cross the threshold. Moir and Ousby both argued that the Georgians regarded 'old' buildings as largely unacceptable unless they had significant historical, literary or romantic associations, or had been improved.[37] Without these attributes, tourists tended to avoid them. Ronnes and Koster, however, believe this view to be overstated and point towards an increasing interest in 'old' houses predicated upon a more general appreciation of the past.[38] 'New' or 'modern' were sometimes given specifically as reasons not to visit. As for architectural styles, baroque was generally reviled for its excesses reminiscent of the 'unhealthy ... fancies of the rest of Europe', yet in England its two most famous examples, Castle Howard in Yorkshire and Blenheim Palace, were much visited.[39] An emerging 'national' style of architecture in England, inspired by cooler, more rational Palladian and neoclassical models, did not escape censure

37 Moir, *The discovery of Britain*, p. 63; Ousby, *The Englishman's England*, pp 66–7.
38 Ronnes and Koster, 'A foreign appreciation of English country houses', pp 109, 112, 115.
39 Steven Parissien, *Palladian style* (London, 1994), pp 17, 24, 94.

either. Like baroque, they were imported styles but also carried with them overtones of power and authority.[40] For nineteenth-century architect George Gilbert Scott classically inspired mansions were 'the greatest drawback' to beautiful parkland. 'One is apt to wish them away' because 'their cold, and proud Palladianism, so far from inviting, seems to forbid approach; one feels under painful restraint so long as they are in view and the only rural thoughts they suggest are of game-keepers and park-rangers, whom one fancies ready at every turn to repel the timorous steps of the intruder'.[41] In the early nineteenth century, the brief revival of symmetrical, castellated properties including Lowther Castle, Cumbria, and Eastnor Castle, Herefordshire, signalled, in part, an authoritarian response by owners to the upheavals of the French Revolution.[42] These, and Thomas Dearn's unexecuted design of 1811 for the gatehouse at Bayham Abbey on the borders of Kent and Sussex with its towers, crenellations, battlements, arrow slits, moat and bridge may have been intended to evoke the same sense of dread that writer and caricaturist George Woodward found at the late sixteenth-century Wollaton Hall, Nottingham.[43] 'The long gloomy vista', he wrote, 'aided by the cawing of the rooks, gives to the pedestrian visitor the sombre idea of feudal vassalage, approaching the domains of arbitrary power!'[44] The construction of Lenton Lodge and a seven-mile perimeter wall enhanced Wollaton's sense of 'arbitrary power'. Completed in 1825, the monumental lodge, with its three storeys, towers and turrets, imitates the hall's architecture.

Travelling around Derbyshire in 1790, John Byng condemned Foremarke Hall, 'a house built, within these thirty years ... which is of vile architecture ... I never wish to enter these Venetian vanities', and he did not go inside.[45] This was not the only occasion when his ideas on architecture resulted in his refusal to enter some houses, even when considerable effort had been made to get there. In 1790, at Dunham Massey, Cheshire, Byng had expected to see an 'old magnificent mansion' but such was his dismay at finding a 'modern, red brick, tasteless house' that he had 'not a wish to enter it'.[46] Neither was he 'sorry at being refused admittance' to Sandbeck Park, in 1792, partly because the family was present but also because, fatigued after seeing many, 'A modern house cannot be worth the trouble'.[47]

When country houses displayed architectural features usually found adorning public buildings, particularly those associated with power and incarceration, it is unsurprising that visitors sometimes regarded them as forbidding and were consequently wary of approaching them. In York, the female prison, assize and crown courts, with their porticoes, entablatures, recessed arches and symmetrical

[40] Parissien, *Palladian style*, p. 17. [41] George Gilbert Scott, *Remarks on secular & domestic architecture, present & future* (London, 1857), p. 147. See also Girouard, *English country house*, p. 242. [42] Girouard, *English country house*, p. 242. [43] Mowl and Earnshaw, *Trumpet at a distant gate*, pp 36, 73. [44] G.M. Woodward, *Eccentric excursions: or literary and political sketches of countenance, character and country* (London, 1796), p. 184. [45] Byng, *Diaries*, ii, p. 163. [46] Ibid., p. 205. [47] Ibid., p. 20.

6.2 Former female prison, York (photograph by the author).

facades could easily pass for country houses.[48] Indeed, John Carr, responsible for these buildings, incorporated the same features in his country house designs. Porticos adorning gaols were so commonplace by the early nineteenth century that they became, in Dan Cruickshank's phrase, 'an awe-inspiring symbol of penal servitude'.[49] Samuel Johnson was aware of the architectural similarities between public buildings and country houses. Kedleston, with its portico, he declared, 'would do excellently for a town hall. The large room with pillars ... would do for the Judges to sit in at the assizes, the circular room for a jury chamber; and the rooms above for prisoners.'[50]

Interiors too could have an impact on an individual's decision to enter a property. Byng 'did not think it worth our trouble to go into' the remodelled Staunton Harold, Leicestershire (1763), as it promised 'nothing curious, old or new'.[51] In her *Companion, and useful guide* the Hon. Sarah Murray expressed a sentiment not restricted to eighteenth-century travellers: 'My search was not for what is to be seen in the interior of fine houses; for when one has seen half a dozen, they are in a manner all seen; I therefore refused to run over the house at Taymouth.'[52]

---

48 Dan Cruickshank, *A guide to the Georgian buildings of Britain and Ireland* (London, 1985), pp 157, 160. **49** Cruickshank, *Georgian buildings*, p. 158. **50** James Boswell, *The life of Samuel Johnson*, ed. Rodney Shewan, 2 vols (London, 1968), ii, p. 159. **51** Ibid., p. 72. **52** Sarah Murray, *A companion, and useful guide to the beauties of Scotland, to the lakes of Westmoreland, Cumberland, and Lancashire* ... (London, 1799), p. 315.

MISINFORMATION, ACCESS AND MISTIMED VISITS

Expectations prompted by advance reading of guidebooks and personal recommendations could be confirmed or confounded by a visit. Properties that failed to match perceptions and taste were particulalry irksome to visitors. At Wilton House, Wiltshire, MP and writer Richard Sullivan was initially underwhelmed.

> From whom I had derived my information ... I know not; but I honestly confess, I had formed an idea of this place which scarcely can be exceeded by imagination. But how I was disappointed! ... Substantial in appearance, but devoid of every principle of elegance or taste. We however alit, and ... proceeded to the investigation of this wonderful collection of antiquities.[53]

After a visit to Berkley Castle, Gloucestershire, Sullivan noted, 'How travellers can be so infatuated themselves, or how they can venture to impose upon the credulity of the world, in loading objects with praise in every respect unworthy of them, is to me astonishing.'[54] Enville, Staffordshire, elicited a similar sentiment from him: 'I will confess, from the accounts I had heard of it, to my disappointment.'[55] Having heard much about Downton Castle, Shropshire, James Plumptre was disappointed but conceded that it was 'infinitely above the run of modern built mansions'.[56] Inevitably, when faced by the reality, some tourists made the decision not to seek admittance to a property. In 1797, Johnson Grant, from the University of Oxford, had been informed that 'Chatsworth was worth seeing', but on encountering the 'vile lawns and belts and summer seats' and asking 'what curiosities it contained', only to be told, 'Nothing but what you see', went no further.[57] Staying at Farnham in 1782, John Byng asked an innkeeper whether the Bishop's Palace was worth seeing. The innkeeper believed not as no one ever went there.[58]

It was advisable for those planning to make special excursions to check opening arrangements. Chatsworth was open 'two public days in the week' by the 1760s and Blenheim every afternoon in the 1780s, except Sundays, between two and four.[59] The grounds of Willersley Castle, Derbyshire, were open on Mondays and Thursdays and Corsham Court, Wiltshire, on Tuesdays and Fridays.[60] For a long time Kedleston's opening hours remained unchanged;

---

[53] Richard Sullivan, *Observations made during a tour through parts of England, Scotland, and Wales. In a series of letters* (London, 1780), pp 68–9.   [54] Sullivan, *Observations*, p. 111.
[55] Ibid., p. 130.   [56] Plumptre, *Journals*, p. 174.   [57] Johnson Grant, 'Journal of a three weeks' tour in 1797 through Derbyshire to the lakes' in William Fordyce Mavor, *The British tourists; or træveller's pocket companion*, 6 vols (London, 1809), v, p. 245.   [58] Byng ignored the advice but upon inspection concurred with the innkeeper; Byng, *Diaries*, i, p. 73.   [59] Quoted in Ousby, *The Englishman's England*, p. 79; Byng, *Diaries*, ii, p. 127.   [60] Richard Warner, *A tour through the northern counties of England and the borders of Scotland*, 2 vols (Bath, 1802), i,

6.3 Kedleston Hall, Derbyshire (photograph by the author).

'if you have a mind to see Lord Scarsdale's', Richard Sullivan was advised in 1778, 'you must go directly; it is now noon, and travellers have no admittance but from ten till two'.[61] Hours of admittance published in local newspapers could not necessarily be relied upon. On 13 and again on 20 June 1805, Ann Stevens, proprietor of the Kedleston Inn, announced in the *Derby Mercury* that 'Kedleston House is now shewn as usual from ten o'clock till two every day, Sundays excepted'.[62] On 27 June, the advert contained an alteration: 'Kedleston House will be shewn as usual from eleven o'clock till three every day, Sundays excepted'.[63] Restricted access arrangements of a different kind were put in place in 1823 at Fonthill, Wiltshire. Advertisements announcing the auction of the abbey's contents made it explicit that, notwithstanding the sale, the abbey and grounds could be viewed until October. For those wishing to view the lots and attend the sale itself, however, 'tickets for visiting (12s. 6d. each) on any two days ... may be had at the Abbey Gates; and at Mr Phillips's No. 73 Bond Street; where catalogues of the forty days sale may be had, (and which alone admit to the sale)'.[64]

Choosing the wrong day, arriving late, not allowing sufficient time for a viewing, or relying on others could all lead to disappointment. At Leeds Castle,

p. 145; Stephen Bending, 'One among the many: popular aesthetics, polite culture and the country house landscape' in Arnold, *The Georgian country house*, p. 65. 61 Sullivan, *Observations*, p. 143. See also, Moir, *Discovery of Britain*, p. 59. 62 *Derby Mercury*, 13, 20 June 1805. 63 *Derby Mercury*, 27 June 1805. 64 Ibid., 15 Oct. 1823.

Kent, Byng bemoaned 'our ill choice of Day (Sunday), [and] the Rudeness of Ld F[airfax] in refusing us admission'.[65] As an experienced traveller, he should have known better. Virtually all properties excluded Sundays from their opening days. This effectively denied entry to any for whom it was their only day off. James Plumptre was denied admission to Chatsworth due to the lateness of his arrival, but was admitted the following day.[66] Byng arrived late in the day and in the rain to see the woods at Hackfall, Yorkshire, only to declare 'an evening inspection is wrong'.[67] Lady Carlow's journey north in 1781 involved viewing Thoresby Park, Clumber Park, Wellbeck Abbey and Worksop Manor in Nottinghamshire and Wentworth Woodhouse, Wharncliff and Wentworth Castle, Yorkshire, in quick succession. The result was that she had little or no time to appreciate all they had to offer and was not always sure of what she had seen or where. In one case, she got no further than the lodge.

> We were in such a hurry we hardly saw any of them with comfort, as they all lie close together, and four is rather too many to see in one day ... so at the Duke of Portland's [Welbeck] we only saw the gardens and the plantations, and the same I think of the Duke of Norfolk's [Worksop] ... Lord Rockingham's came next [Wentworth Woodhouse] ... but could not stay long enough ... to see anything but the offices ... because we had Wharncliff and Lord Strafford's to see that day; but our schemes were frustrated by the postilion not knowing the way, by which means it was near six o'clock when we arrived at the lodge ... We proceeded to Wentworth Castle, but to our sorrow did not arrive until it was too late to attempt seeing it that night ... so we agreed to give up Lord Strafford's altogether.[68]

James Plumptre's long-standing desire to see The Leasowes, Shropshire, was foiled again in 1799 because it would have meant missing his coach.[69] Writer and traveller Thomas Pennant was told that Lumley Castle, near Chester-le-Street, was 'very well worth seeing', but in a spectacular example of elitism declared, 'unfortunately it proved a public day, and I lost sight of it'.[70]

BARRIERS AND IMPEDIMENTS TO ADMISSION: NOTICES AND ANNOUNCEMENTS, OR THE LACK THEREOF

In his *Lectures on architecture,* Sir John Soane pronounced that 'A villa should not be placed too near a city or populous town so as to occasion those who occupy it

65 Byng, *Diaries*, iv, p. 156.   66 Plumptre, *Journal*, p. 72.   67 Byng, *Diaries*, iii, p. 52.
68 Lady Carlow to Lady Louisa Stuart, 7 July 1781 in Clarke, *Gleanings*, i, pp 127–8.
69 Plumptre, *Journals*, p. 177.   70 Thomas Pennant, *A tour in Scotland, 1769* (Chester, 1771),

to be eternally annoyed by troublesome visitors.'[71] Ian Gow drew attention to the troublesome visitors to St Bernard's House, Edinburgh, which prompted Walter Ross to adopt an unconventional approach to deter the unwanted. Having enclosed his grounds but still 'much annoyed by nightly depredators', he set mantraps and spring guns, advertising the fact in local newspapers – all to little effect. Next, he procured 'an old human leg from the Royal Infirmary', had it 'dressed up in a stocking, shoe and buckle' and clenched in the teeth of a trap. It was carried through the streets by the town crier 'who exhibited it aloft to public view proclaiming that it had been found' at Ross' house. The town crier offered to return the leg to its rightful owner.[72] As Ross found, to his cost, and as Robert Lloyd's satire, *The cit's country box*, illustrates, the visibility of villas 'from public rights of way, and relative ease of access ensured less select uninvited viewers'.[73] Lloyd's poem concludes with how, 'Common-council men by dozens' did nothing but stare at Sir Traffic Thrifty's country box each week.[74]

Simple notices were sometimes effective impediments to admission. In 1824, the gardener at Ilam Hall, Staffordshire, showed the grounds on Mondays and Thursdays.[75] This arrangement may have been instituted in response to the 'considerable damage' done to the grounds the previous year as a consequence of which the *Derby Mercury* announced 'that all persons found on the said premises will be prosecuted according to Law'.[76] Approaching a house near Windsor, Carl Philip Moritz, the German writer and traveller, was put off after reading, 'Take care! Steel traps and spring-guns are laid here!'.[77] James Plumptre was stopped from venturing further by a sign at Dalhousie Castle in Scotland: 'So severe a prohibition against approaching the house or entering the grounds was placed against a tree near the gate, that I did not even dare to look over.'[78] Moritz and Plumptre knew their place, but Lady Carlow was not so easily deterred, even if it did ultimately result in disappointment. As she recalled of her visit to Scotland in 1781: 'I think it was to Lord Abercorn's we went ... It's a new-built house, but there is a board put up to desire strangers not to ask to see it; however, he invited us in, [but] I never saw anything look so uncomfortable.'[79]

Unverified reports indicating that properties were not open could be explained by rumour, but at Hawkstone Park, Shropshire, it appeared misinformation about visiting arrangements was being deliberately circulated. The *Staffordshire Advertiser* included a rebuttal by a local innkeeper: 'having

p. 29. 71 Quoted in David Watkin, 'Soane's concept of the villa' in Arnold, *The Georgian country house*, pp 94–104 at p. 95. 72 Cumberland Hill, *Historic memorials and reminisces of Stockbridge* (2nd ed.; Edinburgh, 1887), pp 14–15. See also, Ian Gow, 'The Edinburgh villa revisited: function not form' in Arnold, *The Georgian country house*, p. 148. 73 Bryant, 'Villa views and the uninvited audience', pp 12, 22. 74 I am indebted to Christopher Ridgway for this reference; Robert Lloyd, *Poems* (London, 1757), p. 49. 75 *Staffordshire Advertiser*, 18 Sept. 1824. 76 *Derby Mercury*, 17, 24 Sept., 22 Oct. 1823. 77 Carl Philip Moritz, *Journeys of a German in England: a walking tour of England in 1782*, trans. Reginald Nettel (London, 1983), p. 118. 78 Plumptre, *Journals*, p. 107. 79 Lady Carlow to Lady Louisa Stuart, 18

received Letters from some Friends, requesting to be informed if Hawkstone Park was really "shut against the public" (as reported)', John Morris of the Hawkstone Inn, had

> great pleasure in assuring those friends and the public, that the Park is open ... J.M. further begs leave to caution those families who are on the road to visit Hawkstone, against reports that are too often circulated, that the Inn is so full they cannot be received; many have thus been disappointed of seeing the Park.[80]

This did not resolve the issue. Eight years later Morris published further denials: 'As a report has been circulated that this park will not in future be open ... I take the liberty of saying ... that such report is wholly unfounded ... Tickets of Admission may be obtained as usual at Hawkstone Inn.'[81] Behind the cause of Morris' announcements, one suspects, lay a disgruntled neighbour or commercial rival.

Richard Wilson and Alan Mackley, and Rosemary Sweet have demonstrated that although many great estates were open to a genteel public by the end of the eighteenth century, owners who failed to open their houses or publish the fact were roundly criticised.[82] Ronnes and Koster argue, however, that it was not always necessary to publish opening times because, even if families were not in residence, servants would still be available to show unexpected visitors around.[83] John Byng reserved his ire for those owners whose properties were widely known to be open but who failed to grant access or who changed arrangements at the last moment, rather than for places that were rarely or did not open at all. At Wroxton Abbey, Oxfordshire, after regretting the passing of traditional hospitality, he vented his spleen on the lack of publicized admission arrangements:

> Unluckily for us Ld G[uildford] was just arrived from London, and denied us admittance. Very rude this and unlike an old courtly Lord! Let him either forbid his place entirely; open it always; or else fix a day of admission: but for shame don't refuse travellers, who may have come 20 miles out of their way for the sight of the place.[84]

A few days later Byng was also refused admission to Shirburn Castle, Oxfordshire, because Lord Macclesfield was in residence. It generated another

July 1781 in Clarke, *Gleanings*, i, p. 133. 80 *Staffordshire Advertiser*, 17, 24 Aug. 1816. 81 *Aris' Birmingham Gazette*, 19 July 1824; *Manchester Mercury*, 17 Aug. 1824. 82 Wilson and Mackley, *Creating paradise*, p. 81; Rosemary Sweet, 'Domestic tourism in Great Britain', www.bl.uk/picturing-places/articles/domestic-tourism-in-great-britain, accessed 2 Jan. 2021. 83 Ronnes and Koster, 'A foreign appreciation of English country houses', p. 118. 84 Byng, *Diaries*, i, p. 231.

outburst: 'Let people proclaim that their great houses are not to be viewed, and the travellers will not ride out of their way with false hopes.'[85] These examples are well-known, but he returned often to this theme: 'A refusal of the sight of any house known commonly to be seen, is very unpolite, and cruel upon the tourist.'[86]

Over the course of the eighteenth century, information about houses open to the public was increasingly available in guidebooks. Those aimed at being truly practical alerted readers about the best things to see, circular tours, day trips, food, and accommodation and whether visitors were expected to tip the servants who showed them around the properties. The practice provoked vociferous complaints, Arthur Young calling it a 'vile custom', but few writers openly criticized the owners of properties who permitted their servants to charge admission fees.[87] The travel writer Sarah Murray, however, did point the finger. After noting that Chatsworth's housekeeper and gardener expected 'at least five shillings each', Murray commented that 'When noblemen have the goodness to permit their fine seats to be seen by travellers, what a pity it is they suffer them to pay their servants' wages'.[88] Tourists might complain but whether staying as a guest in a country house or in a genteel lodging house, the giving and receiving of vails was widely practised.[89] The extent to which advance awareness of this practice deterred potential visitors is unknown, but in 1844, Henry Colman from Boston, Massachusetts, believed fees were necessary. Without them, owners 'would be wholly overrun, and could have no quiet'.[90]

BARRIERS AND IMPEDIMENTS TO ADMISSION: PHYSICAL

If simple notices, less-than-glowing reports in guidebooks, or the prospect of vails failed to deter unexpected visitors, owners could implement a range of alternative tactics. Amanda Vickery described the thresholds of urban houses as frontiers 'in custom and law', with the basement area as a 'domestic moat, defended with iron railings', complemented by 'bars, bells, trip wires, servants sleeping across doorways … guard dogs … [and] … firearms'.[91] The same features, and more, were to be found in grander establishments. Closed off driveways, triumphal arches, mock-fortified structures, the removal of villages and the re-routing of roads all constituted part of wider moves to enclose land and landscape parks, but also functioned as symbols of authority extending the distance between properties and the public.[92] Kedleston's North Lodge,

85 Ibid., p. 237. See also, Ousby, *The Englishman's England*, p. 76.   86 Byng, *Diaries*, iv, p. 124.   87 Arthur Young quoted in Bending, 'One among the many', p. 76.   88 Murray, *Companion, and useful guide*, pp 6–7.   89 Pamela Horn, *Flunkeys and scullions: life below stairs in Georgian England* (Stroud, 2004), pp 14–15.   90 Henry Colman, *European life and manners*, 2 vols (Boston, 1850), i, p. 203; Arnold, 'The country house and its publics', p. 29.   91 Amanda Vickery, *Behind closed doors* (London, 2009), pp 28, 31–2.   92 Girouard, *English country house*,

6.4 North Lodge, Kedleston, Derbyshire (photograph by the author).

6.5 Humphry Repton, *Sketches and hints on landscape gardening* (1795). (Metropolitan Museum of Art, New York, Harris, Brisbane, Dick Fund, 1945, Accession no. 45.10.1).

designed by Robert Adam, has tall iron gates set within a triumphal arch, and attached lodges, all linked to a perimeter fence of spiked iron railings.[93] A 'before' image in Humphrey Repton's *Sketches and hints in landscape gardening* shows three fashionably dressed tourists outside landscaped grounds surrounded by a high wooden fence with no obvious entry point. To compensate, a man stands on the cross rail of the fence peering over the top to view the landscape within; a woman peeps through a hole in the fence.[94] John Byng had no desire to enter Attingham Park near Shrewsbury, but commended Lord Berwick's decision to construct a wall around it: 'I ... passed Ld B's great, tasteless seat ... but I visit not such houses ... He does right to begin building a wall, for were I obliged to live near a great town, I would wall, as high as walls could be built, to keep out insolence, and roguery'.[95] Perhaps, as occurred at Canons in Middlesex in 1722, Lord Berwick could have provided lodgings for 'old sergeants of the army' whose function was to 'guard the whole, and go their rounds at night and call the hours ... to prevent disorders'.[96]

With such barriers in place, few visitors were prepared to adopt the determined, and ultimately successful, tactics employed by John Byng and his travelling companion at Bolton Hall, Yorkshire, in 1792. There, they were

> directed to a single house where the key was kept; but unluckily there was no place within; the first gate that we found locked – we contrived to pass beyond by scrambling over a hedge; but the second [gate] ... was not to be forced, neither were the pales to be surmounted: so we were obliged to take a roundabout course through fields, before we arrived ... We have been five hours in our ramble.[97]

Sometimes entry was impossible, especially where properties were ruined or abandoned. Byng noted that half of the castles and abbeys he tried to visit in Wales were 'unapproachable, and inaccessible, tho' a man with a mattock, and spade, might make a comfortable walk of inspection ... And they are all, even the most noted, choked by impediments; and only to be surveyed in danger.'[98] At Chepstow Castle, courtyards were so overgrown with nettles and brambles that walking around the ramparts was out of the question.[99] Even places known to be open could be problematic. In 1781, Byng noted a number of potential impediments at Hagley, Worcestershire. The gates were locked, an hour was spent locating the key; the servants lacked both 'attention' and 'civility', and entry to the house was via 'a flight of steps, inconvenient and unsafe, in summer

p. 242; Mandler, *Stately home*, pp 1–2; Ousby, *The Englishman's England*, p. 61.   [93] Leslie Harris, *Robert Adam and Kedleston: the making of a neoclassical masterpiece* (London, 1987), p. 76.   [94] Moira Goff, John Goldfinch, Karen Limper-Herz, Helen Paden and Amanda Goodrich, *Georgians revealed: life, style and the making of modern Britain* (London, 2013), p. 37.   [95] Byng, *Diaries*, iii, pp 232–3.   [96] J. Macky quoted in Mowl and Earnshaw, *Trumpet at a distant gate*, p. 21.   [97] Byng, *Diaries*, iii, p. 60.   [98] Ibid., pp 266–7.   [99] Ibid., i, p. 27.

and in winter'.[100] At The Leasowes, near Halesowen, Byng provided an early acknowledgment of different visitor needs; he wished the walk was wider so as to 'admit small chaises, that the weak and infirm might enjoy its charms'.[101]

Locating key holders, who included owners, vicars, parish clerks, innkeepers and gatehouse keepers, and getting them to part with the keys was not always straightforward. Each could potentially thwart attempts to gain access through nothing more than absence. At Conisbrough Castle, Yorkshire, 'after much hunt and vexation', Byng discovered that the key was kept at the local inn.[102] At Bodiam Castle, Sussex, Sir Godfrey Webster had 'locked up the gate leading to the interior of the square; and from a narrowness of possession does not allow a key to any neighbour'.[103] In Killin, Scotland, Sarah Murray fruitlessly attempted to gain access to an island on the Dochart river: 'the entrance to the island is closed by a gate, kept fastened by the owner of it ... I had a strong desire to go upon the forbidden island, but bars and locks denied me entrance'.[104] Locked park gates at Poynton Hall, Cheshire, compelled John Byng 'to make a long detour' in 1790.[105] After passing through several gates at Hardwick Hall, Derbyshire, Byng noted, 'we were much vexed, at finding one fast locked, [and forced] to return back, and to seek another way by a blind lane'.[106] Other places had less restricted key arrangements. Without saying precisely where a key could be obtained from, Sarah Murray advised that when travelling through Westmorland, 'If at Leven's Hall you can get a key to go through Leven's Park ... If you cannot procure a key ... you must go on by Sizergh Hall'.[107] Caroline Lybbe Powys' visit to Chatsworth in 1757 was made considerably easier because the family with whom she was staying held 'a key to go through his Grace's grounds'.[108]

ENCOUNTERS WITH OWNERS AND SERVANTS

Entry to country houses often depended upon how you and your entourage were dressed and, as Stephen Clarke observes, on whether, as a result, servants thought their effort would be well-remunerated.[109] Staff appraised outfits, one's mode of transport (a chaise was preferable to a horse, a horse preferable to arriving on foot) and checked one's letters of introduction and calling cards. Arthur Young carried a letter to increase his chances of getting into Worksop Manor, Nottinghamshire.[110] In Scotland, James Plumptre, 'favoured with many a letter, to facilitate my progress', found his journey eased considerably.[111]

100 Ibid., i, pp 46, 48. 101 Ibid., i, p. 48. 102 Ibid., iii, p. 27. 103 Byng, *Diaries*, i, p. 351.
104 Murray, *Companion, and useful guide*, pp 329–30. 105 Byng, *Diaries*, ii, p. 180.
106 Ibid., p. 30. 107 Murray, *Companion, and useful guide*, pp 14–15. 108 Emily J. Climenson (ed.), *Passages from the diaries of Mrs Philip Lybbe Powys of Hardwick House, Oxon: A.D. 1756–1808* (London, 1899), p. 28. 109 Clarke, 'A fine house richly furnished', p. 203.
110 Ousby, *The Englishman's England*, pp 66–7. 111 Plumptre, *Journals*, p. 87.

6.6 Chatsworth, Derbyshire (photograph by the author).

Without letters of introduction, in 1835 the German art scholar Dr Gustav Waagen made no attempt to see the interior of Duncombe Park. Waagen was granted only limited access to Temple Newsam, while at Wentworth Woodhouse, he had only a 'very superficial view' because the housekeeper had no instructions regarding his admittance.[112] When John Byng's trunk failed to arrive in Buxton in 1790, he felt unable to mix in company. Instead, he occupied his time touring the surrounding country on horseback for a week dressed in the same clothes; this may help to explain why he failed to gain access to Lyme Park in Cheshire. Byng made another unsuccessful visit to Lyme in 1792. When the housekeeper appeared Byng asked, 'Is there any family here?' She responded, 'Yes, to be sure.' After enquiring, 'Mr Legh's?', only to receive a straight 'No', Byng then asked to see the house. The housekeeper replied, 'Indeed you can't. I should have enough to do then.' Hoping to tempt the housekeeper with the prospect of a fee, he countered, 'Pleasing business, surely for a housekeeper?' only to be rebuffed once again by the housekeeper, 'We never shew it but to those we know'.[113] He received the same treatment in 1790 at Wimpole, Cambridgeshire: 'I sought, in vain, for admission; and after waiting twenty minutes (a sufficient time for a

---

[112] Quoted in Arnold, 'The country house and its publics', p. 28.   [113] Byng, *Diaries*, iii, p. 120. See also Clarke, 'A fine house richly furnished', p. 199.

view) was refused by the servants ... I did, to be sure, feel a little vexed but what can be seen in such an ugly modern house?'[114] It was not just at the grandest places that admittance was refused. In 1790, at Hanson Grange, Derbyshire, Byng 'trusted to the hospitality of Mr Gould, the rich farmer; but this sullen hunks suffered us to remain at his stable door ... tho' our worthy guide spake every broad hint to him!'[115] Six years later, Robert Clutterbuck was more forgiving. Having travelled a considerable distance to Mamhead in Devon, only to be denied admittance, Clutterbuck accepted that some owners did not wish to lay their homes open to inspection either because they were at home or because there was little to see.[116] The antiquary William Bray's experience at Wollaton, however, was one he deemed unusual: 'Strangers are not permitted to see the inside, even when the family is absent; a piece of pride or gloomy inhospitality, which for the credit of our country is rare.'[117]

Owners and servants, especially housekeepers, held enormous power over those who came in the hope of seeing a house. They might grant full, partial or no access at all, or could ensure that the visitor experience was less than impressive: Okeover Hall, Staffordshire, featured in many guidebooks, but one room only was on view.[118] If unexpected visitors were admitted to a property, they could be made to feel unwelcome. Byng's eventual access to Aston Hall, near Birmingham, was 'as difficult as into a garrison town, from the sulkiness of the porter'.[119] In Yorkshire, James Plumptre went to see Aldborough's Roman remains, but 'The man of the house was not very civil, and on my enquiry whether there was anything else to be seen, said there was another pavement ... and discouraged my going to see it.'[120] The earl of Warwick permitted Plumptre to see Warwick Castle, but was told by a servant that his lordship denied access to the battlements.[121] John Scattergood visited Chatsworth in 1719 in the company of Thomas Hanbury of Kelmarsh estate, Northamptonshire, and a Mr Isted, a lawyer, and toured the house, but not the kitchens, cellars nor roof. On hearing of their visit, the duke of Devonshire invited Hanbury and Isted to dinner, but as a clergyman's son, Scattergood was not included. *Noblesse oblige* extended only so far.[122] Before being granted limited access to Raby Castle, Byng was first 'obliged to send in my name to Lady D[arlington] and ask permission for entrance. I am told that many are Refused! Why not a fix'd day, or fix'd hours?' He was then met by the housekeeper who showed him the cold great hall and a number of 'Frenchifi'd apartments'. Hoping to see more, he enquired, 'Have you any picture gallery?', only to receive a flat 'No'; 'No chapel?', 'No. That was taken with the hall'; 'No library?', 'Yes, one upstairs, kept lock'd.'[123]

114 Byng, *Diaries*, ii, p. 239. 115 Ibid., p. 56. 116 Tinniswood, *Polite tourist*, p. 93.
117 William Bray, *Sketch of a tour into Derbyshire and Yorkshire, including part of Buckingham, Warwick, Leicester, Nottingham, Northampton, Bedford, and Hertford-Shires* (London, 1778), pp 215–16. 118 Warner, *A tour through the northern counties of England*, i, p. 129. 119 Byng, *Diaries*, iii, p. 221. 120 Plumptre, *Journals*, p. 95. 121 Ibid., pp 26–7. 122 MacArthur, 'Gentleman tourists', p. 101. 123 Byng, *Diaries*, iii, p. 74.

CONCLUSION

The 'gloomy inhospitality' Bray encountered at Wollaton was replicated to varying degrees across the country. As Queen Charlotte discovered, even if you were of the 'right sort', appropriately dressed and arrived in suitable style, access to houses was not always granted to those without an appointment.[124] Status still determined how far the majority of visitors could penetrate an interior, but even for the elite access was not guaranteed.[125] Notices, warnings and physical barriers all carried their own messages about the likelihood of admission and potential visitors responded accordingly. What is most evident, however, is that visitor preference, based on the age and characteristics of a property and the signals its architecture conveyed, could act as a powerful deterrent. As a consequence of visitors' tastes, houses, estates and their owners, for all their show and claims of welcome, often appeared distant, disdainful, daunting or dangerous and sometimes all four.[126]

---

[124] Arnold, 'The country house and its publics', p. 22.   [125] Ronnes and Koster, 'A foreign appreciation of English country houses', p. 118.   [126] Girouard, *English country house*, p. 242.

'By far the greatest & most perpetual source of happiness in my life has been, & is, seeing': Christopher Hussey's visits to country houses, 1920–70

OLIVER COX

In the ground floor study at Scotney Castle sits the working library of one of the most significant, and yet understudied, visitors to country houses of the twentieth century. On densely packed shelves a lifetime's accumulation of books speaks to a deep intellectual engagement with mainly European histories of art, architecture and design. On one shelf, a copy of Clough Williams-Ellis' *England and the octopus*, so well used that its original cover has disintegrated, is sandwiched between the first volume of John Ruskin's *The stones of Venice* and a copy of Sir Thomas More's *Utopia*; on the shelf below, M.S. Briggs' *The architect in history* nestles next to Vita Sackville-West's *English country houses* and alongside Danish architect and town planner Steen Eiler Rasmussen's *Experiencing architecture*. In the adjacent bookcase, held together by scraps of sellotape, sits an extensively annotated pamphlet printed in 1950 and labelled 'Confidential – Not for Publication'. This proof copy of *Houses of outstanding historic or architectural interest: report of a committee appointed by the chancellor of the exchequer*, better known as the Gowers Report, hints at the centrality of Christopher Hussey to the story of country houses and their visitors.

Hussey was a pivotal thinker in shaping the position of the country house in both academic and contemporary popular culture. In a letter addressed to Hussey's widow, Betty, and accompanying a bibliographic tribute, Professor Joseph Mordaunt Crook (the then editor of the journal *Architectural History*) reflected on the bibliography of Hussey's writing he had compiled three years earlier:

> Compiling it was a pleasure as well as a duty: my generation of historians owe him a very great deal. As a schoolboy his writings opened up for me a new world of buildings and landscapes.[1]

Mordaunt Crook was not alone in citing Hussey as a foundational figure in the country house movement. Dorothy Stroud, the author of the first biography of

---

[1] Scotney Castle, Christopher Hussey's study: J. Mordaunt Crook to Elizabeth Hussey, 13 Nov. 1973, letter included inside *Architectural History: Journal of the Society of Architectural Historians of Great Britain*, 13 (1970), pp 5–29. Christopher Hussey's archive and working library spreads out across Scotney Castle.

7.1 Christopher Hussey's study at Scotney Castle (photograph by the author).

Capability Brown, inspectress of the Sir John Soane's Museum, and one time secretary to Christopher Hussey during his time at *Country Life*, wrote on the occasion of his CBE in May 1956:

> Dear Christopher,
> I am delighted to read the good news about your CBE. Now that everyone seems to be country-house-conscious, it is very proper that they should be reminded of how much your articles have achieved in this direction.[2]

Stroud also included a pen sketch of a country house shaped like a person in the act of clapping hands:

> CH is now a CBE
> And all the country's houses
> Whatever their century –
> Are loud in their applauses.

2 'Correspondence relating to Christopher CBE': Dorothy Stroud to Christopher Hussey, 31 May 1956 (Scotney Castle Archives, Christopher Hussey Papers, 2/2/6/1).

7.2 Scotney Castle Archives, Christopher Hussey Papers: 2/2/6/1, Dorothy Stroud to Christopher Hussey (31 May 1956) (photograph by the author).

> SIR JOHN SOANE'S MUSEUM
> 13 LINCOLN'S INN FIELDS LONDON WC2 : HOLBORN 2107
> Curator: John Summerson, C.B.E., F.B.A.
>
> May 31st 1956.
>
> Dear Christopher.
>
> I am delighted to read the good news about your CBE. Now that everyone seems to be country-house-conscious, it is very proper that they should be reminded of how much your articles have achieved in this direction.
>
> Yours ever,
> Dorothy.
>
> CH is now a CBE and all the country houses – whatever be their century – are loud in their applauses.

It is possible to reconstruct Hussey's visits to country houses due to the remarkable archive in the care of the National Trust at Scotney Castle. A decade-long programme of cataloguing has rescued a lifetime of correspondence, scrapbooks, annotated books and diaries from cupboards, shoeboxes and sideboards, and reveal a man whose approach to country house visits was informed in an equal measure by an intellectual impulse to understand the architectural evolution of Britain's building stock and a desire for fun and sociability. The professional and personal frequently intertwine. For over fifty years, Christopher Hussey was at the heart of a fluid and exciting social, aesthetic and intellectual milieu, where it was possible to be an enthusiast for the modern, the contemporary, the scary and the new, as well as find a deep affinity with the layered pasts of England's houses and landscapes.

Hussey was, at heart and by inheritance, a patrician figure. His understanding of the country house was that of a method actor – he lived it. First, in other peoples' country houses, and then, after thirty years of being a weekend guest, from 1952 in his own country house, Scotney Castle, which he inherited upon

7.3 R. Tait McKenzie, *Christopher Hussey*, 1930 (NT791403, by kind permission of the National Trust).

his uncle's death. While in later life a pillar of the cultural establishment, Hussey's life in the 1920s and 1930s placed him at the heart of a homosocial group of aesthetes. Sending Hussey a portrait medallion to mark his thirtieth birthday, the Canadian sculptor R. Tait McKenzie wrote flirtily: 'Enclosed is a picture of a recently exhumed medallion of Apollo some think it has a certain resemblance to you'.[3]

This essay explores how Christopher Hussey's visits to country houses were significant in three ways. First, they provided an insight into the creation of three whole new academic disciplines: architectural history, country house studies and garden history were in their infancy in the 1920s and 1930s, and Hussey was one of their founding fathers. Second, his visits documented the birth, scrappy

3 R. Tait McKenzie to Christopher Hussey, 15 Sept. 1930 (Scotney Castle Archives, Christopher Hussey Papers, 2/2/6/1 Box 2). Hussey had published a laudatory biography of Tait McKenzie the previous year, arguing that 'the importance of Tait McKenzie's sculpture lies in its being the first considerable oeuvre since the time of the Greeks' to consider the athletic male form; Christopher Hussey, *Tait McKenzie: sculptor of youth* (London, 1929),

adolescence, and anxious middle age of what would now be called the heritage industry. Hussey was in the rooms where the National Trust's approach to country houses developed and he was an influential lobbyist and activist for new legislative approaches to privately owned heritage. Third, as illustrated by Stroud's letter, Hussey was the instigator of a scholarly and popular discourse that situated country houses as part of a national history accessible – in theory – to all.

Running across these three themes, and powered by innumerable country-house visits, was the idea that country houses were neither dead nor inert. Rather, their architecture and landscapes offered an intellectual approach, a way of seeing, that Hussey believed could be profitably adapted and adopted to confront, as well as provide answers to, the most contemporary of challenges. In so doing, Hussey managed to bridge the gap between the insular worlds of the country house set and high society aesthetes, and find clues in their houses and landscapes as to how the largest of contemporary challenges – interwar suburban sprawl and post-war reconstruction – could be responded to through a native, English, style.

Christopher Hussey was born at 113 Park Street, Grosvenor Square, Mayfair on 1 October 1899, the only son and elder of the two children of Major William Clive Hussey of the Royal Engineers and his wife, Mary Ann, eldest daughter of the Very Revd George Herbert, dean of Hereford Cathedral. Hussey's uncle was Edward Hussey of Scotney Castle.

Hussey's upbringing was a privileged one. The earliest items in the archive at Scotney include an album of postcards sent to him between the ages of five and six, as well as a set of letters from his parents while he was at Eton during the First World War. In 1918 Hussey served as a second lieutenant in the Royal Field Artillery. After the war, Hussey moved on to Christ Church, Oxford, to read modern history (receiving second-class honours in 1921), but surprisingly little remains in terms of archive material for this period. Invites to 'The Medieval Club' to hear G.K. Chesterton, and to a lecture given by Hussey on 'The chair and the sofa' to the Oxford Canning Club suggest a heady cocktail of intellectual performance and well-heeled loutishness that characterized much of Oxford in the 1920s.[4]

It was this Oxford milieu that provided Hussey with his first sustained period of country house visiting, as his university set were the scions of country house owners up and down the country. Edward Marjoribanks, Hussey's roommate, writing from the house of his step-father, Douglas, first Viscount Hailsham, at Carter's Corner Place in Sussex, invited him to, 'Come and find some forgeries

preface [no page number].   4 Oxford between the wars owes much to the literary imagination of Evelyn Waugh in *Brideshead revisited*. For recent analysis of the social and cultural milieu in which Hussey was a part, see, Leslie Mitchell, *Maurice Bowra: a life* (Oxford, 2009) and Daisy Dunn, *Not far from Brideshead: Oxford between the wars* (London, 2022).

in the furniture on which my poor parents have literally lavished thousands.' Turning from furniture to gossip, Marjoribanks confided to Hussey how, 'In London I have a continual longing to bring young women to bed', and that he had just purchased a 'heather-mixture' knicker-bocker suit to match his pink shirts, which would make Hussey 'green with envy'.[5] Hussey seems to have been able to balance hedonism with hard work in his early twenties. Letters to his parents during a trip to the Dalmatian coast, for example, contain standard filial reportage, but are also rich in architectural and historical detail.

In his second year at Christ Church he submitted his first article for *Country Life*, on his uncle's home, Scotney Castle, which appeared in July 1920.[6] Cecil Gwyer, whose parents were busy remodelling Eywood House in Herefordshire, wrote to Hussey that spring: 'How frightfully nice having to write Scotney for *Country Life*. You ought to do it artfully well knowing the place as you do and loving it. I expect you will. You <u>are</u> becoming a literary gentleman.'[7] Gwyer wasn't wrong, as the twenty-year-old Hussey played to the gallery in his opening paragraph:

> Words and – with all due deference to the gentleman who takes them – photographs are not a good medium for describing a gem such as the old buildings of Scotney Castle, the setting of which is so exquisite and the whole effect so unexpected that it seems for a moment that it must be a little fairy castle that will melt when the sun shines on it.[8]

Having spent significant time in his uncle's country house and weekends engaging in country pursuits was one thing, writing about this for *Country Life* was something different, and required a particular approach. A set of letters from *Country Life*'s proprietor, Edward Hudson, indicate how Hussey was schooled in a particular way of looking at, and understanding, country house spaces. In August 1921, Hudson wrote from his home on Lindisfarne to explain the house style ahead of visits to Carter's Corner and Herstmonceux Place in East Sussex:

> I should just make notes & plans of Rooms showing what you propose to Photo. Keep them in Books. I have written Mssrs Richards to order some Books such as I use ... I make plans of the Rooms – or House or Garden with arrows showing what I want photographed. Some of the arrow points I mark A-B-C &c & under give explanatory notes of what I want. I also

---

5 Edward Marjoribanks to Christopher Hussey [1920] (Scotney Castle Archives, Christopher Hussey Papers, 2/2/6/1 Box 1).   6 Christopher Hussey, 'Scotney Castle', *Country Life*, 48:1226 (3 July 1920), pp 12–19.   7 Cecil Gwyer to Christopher Hussey [1920] (Scotney Castle Archives, Christopher Hussey Papers, 2/2/6/1 Box 1).   8 Hussey, 'Scotney Castle', p. 12.

note the furniture about the house & suggest moving it to particular rooms if necessary & I also note what they are <u>not</u> to bring into a picture.[9]

Interest in Hussey's architectural writings was not just limited to *Country Life*. In spring 1923, the publisher John Murray wrote to Hussey in the hope that he might consider writing 'an article on the decadence of English Country Homes' for the *Quarterly Review*:

> It seems to me that a very interesting article might be made about the passing of these great houses and the great work which the best of their proprietors has done in the country in years gone by. I have very little doubt that in the long run the wage-earning classes will be heavy sufferers by this; but at present they do not recognise it.[10]

By the middle years of the 1920s, Christopher Hussey had established himself as a new voice on the aesthetic and architectural scene. He was, as Peter Mandler has noted, not alone as one of 'the more aesthetic children of the squirearchy and aristocracy, who rebelled against their parents' philistinism or Victorian tastes, and came to love the remaining classical houses of their friends and neighbours'.[11] Unlike several contemporaries, Hussey's architectural tastes were thrillingly eclectic. His was not an appreciation limited only to volutes and Doric friezes, as his Christ Church contemporary Noel Carrington recalled in a letter to John Cornforth in 1979:

> After your first letter I continued to think about Christopher Hussey and was annoyed that my memory of the twenties & thirties had been so poor, because I do recall clearly enough that his interests were always much wider than he was generally credited with … about 1924 after I had returned to England [from India] he gave me a copy of Corbusier's 'Vers Une Architecture' and advanced my interest in modern design. This he retained, and persuaded Hudson to admit specimens of it (reluctantly enough) into the pages of C.L …[12]

Hussey was in the vanguard of architectural criticism, with Carrington recalling in a subsequent letter to John Cornforth that Hussey had owned Le Corbusier's book in the original French 'before Etchells translated it'.[13] As Elisabeth Darling

9 Edward Hudson to Christopher Hussey, 8 Aug. [1921] (Scotney Castle Archives, Christopher Hussey Papers: 2/2/6/1 Box 1).   10 John Murray to Christopher Hussey, 17 May 1923, ibid.   11 Peter Mandler, *The fall and rise of the stately home* (New Haven and London, 1997), p. 286.   12 'Material collected by John Cornforth of *Country Life* for a monograph on CH 1979'; Noel Carrington to John Cornforth, 14 Mar. 1979 (Scotney Castle Archives, Christopher Hussey Papers: 2/2/7/6).   13 Noel Carrington to John Cornforth, 30 Mar. 1979, ibid.

has demonstrated, it is possible to trace the origins of 'collective activity around the promulgation of a modern design or architectural culture in England' to the circle of architects and writers who increasingly clustered around Hussey during the mid- to late 1920s. Hussey, influenced by his membership of the Architecture Club, formed his own group, named either the 'Vers Group' or the '63 Club', to promote the Corbusian message.[14]

The most significant manifestation of Hussey's enthusiasm for the modern was the intellectual and financial underpinning of the *Exhibition of British industrial art in relation to the home* held at Dorland Hall in 1933. Hussey contributed £525 towards the expenses of the exhibition, and the surviving correspondence at Scotney praises, in the architect Wells Coates' words, 'the qualities of generalship which you displayed as Chairman'.[15] In a letter to the historian Christian Barman in 1968, Hussey recalled his involvement:

> The idea of organising this pioneer display of selected industrial art 'In Relation to the Home' was due to Oliver Hill, FRIBA, with whom I shared his weekend cottage, Valewood Farm, Haslemere, 1931–1936. With his enthusiasm both for design and display, we hatched the scheme together, on the understanding that he should be the Exhibition's Architect, with scope to ensure its expressing his own characteristic enjoyment of materials imaginatively handled. But he felt that he himself neither could nor should sponsor it directly, so pressed me to do so, owing to my connection with *Country Life* etc., and my independent status.[16]

Hussey's enthusiasm for the modern was well known among his social circle; one correspondent begged him for advice on buying 'good modern furniture in London' and queried whether there 'is good modern design English table silver to be had' as she regarded him as 'a criterion of good taste & an encyclopaedia of all the nicest sorts of knowledge'.[17]

His was a social circle that was nurtured in both London and the countryside, combining, in John Betjeman's words, 'all those phases of Wells Coatsism & Chermayeffectics in the Archie Rev',[18] with weekends at Owlpen Old Manor,

14 Elizabeth Darling, 'Institutionalising English modernism 1924–1933: from the Vers Group to MARS', *Architectural History*, 55 (2012), pp 299–320.   15 Wells Coates to Christopher Hussey, 18 July 1933 (Scotney Castle Archives, Christopher Hussey Papers).   16 'Notes on the production of the Exhibition of British Industrial Art at Dorland Hall, 1933' [June 1968] (Scotney Castle Archives). Barman was midway through his research for a biography of the London Transport director and modern design impresario Frank Pick. This work appeared 11 years later in 1979 as *The man who built London transport: a biography of Frank Pick* (Newton Abbot, 1979).   17 Catherine [?] to Christopher Hussey, Stonesfield Manor, 27 Dec. 1933 (Scotney Castle Archives, Christopher Hussey Papers, 2/2/6/1).   18 John Betjeman to Christopher Hussey, 11 May 1945 (Scotney Castle Archives, Christopher Hussey Papers, 2/2/6/1). John Betjeman was referring to the work of the architects Wells Coates and the Russian-born Serge Chermayeff. For details of Betjeman's time at the *Architectural Review*,

Gloucestershire, where his hostess, Barbara Crohen (née Bray), could offer a world far removed from functionalism: 'Sezincote's too far, but you shall go to Doughton [Manor] & meet Chris More Molyneux again, & go coursing, and if it please you, also we will laugh & play in a nice warm house full of young folks, of whom as you know, I like you not least!'.[19]

Hussey clearly had form at a house party. Recalling his visit to Crosswood in Cardiganshire, Elizabeth Inglis Jones wrote to Hussey how:

> I am sure it will interest you to learn what a hive of interest, &, if I may say so, delight you stirred up when you lay here last Easter. Delight, that is, in the Charming plans which you drew for the beautification of the front aspect of this mansion ...
>
> I have stayed here many times this summer, & unfailingly, on the Evening of my arrival my fellow guest says: 'Reggie,[20] what are you doing in front'. 'Ah, Christopher Hussey stayed here, & he was so helpful & kind, & this is the result ... They go together & with rapt interest more is told by the young man, about that Christopher Hussey who while visiting his friends improves their 'fronts' & no doubt if necessary, wouldn't be above tampering with their 'behinds'.[21]

This close social network that sustained weekend house parties at country houses, combined with an intense interest in contemporary architecture, enabled Hussey to write sympathetically about both. It was a skill recognized by his contemporaries. Oliver Hill, with whom Hussey shared a weekend house for five years between 1931 and 1936, reflected on their time spent together:

> I must let you know how very much I for my part enjoyed your sojourn at Vale. Your being there meant a great deal to me, because, I have long felt, that at core, both in yourself and in your work, you symbolize to me that England that I love, more I suppose, than anything else.[22]

From the summer of 1936 onwards, Christopher Hussey also created a visual record of his visits to country houses. The impetus for this new approach to documenting his visits was likely his marriage to Elizabeth (Betty) Kerr-Smiley. These six richly coloured and hugely atmospheric watercolour albums provide

---

see: Karin Hiscock, 'Modernity and "English" tradition: Betjeman at the *Architectural Review*', *Journal of Design History*, 13:3 (2000), pp 193–212. **19** Barbara Crohen to Christopher Hussey, 15 Nov. 1931 (Scotney Castle Archives, Christopher Hussey Papers, 2/2/6/1). **20** Most likely the nickname given to Elizabeth's aunt, the Chilean heiress, Maria Isabel Regina Aspasia de Bittencourt. **21** Elizabeth Inglis Jones to Christopher Hussey, 13 Sept. 1927 (Scotney Castle Archives, Christopher Hussey Papers, 2/2/6/1). **22** John Cornforth, 'Qualities of generalship: Christopher Hussey and modern architecture – II', *Country Life*, 170:4393 (29 Oct. 1981), pp 1468–9.

a snapshot of country house life in the final years before the Second World War. The albums share a format. Each page presents a visit to a country house. The house's name is either handwritten, or provided by a stuck-in piece of headed notepaper from the Husseys' hosts. Each host, and guest signed their names, and either a set of photographs or a small watercolour sketch (by Hussey) provided a visual snapshot of the house and the guests. These albums act as a visitor book in reverse – fitting for a peripatetic couple yet to inherit their own country house.

The first album in the series gives a cross-section of the Husseys' social and intellectual milieu. Their stamina for country house weekends is remarkable. The first scrapbook begins with a visit to Reginald Cooper's Cothay Manor, Somerset, on 10 July 1936,[23] followed by a trip to see his uncle at Scotney Castle (23 July 1936), a jump across the Irish Sea to Lambay off the coast of County Dublin (31 July 1936), before heading to Scotland to visit Glenthromie Lodge (22 Sept. 1936), Fremantles at Ceannacroc, Inverness-shire (27 Sept. 1936) and the Austruthers at Balcaskie (1 Oct. 1936), heading back south to Buckinghamshire to stay at Lillingstone Lovell Manor (9 Oct. 1936), followed by Dumbleton Hall, Evesham, Worcestershire (16 Oct. 1936), Helsington Hall, Yorkshire (23 Oct. 1936) and Owlpen Old Manor (30 Oct. 1936). In November, the Husseys stayed at Easington Manor, Northleach, Oxfordshire (13 Nov. 1936) before heading to Sussex two weeks later, where they hunted at Burton Park, Petworth (27 Nov. 1936), which had been purchased by the Courtauld family in 1919. The house had been written up for *Country Life* in July of the same year, perhaps resulting in a more social visit. Christmas was spent with the Kerr-Smileys at Bentley Park in Suffolk. The thirteen different country houses that the Husseys visited between July and December 1936 provide a remarkable cross section of interwar country house society, some of which Hussey was very familiar with. He described Cothay Manor as 'the most perfect small fifteenth-century house that survives in the kingdom' in a 1927 article for *Country Life*.[24] Owlpen Old Manor, which the Husseys would visit frequently, did not make it into the pages of *Country Life* until 1951.[25] On Lambay Island, home of Rupert, fourth Baron Revelstoke, one of the Husseys' fellow guests was the architect Edwin Lutyens. Lutyens had worked on different projects at Lambay since the mid-1920s. For Christopher Hussey, this opportunity to spend significant amounts of time with Lutyens in a social setting must only have reinforced his contextual understanding of the architect whose *Life* he would publish in 1950.[26]

Two weeks into the new year, the Husseys were on the road again. The Hendersons hosted them at Barnsley Park, Gloucestershire, on 15 January 1937, after which they visited Stoke Rochford in Lincolnshire on 22 January 1937.

---

23 Scotney Castle Collection: NT790773.   **24** Christopher Hussey, 'Cothay, Somerset', *Country Life*, 62:1605 (1927), p. 596.   **25** Christopher Hussey, 'Owlpen Old Manor, Gloucestershire', *Country Life*, 110:2859–60 (1951), pp 1460–3, 1544–7.   **26** Christopher Hussey, *The life of Sir Edwin Lutyens* (London, 1950).

Christopher Hussey's visits to country houses, 1920–70   167

7.4 A visit to Buscot Park, 12 Nov. 1937 (NT790773, by kind permission of the National Trust).

Three visits in February and March – Lillingstone Lovell, Wheler Lodge and the Tides Reach Hotel, Salcombe, Devon – were followed by successive weekends away at New Hall, Bodenham, Worcestershire (9 Apr. 1937), Owlpen Old Manor (16 Apr. 1937), Cothay Manor (23 Apr. 1937) and Eltham Hall with the Courtaulds (30 Apr. 1937). On 7 May 1937 the Husseys were at Standsted Hall in Essex, followed by another visit to his uncle at Scotney Castle (14 May 1937). Visiting Ralph Dutton at Bedhampton Manor, Hampshire (28 May 1937), the Husseys saw Hinton Ampner in the process of losing its Victorian Gothic pitches and pinnacles before returning for a third time to Lillingstone Lovell Manor. The summer saw visits to Sudeley Castle, Gloucestershire (18 June 1937), Valewood Farm, Surrey (25 June 1937), Merdon Manor, Hampshire (2 July 1937), The New House, Wildhern (Hampshire) (9 July 1937), Holywell Manor, Hatfield, Hertfordshire (16 July 1937), Littlewood House, Malvern, Worcestershire (23 July 1937), Lambay, County Dublin (29 July 1937),

Danmore, Hampshire (6 Aug. 1937), Rake Manor, Surrey (13 Aug. 1937), Ince Castle, Cornwall (20 Aug. 1937) and Cassia House in Winsford, Cheshire (2 Sept. 1937). The Husseys were then sedentary for all of six weeks before visiting Oddington House, Gloucestershire (15 Oct. 1937), Dane End, Hertfordshire (22 Oct. 1937) and Owlpen Old Manor (29 Oct. 1937).

Their perambulations were occurring at a significant moment in the history of the country house preservation movement. In 1934, Philip Kerr, marquess of Lothian, had ventriloquized a decade of Christopher Hussey's writings in *Country Life* as the basis of what would become the National Trust's Country Houses Scheme. By the start of 1936, the National Trust was actively involved in drawing up lists of those houses deemed most worthy of preservation. The vehicle for achieving this was the Country Houses Committee, which appointed James Lees-Milne as secretary.[27] The Husseys' hosts, however, tended to be owners of smaller country houses, which were not included on the lists being drawn up under the aegis of the National Trust.

At least two visits to Gavin Faringdon's Buscot Park, Oxfordshire, are recorded, which help give a sense of the vibrant social and intellectual world the Husseys inhabited. In November 1937 (12 Nov. 1937) the Husseys were in the company of the poet Robert Byron and the novelist Raymond Postgate, who at the time was editing the left-wing monthly serial *Fact*. Other guests included Peter Rodd and Nancy Rodd (née Mitford). Byron had co-founded the Georgian Group of the Society for the Protection of Ancient Buildings in April that year, and Hussey had recently agreed to join the group's executive committee.[28] In July 1938 the Husseys were joined by the sculptor Dora Gordine Hare, recently married to her third husband, the Hon. Richard Gilbert Hare. Gordine would later write to Hussey thanking him for 'the intelligent article and lovely photographs', noting that 'many of my friends tried to get a copy near the Leicester Gallery but could not'.[29]

April 1938 saw the Husseys visiting Furzebrook House, Dorset (2 Apr. 1938), where the entrepreneurial owner Tom Barnard had built a tearoom and created a tourist attraction around a flooded clay pit,[30] his new father-in-law Peter Kerr-Smiley at the Mill House, Astwick, Bedfordshire (9 Apr. 1938) and Tom and Helen Foley at Stoke Edith Park, Hereford (14 Apr. 1938), before embarking on a Welsh tour to Pwll-Y-Faedda in Breconshire (15 Apr. 1938), Stackpole Court (18 Apr. 1938), Llanmaes House (20 Apr. 1938) and Fonmon Castle (21 Apr. 1938), and then returning towards London with Corsham Court (23 Apr. 1938).

---

27 Michael Bloch, *James Lees-Milne: the life* (London, 2009), pp 92–3.   28 Gavin Stamp, 'How we celebrated the coronation: the foundation and early years of The Georgian Group', *Georgian Group Journal*, 20 (2012), p. 9.   29 Dora Gordine Hare to Christopher Hussey (Dorich House [1938]) (Scotney Castle Archives, Christopher Hussey Papers 2/2/6/1 Box 1); in the same year an article featuring Gordine and her new home-cum-studio appeared in *Country Life*, 84:2181 (5 Nov. 1938), pp 456–7.   30 Hussey includes a sketch of the blue pond, and two photographs of the new tearoom.

Over successive weekends in Autumn 1938 they were guests of Ralph Dutton, along with Charlotte Bonham Carter, in Dutton's newly rebuilt Hinton Ampner House; stayed with Osbert Sitwell, David Horner and Christabel, Lady Aberconway at Renishaw Hall; and visited Bentley Park (28 Oct. 1938), Scotney Castle (18 Nov. 1938), Earnshill (4 Nov. 1938), Stoke Edith (11 Nov. 1938) and Merdon Manor (25 Nov. 1938). This extraordinary series of social engagements hints at the Husseys' popularity as house guests, but also helps explain Christopher Hussey's ability as an architectural writer. He was seeing different types and scales of buildings almost every weekend. Social interactions in different architectural spaces combined with the close looking that characterizes his watercolour sketches of country house interiors and exteriors. As John Cornforth has noted, the albums provide an insight into the way in which Hussey organized his working life, how 'articles grew out of visits and how articles led to books; and, conversely, how books stimulated articles and visits'.[31] The way in which Hussey sketches interiors can be mapped onto the early instruction from Edward Hudson to think pictorially, and this painterly approach to composition, which is particularly evident in Hussey's earliest – and most acclaimed – work, *The picturesque: studies in a point of view*, would remain a core component of his approach to architecture.

After the war, the type of visit appears to shift.[32] The exact dates are no longer included, marking a change in the compiler's approach. The Husseys visit Elsie Bainbridge at Wimpole Hall with Ralph Dutton, and then Marcia and Joe Lane Fox at Bramham Park. One page in particular is striking, a family shot of the Pipers at Fawley Bottom compared with the earl of Radnor at Longford Castle. Alongside these scrapbooks, Hussey recorded his visits to country houses in a series of pocket-sized notebooks and appointment diaries that survive from the mid-1920s through to his death in 1970.[33] His notes from 1954 are instructive. Thirty years after his first instructions from Edward Hudson, Hussey maintained the same approach, preparing for his article on Holkham Hall with a photographer's eye. He first sketches the chapel ('one view only') and notes that the Claude Room provides a 'view through all doors to W end'. He then moves on to the Green State Bedroom (with a note to 'remove sofa from foot of bed'), and the Brown State Bedroom, before suggesting the best angles to photograph the State Sitting Room and Great Hall.

Hussey's writing on country houses, whether in *Country Life* or his three-volume history of Georgian houses,[34] was therefore the product of both lived experience and intellectual endeavour, blending the personal and professional.

---

31 John Cornforth, 'Country house enthusiasms: Christopher and Betty Hussey's visiting albums, 1936–70 – I', *Country Life*, 175:4510 (1984), p. 199.   32 Scotney Castle Collection: NT790774.   33 Scotney Castle Archives: 2/6/6/3.   34 The three volumes of Hussey's *English country houses* appeared in 1955, 1956 and 1958. The descriptions of houses featured were distillations of his own writings from *Country Life*, along with choice citations from work

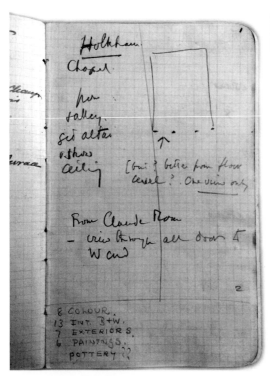
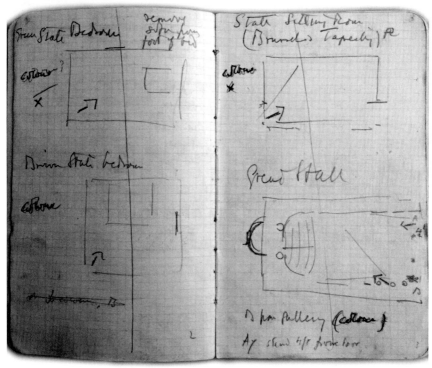

7.5 a&b Christopher Hussey's Holkham notebook entries (photograph the author).

On receipt of his proofs for his article on Uppark for *Country Life*, Meg Fetherstone expressed the appreciation that would come to be shared by many country house owners for Hussey's sympathetic portrayal of the house:

> You have paid me such a charming tribute at the end of this Proof – with a delicacy that delights me, in a tone that touches me, and a kindness that will kindle my efforts to fresh endeavours to carry on the work we have begun here. If 'There will always be an England', Uppark will outlive these troublous times; I have faith in the future.
>
> Thank you with all my heart, you have achieved a perfect picture of Uppark, of its intangible atmosphere, its Timeless mystery, its matchless setting for Romance & Adventure.[35]

Hussey's writings clearly had appeal to country house owners and the coteries of country house connoisseurs who engaged with his articles in *Country Life*. But they were also aware of the new audiences for country houses. By the fourth edition of his *English country houses open to the public* in 1964, Hussey could reflect on his methods:

> From the outset of putting together these notes and illustrations of the principal country houses of England and Wales open to the public, the idea was that they should provide a handy 'picture history' of country house architecture and decoration which people could see for themselves. That remains the purpose of this new edition, expanded to include many of the notable houses which have since opened their doors.[36]

Hussey believed that the country house was the ideal unit for understanding British history more broadly, noting how architecture could be a mirror to social, economic and political change, enabling 'the country houses now accessible [to] form a continuous series illustrating every important stage in this aspect of national history'.[37] In many ways, Hussey embodied an English antiquarian tradition that sought to set each individual building firmly and precisely in its immediate time and place. Yet, particularly in his writings concerning the picturesque, Hussey was also capable of imaginative leaps to join distinct historical epochs together. Lecturing to the Leeds and Lower Dales branch of the Campaign for the Protection of Rural England in May 1954, he argued that

---

by Arthur Oswald and H. Avray Tipping.   **35** Meg Fetherstone to Christopher Hussey, 16 June 1941 (Scotney Castle Archives, Christopher Hussey Papers, 2/2/6/1 Box 1). **36** Christopher Hussey, *English country houses open to the public* (4th ed.; London, 1964), p. 5. **37** Ibid.

Picturesque, is really the specialized, aesthetic, aspect of the leading trait in the English character, which, if we stand back and look at ourselves down the ages, we see has provided the mainspring of our destiny and our politics, and indeed whole attitude to life. This outstanding trait is surely our national Freedom, our mistrust of principles and systems, and instinctive reliance on finding the natural way to solutions by experiment, compromise, democracy, – in a word by empirical methods.[38]

His writing also offered the potential to bridge the gap with more academically inclined authors. Nikolaus Pevsner, for example, relied on Hussey's writings when starting his initial research for the *Buildings of England* series.[39] There is also a similarity in Pevsner and Hussey's approaches to English exceptionalism, with both authors seeking to locate the Englishness of English art within the interplay of language, topography and climate.

While Pevsner's use of new media (in particular his series of Reith Lectures for the BBC) has been the subject of scholarly discussion, Hussey's radio appearances have gone unremarked upon.[40] He was a contributor to The Third Programme, which, when launched in 1946, was described by the then BBC Director General Sir William Haley as being directed 'to an audience that is not of one class but that is perceptive and intelligent'.[41] In 1949, Hussey wrote the script for a forty-five-minute television documentary on Longleat, with the *Radio Times* noting, 'Lord and Lady Bath have a plan for the future which they explain in this programme'. This occasioned a meeting with James Lees-Milne, who noted in his diary how he, 'Lunched with Christopher Hussey at the Garrick Club in order to talk about my discoveries among the Longleat Papers. It transpired that I was unable to impart much that he did not know already.'[42] Hussey reprised his scriptwriting skills in 1950, contributing to documentaries on Luton Hoo and Penshurst Place.

His visits also help to illustrate the shifting position of the country house in post-war Britain. Hussey became both a house guest and an early pioneer of high-end heritage-sector consultancy. The duke of Bedford at Woburn, for one, was eager to source Hussey's advice:

> You have such vast knowledge of so many subjects connected with houses and their contents and I would like you, if you will be kind enough, to give

---

38 Christopher Hussey, *Formal landscapes in Yorkshire: a talk given to the Leeds and Lower Dales branch of the Council for the Preservation of Rural England at Bramham Park on May 15th, 1954* (Leeds, 1954), p. 4.   39 Susie Harries, *Nikolaus Pevsner: the life* (London, 2011), p. 390.   40 Pevsner gave 113 talks on radio and television between 1945 and 1955; Stephen Games (ed.), *Pevsner: the complete broadcast talks: architecture and art on radio and television* (Burlington, VT, 2014).   41 Hussey presented a programme on: 'Landscape and the picturesque' (29 May 1950), as part of the series 'Aspects of Art in England, 1700–1840'. 'The beginnings of The Third Programme', bbc.com/historyofthebbc/anniversaries/september/third-programme, accessed 6 Nov. 2022.   42 James Lees Milne, entry for 21 Jan. 1949,

me some idea of what you think I should do regarding restoration work here with the thought of applying to the Historic Buildings Council for a grant, should you think that the place or its contents warrant it. You will see many changes since your last visit and we have unearthed a great deal more over the years. The more I learn about houses, pictures, porcelain etc, the more I realise how appallingly ignorant I am and how much I would appreciate the advice of someone like yourself who has so much valuable experience.

George Landsdowne at Bowood told Hussey that 'I am relying on you to supply all the knowledge about Capability Brown. I will provide food, bed and a means of transport!', while Richard Sykes at Sledmere thanked Hussey for discovering historic textiles related to the house, noting that 'the house is now open to the public during the summer months and your present will make very interesting exhibits'.[43] It was not just dukes who consulted Hussey. R.W.B Howarth, from the Ministry of Works, wrote that at Wrest Park 'we do not get a large attendance here', hoping that the new leaflet he enclosed would encourage more visitors for 'the gardens deserve to be so much better known than they are'.[44]

As well as helping owners and managers of newly publicly accessible country houses, Christopher Hussey was assiduous in promoting the value of these houses as part of national heritage. A lecture he gave in the 1950s, 'Adventures in country houses', gives an indication of the way he marshalled his decades of country house visiting to a new, more public-facing purpose. His lecture opened with the hope that he might 'inspire or help some of you to undertake the adventure of visiting some of our historic country houses'. He argued that there were different ways of enjoying these spaces: 'as showing the way people lived here at different times, – and still try to live for choice; for the treasures of art which many contain; for the beauty of their settings in their surrounding landscapes; and as illustrating how the art of living has developed through the centuries'.[45]

This was also a lecture that sought to make a plea for the significance of the country house as a public asset. Hussey suggested that 'these family homes are not dead relics of what one of your most eminent citizens once described as "bunk", but they fit in with the pattern of English life and the pattern of English scenery'. In the lecture, phrases that have echoed through the scholarship on the country house for subsequent decades crop up with a regularity that suggests the extent to which Hussey formed the language around which the country house preservation lobby coalesced.

Midway on the waves (London, 1985), p. 148.   **43** Richard Sykes to Christopher Hussey, 17 Feb. 1968 (Scotney Castle Archives, Christopher Hussey Papers, 2/2/6/1 Box 3).   **44** R.W.B Howarth to Christopher Hussey, 2 June 1961 (Scotney Castle Archives, Christopher Hussey Papers, 2/2/6/11/1 Box 5).   **45** 'Typescripts Various 1950–1956' (Scotney Castle Archives, Christopher Hussey Papers, 2/2/6/11/1 Box 1); the venue and audience are not listed in

'It is', he remarked, 'true to say that the country house is the most notable English contribution to the visual arts of Europe'. It was through these houses, not the vernacular architecture of towns and villages, nor the communal ecclesiastical space of the parish church, that 'the English spirit and way of life is seen at its best'. Lecturing in the post-war context, Hussey noted how the country house contributed to the political vitality of the nation – Churchill was born at Blenheim; Hatfield House produced three prime ministers; and Sir Philip Sidney's descendant at Penshurst, Lord de Lisle and Dudley, served as the secretary of state for air – and also to the needs of the 'welfare state', through the transfer of ownership to local councils. Hussey's concern over the latter arrangement was that 'this development at least ensures the preservation of their fabric, but ends for ever the use and life of these houses as cells in the living tissue of the nation's history'.

Hussey used his lectern to advocate for the new forms of country house preservation gaining pace in postwar Britain, 'to help us maintain as much as possible of the country house way of life, which has been the background and birthplace of so much of our civilization and tradition'. His final sentence before switching the lights off so his audience could better see the slides was powerfully evocative: 'These scenes do represent visually the union in time, the unity formed by architecture and landscape and history, which to my mind is the most fascinating aspect of the country house, whether regarded as a work of art, or a family's home, or as a living fragment of national history framed in living beauty.' The lecture continued with a set of slides illustrating key moments in the architectural evolution of the country house – Scotney, Uppark, Alnwick, Powis, Brympton, Little Wenham, Stokesay, Great Chalfied, South Wraxall, Haddon Hall, Longleat, Montacute, Hardwick, Chastleton, Blickling, Hatfield, Parham, Bramshill, Cranbourne, Wilton, Little Moreton, Cold Ashton and Sulgrave Manor – before concluding with an encouragement to join the National Trust: 'it is a pound well spent in your own interest'. Hussey had been an influential champion of the National Trust throughout his life, and would go on to leave Scotney Castle to the Trust after his death in 1970.

This roll-call of architectural heavyweights has remained largely unchanged when it comes to narrative histories of the country house, and Hussey's phraseology recalls his statement in front of the Gowers Committee that these houses and their surroundings 'remain a living element in the social fabric of the nation, uniting visibly the present with national history'.[46] Hussey's contribution came after that of the duke of Wellington, who stated that 'the English country house is the greatest contribution made by England to the

---

Hussey's notes.   **46** Sir Ernest Gowers, *Report of the committee on houses of outstanding historic or architectural interest* (HMSO, 1950), p. 3.

visual arts'.[47] Eighteen years earlier, Hussey had rented the then Gerald Wellesley's house in Buckinghamshire for £30.[48]

This essay has used Christopher Hussey's extensive travels across England, Wales, Scotland and Ireland to explore how a combination of close looking and patrician sociability provided the backbone for his foundational articles on the history of country houses for *Country Life*. Hussey was an unusually alert visitor, who from his late teenage years had been schooled in a way of seeing by *Country Life*'s proprietor, Edward Hudson, and he did more to shape the way in which the country house has been consumed – by scholars and the public alike – than almost any other author. Partly this is due to his prolific output. But writing alone does not capture the impact of Hussey's visits to country houses. His extensive knowledge of houses spread across the length and breadth of the country meant that, when thoughts turned to new approaches to preservation, Hussey was present in the rooms where the big decisions were made.

However, like any catalytic substance, Hussey's personality and intellectual approach has yet to be absorbed into the histories of architecture and preservation. This is not due to any intellectual snobbery on the part of professional historians, more the fact that the raw materials for reconstructing Hussey's life and intellectual worldview have remained unavailable, but now, thanks to the dedication of National Trust cataloguing volunteers at Scotney Castle, they are being arranged to enable scholars to reappraise the importance of Hussey's visits in fostering both the vibrant scholarship on, and the appeal of, country houses to the millions of visitors who visit them today.

[47] Ibid. [48] Gerald Wellesley to Christopher Hussey, 12 June 1931 (Scotney Castle Archives, Christopher Hussey Papers, 2/2/6/1).

'There seem to be many more people here than I thought we'd asked': building collections of visitors in the Irish country house

IAN D'ALTON

INTRODUCTION

The Irish country house, like country houses everywhere, was always full of *things* – decorated firescreens, shot and stuffed animals, paintings, telescopes, coins, vases, books. It was also full of *people* – servants and families of course, and visitors as well.[1] As a sort of spacious human zoo, the big house was made for peacock-like narcissistic display, with an intricate and complex social interplay between hosts and visitors. The life of the house often revolved around these guests – why they were there, what they did and how they fitted in are important lines of enquiry. This chapter suggests one conceptual framework within which the choice of guests and visitors can perhaps tell us something of how the Irish landed classes positioned and triangulated themselves within their Lilliputian society. Through the lens of a collector's eye, using the taxonomy of collecting – choosing and acquiring; cataloguing and classifying; framing and displaying; arranging and curating – it offers an analysis of how and why the gentry and aristocracy chose their guests and attracted visitors. Outside its scope are those uninvited tourists who might have turned up to view the house's treasures or gardens (an activity common in Georgian England, but relatively unusual in Ireland), and unwanted 'guests', an extreme example of whom are those who came to raid or burn country houses during the 1919–23 period.[2]

Acquiring related things is in our DNA, it seems; it reinforces our identity. Psychologist Christian Jarrett highlights what he calls an endowment effect, wherein we value things we collect more than those we do not. Humankind's propensity to create collections could only start when permanent abode

---

1 The quotation in the chapter title is by Lady Naylor, chatelaine of Danielstown, in Elizabeth Bowen, *The last September* [1929] (London, 1998), p. 36. My thanks go to Fergal Browne, Marcia Johnson, Felix Larkin and David Nolan for their comments on earlier drafts. 2 Mark Rothery, 'Country house visiting: past, present, and future', blog.oup.com/2016/10/country-house-visiting-jane-austen, accessed 28 Apr. 2021; Lennox Robinson's 1926 play, *The Big House*, where the house is invaded by an arson party facilitated by a sympathetic servant – Christopher Murray (ed.), *Selected plays of Lennox Robinson* (Gerrards Cross, 1982), pp 185–7; also Terence Dooley, *Burning the big house: the story of the Irish country house in a time of war and revolution* (New Haven and London, 2022). 3 Christian Jarrett, 'Why do we collect things? Love, anxiety or desire', *Guardian*, 9 Nov. 2014, theguardian.com/lifeandstyle/2014/

supplanted nomadic existence.³ As country houses have a particular permanence, they are well placed to be the locus of long-term collecting, such as the nineteenth-century craze for acquiring exotic and unusual botanical specimens, often from far afield. The big house – usually with plenty of rooms, large gardens, all well-serviced – was ideal to bring together sparkling collections of guests even if, unlike plants and paintings, these were temporary rather than permanent exhibits.

The zeal of the collector of things is not always a constant. A collection of coins or stamps, for instance, may require the acquisition of specimens to complete a set; that set may contain desirable and not-so-desirable items. Acquiring the latter is often treated as a necessary but essentially a journeyman's chore. In a collection of twentieth-century Irish pennies the great rare date is 1938. This coin looks no different to the rest of the series, but it will be hunted down by the avid collector with all the resources at their disposal. Thus it was with country house visitors. Where one was well-connected or wealthy enough, prestigious trophies were to be had. However, most visiting took place as the result of simple neighbourliness, reciprocating hospitality, and observing dutiful family responsibilities.

THE GUESTS

The quantum of guests at Irish country houses could vary depending on the whims, resources and possibly the mental resilience of the owners. Writer Elizabeth Bowen described Eddy Sackville-West (who lived at Cooleville, County Tipperary, not too far away from Bowen's Court) in the autumn of 1956 as 'cracking up' under a tsunami of visitors over a seven-week period. Apparently, he could not say no to self-invitees.⁴ By contrast Homan Potterton's father was not fond of guests and thus 'no one was ever asked to stay the night' at Rathcormick, County Meath.⁵ The fictional Alcocks in Lennox Robinson's 1926 play *The Big House*, reduced by poverty, are 'shrinking' – withdrawn to one or two rooms in a draughty and servantless house where 'no one ever calls'.⁶ But most owners were happy to entertain as lavishly as their resources would permit. It was expected of them: 'The pleasure and duty of dispensing and receiving hospitality' was one of F.M.L. Thompson's 'five main activities' of the aristocracy and gentry.⁷

Sir Algernon and Lady Coote at Ballyfin in Queen's County had 147 guests in 1902, 106 in 1903 and 161 in 1904.⁸ Castle Hyde in County Cork had sixty-

nov/09/why- do-we-collect-things-love-anxiety-or-desire, accessed 2 Apr. 2019.   4 Victoria Glendinning (ed.) with Judith Robertson, *Love's civil war: Elizabeth Bowen & Charles Ritchie: letters and diaries from the love affair of a lifetime* (London, 2009), p. 247.   5 Homan Potterton, *Rathcormick: a childhood recalled* (London, 2004), p. 191.   6 Murray (ed.), *Selected plays of Lennox Robinson*, pp 183, 184.   7 F.M.L. Thompson, *English landed society in the nineteenth century* (London and Toronto, 1963), p. 95.   8 Mark Bence-Jones, *Twilight of the ascendancy*

eight visitors in 1936,⁹ and the Bruens at Oakpark, County Carlow, had between thirty-two and sixty guests per annum in the years from 1919 to 1927, with only a slight, but not catastrophic, decline after Irish independence.[10] Between 1860 and 1900 the earls of Portarlington entertained an impressive total of 1,327 guests at Emo Court, Queen's County.[11] That was a relatively modest average of some thirty-three each year – but at Emo, as we shall see, quality tended to trump quantity. Such patterns were a function of class and wealth as much as anything else – for example the well-off Catholic Grehans of Clonmeen, Cork, had 266 overnight visitors between 1887 and 1893.[12]

Collectors usually start by identifying what they want to collect – and why. Where hosts had discretion over their choice of guests, amiability was of paramount importance. Eddy Sackville-West was described by Elizabeth Bowen as 'house-trained and considerate and amenable'.[13] Somerville & Ross' fictional Major Yeates' step-brother-in-law never gave his host 'a moment's anxiety', possessing 'the attribute, priceless in guests, a good portable hobby' (in this case, the major was enamoured of the Celtic movement and desirous of practising Irish).[14] He would have presumably fulfilled the criteria set out in this admonitory ditty by Rose Henniker Heaton rather ostentatiously pasted into the front pages of the Bruens' visitors' book at Oakpark, Carlow:[15]

> '*The Perfect Guest*'
> She answered by return of post
> The invitation of her host.
> She caught the train she said she would,
> And changed at junctions as she should.
> She brought a light and smallish box
> And keys belonging to the locks.
> Food, strange and rare, she did not beg.
> But ate the homely scrambled egg …

As if to emphasize the point, the Bruens also felt they should point out the yin to this yang:

(London, 1987), p. 97. **9** Photostat of Castle Hyde visitors' book (courtesy of Professor Terence Dooley, Maynooth University), pp 19–24. **10** Oakpark visitors' book, 1914–28 (NLI, MS 23,050). **11** John Stocks Powell, *The royal palace of Emo. Emo Court, County Laois, its connections with royalty, and the proposal for a royal residence in 1872* (York, 2012) (typescript in NLI, MS 49,540), p. 112. **12** Maeve O'Riordan, 'Home, family and society: women of the Irish landed class, 1860–1914: a Munster case study' (PhD, UCC, 2014), p. 40. **13** Glendinning with Robertson, *Love's civil war*, p. 134. **14** Edith Somerville and Martin Ross, *Experiences of an Irish R.M.* (1908; London, 1970), p. 261. **15** Oakpark visitors' book. The poem was originally published in London, 1931.

Building collections of visitors in the Irish country house 179

> *'The Perfect Pest'*
> She merely sent a wire to say
> That she was coming down to stay.
> She brought a maid of minxsome look,
> Who promptly quarrelled with the cook.
> She smoked, and dropped with ruthless hand
> Hot ashes on the Steinway grand ...
> She snubbed the wealthy, dull relations
> From whom my wife had expectations ...
> And when at last with joyful heart
> We thrust her in the luggage cart,
> In half an hour she came again,
> And said 'My dear, I've missed the train'.

This was the essential difference between collecting things and people – inanimate objects did not make unreasonable demands or cause trouble. Very occasionally guests, through no fault of their own, disrupted the even tenor of a visit. In December 1889 an English clergyman is recorded as having died at Dromoland of typhoid fever;[16] while in Glaslough's visitors' book there are dramatic pictures of 'Lady Tweedale's car smashed near Steward's House, 12 August 1935'.[17] Likewise events could impose on the country house guests who might otherwise not have been usually invited. War was an obvious disrupter. During the Great War, Richard Longfield at Longueville, County Cork, billeted Australian officers on leave, where they were treated as part of the usual guest-list.[18] They were the accidental and exceptional overspills of wartime. They didn't always want to be there, either – as Kate Alcock, heroine of *The Big House*, lets slip: 'We tried having colonials here for their leave, men, you know, who had no relations or friends to go to ... the Australians always, after one day, sent themselves telegrams recalling themselves to the front.'[19] Glaslough visitors' book records that 'All of K Battalion, Royal Inniskilling Fusiliers' (Sir John Leslie's regiment) were marked as being there on 19 and 20 October 1917. It is unlikely that those sergeants, corporals and cadets who signed the book dined with Sir John and Lady Leslie.[20] These were not guests in the sense that the owners and their families would have understood the term.

---

[16] Dromoland visitors' book, Dec. 1889 (NLI, Inchiquin Papers, MS 14,500). [17] Glaslough visitors' book, 12 Aug. 1935 (NLI, Leslie Papers, MS 49,495/2/170). [18] Victoria Glendinning, *Elizabeth Bowen: portrait of a writer* (London, 1977), p. 172. [19] Murray (ed.), *Selected plays of Lennox Robinson*, pp 143–4. [20] Glaslough visitors' book, 19 and 20 Oct. 1917.

THE HOSTS

No matter what was the social status of each guest it was always expected that hosts would cosset their curations even when money was tight. Hubert Butler noted Elizabeth Bowen's 'unstinted hospitality';[21] likewise Bowen's biographer Victoria Glendinning wrote that 'Visitors to Bowen's Court ate and drank royally'.[22] Bowen's collection of characters came at some considerable cost – even modest entertaining could be expensive. Yet for Bowen, in the straitened 1950s, after husband Alan Cameron's death, visitors were still part of the warp and weft of an Irish gentry existence, and not to be lightly abandoned.

Most hosts took their duties seriously. It is hoped that not many visitations reflected the experience of Somerville and Ross' Major Yeates at Knockeenbwee, with guests 'incarcerated in a dungeon-cold drawing-room' and enduring 'A meal that had opened at six with strong tea, cold mutton, and bottled porter' and which was still in progress at eight o'clock, 'suggesting successive inspirations on the part of the cook'.[23] The Oakpark visitors' book had a workshop manual for the perfect host as well as guest:

> She makes you feel when you arrive
> How good it is to be alive;
> She pours you out a cup of tea
> Exactly as it ought to be …
> Your hostess talks of *you* through dinner
> 'How well you look, but growing thinner!' …
> She sends you up a breakfast tray
> As soon as you're awake next day,
> And says: You're not to stir from here
> 'Till nearly luncheon time, my dear'.
> What better way to please her guest?
> A Perfect Hostess lets you REST.

The countess of Rosse suggested that 'The vital thing was to keep people amused without making them feel too organized.'[24] Ennui was always a constant danger; in 1820 at Gorhambury the grandeur of Lord Verulam's royal guest, the duchess of Gloucester, was offset by having to play interminable board and bored games with her, as well as pretending not to notice the appalling shooting of fellow guest the duke of York.[25] Some hostesses seemed to work a little too hard at their hospitality. Lady Carysfort at Glenart, County Wicklow, sighed to

---

21 The phrase is Hermione Lee's in her *Elizabeth Bowen* (London, 1999), p. 37. 22 Glendinning, *Bowen*, p. 203. 23 Somerville and Ross, *Experiences of an Irish R.M.*, pp 234, 241. 24 Quoted in Adrian Tinniswood, *The long weekend: life in the English country house between the wars* (London, 2016), p. 280. 25 Thompson, *English landed society*, p. 98.

her sister: 'Our parties never seem to be quite a success, though we take so much trouble over them.'[26] Successful hosting required attention to detail and constant policing – 'A disembodied eye/Roves through the big house' as poet Michael Davitt wrote.[27] Lady Latterly, in Bowen's novel *A world of love*, was a fascinating character, but (like her creator) managing visitors does not appear to be one of her strengths, given 'the failure of her house parties to arrive or, still worse, leave again'.[28]

CHOOSING AND ACQUIRING

Appropriate choice and acquisition are the foundation stones of any successful collection. Thus it was with guests. Choosing them was one thing; actually acquiring them was another issue altogether. Like the collectors of artefacts, unless stratospherically wealthy, collectors of guests found there often had to be a compromise between quantity and quality; it is easy enough to build up a large collection of cigarette cards, less so paintings by Old Masters. For aristocratic grandees, the peerage was an obvious and prestigious collectible category, more or less guaranteeing that these 'people like us' would at least be relatively talkable-to. As an English example, the marquess of Bristol's visitors' book at Ickworth in Suffolk for house parties in the 1930s shows whole weekends with very few guests who were not members of the peerage.[29] While any host would doubtless have liked to bag the sovereign or a prime minister, it was unrealistic to aim for such exalted creatures unless one were high of status and deep of pocket. Only someone of the social elevation and wealth of the duke of Devonshire could assemble the sort of party he did in 1947 at Lismore Castle, County Waterford, with a future British prime minister, Anthony Eden, John F. Kennedy and his sister Kick, and Pamela Churchill, ex-wife of Randolph.[30] Only someone of Lord Portarlington's resources and influence could be assured of entertaining such as the duke of Connaught (1876) and the lord lieutenant of Ireland (1879).[31]

If royalty was the great prize it carried pitfalls, principally because of its high visibility, the demands it made on preparation, time and money, and an often regal indifference to what we would now call scheduling. In the 1820s George King, third earl of Kingston, set his sights on acquiring George IV, the friend of his wild youth, as his guest at Mitchelstown, County Cork. As we shall see,

26 Bence-Jones, *Twilight of the ascendancy*, p. 80. 27 Michael Davitt, 'Third draft of a dream', trans. Paul Muldoon, in Tim Pat Coogan (ed.), *A special issue of Literary Review: Ireland and the arts* (London, 1982), pp 161–3. 28 Elizabeth Bowen, *A world of love* (1954; New York, 1978), p. 72. 29 Observable in a graphic presentation at the house, which is now a UK National Trust property. 30 Frederik Logevall, *JFK: coming of age in the American century, 1917–1956* (New York, 2020), pp 452–3. 31 Stocks Powell, *The royal palace of Emo*, pp 51, 72, 76.

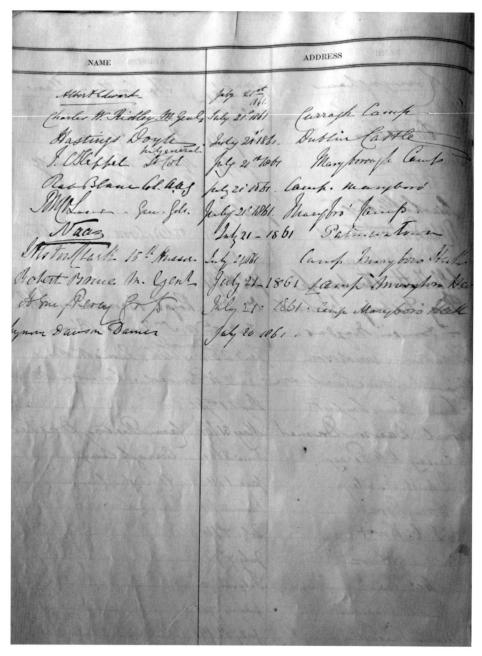

8.1 The signature of 'Albert Edward' in the Emo Court visitors' book, at the top of the page (National Library of Ireland, MS 42,100).

Kingston spent an enormous amount of money building a castle for a king who never visited it. Similarly, but more modestly, in 1904 Edward VII failed to turn up for tea with the Langrishes at Knocktopher, County Kilkenny, where expensive new carpets had been laid for the occasion.[32]

Other hosts of royalty were more fortunate – or cannier. In April 1899, the marquess of Ormonde entertained the duke and duchess of York (the future King George V and Queen Mary) for five nights at Kilkenny Castle. Also present were Lord Frederick Fitzgerald (of the ducal Leinster family) and Lord Ava (son of the marquess of Dufferin and Ava).[33] The entertainments on offer included a water-picnic on the river Nore. The Ormondes regularly hosted royalty; when King Edward VII and Queen Alexandra came to Ireland in 1904 and stayed at Kilkenny, it prompted the marquess finally to install proper baths with hot and cold running water.[34] At least, though, it seems that Edward's visit to Emo Court as a guest of the earl of Portarlington passed off without incident.[35] Apart from the prince of Wales, other visitors to Emo with royal connections included two descendants of William IV born on the wrong side of the blanket, George and Aubrey FitzClarence (who also were guests at Headfort House, home of the marquess of Headfort, near Kells, County Meath) who visited in 1870 and 1891, respectively.[36] Another royal – a minor German, but well-connected – was Francis, duke of Teck, who stayed at Emo in October 1893. Teck had been somewhat *déclassé* in the 1880s, but by 1893 had been rehabilitated as the father-in-law of the duke of York, later George V.[37]

The earl of Listowel had the same prince of Wales as a guest in 1885 at his mansion, Convamore, on the river Blackwater in County Cork. The prince's visit was in the midst of a land war, so crowds of adoring tenantry were missing on this occasion, as a contemporary account attested:

> On April 17th 1885, their Royal Highnesses the Prince and Princess of Wales and Prince Albert Victor, accompanied by the Earl and Countess of Listowel, the Marquis of Ormond, Lord and Lady Lismore, paid a short visit to Lord Waterford at Curraghmore. The one thing that was commented on generally was the all but total absence of the farming classes at Kilmeadan, along the road to Portlaw and Curraghmore. The only men of this class were some dozen who stood in a field some distance from Kilmeadan with a black banner on which the words 'Evicted tenants – Will the Prince reinstate them?' were printed.

32 Bence-Jones, *Twilight of the ascendancy*, p. 101.   33 Ibid., pp 85–6.   34 Ibid., p. 100.
35 Stocks Powell, *The royal palace of Emo*, pp 9, 24.   36 Headfort House visitors' book, 10 Apr. 1889, 1 Mar. 1890, 13 July 1890 (NLI, Headfort Papers, MS 25,369).   37 Teck lived off his wife's money (she was a descendant of George III), and they had to flee to the continent in 1883 to escape their debts.

Boys stood at the roadside shouting 'up the Mahdi!', the killers of General Gordon at Khartoum.[38]

For guests of this status, the authorities helpfully stepped in to provide some sense of occasion:

> At Kilmeadan Railway Station extensive preparation had been made for the Royal Reception. The Station was decorated with flags, flower, festoons and garlands and a large awning was erected at a point where it was arranged that the Royals would alight. There were a large number of soldiers and police present. There were up to two hundred people on the platform of the station. There was a military escort in waiting consisting of a squadron of the 21st Hussars under Captain Montague, a detachment of Waterford artillery under Captain Cuffe and a large force of Police under County Inspector Owen, and District Inspectors Milling and Higgins. Mr Connington, the Station Master had everything in admirable order. A large crowd of local people greeted the Royals in respectful silence on the railway bridge. The Royal party were taken to Curraghmore in Lord Waterford's carriage, drawn by two grey horses.[39]

It is difficult to establish the extent to which people were invited to country houses because of *what* they were rather than *who* they were. Henry Laughlin at Castle Hyde, in common with many big house owners, entertained hunts en masse; but more exotically in a notable coup he managed to bag the entire Boston Symphony Orchestra when it visited Ireland in 1956.[40] Glaslough has a governess or two in its visitors' book,[41] and a striking entry at Emo shows one Henry Eacrett, 'a local name belonging to farmers and carpenters', on 13 September 1890.[42] Here was a serious outlier, and how Eacrett came to leave his signature is a mystery. It could be held that the earls of Portarlington exhibited some elements of collecting 'whats', or titles, rather than 'whos' or individuals, in their accumulation of minor royals and near royals, and the occasional lord lieutenant or two.[43] That may have led to a certain disengagement with the whole process of collection. The chronicler of Emo, Stocks Powell, was perhaps correct when he wrote that the Portarlingtons' 'encounter with royalty, and royalty's with them were sporadic, non-specific, and with no major significance to either party'.[44]

---

38 Bence-Jones, *Twilight of the ascendancy*, p. 65. 39 *Waterford News*, 19 Apr. 1885. For 'respectful silence' probably read 'hostile indifference'. 40 Terence Dooley, '"It was like a scene from the ball in *Gone with the wind*": social life in Castle Hyde, 1931–88' in Terence Dooley and Christopher Ridgway (eds), *The Irish country house: its past, present and future* (Dublin, 2015), p. 157. 41 Glaslough visitors' book, 29 July–16 Sep. 1927 (Dulcie E. Swinford). 42 Emo Court visitors' book, 13 Sep. 1890 (NLI, Portarlington Papers, MS 42,100). 43 George FitzClarence in 1870; the duke of Connaught in 1876; the duke of Marlborough in 1879; Aubrey FitzClarence in 1891 – Stocks Powell, *The royal palace of Emo*, pp 24, 72, 76. 44 Stocks Powell, *The royal palace of Emo*, p. 25.

Building collections of visitors in the Irish country house 185

8.2 Iris Murdoch at Bowen's Court, 1956 (Noreen Butler).

One-off specimens or small parties were a lot more intriguing. Philosopher and novelist (and self-declared Irishwoman) Iris Murdoch stayed at Bowen's Court in 1956. It seems that this was one instance where Bowen felt that she might find her invited guest difficult to deal with: 'an Existentialist – I feared she might be gaunt, scornful, unaccommodating or bleak'. As it turned out, Murdoch showed a touching vulnerability with regard to her impending marriage to John Bayley, and Bowen 'after all very much did enjoy her being here'.[45] Wits and conversationalists were always popular. The Leslies entertained Oliver St John Gogarty at Glaslough on four occasions between 1918 and 1936; he stayed for two days each time.[46] Gogarty was a serial visitor to country houses: writing poetically of Dunsany Castle, he 'found there pleasant chambers filled with song'.[47]

45 Glendinning with Robertson, *Love's civil war*, p. 244. 46 Glaslough visitors' book, 4–5 Oct. 1918; 30–1 Aug. 1919; 6–8 Nov. 1927; 20–1 Sep. 1936. 47 Oliver St J. Gogarty, 'Dunsany Castle'; also Oliver St J. Gogarty, *The green book: writings on Irish Gothic, supernatural and*

Socially acceptable Catholic priests occasionally feature at house parties. Lady Portarlington (a Catholic) entertained Catholic bishops at Emo in the 1880s.[48] In 1903, parish priest and novelist Canon Sheehan was at Lord Castletown's Doneraile Court in County Cork in the company of American author Oliver Wendell Holmes.[49] Sheehan was urbane and well-read. As was Father Healy, a socialite Catholic priest often found at country houses, and who stayed at Headfort House between 13 and 19 November 1892, where other guests included Sir West and Lady Ridgeway, the duchess of Abercorn and the earl and countess of Kilmorey.[50]

Unlike some who more carefully curated their guest lists, the Leslies at Glaslough exhibited a seriously eclectic approach. The entries in their visitors' book covering the period of the first and second baronets' lifetimes (1871 to 1944) belie their rather conventional lives as landlords and military men. The book provides revealing vignettes about how the guests viewed their stay, as well as placing their own characters within the house's purview. Playwright Lennox Robinson stayed at Glaslough, and presumably knew the form. In his 1926 play *The Big House* he has British officer Captain Montgomery Despard – only a guest at the eponymous house for a day and two nights – demonstrating an accidental acuity about the house and its place in the landscape of Irish identity, when he divines that the house (and how it is run) is not typical of the generality of gentry residences.[51] Perhaps reflecting cultural shifts, in 1918 one visitor to Glaslough wrote in Irish, as did another (Celticist Robin Flower) in 1931. Between 1916 and 1963, guests included such as Sir Peter Scott the naturalist; artists Sir John Lavery and the lesser-known Frank Wilson; and poets W.B. Yeats and John Betjeman. Basil Brooke (later Stormont prime minister), recently elected an MP in the Northern Ireland Parliament, stayed between 2 and 4 December 1930, narrowly missing the governor-general of the Irish Free State, James McNeill, two days later, who signed himself in Irish and English.[52] Alice Milligan, Methodist advanced nationalist and writer, was an exotic guest in October 1917.[53]

---

fantastic literature, no. 10 (Samhain 2017), p. 99.   **48** Stocks Powell, *The royal palace of Emo*, p. 53 (bishop of Kildare and Leighlin); p. 59 (bishop of Kerry).   **49** D.H. Burton (ed.), *Holmes-Sheehan correspondence: letters of Justice Oliver Wendell Holmes, jnr. and Canon Patrick Augustine Sheehan* (New York, 1993), pp 9–10.   **50** Headfort visitors' book, 13–19 Nov. 1892. See also James Healy, *Memories of Father Healy of Little Bray* (London, 1904), pp 309–10.   **51** Murray (ed.), *Selected plays of Lennox Robinson*, pp 141–2.   **52** Glaslough visitors' book, entries for 19–20 Sep. 1919 (Scott); 14 Sep. 1926 (Yeats); 4–5 Aug. 1929 (Lavery); 4–6 Jan. 1930, 6–9 Dec. 1930 and 25 Apr. 1940 (Robinson); 8–10 Sep. 1931 (Flower); 18–21 Apr. 1941 (Betjeman); 6–9 Dec. 1930 (McNeill).   **53** Glaslough visitors' book, 19 Oct. 1917. For Milligan's strange, peripatetic life, see Catherine Morris, *Alice Milligan and the Irish cultural revival* (Dublin, 2013).

CATALOGUING AND CLASSIFYING

How could a collection of guests – by definition ephemeral – be marked and recorded? In the case of inanimate objects, their permanent presence in the house was a self-evident record exemplified by such as trophies of big game hunts (at Sandringham, for instance); cabinets of coins; sculpture galleries (as at Petworth in Sussex) and libraries. In the country house visitors' books were the sturdy records of the presence of guests and the holding of parties. The solidity and physical size of some of these bore testament to their evidentiary importance. Those for Dromoland Castle, Emo and Glaslough – residence of the Leslie baronets of County Monaghan – were massive volumes.[54] Those for Vevay House near Bray, County Dublin, and Castle Hyde were more modest tomes.[55] All were kept carefully. In the case of Dromoland and Glaslough, these books were more than just a list of names – they acted as records of the gatherings there, emphasizing social events as well as characters, often supplemented with photographs of parties, anniversaries, children and dogs: as guestbooks they begin to morph into scrapbooks.[56] Here is where a later visitor leafing idly through the book could be suitably impressed (or maybe otherwise) by those who had preceded her, and where she could bask in the reflected glory of being among acceptable guests. She could, in turn, add her individual presence to the parade of ghostly inhabitants in the pages.

Visitors' books were chronicles of a generic country house social discipline. Since convention dictated that guests would never write criticisms of the hospitality afforded them, complimentary comments always have to be seen through the prism of politeness and etiquette.[57] However, the intensity of arrivals and departures can go some way towards gauging the enjoyment (or otherwise) of visiting, as can the frequency of repeat visits – Gogarty and Robinson at Glaslough are examples – which indicated that accepted and acceptable guests were not to be lightly discarded. Novelists and poets from Maria Edgeworth to John Banville have usefully picked up on this trope; in Elizabeth Bowen's *The last September* the 'agitation of greeting' was often matched by an agony of goodbyes.[58] In the novel, the Montmorencys' arrival at Danielstown in a veritable 'moment of happiness, of perfection' is countered by Mrs Trent's leaving Lady Naylor after a very short visit – 'they sighed at each other their resignation to parting'.[59] Applying the 'collections' trope to Bowen's novel means seeing it, in effect, as the story of a series of acquisitions (arrivals) and disposals (departures).

---

54 NLI, MS 14,500 (Dromoland Papers); MS 42,100 (Emo, Portarlington Papers); MSS 49,495/2/169–70 (Glaslough, Leslie Papers). **55** NLI, MS 34,975 (Vevay House); photostat of Castle Hyde visitors' book (Prof. Terence Dooley). **56** For an example of a scrapbook see Maeve O'Riordan, 'Lady Castletown's scrapbook: making memories for leisure' in Terence Dooley and Christopher Ridgway (eds), *Sport and leisure in the Irish and British country house* (Dublin, 2019), pp 198–216. **57** Headfort, Dromoland and Glaslough visitors' books. **58** Bowen, *The last September*, p. 7. **59** Ibid., pp 7, 205.

8.3 Glaslough House visitors' book, *c.*1930, by artist Frank Wilson (National Library of Ireland, MS 49,495/2/170).

One of these is terminal – the death of soldier Gerald Lesworth, who is killed in an ambush; and another is, ultimately, the house itself, when it is destroyed by its 'executioners'.[60] Visitors were often reluctant to leave, as for example depicted by Frank Wilson's sketch in the Glaslough visitors' book, *c.*1930, on his departure from the Leslies' generous hospitality:[61] Wilson's sketch typified a sort of sentimental nostalgia for place, similar to Gillian Bence-Jones' poetical lauding of Drishane (home of the Somervilles in south-west County Cork) as 'Wrapped in a gentle Georgian dream'; and echoed in Francis Warner's words about Castle Leslie:

> wherever I may be,
> All will come back; the laughter, lake, the rain,
> This overflowing, peace-grown memory.[62]

FRAMING AND DISPLAYING

Framing and display are important parts of the collecting culture. For visitors, the big houses themselves performed the function of galleries and display cabinets. An extreme example of this was the earl of Kingston's version of a collector's bespoke cabinet – the extraordinary Mitchelstown Castle in County Cork, started in 1823, and built explicitly for a visit by King George IV. Trollope,

---

60 Ibid., p. 206. 61 Glaslough visitors' book, 1916–63. 62 Gillian Bence-Jones, 'Drishane' in *Ostrich Creek: Tom and other survivors* (Cheshire, 1999), p. 23; Francis Warner, 'Castle

in *Castle Richmond*, has a thinly disguised description of the pile as 'huge, ungainly and uselessly extensive'. He captured its alien presence in the landscape – its 'great hall door opens out upon a flat, bleak park, with hardly a scrap around it which courtesy can call a lawn',[63] although one 1825 description was kinder – 'the Mansion presents a magnificent appearance'; it 'harmonizes with the surrounding landscape, and gives a dignity to the scene'.[64]

Designed by the Pain brothers, Mitchelstown was a neo-Gothic fancy of immense proportions, consciously modelled on Windsor Castle. Everything about it was on a grand scale. The cost was enormous, variously estimated at between £100,000 and £220,000 (many tens of millions now). It was erected in two years, with the employment of hundreds of workmen.[65] The castle was run lavishly, even for the spendthrift aristocracy of the south of Ireland. This was emphatically a house for entertaining – there were parties, balls, vast quantities of plate, liveried footmen, large chandeliers, and great chefs (one was young Claridge, later of London hotel fame).[66] It bankrupted the estate and contributed to Kingston's eventual insanity.[67]

The earls of Portarlington lived at Emo Court, Queen's County (County Laois), a magnificent neoclassical house designed by James Gandon and touted for a time as a possible royal residence for the prince of Wales if he were to become viceroy. While the journal kept by the second earl covering the period 1816–33 shows very few visitors (and those who did turn up could hardly be called stellar),[68] the third and fourth earls were the Irish equivalents of William Vanderbilt or Andrew Carnegie in terms of wealth.[69] They had the financial clout to aim high; but the third earl, Henry Dawson-Damer (1822–89), may have been driven by deeper psychological motives. According to his successor he was 'diminutive and fussy' and seemed to suffer from a sort of inferiority-superiority complex; on his English properties it was alleged by one of his descendants that he was unpopular.[70] At Emo Court 'he lived like a king'[71] and entertained appropriately. For instance on 25 and 26 January 1872 he hosted a glittering

---

Leslie' in *Poetry of Francis Warmer* (Philadelphia, 1970), p. 41.   **63** Anthony Trollope, *Castle Richmond*, 3 vols (London, 1860), i, pp 5–6.   **64** John Neale and Thomas Moule, *Views of the seats of noblemen and gentlemen, in England, Wales, Scotland, and Ireland* (London, 1825), n.p.   **65** Mr and Mrs S.C. Hall, *Hall's Ireland*, ed. M. Scott (London, 1984), pp 1, 40; R.D. King-Harman, *The Kings, earls of Kingston* (Cambridge, 1957), p. 82; [N.L. Beamish], *Peace campaigns of a cornet*, 2 vols (London, 1829), ii, p. 33.   **66** *Cork Constitution*, 12 Dec. 1829; King-Harman, *The Kings, earls of Kingston*, pp 82–3.   **67** *Cork Constitution*, 27 July 1833; David Murphy, 'King, George', *DIB*, v, pp 202–4.   **68** John Stocks Powell, *'Shot a buck ...': the Emo estate, 1798–1852*, Documents of Portarlington 3 (Portarlington, 1998).   **69** For the great American collectors of the nineteenth and early twentieth centuries, see Michaël Vottero, 'To collect and conquer: American collections in the gilded age', at journals.openedition.org/transatlantica/ 6492, accessed 20 Apr. 2019.   **70** John Bateman, *Great landowners of Great Britain and Ireland* (London, 1883), p. 364, does not list the earl as possessing property outside Ireland, but there is a listing for lands in Dorset (2,295 acres) by Captain Lionel Dawson-Damer (Bateman, *Great landowners*, p. 118).   **71** Stocks Powell, *The royal palace of Emo*, p. 16.

gathering of titled aristocracy comprising Lords Spencer, Hartington, Langford, Antrim, De Vesci, Clonmell, Ormonde, Cloncurry and Offaly.[72]

It was not always necessary to have the magnificence of an Emo Court or a Mitchelstown Castle as a 'display case'. Not far away from the castle was Elizabeth Bowen's plain mansion, Bowen's Court, where, reflecting her cultural and social predilections, the writer collected an idiosyncratic mix of intellectual and literary types at various house parties between the 1930s and 1950s.[73] Here she lived a somewhat decayed existence – in 1934 novelist Virginia Woolf described Bowen and her husband as 'keeping up a ramshackle kind of state, dressing for dinner and so on'.[74] Yet despite a deficiency in decent sanitation and a general shabbiness, guests did not seem to be deterred – or at least those who inhabited Elizabeth's *demi-monde*.[75]

Castle Hyde, near Fermoy, County Cork, was grander than Bowen's Court, but in a somewhat similar condition of disrepair. Acquired by American publisher Henry Laughlin in 1931, its top floor and basement were uninhabitable. To camouflage the state of the building inventiveness was the order of the day: huge flower arrangements were utilized to hide the lack of pictures and the cracks in the walls.[76] Unlike Lords Kingston, Ormonde and Listowel, who clearly had specific targets for acquisition, Laughlin's aim was more scatter-gun than rifle. Specializing in 'his people' – 'if you are travelling back to the USA through Ireland why not come to Castle Hyde?'[77] – the visitors' book shows that the vast majority of guests were from the eastern part of the USA. John Montague's words might have been written for Castle Hyde:[78]

> I dwell in this leaky Western castle.
> American matrons weave across the carpet,
> Surefooted as camels, and less useful.

Its general decrepitude might have held some attractions for those seeking a sort of Gothic descendancy experience but twentieth-century Americans abroad liked their creature comforts (William Randolph Hearst's St Donat's Castle in Wales had thirty bathrooms[79]). Like Bowen's Court, Castle Hyde's ablutionary plumbing was in a parlous state. Curiously, though, none of this seems to have put off guests. Despite the Castle's dampness, its alarming cracks and a gentle slide towards the river Blackwater, Laughlin collected a broad-based and impressive list of guests, including Lady Mary Bowes-Lyon (sister of Queen

---

72 Ibid., p. 58; Emo Court visitors' book.   73 Glendinning, *Bowen*, p. 109.   74 Woolf to Vanessa Bell, in Nigel Nicholson (ed.), *The sickle side of the moon: the letters of Virginia Woolf, 1932–1935* (London, 1979), pp 299–300, quoted in Lee, *Bowen*, pp 37, 232–3. Bowen wrote of her Irish life being 'more than a bit ramshackle' (18 Jan. 1953) – Glendinning with Robertson, *Love's civil war*, p. 202.   75 Glendinning with Robertson, *Love's civil war*, p. 133n. 76 Dooley, 'Castle Hyde', p. 157.   77 Ibid., pp 157–8.   78 John Montague, 'Dowager' in *Collected poems* (Oldcastle, 1995), p. 268.   79 Tinniswoood, *The long weekend*, p. 284.

Elizabeth, the wife of George VI); George Putnam, the publisher; and Burton Holmes, a pioneering American film-maker.[80] After a hiatus in the 1940s, when the house was commandeered by the Irish Army, the guests he attracted continued to be wonderfully wide-ranging – actor and dancer Fred Astaire; Lord Moran, Winston Churchill's physician; Sybil Connolly, fashion designer; and of course his neighbour Elizabeth Bowen.[81]

To be aesthetically pleasing, collections – and individual objects – often require framing, most obviously in the case of paintings. People, framed within an occasion, are in effect animated portraits, beautified by their setting and occasionally adding life and glamour to that setting. As at one end of the scale small art medals are much enhanced by cases, so at the other are monumental sculptures placed in imposing galleries or set in landscaped parkland. The frame is not just a container; its aesthetic function also serves as an introduction for the observer or connoisseur. It creates an effect that is both separate from, and complementary to, that being framed. Thus the act of visiting the country house had its rituals of entrance and arrival that framed the visitors, measuring their status and importance. In the fictional televised world of Downton Abbey, very important people – not only family but staff too – were placed on parade at the entrance, in the manner of a guard of honour. In Bowen's novel *A world of love*, the opposite is the case. The guests on arrival are left to greet each other on the steps of the castle,[82] reflecting the informality of hostess Lady Latterly – or possibly that she did not set much store by any of them. When Americans call at the big house in Jennifer Johnston's *The gates*, the Major will not step outside to greet them. That was a job for the one remaining servant in this disintegrating house.[83] Doubly alien, they are not only strangers, but *American* strangers.

ARRANGING AND CURATING

The essence of any collection lies in its arrangement. For country house guests their host had to be expert in making sure that they matched harmoniously and could be carefully managed or choreographed correctly to provide interest and entertainment. Prince Arthur, duke of Connaught's visit to Emo Court on 9 December 1876 coincided with that of Sir John and Lady Leslie – Sir John was related to Lord Portarlington.[84] From a host's point of view the circumstances cannot have been without peril – the duke was seriously sweet on Sir John's wife. Such delicate situations required a sure touch; not every hostess could hope to get her ducks in an ordered and well-behaved row. An indiscreet Lady

80 Dooley, 'Castle Hyde', p. 157.   81 Ibid., pp 160–3. All this speaks to Laughlin's apparent desire – not uncommon among Americans living in the interwar British Isles – to be 'lord of the manor'; Dooley, 'Castle Hyde', p. 157.   82 Bowen, *A world of love*, p. 73.   83 Jennifer Johnston, *The gates* (London, 1974), p. 119.   84 Stocks Powell, *The royal palace of Emo*, p. 72.

Londonderry nearly caused an unpleasant incident at a house party at Mount Stewart when she told another guest – Edward Carson – that Daisy Fingall thought he had 'an awful face'.[85] Despite her reputation for sociability, Elizabeth Bowen's parties 'did not always work for all of the guests, who tended to be mixed indiscriminately; sometimes one could find no one to talk to'.[86]

Interlopers could also upset delicate social and personal balances. Occasionally, boarders had to be repelled. The fictional Irish detective who has to infiltrate the big house in John Banville's novel *Snow* is an unsettling intruder to its inhabitants because he too, unusually for an Irish policeman, is a Protestant. He is there to help in solving the gruesome murder of a Catholic priest in the house; but he is also the family's enemy, as he proceeds to uncover uncomfortable secrets.[87] Likewise, in Bowen's novel *The last September* the British Army officers' wives are 'vaguely but unmistakably frozen off on the steps of Danielstown'[88] by the house's Lady Naylor – even though their husbands are there to protect the Irish gentry families and preserve their political connectivity with Britain.

In real life, though, hangers-on could not be so easily kept out. Philosopher Isaiah Berlin was at a Bowen's Court party in 1935. When two undergraduates arrived unexpectedly to pay homage to the great man, apparently they were acceptable since they were of Bowen's (and Berlin's) world. But they brought a ditzy and sharply iconoclastic blonde friend with them, who set little store by either Bowen or another distinguished visitor, historian Veronica Wedgwood. The blonde lady, almost insolent to Wedgwood, did not impress Bowen who was provoked into waspishly remarking that 'Some people really ought to be left in the car with the dogs.'[89] Bowen's husband, Alan Cameron, was often much kinder to these brought-alongs – he probably found them easier to talk to than Bowen's literary friends.[90]

One of the principal satisfactions to be gained from object collecting is to place them within a structure of reference, to curate a relationship between them, or groups of them. In country houses, this can be observed in how collections of guests were put together. Hunting and shooting parties probably best exemplified the common group idea. At Dromoland in the early 1890s sporting guests accounted for a significant proportion of Lord Inchiquin's annual hospitality.[91] In November 1891, one such party was a wholly north Cork

---

85 Bence-Jones, *Twilight of the ascendancy*, p. 74.   86 Glendinning, *Bowen*, p. 103.   87 John Banville, *Snow* (London, 2020); see perceptive reviews in the *New York Times*, 5 Oct. 2020 at nytimes.com/2020/10/05/books/review/john-banville-snow.html and the *Financial Times*, 21 Oct. 2020, ft.com/content/3908cac1-6cc8-4f34-86af-66c242b116a6, accessed 28 Apr. 2021. J.B. Priestley's play *An inspector calls* (1945) has a similar construction, with the policemen in both cases represented as being a sort of 'avenging angel'.   88 Glendinning, *Bowen*, p. 203.   89 Ibid., *Bowen*, pp 103–4.   90 Ian d'Alton, '"My name is Alan Charles Cameron": The Farahy address, 9 September 2007', *Irish Review*, 40–1 (Winter 2009), p. 174; Glendinning, *Bowen*, p. 105.   91 Showing the interweaving of the gentry's social fabric, Lord Headfort

affair – Aldworths, Purdon Cootes and Listowels – with a careful record of the day's kill also entered into the visitors' book.[92] Tennis was always a popular excuse for day visits where sport could be supplemented by gossip, flirting and trysts.[93] And there were few country houses in either Britain or Ireland without some sort of tennis court.[94]

Forming any collection of guests, no matter how well-curated, always held an element of risk. 'Fast' guests were a potential problem, especially when quantities of drink were involved. At a house-party at Castle Bernard, County Cork, Mrs Sadlier-Jackson was dumped, as a prank, fully clothed into a bath – it was jokingly claimed that her subsequent language heated the water. Dorothea Conyers shocked her hosts and other guests at a party when she smoked after dinner.[95] On 7 September 1948 Elizabeth Bowen reported to her lover Charles Ritchie that 'The house party goes on well: everybody seems very happy and harmonious';[96] but it was not always thus. Her parties sometimes seemed to have had the potential to turn out like an Agatha Christie novel – marked not by murder but by social mayhem. Her more bohemian guest list, often with louche characters and loose morals, was doubtless a factor. But she was in good company; it has been written that 'The great nocturnal pastime of the country-house party was sex.'[97]

Thus it was that one Bowen's Court house party in 1936 went awry. Present were writer and beauty Rosamond Lehmann, and Oxford scholar Isaiah Berlin, with two of his undergraduates who would later shine – Con O'Neill, diplomat, and Stuart Hampshire, philosopher. Architectural historian John Summerson, solicitor Michael Gilmour and Bowen's cousin Noreen Colley made up the party. Finally, Welsh journalist Goronwy Rees, then assistant editor at the *Spectator*, turned up late. Rees, much younger than the other guests, arrived, in Berlin's phrase, 'like the Toreador in *Carmen*', and soon had the entire house party in chaos. Young, attractive, oozing sex appeal and knowing it, he had been invited by Bowen in the hope of kindling something between the two of them. Bowen, on this occasion, would have failed the Oakpark test: to remain a hostess who 'lets you REST'. It might have seemed a clever and calculated move on Bowen's part to ask Rees to her house and, hopefully, inveigle him into her bed, but she had miscalculated.

attended shooting parties in Dromoland; Grania O'Brien, 'The visitors book', *The Other Clare*, 33 (2009), p. 53. **92** In 1892, the guest list was widened in scope and numbers – ten, including Lord Shaftesbury – and in 1893, fourteen. In 1921 no shoots were allowed, and it seems that no more took place on the estate; O'Brien, 'The visitors book', p. 51; also Dromoland visitors' book, entries for 2/3 Nov. 1891, 1 Nov. 1892, 2 Nov. 1893. **93** Bowen, *The last September*, pp 35–53. **94** Tinniswoood, *The long weekend*, pp 105, 147, 203. **95** Bence-Jones, *Twilight of the ascendancy*, p. 98. **96** Glendinning with Robertson, *Love's civil war*, p. 134. **97** Tinniswood, *The long weekend*, p. 284. He goes on to chronicle the carry-on in English country houses in the 1920s and 1930s, pp 284–8. See also Molly Keane's novels *Devoted ladies* (1934) and *Loving and giving* (1988).

Something did indeed kindle, but it turned out to be not with Bowen but with Rosamond Lehmann. Bowen did not take kindly to what she described as 'the prosecution of a love-affair so ruthless that it crashed across the sensibility and dignity of everyone else here', and in Victoria Glendinning's colourful phrase, 'Elizabeth suffered, and she made Goronwy suffer'.[98] If this is an example of someone not playing the expected part, or acting as a rogue piece in the collection, the fictional world too picks up similar stories of confounded expectations. Somerville and Ross in the 'Irish R.M.' stories relate what happened when Major Yeates invited an old college chum, the politician Leigh Kelway, to stay. Condescending and patronizing in a particularly irritating English way and wanting to 'master the brogue', Kelway leads Yeates to realize that his friend had changed since student days: 'I had at the end of three days arrived at the conclusion that his society, when combined with a note-book and a thirst for statistics, was not what I used to find it at Oxford.'[99]

CONCLUSION

Observing country house visiting through the prism of collecting goes some way towards interpreting the purpose and rationale of the phenomenon. But it is not an all-encompassing conceptual framework. The evidence in some visitors' books suggest some degree of conscious collecting: for those who stayed at Emo Court, and to a lesser extent Dromoland, Headfort and Glaslough, and at the more modest Vevay House near Bray, County Wicklow, the hosts seem to have made the entries for their guests, as if asking visitors to record their stay themselves was somehow vulgar.[100] Most of Vevay's visitors were family and close friends. It remains the case that the sociable life was what drove many to entertain in the Irish country house, and what determined the guest list was not necessarily entertaining the great and the good just to show off.

Irish country houses were alien in the landscape; William Trevor's 'uneasiness of possession' always haunted these residences in a way it did not for their Scottish and English equivalents.[101] Over the course of the nineteenth century the house grew ever more important as a sanctuary for the gentry in their troubled search for identity. Usually regarding Ireland as, in Joseph Hone's phrase, 'a country, rather than as a nation', the gentry increasingly 'turned to geography in the attempt at patriotization'.[102] Largely centred on the big house, this was a congenial and secure course for them. As a social elite they relished the

---

98 Selina Hastings, *Rosamond Lehmann* (London, 2002), pp 172–3; Glendinning, *Bowen*, pp 113–16; Lee, *Bowen*, p. 116.   **99** Somerville and Ross, *Experiences of an Irish R.M.*, pp 57–8. **100** Vevay visitors' book, 1901–3.   **101** William Trevor, 'Introduction' in Potterton, *Rathcormick*, p. xiii.   **102** J.M. Hone, 'Five strains', *The Bell*, 2:6 (Sept. 1941), p. 26; Declan Kiberd, *Inventing Ireland* (Dublin, 1996), p. 107.

exclusivity and otherness that it represented – exemplified by an interior gathering of the favoured few among their own kind. Those who visited also played their part as the outward and visible material sign of an uncertain inward and spiritual social grace.

There were those who 'visited incorrigibly'.[103] The Leslies and the Bandons (who feature heavily at Emo, Vevay, Dromoland and Glaslough in the period between 1880 and 1920) could be counted upon to be reliable. Knowing your guests well brought comfort. As she awaits her visitors, Lady Latterly, in Bowen's novel *A world of love*, startlingly declaims that 'Any moment, these bastards will be arriving!' – but it is said with affection.[104] The opposite was the case for the fictional Major Yeates anticipating the visitation of a 'coloured potentate' from the East, where trepidation is the dominant emotion.[105] Lord Inchiquin, on the other hand, probably coped capably with Ali Bin Salem bin Kalfasi, the Wali of Gazi (whose name in the visitors' book is signed in Arabic as well as in English), when he visited Dromoland in 1896.[106] Nevertheless, even in Dromoland the Wali of Gazi was both exotic and exceptional; the core of Inchiquin's collection of visitors lay in the local Clare, Limerick and north Cork gentry and aristocracy.[107] Value was placed upon people like those. They grounded the guest-list, providing a sense of continuity to country house life and a deep connection to an adamantine class structure that operated within an intricate and filigreed social network. The appreciation of wit, shared interests, and family and tribal connection could, and almost certainly did, trump the temporary trophies of unknowable Walis, feckless Tecks and peripheral FitzClarences:

> We never know when we go, when we are going
> We jest and shut the door;
> Fate following behind us bolts it,
> And we accost no more.[108]

---

103 Bowen, *The last September*, p. 81.   104 Bowen, *A world of love*, p. 78.   105 Somerville and Ross, *Experiences of an Irish R.M.*, p. 194.   106 Dromoland visitors' book, 14 Nov. 1878 (Churchill); 12 July 1896 (Gazi).   107 O'Brien, 'The visitors book', pp 51–4.   108 *The complete poems of Emily Dickinson, with an introduction by her niece, Martha Dickinson Bianchi* (Boston, 1924), poem 131.

'An antient seat of a gentleman of Wales': the place of the *plas* in Thomas Pennant's *Tour in Wales* (1778–83)

SHAUN EVANS

INTRODUCTION: PENNANT'S 'TOUR' AND THE COUNTRY HOUSE IN
HISTORIOGRAPHICAL CONTEXT

'I now speak of my native country.' So Thomas Pennant (1726–98) began his *A tour in Wales*, published in three parts between 1778 and 1783, reflecting on earlier journeys and knowledge accumulated over the course of his lifetime.[1] By this period, he had already established a European reputation as a naturalist, antiquarian and travel writer.[2] His *A tour in Wales* has been credited as 'the single most important textual influence upon English attitudes towards travel in Wales', with Pennant seen as the pioneer in a great outpouring of topographical literature on the country, which exerted a lasting influence on how the country was perceived and experienced by an influx of visitors from the late eighteenth century.[3] It earned for Pennant the accolade of 'father of Cambrian tourists'.[4] The insight he provides into the character of his 'native country' – a rich compendium of landscape, history, culture, built heritage, tradition and natural history – is perhaps unsurpassed for the period. Pennant's Wales is one where the *plas* – the Welsh country house – had an ubiquitous presence. They pepper his narrative: dozens of them feature across the six historical counties of north Wales (Anglesey, Caernarfon, Denbigh, Flint, Merioneth and Montgomery) and the adjoining English border regions which formed the focus of his observations.

1 Thomas Pennant, *A tour in Wales* (London, 1778); idem, *A journey to Snowdon* (London, 1781); idem, *Continuation of the journey* (London, 1783). A second edition, combining all three journeys in two volumes, with additions and corrections, was published as *A tour in Wales* in 1784. All references in this paper are taken from *Tours in Wales*, 3 vols (London, 1810). 2 For Pennant's career see Mary-Ann Constantine and Nigel Leask (eds), *Enlightenment travel and British identities: Thomas Pennant's tours in Scotland and Wales* (London, 2017); R. Paul Evans, 'The life and work of Thomas Pennant (1726–1798)' (PhD, University of Wales, 1993). The *Curious Travellers* website features an array of useful information on Pennant, his correspondence and published works: curioustravellers.ac.uk. 3 Shawna Lichtenwalner, *Claiming Cambria: invoking the Welsh in the Romantic era* (Newark, 2008), p. 97. See also Elizabeth Edwards, '"A galaxy of blended lights": the reception of Thomas Pennant' in Constantine and Leask (eds), *Enlightenment travel*, pp 141–59; Kathryn Jones, Carol Tully and Heather Williams, 'Travel writing and Wales', *Studies in Travel Writing* 18:2 (2014), pp 101–6. For European travel to Wales see Kathryn Jones, Carol Tully and Heather Williams (eds), *Hidden texts, hidden nation: (re)discoveries of Wales in travel writing in French and German (1780–2018)* (Liverpool, 2020). 4 R. Paul Evans, 'Thomas Pennant (1726–1798): "the

The place of the plas *in Thomas Pennant's* Tour in Wales

9.1 Title page of Pennant's *A tour in Wales*, vol. 1, 1784 (with thanks to Bangor University Archives and Special Collections, BUASC, Rare Book, X/AA 7 PEN).

For Pennant, the *plas* represented one of the core features of Wales, integrally connected to its history, culture and landscape – a physical link between past and present.

This centrality of the country house has tended not to feature as a major theme in the burgeoning scholarship centred on Pennant's *Tour*, nor has the Welsh context been considered in the growing corpus of literature focusing on travel and the country house.[5] This essay is an attempt to address these deficits.

Father of Cambrian tourists'", *Welsh History Review*, 13 (Jan. 1986), pp 395–418.   5 Jon

As Jon Stobart has noted, 'travel was something that placed the country house into social, spatial and cultural context'.[6] It is here argued that Pennant's *Tour* augments, and makes significant points of departure from, established historiographical assessments of the country house in eighteenth-century Wales, offering new insights into how the *plas* was imagined, constructed and perceived, and how it was connected, both culturally and physically, with the fabric of Wales.[7]

Pennant's impulse to travel, observe and collect information about Wales, and shape it into a readable form, was immediately informed by the success of his two published tours of Scotland of 1769 and 1772. His Welsh *Tour* was first thrust into public circulation in the decade prior to a period when warfare in continental Europe disrupted access to the Grand Tour.[8] Linda Colley sees the resultant 'internal tourism', involving unprecedented domestic exploration of 'the remotest parts of Britain' – including north Wales, the Highlands of Scotland and the Lake District – in search of antiquity, the sublime and picturesque, as making an important contribution to the expansion of British consciousness and cohesion among the ruling class.[9] Pennant, writing in English, helped to facilitate this external access to and engagement with Wales as a part of Britain.[10] But his celebratory depiction was unashamedly one of Welsh national distinctiveness. He was living and writing during a period of pronounced historical and cultural revival in Wales, what Prys Morgan has called 'an unprecedented outburst of interest in all things Welsh and highly self-conscious activity to preserve and develop them'.[11] Pennant's *Tour* was at the forefront of this movement to celebrate and reinvent Wales; to 'ransack the past and transform it with imagination, to create a new Welshness which would instruct, entertain, amuse and educate'.[12] In this respect, the impact of Pennant's

---

Stobart (ed.), *Travel and the British country house: cultures, critiques and consumption in the long eighteenth century* (Manchester, 2017); Jocelyn Anderson, *Touring and publicizing England's country houses in the long eighteenth century* (New York, 2018); Adrian Tinniswood, *The polite tourist: four centuries of country house visiting* (London, 1998). **6** Stobart, *Travel and the British country house*, p. 1. **7** The principal works on Welsh landed society in the eighteenth century are Philip Jenkins, *The making of a ruling class: the Glamorgan gentry, 1640–1790* (Cambridge, 1983); David Howell, *Patriarchs & parasites: the gentry of south-west Wales in the eighteenth century* (Cardiff, 1986); and Melvin Humphreys, *The crisis of community: Montgomeryshire, 1680–1815* (Cardiff, 1996). **8** James Buzard, 'The Grand Tour and after (1660–1840)' in Peter Hulme and Tim Youngs (eds), *The Cambridge companion to travel writing* (Cambridge, 2002), pp 37–52; Malcolm Andrews, *The search for the picturesque: landscape aesthetics and tourism in Britain, 1760–1800* (Aldershot, 1989). **9** Linda Colley, *Britons: forging the nation, 1707–1837* (New Haven, 1992), pp 172–4. **10** Mary-Ann Constantine and Nigel Leask, 'Introduction: Thomas Pennant, curious traveller' in Constantine and Leask (eds), *Enlightenment travel*, pp 2–4. **11** Prys Morgan, 'From a death to a view: the hunt for the Welsh past in the Romantic period' in Eric Hobsbawm and Terence Ranger (eds), *The invention of tradition* (Cambridge, 1983), pp 43–100, quote at p. 43. **12** For more on this theme see Prys Morgan, *The eighteenth-century renaissance* (Cardiff, 1981); Geraint Jenkins, *The foundations of modern Wales: Wales, 1642–1780* (Oxford, 1987), pp 386–426; Damian

writings on his fellow landowners *within* Wales should not be underestimated. Volumes of his works filled the shelves of Welsh country house libraries, influencing how landowners viewed their own family and local histories, the cultural significance of their country houses and estates, and the nature of their identification with Wales as an 'imagined community'.[13]

Pennant's picture of Wales also has historiographical significance. In the second half of the nineteenth century a powerful political campaign, spearheaded by a nationalist nonconformity, succeeded in presenting country houses and their occupants as somehow detached from Wales: enclaves of anglicization and Anglicanism that did not belong to the idealized picture of Welshness characterized by an imagined *gwerin* community – portrayed as continuously at odds with the gentry since the Act of Union of 1536 and 1543.[14] This nineteenth-century narrative of deep-seated social, cultural, political, religious and linguistic division in Welsh communities has occupied a pervasive presence in historiographical analyses of post-medieval Wales. For Pennant's age, Geraint H. Jenkins has concluded that the 'ruling landed classes severed themselves from native Welsh culture ... and were only too willing to lose the valuable culture bequeathed to them by their ancestors'.[15] Pennant's *Tour* contradicts this assertion. Furthermore, in their regional studies of Glamorgan, Montgomery and Merioneth, Philip Jenkins, Melvin Humphreys and Peter Roberts all observe degrees of 'demographic catastrophe' across the eighteenth century, which, they argue, fundamentally altered the composition and nature of traditional landed society, epitomized by the disappearance of long-established lineages of *uchelwyr* (gentry) from the countryside and an associated decline in Welsh cultural outlook.[16] While demonstrating awareness of, and occasional frustration with, the impacts of dynastic discontinuity and associated inheritance patterns (which affected ruling elites across all parts of Britain and Ireland), Pennant paints a very different picture of the cultural character of the

---

Walford Davies and Linda Pratt (eds), *Wales and the romantic imagination* (Cardiff, 2007); Mary-Ann Constantine, 'Beauty spot, blind spot: romantic Wales', *Literature Compass* 5:3 (2008), pp 557–90.   13 For Welsh country house libraries see Shaun Evans, 'Book cultures, gentry identities and the Welsh country house library: problems and possibilities for future research', *Welsh History Review* 31:1 (June 2022); Eiluned Rees, 'An introductory survey of 18th-century Welsh libraries', *Journal of the Welsh Bibliographical Society*, 10:4 (1971), pp 197–258; T. Lloyd, 'Country-house libraries of the eighteenth and nineteenth centuries' in Philip Jones and Eiluned Rees (eds), *A nation and its books: a history of the book in Wales* (Aberystwyth, 1998), pp 135–46.   14 This is discussed in Paul O'Leary, 'The languages of patriotism in Wales, 1840–1880' in Geraint Jenkins (ed.), *The Welsh language and its social domains, 1801–1911* (Cardiff, 2000), pp 533–60; Prys Morgan, 'The *Gwerin* of Wales – myth and reality' in Ian Hume and W.T.R. Pryce (eds), *The Welsh and their country* (Llandysul, 1986), pp 134–52; Matthew Cragoe, *Culture, politics and national identity in Wales, 1832–1886* (Oxford, 2004).   15 Jenkins, *Foundations*, p. 386.   16 Jenkins, *Glamorgan gentry*; Humphreys, *Montgomeryshire*; Peter Roberts, 'The decline of the Welsh squires in the eighteenth century', *National Library of Wales Journal*, 13 (1963–4), pp 157–73. See also Jenkins, *Foundations*,

eighteenth-century Welsh *plas*. In his *Tour*, country houses were celebrated as integral components of Wales: storehouses of an esteemed Welsh ancestral consciousness; one of the vital elements for articulating the distinctive character, history, culture, and identity of the country – and deemed as important as the ancient monuments and antiquities, historical characters and legends, landscape features, events, traditions, and myths that combined and intertwined to make up his multi-layered description of Wales.

The *Tour* highlights that along with parish churches, medieval castles and monastic ruins, country houses usually were among the most prominent structures in their localities. In some parts of the *Tour* country houses dominated Pennant's attention: from a viewpoint at Llanerch he described the 'charming view of the vale of Clwyd' in which 'churches and neat mansions enliven the scene'.[17] Along the north Wales coast the houses of Kinmel, Faenol Fawr, Bodelwyddan and Pengwern were highlighted as the key features in quick succession: Faenol Fawr, 'one of the best old houses in the county of Flint ... built in 1595 by John Lloyd'; Bodelwyddan, 'the seat of John Williams ... a purchase of his grandfather'; and Pengwern, 'an excellent new house built on the site of an old one'.[18] Pennant's description of Ystrad Alun, the area surrounding the town of Mold in Flintshire, was also packed with references to its country houses: 'a tract filled with numerous seats of gentlemen of independent fortunes, as yet not caught and absorbed in the gulphy vortex of our Leviathans', those great landowners who were swallowing up numerous smaller estates.[19] Fron, 'the seat of the ingenious reverend Richard Williams'; Leeswood, 'rising palace-like' and adorned with its 'magnificent gates'; Nerquis, 'a good old seat, built in 1638 by John Wynne', now the home of Robert Hyde 'who enjoys it with great hospitality'; Tower, where Pennant enjoyed the 'witty, the lively and agreeable conversation of William Wynne'; Pentrehobyn, 'a good old house built in 1540'; Coed-llai, 'the antient seat of my worthy relation Thomas Eyton'; Hartsheath, 'most beautifully situated'; Plas Teg, 'a singular house, belonging to the Trevors'; and Rhual, 'the pleasant seat of Thomas Griffith'.[20] Few houses of significance escaped Pennant's attention.

The prominence afforded to these places by Pennant reflects the influence they exerted in eighteenth-century society. They were the powerbases at the heart of landed estates – large and small – which adjoined and intermixed with one another to create a patchwork of interest and influence that enveloped much of the landscape described by Pennant. The structure of society underpinned by the *plas* and its surrounding estate ruled supreme. The owners of these places were the dominant force in the life of the country, capable of exerting influences that straddled local, regional, national and global concerns in areas as diverse as politics, law and order, defence, architecture, agriculture, music, literature,

pp 93–102, 261–72. **17** *Tours*, ii, p. 138. **18** *Tours*, iii, pp 162–5. **19** *Tours*, ii, p. 41.
20 Ibid., pp 29–58.

industry, empire and colonialism. There were very few areas of Wales covered by the *Tour* where country houses and their owners did not hold sway; an exception was Nant Eglwyseg, near Llangollen, which Pennant described as being 'chiefly inhabited (happily) by an independent race of warm and wealthy yeomanry, undevoured as yet by the great men of the country'.[21] His occasional references to the 'Leviathans' of the country provided evidence that Welsh landed society incorporated vast gradations in acreage, wealth and status. The occupants of Wales' country houses were a mixed group, including families of varying degrees of prosperity and indebtedness, descendants of the old *uchelwyr* and families who had more recently acquired their estates and houses through marriage, inheritance, or purchase. Notwithstanding this diversity, they were held together by bonds of landownership and status, and, in Pennant's portrayal, as representatives of the esteemed ancestral heritage affixed to their houses.

COMPILING THE 'TOUR': WELSH GENTRY CULTURE AND THE HERITAGE OF WALES

The esteem in which the *plas* was held by Pennant is perhaps unsurprising: he was part of this world. The Pennants of Downing and Bychton were long-established members of the Flintshire gentry. Though not of the same status as major landholding dynasties such as their parochial neighbours at Mostyn, they nevertheless bore all the hallmarks of a family of gentle status: a strong ancestral identity, myriad connections to other landowning families across Wales (Pennant regularly refers to kinsmen in the *Tour*), a record of office-holding in the county of Flint since the seventeenth century, an estate surveyed at just over 1,700 acres in 1772 and country houses in the parish of Whitford which physically symbolized a claim to local status and authority.[22] Pennant's *History of the parishes of Whiteford and Holywell* outlines the influence and role exerted by his ancestors within the locality over generations.[23] He inherited this patrimony on the death of his father in 1763. Thereafter, in his own words, he was the 'father of a family, landlord of a small but very numerous tenantry and a not inactive magistrate' as well as a naturalist, travel writer and antiquarian.[24] Appreciating Pennant's identity as a Welsh squire and landowner is critical for understanding his interpretation and depiction of his 'native country'.

This background not only induced him to paint the *plastai* (mansions) of Wales in a celebratory light; it permitted him unfettered entry to these places –

---

21 *Tours*, ii, p. 11.   22 R. Paul Evans, 'Thomas Pennant and the influences behind the landscaping of the Downing estate', *Flintshire Historical Society Journal*, 35 (1999), pp 57–84.   23 Thomas Pennant, *The history of the parishes of Whiteford and Holywell* (London, 1796), esp. pp 1–52 (hereafter Pennant, *History*).   24 Thomas Pennant, *The literary life of the late Thomas Pennant esq., by himself* (London, 1793), p. 35.

a degree of access that, from the complaints of antiquarians such as Evan Evans (*Ieuan Fardd*, 1731–88), may not have been automatically granted to writers from other sections of society.[25] This access to country houses and their owners played an integral role in the construction of the *Tour*.[26] Pennant's indebtedness to the squirearchal network of north Wales – his friends, relations, neighbours and fellow magistrates – is evinced in the advertisement for the first part of his *Tour*:

> I implore the aid of my countrymen to assist me in the attempt; and to favor me with the necessary materials ... I look up to my friends for history and anecdote latent among their papers; or references to our writers ... Among the gentlemen I am chiefly indebted to for information respecting the present work, I cannot pass unthanked, Philip Yorke Esq. of Erddig; John Mytton Esq. of Halston; Thomas Mostyn Esq. of the house of Trelacre; Peter Davies Esq. of Broughton; Kenrick Eyton Esq. of Eyton; Paul Panton Esq. of Bagilt; Lloyd Kenyon Esq. of Gredington; Mr Roger Kenyon of Cefn; to Owen Brereton Esq. I owe the loan of the curious antiquities found in his estate near Flint ... To the reverend Richard Williams of Fron, I am highly obliged for his poetical translations.[27]

This roll-call of country houses and their owners points to a much deeper body of correspondence and exploration within gentry libraries, which underpinned Pennant's descriptions of Wales and its localities, supplementing and clarifying his own field notes and the major contributions made by his faithful and learned travel companion Revd John Lloyd (1733–93).[28] As Paul Evans has shown, in the early 1770s Pennant composed a questionnaire for inclusion in the main north Wales (Chester) newspapers, so that local gentry and clergy could submit information about the history and antiquities of their parish – replicating a methodology used generations earlier by Edward Lhuyd (1660–1709) for the compilation of his *Archaeologia Britannica* (and following the practice in his earlier tours of Scotland).[29] The *Tour* was very much a collaborative endeavour. These research practices not only point to the significant interest in Welsh antiquities, history, genealogy, archaeology and manuscripts exhibited by landowners during this period, they also recognize the country houses of Wales as important repositories of Welsh cultural heritage.[30]

---

[25] Bethan Jenkins, *Between Wales and England: anglophone Welsh writing of the eighteenth century* (Cardiff, 2017), pp 150–1.   [26] This theme is discussed extensively in Evans, 'Cambrian tourists', pp 395–418.   [27] *Tours*, i, pp v–vi.   [28] R. Paul Evans, 'The Rev. John Lloyd of Caerwys (1733–93): historian, antiquarian and genealogist', *Flintshire Historical Society Journal*, 31 (1983–4), pp 109–24. Examples of Pennant's correspondence with other Welsh landowners are available at editions.curioustravellers.ac.uk/letters, accessed 26 Feb. 2023.   [29] Evans, 'Cambrian tourists', pp 404–5.   [30] This theme is advanced in Shaun Evans, 'Inventing the Bosworth tradition: Richard ap Hywel, the "King's Hole" and the Mostyn family image in the nineteenth century', *Welsh History Review* 29:2 (Dec. 2018), pp

Another important role that country houses played in Pennant's writings is that they very often framed his journeys. His *Tour* can be seen as a ride from country house to country house, visiting relations, friends, kinsmen and fellow landowners. Plas Gwyn, the seat of his friend, the antiquarian squire Paul Panton (1727–97), was used as the base for exploring Anglesey, which also included a visit to John Griffith (*c.*1732–76) at Carreglwyd.[31] Pennant stayed with his kinsman Peter Davies at Broughton while exploring the border region connecting Flintshire, Cheshire and Shropshire.[32] He was hosted at Bodfach and Gregynog during his journeys around Montgomeryshire with Bell Lloyd (d. 1793) and Arthur Blayney (1716–95) acting as guides for their estates, localities and territorial spheres of influence.[33] Blayney was praised as a 'good host, the best shower of a country I ever had the good fortune of meeting'; Pennant continued, 'Under his conduct I saw everything in the neighbourhood which merited attention'. Pennant was entertained 'for some days' by William Vaughan (1707–75) of Corsygedol during his explorations of Merioneth.[34] Hugh Griffiths (1724–95) of Brynodol provided 'a hospitable reception for two nights', allowing Pennant to explore Llŷn; and while staying at John Myddelton's seat of Gwaenynog, near Denbigh ('my headquarters for this neighbourhood'), Pennant 'rummaged over the family papers of this house'.[35]

These visits exhibited hospitality as one of the core virtues of the *plas*, perpetuating a strand of *uchelwriaeth* (gentility) traditionally praised by the Welsh bards who had in previous centuries enriched the cultural life of such houses with their poetic performances.[36] As well as providing good hospitality, entertainment and a more comfortable bed than the local inn, these country-house visits served a practical purpose. Pennant's vivid commentary on his own landed patch, his '*Milltir Sgwâr*' – as delineated in his *History of Whiteford and Holywell* – relied on his embeddedness in the area; he was part of the locality that he was attempting to describe. His visits to country houses across north Wales allowed him to tap into the knowledge and experience of the local landowner, whose family had occasionally resided there for centuries. Landowners like Arthur Blayney and William Vaughan – alongside the archives and collections of houses such as Gwaenynog, Hengwrt, Mostyn and Plas Gwyn – were viewed by Pennant as valuable repositories of 'anecdote'.[37]

218–53. **31** *Tours*, iii, pp 43–4, 55, 69. **32** *Tours*, i, p. 289. **33** *Tours*, iii, pp 175–6, 178, 184–5, 197–8. Pennant used a similar methodology in the compilation of his Scottish tours: see R. Paul Evans, '"A round jump from ornithology to antiquity": the development of Thomas Pennant's *Tours*' in Constantine and Leask (eds), *Enlightenment travel*, p. 23. **34** *Tours*, ii, pp 268–9. **35** Ibid., pp 174–6, 385–6. **36** Pennant discusses hospitality in *Tours*, ii, pp 242–3. For context see J. Gwynfor Jones, *Concepts of order and gentility in Wales, 1540–1640* (Llandysul, 1992). **37** For Pennant's own library see Eiluned Rees and Glyn Walters, 'The library of Thomas Pennant', *The Library*, 25:2 (June 1970), pp 136–49.

THE 'ANTIENT SEAT OF …': PENNANT'S PORTRAYAL OF THE 'PLAS'

Pennant used a variety of terms to describe the country houses of Wales: Bodidris, 'a large and antient place'; Chirk, an 'exalted pile'; Erddig, an 'elegant seat'; Gregynog, 'a most respectable old house'; Lleweni, with its 'magnificent old hall'; Pentrehobyn and Nanytclwyd, 'good old houses'; Plas Teg, 'a singular house'; Cadwgan, 'a very large old house'; and Plas Newydd, Anglesey, simply a 'mansion'.[38] His most common way of referring to these places was as 'the seat of' a particular family, frequently 'the *antient* seat of …' (as applied to Bodychan, Caer Gai, Corsygedol, Foxhall, Gwydir, Hafodunos, Mostyn, Nannau, Penrhyn, Rhiwlas).[39] The 'antient' designation is key to understanding Pennant's portrayal of these houses. They were built in a variety of architectural styles, from former medieval castles such as Chirk and Powis to sprawling mansions such as at Wynnstay and Lleweni, and smaller houses like Corsygedol and Pentrehobyn. These buildings were recognized as primary public statements of their owners' positions within the localities. Commenting on the principal houses in his own parish of Whitford, Pennant concluded that Mostyn gives the appearance of 'the seat of a gentleman of large fortune in antient times. In that of Bychton one of middling fortune. In that of the late Mr Parry of Merton one of small fortune.'[40] Despite significant differences in size and status, all three houses were recognized by Pennant as gentry residences. Judging by the length and nature of his descriptions, Pennant viewed Baron Hill, Chirk, Gwydir, Lleweni, Mostyn, Nannau, Penrhyn, Plas Newydd, Powis and Wynnstay as the chief houses of north Wales.[41]

What significance did Pennant attach to the Welsh country house? In the twentieth century especially – a period that witnessed the destruction, demolition or desertion of hundreds of houses – it was fashionable to interpret the importance of these places in terms of the 'loss' of their architectural splendour and the break-up of the rich treasures and collections they housed.[42] The significance attached to these places by Pennant is much more culturally, socially, and landscape orientated. The virtues of 'ancientness' and 'hospitality' have already been mentioned: principally, it was the ancestral heritage attached to the sites, and their position in the landscape, which Pennant celebrated in his portrayal of Wales. In his *Tour* the architectural character of Wales' country houses features only as a secondary concern.

Pennant was nevertheless interested in architecture, commissioning the Hawarden and Chester-based architect Joseph Turner (*c.*1729–1807) to provide

---

38 *Tours*, i, pp 366–70, 394, 396; ii, pp 16–17, 44–6, 144–8; iii, pp 18–19, 170.   39 *Tours*, i, p. 12; ii, pp 138, 177–8, 210, 220, 249–51, 268–9, 306–9; iii, pp 78, 87–100.   40 Pennant, *History*, p. 59.   41 *Tours*, i, pp 12–18, 366–70, 390–4; ii, pp 144–9, 249–51, 306–9; iii, pp 18–19, 42–3, 87–100, 209–14; Pennant, *History*, pp 53–98.   42 For the destruction of country houses in Wales, see Thomas Lloyd, *The lost houses of Wales: a survey of country houses in Wales demolished since c.1900* (2nd ed.; London, 1989).

plans for remodelling his own seat at Downing to achieve greater symmetry.[43] He also made insightful comments on the structure and configuration of Chirk, Gwydir, Penrhyn, Powis and Wynnstay, and included a lengthy account of the complex architectural evolution of Mostyn Hall in his local *History*, but his architectural remarks tended to be short: Broughton, 'a venerable wooden house'; Hanmer, 'a modern brick house'; Llanrhaeadr, 'partly ancient, partly rebuilt'; Brynkinallt, 'the house is of brick, built in 1619'.[44] He occasionally discussed regional architectural characteristics, such as the 'Roman H'-type houses that proliferated in the early seventeenth century, as well as distinctive structures: Tower, 'a true specimen' and the 'great regularity and simple grandeur' of Plas Teg, 'built in 1610 by Sir John Trevor'.[45] Richard Clough's 1560s show house at Bachygraig, Tremeirchion, was sufficiently 'singular' to merit detailed description.[46] He also applauded the improvements made to Plas Newydd, Anglesey, which had been 'altered to a castellated form, by the present owner'; the modifications recently made to Baron Hill by 'that elegant architect Mr Samuel Wyat[t]' (1737–1807); and the same architect's plans for 'restoring [Penrhyn] to its former lustre'.[47] Furthermore, the watercolours made by Pennant's draughtsmen, Moses Griffith (1749–1819) and John Ingleby (1749–1808), which illuminate the extra-illustrated copies of his *Tour*, are important sources for Welsh architectural history.[48] Pennant rarely discussed the interiors or collections of country houses. Exceptions to this are the detailed accounts of Mostyn and Downing included in his local parish *History*. The description of Mostyn – 'the mansion and its antient owners' – highlighted the rich ancestral heritage of the place: its 'great gloomy hall' with dais step, '*nen-bren*',[49] heraldic display, date inscriptions, stained glass, fireplaces, 'antient militia guns, swords and pikes; with helmets and breast-plates', 'funeral atchievements', 'spoils of the chaise', Roman busts, library, manuscripts and various antiquities.[50] The *Hirlas* drinking horn at Penrhyn, which had belonged to the esteemed Gruffydd family, was showcased in a similar manner.[51] Pennant also occasionally made use of family portraits and funerary monuments as vehicles for discussing recent Welsh history and biography: the exploits of Sir John Owen (1600–66) and Sir Thomas Myddleton (1586–66) during the Civil War, the mercantile career of Richard Clough (d. 1570), the scholarly achievements of Humphrey Llwyd (1527–68), the marriages of Katheryn of Berain (d. 1591) and the influence of Sir John

---

43 Evans, 'Downing estate', pp 57–84.   **44** *Tours*, i, pp 289, 291, 368–9, 375–7, 391–2; ii, pp 185, 306–9; iii, pp 209–14; Pennant, *History*, pp 53–98.   **45** *Tours*, ii, pp 42–6, 56–8; Pennant, *History*, p. 2.   **46** *Tours*, ii, pp 139–42.   **47** *Tours*, iii, pp 18–19, 42–3, 90.   **48** Donald Moore, 'Thomas Pennant's vision of the landscape', *Archaeologia Cambrensis*, 146 (1997), pp 138–77, esp. pp 154–61; idem, *Moses Griffith, 1747–1819* (Caernarfon, 1979). An extra-illustrated version of Pennant's *Tour* is available at library.wales/discover/digital-gallery/pictures/a-tour-in-wales, accessed 22 Feb. 2023.   **49** The principal central beam supporting the roof of the great hall; used as a metaphor in Welsh poetry for the lord of the house.   **50** Pennant, *History*, pp 53–98.   **51** *Tours*, iii, pp 91–9.

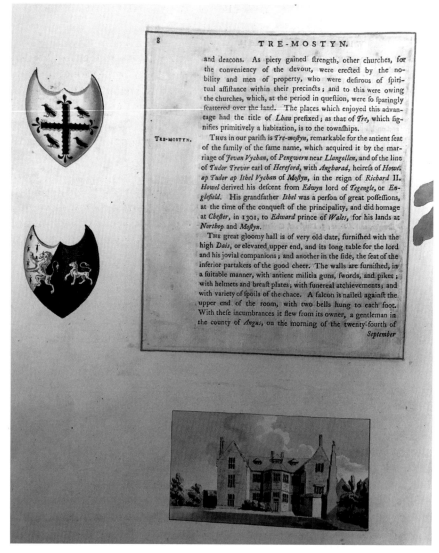

9.2 Extra-illustrated copies of Pennant's *Tour* are often augmented with sketches of Welsh country houses and coats of arms by Moses Griffith. This example shows Mostyn Hall in Flintshire and part of the Mostyn family's heraldic insignia which paraded their claimed descent from Tudur Trefor and Edwin Tegeingl (with thanks to Bangor University Archives and Special Collections, BUASC, Rare Book, X/AA 7 PEN).

Wynn (1553–1627) of Gwydir, for example.[52] The extra-illustrated versions of the *Tour* often include naive reproductions of these portraits by Moses Griffith.

52 *Tours*, i, pp 354–60, 364; ii, pp 140–3, 146–7, 155–6, 312–14.

CWM BYCHAN: ANCESTRAL HERITAGE, WELSH IDENTITY AND THE COUNTRY HOUSE

One of the best entry points for assessing the cultural value Pennant ascribed to country houses is his report of a visit to a small *plas* in Merioneth. While journeying from Corsygedol to Harlech, Pennant was encouraged by his travel companion, Revd John Lloyd, to make a deviation to visit one of Lloyd's relations 'in his antient territories of Cwm Bychan'.[53] Pennant described, in detail, the sublime route they made through 'a wild horizon of rocks and rocky mountains':

> Wind up a rocky stair-case road, and arrive full in sight of Cwm Bychan, embosomed with rocks of magnificent height. After a short ride, high above a lake of the same name, descend, and reach the house of the venerable Evan Llwyd, who, with his ancestors, boast of being lords of these rocks, at least since the year 1100.[54]

Pennant referred to 'the mansion' as 'a true specimen of an antient seat of a gentleman of Wales' and gave a full description of its setting:

> The territories dependent on the mansion, extend about four miles each way, and consist of a small tract of meadow, a pretty lake swarming with trout, a little wood, and very much rock; the whole forming a most august scenery. The naked mountains envelop his vale and lake, like an immense theatre. The meadows are divided by a small stream, and are bounded on one side by the lake; on the other, by his woods, which skirt the foot of the rocks, and through which the river runs, and beyond them tumbles from his heights, in a series of cataracts. He keeps his whole territory in his own hands; but distributes his hinds among the *Hafodtys*, or summer-dairy houses, for the conveniency of attending his herds and flocks: he has fixed his heir on another part of his estates. His ambition once led him to attempt draining the lake, in order to extend his landed property: but, alas! he gained only a few acres of rushes and reeds; so wisely bounded his desires, and saved a beautiful piece of water ... Stools and roots of firs, of vast size, are frequently found near the lake. Mr Llwyd observed one, with the marks of fire on it, which he used to repair the *Tyddyn y Traian*, or jointure-house of his family; an antient customary appendage to most of the Welsh houses of any note.[55]

[53] *Tours*, ii, pp 274–8.   [54] Ibid., p. 275.   [55] *Tours*, ii, pp 277–8.

Pennant proceeded to give the full 'British pedigree' of Evan Llwyd, eighteenth in descent from Bleddyn ap Cynfyn (d. 1075), 'prince of North Wales and Powys'. He wrote: 'I was introduced to the worthy representative of this long line, who gave me the most hospitable reception, and in the style of an antient Briton.'[56] What followed was a romanticized view of the traditional Welsh *uchelwr* and the life of a *plas* as in former days; 'here they have lived for many generations, without bettering or lessening their income; without noisy fame, but without any of its embittering attendants'.[57] Pennant was welcomed with ale and potent beer, to wash down the '*coch yr wden*' (hung goat) and the cheese, made from the milk of cow and sheep. He was shown the ancient family cup, made of a bull's scrotum, and commented on the '*cistiau styffylog*', or great oatmeal chests – the most remarkable pieces of furniture in the house – used to store provisions. While speaking with Mr Llwyd he was told of the family legend: 'Of this house was the valiant Dai Llwyd', the subject of a noted Welsh tune, addressed to him 'on occasion of his going with Jasper Tudor [1431–95] and Owen Lawgoch [d. 1378]' to fight Richard III (he did not recognize the chronological impossibility of this traditional feat).[58]

In this extensive account of Cwm Bychan we get to the nub of why *plastai* feature so prominently in the picture of Wales Pennant created and presented to the readers of his *Tour*. Everything around Cwm Bychan was synonymous with the house and its long lineage of owners, stretching back centuries. The landscape, livestock, food and drink, ancient cup, traditions, customs, place-names and legends were all inextricably connected to the family and its house; this part of Wales could only be understood with reference to the *plas* and its associated pedigree. It was this combination, the relationship between Evan Llwyd's ancestors and their house, which *made* this locality; determining its character, identity and history. Crucially, this process of 'place-making' was still taking shape, through the life and influence of Evan – the contemporary representative of Cwm Bychan.

What Pennant witnessed at Cwm Bychan was to a considerable degree extinct, or at least diluted, across other parts of Wales; it is a romanticized account of a survival from a bygone era. Tellingly, the report of Cwm Bychan flowed seamlessly into an explanation of 'antient hunting' practices, further augmenting the picture of traditional *uchelwriaeth*, or Welsh gentility.[59] In other parts of his *Tour*, Pennant was severely critical of the 'old' nature of the gentry in Wales, best encapsulated in his scathing remarks on fifteenth-century Eifionydd, when 'the feuds among the gentry filled the land with blood'.[60] Nevertheless, there are strong echoes of Pennant's celebration of the Llwyds and Cwm Bychan in his other descriptions of country houses across north Wales.

---

56 Ibid., p. 276.   57 Ibid., p. 276.   58 Ibid., pp 276–7.   59 *Tours*, ii, pp 278–82.   60 Ibid., pp 370–1 (see also pp 183, 232–4).   61 Ibid., pp 42, 268.

At Corsygedol, Pennant was similarly 'entertained ... for some days, in the style of an antient baron', and he described William Wynne of Tower as a gentleman 'who kept the patrimony derived from a long train of ancestors, without increase, yet without impair'.[61] *Plastai* were significant to Pennant – and for his picture of Wales – because they physically and symbolically embodied links between esteemed lineages and localities.

Ancestry was fundamental to Pennant's conceptualization of Welsh identity: 'Now let the whole Welshman arise in me!' he proclaimed, before proudly outlining his own descent from Tudur Trefor via Madoc ap Meilir.[62] In eighteenth-century England a small house like Cwm Bychan might have been degraded to the status of upland farmhouse, with Evan Llwyd perhaps admitted to the inferior rank of yeoman or freehold farmer. However, in Wales the ancestral heritage linking the house and lineage conferred gentry status on both. Therefore, Pennant so often referred to country houses – grand and modest – as the 'antient seat of' a particular family: they were perceived as symbols of continuity in their communities, which provided gateways into the antiquity and the essence of Wales. This is reflected in Pennant's concise account of Glynllifon, near Caernarfon.[63] Its significance to Pennant was that Cilmin Troed-Du, one of the so-called founders or patriarchs of the 'fifteen noble tribes of north Wales' and a supposed nephew of Merfyn Frych (d. 844), king of Gwynedd, had his residence on this spot. Plas Glynllifon was named after its situation beside a small river called the Llifon. The family who had lived there were the Glynnes, who took their name from their house. They claimed descent from Cilmin and bore as part of their heraldic identity his black leg ('*troed du*'), which, according to the legend, had acquired its dark dye while he was escaping from a daemon, running away only to miss the leap over a steam, one of his legs plunging into the water and acquiring its colour. With its emphasis on ancestry and place this legend is representative of many country house accounts in Pennant's *Tour*.

Like his good friend Philip Yorke (1743–1804) of Erddig, Pennant was not a fluent Welsh speaker, yet both were obsessed with Welsh genealogy, especially the groupings of esteemed ancestral figures known as the 'five royal tribes of Wales' and 'fifteen noble tribes of north Wales'.[64] These lists of ancestors, which had been formulated by Welsh poet-genealogists in the fifteenth century, quickly found visual expression in heraldic display.[65] In the world of the medieval *uchelwyr*, where ancestry was the primary marker of status, claiming descent from one or more of these tribes constituted a bold assertion of gentility. Though the practical significance of ancestry had unquestionably declined by Pennant's

---

62 Pennant, *History*, pp 26–32.   63 *Tours*, ii, p. 403.   64 *Tours*, iii, pp 169–70; Pennant, *History*, pp 283–317. See also Eric Griffiths, *Philip Yorke I (1734–1804): squire of Erthig* (Wrexham, 1995), pp 141–65.   65 Michael Siddons, *The development of Welsh heraldry* (Aberystwyth, 1991), vol. 1.

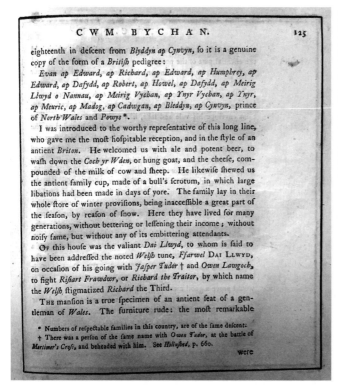

9.3 Extract from Pennant's *Tour* showing part of his description of Cwm Bychan in Merioneth. Ancestry was central to Pennant's presentation of the Welsh country house (with thanks to Bangor University Archives and Special Collections, BUASC, Rare Book, X/AA 7 PEN).

day, it remained an important and distinctive feature of Welsh gentry culture. Whether real or invented, the ancestral heritage attached to the country houses of Wales served to root them in Welsh history. The coats of arms retrospectively invented for the tribal patriarchs, and other esteemed Welsh ancestral figures, were often depicted in the margins next to Pennant's written descriptions of houses in the extra-illustrated versions of his *Tour*. Moses Griffith, Pennant's draughtsman, offered his services as a heraldic painter to the landowner network of north Wales, contributing like his master towards a perpetuation of this culture. For Pennant it was common enough for a house to be associated with one of the tribes, or some other ancient or eminent ancestral figure, to merit inclusion in his *Tour*. Rhug allowed him to discuss the lives of the medieval rulers of Gwynedd and Powys, Gruffudd ap Cynan (c. 1055–1137) and Owain Brogyntyn (fl. 1160–88).[66] Presaddfed in Anglesey was worthy of note because it stood on the site of a mansion purportedly belonging to the prominent ancestral figure, Hwfa ap Cynddelw.[67] Pennant's account of Newtown in Montgomeryshire emphasized that the Pryces, the principal family in the vicinity, 'derives itself

---

66 *Tours*, ii, pp 200–1.   67 *Tours*, iii, p. 77.

from Elystan Glodrydd, one of the five royal tribes of Wales'.[68] Llwydiarth was esteemed as 'a large old house ... formerly the property of the great family of the Vaughans, descended from Aleth Hen, king of Dyfed or Pembrokeshire'.[69] Wigfair, near St Asaph, was presented as the seat of John Lloyd (1749–1815), 'who is derived paternally from Ednowain Bendew, one of the fifteen tribes, and from Hedd Molwynog, by a female ancestor, in whose right he enjoys his ancient seat of Hafodynos'.[70] Maesmynan was deemed worthy of inclusion because of the tradition that Llywelyn ap Gruffudd (c.1223–82), last prince of Gwynedd, had a *llys* (royal court) there, 'whose foundations, till within these few years, were to be seen in an adjacent meadow'.[71] As with the confused legend of Dai Llwyd at Cwm Bychan, many of these ancestral traditions served not only to embed a house in a local historical consciousness, but also in events of national historical significance. Pennant's *Tour* is widely credited for reviving and reframing the legacy of Owain Glyndŵr, who led a major revolt against English rule in Wales during the first decade of the fifteenth century.[72] In his long account of Glyndŵr's revolt, Pennant included the legend of the 'treachery' of Hywel Sele of Nannau, who ended up being stuffed into a hollow oak tree ('*derwen ceubren yr ellyll*') after a failed assassination attempt on his cousin and fellow *uchelwr*.[73] Pennant also articulated the story of Richard ap Hywel's (c.1468–1540) support of Henry Tudor in the lead-up the Battle of Bosworth in 1485, including the dramatic flight of the future king from Mostyn Hall to avoid capture.[74] At Tower, Mold, Pennant's account of the house was dominated by the exploits of Rheinallt ap Gruffydd ap Bleddyn (c.1438–65), renowned for his valiant defence of Harlech Castle during the War of the Roses and the hanging of the mayor of Chester in his great hall.[75] The Nannau, Mostyn and Tower legends, with many others, first substantively appear in print in Pennant's *Tour*. The historical authenticity of some of these legends is questionable; yet following their celebration in print, each of the stories assumed a place of precedence in the heritage of the associated sites, forming primary strands in the resident families' articulations of their ancestral identities.[76] In his recreation and celebration of Wales, Pennant – undoubtedly influenced by the antiquarian and genealogical interests of his correspondents and collaborators, especially Revd John Lloyd – was not averse to augmenting traditions, quarrying the past and transforming it with imaginative twists; the authority and popularity of his work in print gave credibility to such legends, encouraging them to cultivate like Topsy.

---

68 Ibid., p. 189.   **69** Ibid., p. 176.   **70** *Tours*, ii, p. 138.   **71** Ibid., pp 143–4.   **72** *Tours*, iii, appendix VII, pp 310–92; Dafydd Johnston, 'Shaping a heroic life: Thomas Pennant on Owen Glyndwr' in Constantine and Leask (eds), *Enlightenment travel*, pp 105–21.   **73** *Tours*, iii, p. 336.   **74** This is analyzed in Evans, 'Inventing the Bosworth tradition', pp 218–53.   **75** *Tours*, ii, pp 42–3.   **76** Evans, 'Inventing the Bosworth tradition', pp 218–53; Philip Nanney Williams, *Nannau: a rich tapestry of Welsh history* (Welshpool, 2016), pp 32–45, 165–72.

9.4 Watercolour of Y Twr/Tower in Mold, Flintshire, the ancestral residence of William Wynne, included in an extra-illustrated copy of Pennant's *Tour* (with thanks to Bangor University Archives and Special Collections, BUASC, Rare Book, X/AA 7 PEN).

In most cases, ancestors and their associated legends added significant honour and prestige to the house: contributing to its aura of ancientness and historical importance. However, the opposite could also apply. When discussing Acton, near Wrexham, Pennant commented that the former owners of the property – the Jeffreys family – were 'a race that, after running uncontaminated from an ancient stock, had the disgrace of producing in the last century George Jeffries [*sic*], chancellor of England; a man of first-rate abilities in his profession, but of a heart subservient to the worst of actions'.[77] Jeffreys (1645–89) was a successful lawyer, attaining the highest positions in the English legal system, but earned a reputation as 'the Hanging Judge' following the severity with which he pursued the rebels implicated in Monmouth's Rebellion of 1685. For Pennant, Jeffreys' character seems to have lessened the worthiness of the house. In a similar manner, Pennant dismissed the Merioneth residence of the regicide John Jones (*c.*1597–1660) of Maes-y-Garnedd, who had signed the death warrant of Charles I, as a mere 'ordinary house'.[78]

77 *Tours*, i, pp 405–8. 78 *Tours*, ii, p. 273.

CULTURAL CONTINUITY AND CHANGE IN THE WELSH COUNTRY HOUSE

The country houses presented most enthusiastically by Pennant were those that had been inhabited by the same noble lineage for centuries, as exemplified at Cwm Bychan. Ancestry provided strong links to history, tradition and locality. This model also extended to landed families of English origin long settled in Wales, including the various houses associated with branches of the Thelwall family in Denbighshire. Originally from Cheshire, the Thelwalls had settled in Ruthin following Edward I's conquest of Gwynedd, eventually establishing themselves as one of the most prominent *uchelwyr* families in north Wales, with a network of houses and estates including Plas-y-Ward, Bathafarn, Llanbedr, Blaen Iâl, Plas Coch and Nantclwyd.[79] Their immersion in the locality and achievements across the sixteenth and seventeenth centuries – especially the career of Sir Eubule Thelwall (d. 1630) – encouraged Pennant to dedicate more than three pages to their exploits. Similar attention was afforded to another prominent Denbighshire family of English origin, the Salusburys, with their primary residence at Lleweni.[80] Families such as the Salusburys and Thelwalls, the Pulestons of Emral and Bulkeleys of Baron Hill had been part of Welsh society for centuries, fully absorbed into the fabric of their localities, with their houses providing physical statements of their influence. Pennant also discussed houses constructed from 'new money', the most notable example being Bachygraig, erected by Richard Clough in the 1560s with the fortune he had made as a merchant in the service of the Elizabethan financier Sir Thomas Gresham.[81] Pennant referred to the popular saying '*Efe a aeth yn Clough*', or 'He is become a Clough', which describes someone who had attained great riches. Clough was born the younger son of a Denbigh glover; he made a fortune in continental Europe, which on his return to Wales he used to finance his incorporation into gentry society.

Such examples demonstrate that Welsh landed society had long been capable of absorbing new members into its ranks, a point that often goes unnoticed in assessments of the cultural impacts of the 'demographic crisis' experienced by the Welsh gentry across the long eighteenth century. Pennant frequently described in painstaking detail the complex changes in the ownership of Welsh country houses, through marriage, inheritance and purchase, for example:

> Llwydiarth, a large old house ... formerly the property of the great family of Vaughans, descended from Aleth Hen ... The estate was conveyed to Sir Watkin Williams Wynn, by his first wife, daughter and heiress to the last owner.[82]

79 Ibid., pp 193–7. 80 Ibid., pp 144–8. 81 *Tours*, ii, pp 139–43. 82 *Tours*, iii, p. 176.

> Rug ... became the property of Owen Brogyntyn, natural son of Madog ap Meredydd, a prince of Powys ... From the marriage of Margaret Wenn, daughter and heiress of Jevan ap Howel, a descendant of Brogyntyn, with Pyers Salesbury of Bachymbyd, were derived the Salusburies of Rug; a name existing in the male line till the present century.[83]

In most instances the heritage associated with the old lineage was advantageously absorbed into the identity of the new owners, a process that was made easier if there was a blood connection. The *plas*, as a fixed entity in the landscape, provided a continuity across changes in ownership, the house preserving the cultural patrimony of its affiliated ancestors and the new owners succeeding as representatives of such heritage. However, in some instances Pennant gives the impression that the break or breaks with the past were too severe. This is evident in his account of Faenol or Vaynol near Bangor: 'This place had long been the residence of the Williams, a branch of the family of Ednyfed Vychan, and which was honored with a baronetage in 1622. Sir William Williams, the last of the line, was a man of profligate life.'[84] He disposed of the estate 'in a drunken fit', it eventually passing to the great nephew of 'the late Mr Smith of Tedworth, Hampshire', 'by virtue of a grant from King William to his ancestor'. Likewise, after narrating another complex series of changes in ownership, Pennant lamented that Vaynor in Montgomeryshire had been 'alienated to persons foreign to the name and blood'.[85] The overwhelming majority of the 'antient' Welsh houses described by Pennant were still in use, playing active roles in the life of their communities and as powerbases for their mostly resident owners. In his correspondence, however, he expressed frustration with the demographic trends and related inheritance patterns of the period, bemoaning the thirty-five derelict mansions in Merioneth as 'melancholy, deserted and ruinous, once the seat of hospitality and mirth'.[86] In his *Tour* he occasionally lamented the loss of a house through destruction or neglect, including Berth-lwyd, near Llanidloes:

> The poor remains of the antient house of that name stand in the valley; its masters were the old family of the Llwyds, descended from Dyngad, second son of Tudur Trevor. Dafydd, seventeenth in descent from Dyngad, first took the name of Llwyd, and probably gave the additional title to the house. It continued in the family several generations after; and of late years passed, by purchase, to Sir Edward Lloyd, Baronet.[87]

Blodwell Hall in the Welsh marches was described as a 'deserted seat', whereas in his journey near Conwy he passed by Marl, 'a house of fine appearance, but now little more than a case, having suffered by fire about forty

---

83 *Tours*, ii, pp 200–1. 84 *Tours*, iii, pp 21–2. 85 Ibid., p. 199. 86 National Library of Wales, MS 2532B; quoted in Humphreys, *Montgomeryshire*, pp 96–7. 87 *Tours*, iii, pp 195–6.

9.5 Watercolour of Chirk Castle, Denbighshire, by Pennant's draughtsman Moses Griffith (with thanks to Bangor University Archives and Special Collections, BUASC, Rare Book, X/AA 7 PEN).

years ago'.[88] The degeneration of these properties was a consequence of inheritance, the departure of a resident lineage rupturing the status and influence they had once enjoyed in their localities and fragmenting the ancestral heritage they had once embodied.

ESTATE LANDSCAPES: TREES AND THE PICTURESQUE

Pennant was also deeply interested in the landscape settings of Welsh country houses. He was writing during a period when William Gilpin and Uvedale Price's theories on the picturesque, and their manifestation in the designed landscapes of Capability Brown, William Emes, and Humphry Repton, were core features in the intellectual and aesthetic milieus of the British landowning class – including those curious travellers using Pennant as inspiration for their journeys around Wales.[89] Pennant was sufficiently attracted to commission a refashioning of the grounds surrounding his own seat at Downing from the

---

88 Ibid., pp 138–9, 200.   89 Charles Watkins and Ben Cowell, *Uvedale Price (1747–1829): decoding the picturesque* (Woodbridge, 2012); Tom Williamson, *Polite landscapes: gardens and*

1760s: 'to lay out the natural beauties of the place ... enlarging the fine scenery of the broken grounds, the woods and the command of water'.[90] His *Tour* regularly highlighted the picturesque qualities of country houses across north Wales.[91] Penbedw, for example, was esteemed as 'a great ornament to this little valley'; Leeswood, 'rising palace-like along a fine slope on the south side of the vale, surrounded with woods and lawns'; Garthewin, 'commanded a most lively view of a fertile little valley, bounded with hills, covered with hanging woods'; Llanidan, 'finely situated ... commanding upwards a beautiful prospect of Caernarvon and the Snowdon hills'; Fron-yw, 'commands a delightful prospect'; and Tan y Bwlch, 'embosomed in woods, most charmingly situated on the side of the hill'.[92] For Pennant, these settings strengthened the connection of the houses to their landscapes, naturally embedding them deeper into their localities, physically and symbolically. Wynnstay was particularly noteworthy:

> The park of Wynn-stay reaches to the village of Rhiwabon; and is most advantageously situated. The grounds well-wooded; the views distinct and extremely elegant; especially those towards the Berwyn mountains, and the august breach made into them beyond Llangollen, by the rapid Dee, through the country of the irregular and wild Glyndwr.[93]

The picturesque was heavily reliant on trees. Pennant was evidently fond of trees and woods, describing his own ancient favourites, including the 'Fairy Oak' in his grounds at Downing.[94] He introduced Coetmor, near Bethesda, as a property 'seated in the midst of lofty trees, every now and then opening so as to admit a view of the exalted mountains and rocks soaring above with misty tops'.[95] In another example he applauded Bodysgallen as 'a fine situation, environed with woods. From a neglected terrace is a most beautiful view, over the tops of trees, of Conwy, part of the river, and the vast mountains which form the background of the prospect.'[96] Gwaenynog in Denbighshire was also enriched by its trees:

> fronted by the most majestic oaks in our principality. The fine wooded dingles belonging to the demesne are extremely well worth visiting: they are most judiciously cut into walks by the owner, John Myddelton esq.; and afford beautiful scenery in their kind, as any we have to boast. Moel Famma superbly terminates one view; and the ruins of Denbigh Castle burst awfully at the termination of the concluding path.[97]

society in eighteenth-century England (London, 1995). 90 Evans, 'Downing estate', pp 57–84; Pennant, *History*, pp 4–7. 91 Moore, 'Thomas Pennant's vision of the landscape', pp 138–77. See also Bettina Harden, *The most glorious prospect: garden visiting in Wales 1639–1900* (Llangennech, 2017). 92 *Tours*, ii, pp 30, 60–1, 182, 292; iii, pp 8, 170. 93 *Tours*, i, pp 390–4. 94 Pennant, *History*, pp 5–6. 95 *Tours*, iii, p. 108. 96 Ibid., pp 139–45. 97 *Tours*, ii, p. 174.

As with country houses, individual trees were capable of enshrining historical narratives and traditions. At Nannau, Pennant concentrated on the legend of the *Ceubren yr Ellyll* ('oak of the demon'):

> The estate is covered with fine woods which clothe all the sides of the dingles for many miles. On the road side is a venerable oak, in the last stage of decay, and pierced by age into the form of a gothic arch; yet its present girth is twenty-seven feet and a half. The name is very classical, *Derwen Ceubren yr Ellyll*, the hollow oak, the haunt of daemons.[98]

This was the tree into which the body of Hywel Sele of Nannau was stuffed after his failed assassination attempt on Owain Glyndŵr.

THE SPIRIT OF IMPROVEMENT: AGRICULTURE AND INDUSTRY IN THE LANDSCAPE

Woodlands were also an important part of the economy of landed estates. Pennant was disposed to 'make our woods the glory of our estates' and urged his fellow landowners to 'plant, and preserve your woods!'.[99] He heaped praise on Sir Edward Lloyd (d. 1795) of Pengwern for planting 162,000 trees on his Flintshire estates and over 320,000 on his Pantglas estate in Caernarfonshire, 'contributing as a planter more to the benefit of his heir and of the state, than any other in the principality, in this age, or in any past'.[100] With Plas Newydd and Llugwy as exceptions, Pennant lamented that in much of Anglesey, 'it is with great difficulty the gentry can raise a plantation around their houses'.[101] These comments on woodland management are occasionally matched with anecdotes about other aspects of estate management. In his *History* he provided a detailed account of land use on his own and neighbouring estates, referring to soil types, livestock, crops, agricultural practices and also to his relations with his tenant farmers, insisting that 'our rents are moderate, because our gentry would blush to add one dish to their table at the expense of the tenant'.[102] This section on 'husbandry' provided an indication of the wider influence and operation of the landed estate in rural Wales, where agriculture and the relationship between landowners and tenants were still key elements in society. Such observations are rarely repeated in his *Tour*, though he lamented that in Llŷn, 'notwithstanding the laudable example of the gentry, the country is in an unimproved state, neglected for the sake of the herring-fishery'.[103]

---

[98] *Tours*, ii, p. 250. [99] Pennant, *History*, p. 158; *Tours*, iii, p. 189. [100] Pennant, *History*, pp 171–2. [101] *Tours*, iii, pp 18–19, 25, 56. [102] Pennant, *History*, pp 157–72, quote at p. 164.
[103] *Tours*, ii, p. 386.

By the late eighteenth century, parts of Wales were quickly industrializing. Pennant continued his predecessors' efforts to exploit the mineral resources – principally coal and lead – on the Downing estate, and noted that 'the vestiges of antient collieries' remained in the parkland at Mostyn.[104] Across many parts of north Wales, estate owners and others were investing in mineral extraction. The description of Llangynog in Montgomeryshire included notes on lead mining and slate quarrying; remarks on the Grosvenor family's mining interests and endeavours pepper Pennant's journeys around Denbighshire and Flintshire; and Sir Pyers Mostyn (1749–1823) of Talacre's quarry in Gwespyr was 'noted for the excellence of the free-stone'.[105] A full account was also provided of the Parys copper mine on Anglesey, a venture that transformed the fortunes of the Plas Newydd and Llys Dulas estates.[106] Praise was also heaped on Lord Penrhyn for his transformational improvements, centred on the extraction of slate, noting that 'the quarries have become now the source of a prodigious commerce'. This investment included the creation of new transport routes through Nant Ffrancon, an enlargement of Porth Penrhyn, a site for manufacturing writing slates, and the construction of multiple houses and cottages on the estate.[107] Pennant recommended that the curious traveller 'ride to the quarries' to see the works and 'laudable changes in this once desolate country'.[108] This spirit of improvement was also noticeable at Lleweni, where its new owner, Thomas Fitzmaurice (1742–93), was 'animating the country' with his vast bleachery. To Pennant, he was an exemplar: 'May the utility of his life effectually awaken in our gentry a sense of his merit, and the benefits resulting from his labors, and induce them to promote every design of his, calculated for the public good.'[109] In Flintshire too, the 'Holywell' section of Pennant's local *History*, with its detailed account of the booming industries of the Greenfield valley, provides a sharp contrast to the rurality of neighbouring Whitford.[110] Pennant was conscious of the links between these industries, British colonialism and transatlantic slavery: Lord Penrhyn's 'immense' property in Jamaica, the global markets and products of the Greenfield Copper & Brass Co. and in Montgomeryshire, 'the abundance of sheep', their profitable wool used to produce flannel and coarse cloth for the army 'and for covering the poor negroes in the West Indies'.[111] Over the next century, industrialization and empire were to have immense impacts on Welsh country houses and estates, and their social, cultural and economic spheres.

---

104 *Tours*, i, pp 23–6; Pennant, *History*, pp 54, 121–39.   **105** *Tours*, i, pp 100–1; ii, p. 113; iii, pp 172–3.   **106** *Tours*, iii, pp 57–67.   **107** For a full analysis see David Gwyn, *Welsh slate: archaeology and history of an industry* (Aberystwyth, 2015).   **108** *Tours*, iii, pp 87–100; Pennant, *History*, pp 270–2.   **109** *Tours*, ii, pp 147–8.   **110** Pennant, *History*, pp 201–18.   **111** *Tours*, iii, p. 178; Pennant, *History*, pp 211, 270.

The place of the plas *in Thomas Pennant's* Tour in Wales

CONCLUSION: WELSH CONSCIOUSNESS AND THE COUNTRY HOUSE

Pennant's *Tour* underlines the relevance of Jon Stobart's assertion that 'travel was something that placed the country house into social, spatial and cultural context'.[112] Pennant's multi-layered portrayal of Wales emphasized and celebrated a Welsh distinctiveness, with the *plas* as a key ingredient. His presentation of the eighteenth-century country house as an integral part of Wales and Welshness contradicts, or at least complicates, sweeping historiographical generalizations of cultural anglicization and alienation. Notwithstanding an unequivocal sense of attachment to a British polity, both the production and substance of the *Tour* demonstrate continued landowner engagement in the preservation and reframing of Wales as an 'imagined community'. In this respect, Pennant's identity and perspective as a Welsh squire are important: from his standpoint he proudly presents the 'antient' country houses of Wales as living embodiments of a rich Welsh ancestral heritage, deeply embedded in a landscape, history and culture that intertwined to give Wales its character. The extent to which Pennant's portrayal was representative of the views of Welsh landed society overall can be argued, so too the degree to which he romanticized his depiction. But a distinctive Wales and a particular Welsh gentry culture and *plas*, based on connections between pedigree and place, radiates from his narrative. Significantly, the *Tour* was circulated in print, and in the English language, by a writer with a British and European scholarly network and reputation.

In assessing the influence of Pennant's writings, scholars have tended to focus on the role of his *Tour* in inspiring English curiosity and engagement with the fabric of Wales – through reading and travel. The *Tour* – and the boom in travel and travel writing it inspired – contributed towards a further integration of Wales into a British consciousness and cohesion. However, the compilation of the *Tour* suggests that Pennant's fellow landowners *within* Wales should also be viewed as an important part of the work's audience and readership. In this respect, as well as reflecting landowner perceptions towards their family histories, the cultural significance of their country houses and estates, and the nature of their connection with Wales, the *Tour* also had a role in shaping and reframing such attitudes and perceptions into the future – across a period when inheritance, marriage and purchase brought in an array of 'new' owners for the 'antient' country houses of Wales. Pennant thereby inspired both external and internal engagement with his 'native country'.[113]

---

112 Stobart, *Travel and the British country house*, p. 1.   113 A version of this paper was first presented as the annual lecture of Cymdeithas Thomas Pennant (cymdeithasthomaspennant.com) in Holywell, Flintshire (17 Oct. 2019). I am most grateful to Prof. Mary-Ann Constantine for her comments on a draft of this paper.

Visitors and visiting: a Kerry country house, 1912–39

JOHN KNIGHTLY

This essay is based almost exclusively on the papers of Major Markham Richard Leeson Marshall (1859–1939), who lived at Callinafercy House, Milltown, County Kerry. As such, its focus is on one particular family and one particular country house, set against the background of local, national and international events. Callinafercy was not the biggest country house in Kerry, nor were the Leeson Marshalls particularly important, but they had a reputation for being lenient landlords and generally having a good relationship with their tenants. Markham's letters, mostly to his daughter May, and an almost unbroken series of diaries, together with a visitors' book covering the period 1912 to 1939, provide a remarkable and perhaps unique insight into the lost world of the Kerry gentry. These allow us to reconstruct the social rhythm of county society: examine who was invited to stay, when they arrived, how long they stayed for, whom the family visited and why, the impact of war and revolution, and how the Kerry gentry adapted to changing social circumstances after 1923.[1] It was a way of life dominated by country pursuits and local concerns, but part of a wider country house fraternity defined by kinship and friendship.

Markham Richard Leeson Marshall owned an estate of approximately 7,000 acres. His father Richard Leeson, a great grandson of the first earl of Milltown, had adopted the name Marshall as a legal prerequisite to inheriting an uncle's estate in Kerry. Markham's mother Zeena was the daughter of the Ven. Ambrose Power of Lismore, County Waterford. Markham was educated first at Kingstown Grammar School (Dún Laoghaire), before attending Clifton College in Bristol. He studied law at New College, Oxford after which he trained as a barrister at Inner Temple, London, acting in commercial cases. In 1890, he married Mabel, daughter of his neighbour, Sir John Godfrey of Kilcoleman Abbey, Milltown. The couple had one child, May, born in 1891. Mabel died tragically a year later, and Markham only permanently moved back to Kerry in 1903, just prior to selling his estate under the Wyndham Land Act. In 1907, Markham remarried. His bride, Meriel Hodson, was the daughter of Sir George Hodson of Hollybrooke, Bray, County Wicklow.

Built in the early 1860s in a restrained Gothic revival style, Callinafercy House was neither particularly large nor ornate. Nonetheless, it was designed for

---

1 The Leeson Marshall Papers (LMP) is a collection of over 10,000 documents that the author has catalogued over the last number of years. Until recently, the papers were held at Callinafercy House, having accumulated there since it was built in the early 1860s. The

10.1 Markham Richard Leeson Marshall
(The Leeson Marshall Papers, Muckross House Archive Library).

the well-developed rituals of country house entertaining, having a large dining room and drawing room; as Elizabeth Bowen wrote about Irish country houses in general it was, 'planned for spacious living – for hospitality above all'.[2] The house was surrounded by extensive gardens, which included a croquet lawn and a grassed tennis court. It was built on a headland at the confluence of the rivers Maine and Laune, which flowed into Castlemaine harbour. Over forty acres of woodland provided shelter against the prevailing Atlantic winds. Markham had an annual investment income of about £1,000 and also received a yearly salary of £300 as a director of Tomkins, White & Courage, the famous oat-milling company, while Meriel had a separate income of £350 per year. This ample income prompted the couple to commission the architect James Franklin Fuller to add a new wing to the rear of the house in 1911. This increase in its size

collection has recently been acquired by the State and deposited in Muckross House Archive Library (MHL), Killarney, County Kerry. 2 Elizabeth Bowen, 'The big house – from collected impressions' in Eibhear Walshe (ed.), *Elizabeth Bowen remembered: the Farahy addresses* (Dublin, 1998), p. 61.

10.2 Callinafercy House, Milltown, County Kerry (private collection).

allowed the couple to comfortably entertain and host guests, and it is no coincidence that the visitors' book for Callinafercy starts from this date.

Callinafercy was one of approximately seventy-five significant country houses in Kerry at the turn of the twentieth century whose owners collectively comprised county society, referred to by Markham as the 'old families'.[3] The majority were Church of Ireland but even if one includes Catholic families, this social group still only constituted a tiny minority of less than 600 people according to the 1911 census. Callinafercy itself formed part of a subset of mid-Kerry country houses, and an analysis of Markham's diaries shows him visiting these houses on a weekly basis. First and foremost was Kilcoleman Abbey, which was the closest country house to Callinafercy. Six miles away, The Reeks, home of The McGillycuddy, was another well-known rendezvous. At Churchtown lived the two Magill sisters – Nora and Elizabeth – who managed the house and demesne on behalf of their brother, Stephen James Magill (another sister managed Castle Hyde in Cork).[4] Neighbouring Beaufort was home to Edward

---

[3] This number of country houses is based on an analysis of Griffith's Valuation, and *Return of untenanted lands in rural districts, distinguishing demesnes on which there is a mansion ...*, HC, 1906, c.177, and Valerie Bary, *Houses of Kerry* (Whitegate, Co. Clare, 1994). [4] Terence Dooley, "'It was like a scene from the ball in *Gone with the wind*": social life at Castle Hyde,

10.3 Markham (standing on left) at Ballinagroun, 1912, re-enacting a near accident with Anthony MacGillycuddy lying in front of the car (The Leeson Marshall Papers, Muckross House Archive Library).

Nash and his wife Constance, and Lakeview, home of Sir Morgan Ross O'Connell. Near Lakeview was Aghadoe House, formerly the home of Lord Headley but now leased to Samuel Hussey, the infamous Kerry agent. Markham had a deep affection for 'Old Sam', who had been his agent from 1886 to 1900, enjoying his amusing stories, usually about Land War exploits.[5] Markham's closest friend was John MacGillycuddy (a brother of The McGillycuddy – the brothers disagreed over the spelling of the family name), who had a summer house at Ballinagroun near Annascaul. Every year from June to September, Ballinagroun was filled with guests who were invited to lunch, dinner, theatricals and dances which often went on into the early hours. In June 1907, Markham wrote, 'Left 7:30 pm by motor to Ballinagroun where we had an excellent small dance. 7 motors in all. Danced till 4:15'.[6]

Another frequent destination was Kenmare House, seat of Valentine Brown, the fifth earl of Kenmare, who was a close personal friend. With the advent of the railway, Caragh Lake, not far from Killorglin, saw a cluster of small country houses built along its dramatic shoreline in the latter part of the nineteenth century by various retired agents, military and colonial officials. In 1914, Markham's sister, Edith Gordon, built a small Arts and Crafts mansion at

1931–88' in Terence Dooley and Christopher Ridgway (eds), *The Irish country house: its past, present and future* (Dublin, 2011), p. 153.   **5** See Samuel Murray Hussey, *Reminiscences of an Irish land agent* (London, 1904), which recounts Hussey's exploits over a half century as a land agent and landlord in Kerry. The *Reminiscences* were compiled by Home Gordon, brother-in-law of Markham Richard Leeson Marshall.   **6** Diary of MRLM, 7 June 1907 (LMP, MHL).

10.4 Country houses of Kerry mentioned in this essay.

Caragh Lake, which she christened 'Ard na Sidhe Hill', which means 'Hill of the Fairies'. Her autobiography, *The winds of time*, gives a remarkable insight to life in Kerry during 'the Troubles', the common euphemism used in Kerry and elsewhere to describe the period 1919–23.[7] Markham's diaries reveal a yearly average of between forty and sixty visits among this small cluster of families, with Saturday the most popular day for calling and Sunday the least, reflecting perhaps respect for the Christian Sabbath. What comes across very strongly in Markham's correspondence is how this level of social interaction reinforced a strong sense of class cohesiveness, elitism, localism, and identity well into the twentieth century.

7 Edith Gordon, *The winds of time* (London, 1934). Edith was the black sheep of the family due to her nationalist views.

All these houses played host to a small but wealthy cohort of visitors from outside the county. An analysis of the Callinafercy visitors' book reveals that thirty guests came to stay in 1912, twenty-seven the following year and twenty-five in 1914. This number of visitors may not seem very large but in total they stayed a total of 153 days in 1912, 185 days in 1913, and 225 days in 1914. On average, excluding the period 1915–23, Callinafercy hosted visitors 170 days per year. This level of occupancy meant the house effectively operated like a small hotel. Different country houses attracted different kinds of guest. As Adrian Tinniswood notes, 'there were political houses, literary houses, hunting houses, downright weird houses. Some drew their weekend guests almost exclusively from the county, or from extended family networks.'[8] This was very much the case at Callinafercy, whose visitors were drawn from a narrow landed and family network. Of the 257 individuals who stayed between 1912 and 1939, 54 per cent were from a country house background but unrelated to the family, 36 per cent were relatives, 6 per cent were clergymen and their families and 4 per cent were military. This reflects patterns at other country houses. Terence Dooley, for example, writes that of the 278 guests entertained at Headfort, County Meath, in 1887–8, 'all seem to have been landlords, clergymen or army officers and their families'.[9] What is also striking is how 68 per cent of visitors to Callinafercy had an Irish address, 23 percent an English address and 9 percent had an address elsewhere, usually somewhere in the empire. This underlines the insular provincial world inhabited by many Irish landed families. Bowen's observation about the country house being 'an island, and like an island, a world' was in many respects very true.[10]

Visitors came for a variety of reasons. Some were invited to attend family events or visit for Christmas or Easter. Male friends of Markham were specifically invited for shooting or fishing. Visits by clergymen were invariably connected to meetings of the diocesan synod, missions or religious ceremonies. The majority of visitors however came to Callinafercy as part of a sightseeing trip, part of a tourist circuit that in Kerry had its roots in the eighteenth-century.[11] A prerequisite for a visit to any country house was the means to get there and back quickly and with a minimum of effort.[12] Initially it was the rapid expansion of the rail network that provided this. As early as 1853, Killarney was connected to the growing rail network. By 1900, the Great Southern and Western Railway had extended to Dingle, Valentia and Kenmare. Kerry was therefore easily accessible – but what really transformed country house visiting was the introduction of the motor car. Soon after their marriage, Markham and

8 Adrian Tinniswood, *The house party: a short history of leisure, pleasure and the country house weekend* (London, 2019), p. 20.   9 Terence Dooley, *The decline of the big house in Ireland: a study of Irish landed families, 1860–1960* (Dublin, 2001), p. 54.   10 Elizabeth Bowen, *Bowen's Court* (Cork, 1998), p. 19.   11 Finola O'Kane, *Ireland and the picturesque: design, landscape painting and tourism, 1700–1840* (London, 2013), p. 78.   12 Tinniswood, *The house party*, p. 27.

Meriel purchased a car from Chambers of Belfast, the first owned by the family. They were joining a trend, as by 1912 nearly every country house owner in Kerry possessed this new mode of transport.[13] The first run of 233 miles to Kerry from Dublin took two days in the summer of 1908.[14] The introduction of the motor car brought an entirely new dimension to country house visiting – its speed greatly reduced travel time.[15] Unlike previously when visitors would only stay a few days, before moving on to another country house, visitors could now use one house as a base for their entire trip. Planning excursions by motor car became part of the repertoire of a visit, which inevitably included the Ring of Kerry, the Lakes of Killarney, as well as calling at other country houses along the way. Thus, for example, during the summer of 1912, Markham's cousins, Samuel and Mary James, came from Gloucestershire to stay, and during their visit called at Churchtown, 10 miles away, Sillahertane, 37 miles away and Glanleam, 43 miles away, all in a single day. A visit to the Butlers of Waterville, 31 miles away through mountainous terrain which would have previously taken an entire day, now took Markham two and a half hours. A two-day trip around the Dingle Peninsula was now condensed into half a day. Markham could leave Callinafercy at midday, arrive in Dingle by 1.30 p.m., tour Slea Head (a promontory on the westernmost part of the Dingle Peninsula) and be back home at 6 p.m. in time for dinner. The extensive rail network and increase in car ownership after 1910 meant that visitors now enjoyed a new freedom of novelty and choice, a variety of destinations to choose from, and the possibility of longer stays in one location.[16] The most popular days for guests to arrive were Tuesday, Wednesday and Friday (nearly 60 per cent of visitors arrived on these days), followed by Thursday and Saturday – but certainly not Sunday. This, to a degree, reflected the fact that a certain cohort of visitors came to shoot and fish, typically mid-week activities.[17] Not surprisingly, the most popular months for visiting were July to October, which accounted for 57 per cent of visits.

Very few Kerry houses, with the exception of Muckross and Kenmare House (the large Victorian mansion burnt in 1913) and some few others, had sufficient bedrooms to host a large number of guests. Callinafercy at best could host six guests, so house parties were usually intimate affairs. It is possible from diaries and letters to reconstruct how guests occupied their days. The daily routine was organized around set times that were adjusted throughout the year to reflect daylight saving – albeit the decision to move the clock forwards or backwards often depended more on the whims of the local parish priest than on the official calendar, in order to facilitate servants wishing to attend Mass. Guests arose early, often taking a walk before breakfast, which was served between 8 a.m. and

---

13 Henry G. Tempest (ed.), *Irish motor directory and motor annual, 1911–12: a reference handbook for motorists* (Dundalk, 1912), p. 400. **14** Markham Richard Leeson Marshall (MRLM) to May Leeson Marshall, 4 June 1908 (MHL, LMP). **15** Bowen, 'The big house – from collected impressions', p. 60. **16** Tinniswood, *The house party*, p. 18. **17** Ibid., p. 45.

9 a.m. After breakfast, Markham would head out with a gun and hunting dogs and have a morning's sport with his male guests, while Meriel would bring their wives and daughters around the garden. Lunch was served at 12:30, followed by a pre-arranged visit to another country house, a sightseeing tour, a fishing expedition or sports. Lawn tennis, croquet and golf were the most popular outdoor pastimes. Most Kerry country houses possessed tennis and croquet lawns, and most were close to golf links. Golf was popular with both sexes; Edith Gordon was elected the captain of Dooks Golf Club near Killorglin in 1921, the first female captain in Ireland.[18] Afternoon excursions were often organized to coincide with tea or tea parties, served during the summer in the late afternoon between 4 p.m. and 5 p.m. 'Having tea' appears to have been the most regular social interaction in terms of visits to neighbouring country houses. The telegram boy was an indispensable part of arranging these events – usually a local lad employed for a few pence whose job was to cycle to Killorglin post office with telegrams. Dinner was served at 8 p.m., allowing the family and guests ample time to change beforehand. When it came to more sedentary pastimes, the art of conversation clearly prevailed, but playing bridge and chess were popular, and several games tables could be set up in the drawing room. Music was an important part of this social offering. The drawing room at Callinafercy contained a Broadwood piano, with a smaller pianoforte kept on the upper landing, as well as a small church organ. Meriel Leeson Marshall would often sing for her guests, sometimes accompanied by the local rector's wife. Markham liked to sing Irish folk songs, with 'The spinning wheel', a particular favourite of his.[19] Catering for the family, guests and callers were seven indoor staff. In 1912, these comprised the cook, Kathleen Donovan, two kitchen maids, two housemaids, Miss Tucker, who was Meriel's personal maid, and the butler, Richard Jones, always referred to simply as 'Jones', and who was not without a sense of humour. Hearing one guest express the opinion that the children of the gentry were like 'fine china' while the offspring of servants were 'common crockery', he was afterwards asked to fetch some of the visiting children from their rooms upstairs, whereupon he was heard issuing an order to one of the maids: 'Crockery, go up and bring down the china.'[20] A fifty-five-acre home farm supplied the household with milk, cream and butter. A kitchen garden provided a year-round supply of seasonable vegetables and fruit. Surviving receipts show that the house was provisioned almost entirely by Kerry-based merchants, with nearly 80 per cent of supplies sourced locally.[21] Exceptions were more expensive items purchased in Cork, Dublin or in London.

18 Minutes of Dooks Golf Club, 21 Apr. 1921 (Dook Golf Club Archive). 19 Diary of MRLM, 12 Jan. 1904 (MHL, LMP), 'Mary came by 3 train, concert a great success, Miss Power played violin, Kings sang a lot of songs, I sang *Eileen a Carah* ['The spinning wheel'] & the gramophone was much appreciated. Sat down 17 to supper.' 20 Patrick O'Sullivan, *I heard the wild birds sing: a Kerry childhood* (Dublin, 1991), p. 95. 21 An examination of

10.5 Callinafercy Bog 1912, watercolour by William Bingham McGuiness commissioned by Meriel Leeson Marshall (private collection).

10.6 Markham Leeson Marshall, 1928, by Eva H. Hamilton (The Leeson Marshall Papers, Muckross House Archive Library).

In terms of who stayed at Callinafercy, by far the most frequent visitor was a cousin, Louise Hamilton Cox, who stayed on thirteen separate occasions over a twenty-year period for a total of 339 days. She was the daughter of Henry Charles Forde, the famous Irish-born engineer and pioneer in the field of submarine telegraphy.[22] Other regular guests included Gertrude Scott (a Villiers Stuart of Dromana) and Audrey Hodson of Hollybrooke. Lady Barbara Chetwynd-Stapylton, daughter of the fourth earl of Milltown, was another frequent visitor. Occasionally there were guests with a more artistic flair, such as the artist William Bingham McGuinness, who visited in October 1912 for two weeks and returned the following May to give drawing classes. The Hamilton sisters, Eva and Letitia, who were related to the Godfreys of Kilcoleman, also visited, staying four times for a total of forty-five days, with Eva sketching Markham on one occasion as a thank you gift.

These visits were largely informed by personal connections, and the same considerations applied when the Leeson Marshalls themselves travelled. The social year was organized around a regular calendar of trips centred on family, friends and society events, the military season in June and meetings of diocesan and national synods of the Church of Ireland. Markham regularly visited the Blackwater circle of country houses, at the centre of which was Lismore Castle, which belonged to the duke of Devonshire. Markham's mother was from Lismore, and his uncle, Robert Henry Power, was at one time agent to the Devonshire estate. Nearby was Glencairn, home of another uncle, and Dromana House, the home of his aunt, Mary Power, who had married Henry Villiers Stuart. Further north were Dunsany in County Meath and Castle Bellingham, in County Louth, also belonging to relatives. All these houses formed part of an annual circuit of shooting trips, house parties, hunt balls and family events such as weddings and funerals. Markham's marriage to Meriel Hodson introduced two further circuits, in south Cork and Wicklow. Coolfadda, near Bandon, was the home of Meriel's brother, Eddy Hodson, retired agent for the duke of Devonshire's Bandon estate. This connection saw Markham frequently visit Castle Bernard, home of the earl of Bandon, where his last pre-war winter visit included ice skating and a large dinner party.[23] Meriel's strong connection to her old home, Hollybrooke, saw prolonged visits to Wicklow every year, usually in February or March, followed by a short trip to London, returning to Callinafercy in time to see the garden come into blossom. The couple would also visit London every November/December, allowing them to do some shopping, meet old acquaintances and be back in Kerry for Christmas. In their absence the

---

thousands of surviving receipts by this author from the 1860s to the 1920s reveals the extent to which the house was provisioned locally and also what items were purchased from further afield.   22 Irish Architectural Archive, 'Henry Charles Forde', *Dictionary of Irish architects*, https:// www.dia.ie/architects/view/2169/FORDE-HENRYCHARLES, accessed 14 Feb. 2023.   23 Diary of MRLM, 1 Jan. 1914 (MHL, LMP).

house would be thoroughly cleaned, and any repairs and painting carried out. One of the few houses that Markham frequented that was not in some way connected with the family was Mount Talbot in County Roscommon, where he usually went during the winter to take part in a shoot. His hosts, William John Talbot and wife Julia, usually invited between six and ten people to these midweek shoots, often including Lord and Lady de Freyne of nearby Frenchpark.[24]

The personal highlights of Markham's social calendar were probably more ordinary trips with close friends to his hunting lodge at Clydagh, in the Glenflesk valley, bordering County Cork. Visits to Clydagh usually took place every August or September and its thousand acres always supplied a bountiful yield of birds. Clydagh alternated with Castleisland, where Markham retained shooting rights over another 1,000 acres. Castleisland was easily reached by rail, which meant shooting parties could travel from and return to Callinafercy in a day; Clydagh, on the other hand, required more planning and provisions had to be sent in advance. Clydagh was nearly always followed by a visit to remote Sillahertane, high up in the Derrynasaggart mountains where the Lowe family hosted large shooting parties. Sillahertane in turn acted as a half-way house on the way to visit the Kenmare circle of country houses such as Dromquinna, Dromore and Derryquin, whose Scottish owner, Charles Warden, was an equally good shot and fellow gardening enthusiast. Much despised locally because of evictions in the 1890s, Warden was regarded as an excellent host by his coterie of friends, sparing no expense to amuse and entertain his guests, who were waited on by eighteen staff.

Outside of this perpetual circuit of visits to friends and family, there were a series of fixed events that prompted further travelling. One regular event that brought Markham to Dublin was the Punchestown Races every April, when he usually stayed with the Synnots of Furness at Sallins. The Dublin Horse Show every August was another fixed date in the calendar. Markham was a member of the Kildare Street Club, although he usually preferred to stay in the nearby Maples Hotel. The viceregal court was an infrequent destination unless connected with a military or royal visit. Mark Bence-Jones writes of how 'people from further afield tended to come [to court] only when they had debutante daughters to "bring out"'.[25] 'Going to town' inevitably meant London, where Markham usually stayed with his sister Edith Gordon at her town house at 95 Eaton Square. Visits to London were an opportunity to reimmerse oneself in its cultural and social milieu, meet old friends, attend to business and see the latest exhibitions, shows and concerts. For instance, in 1912, Markham went to see the *Ballets Russes* at Covent Garden with the famous ballerina Anna Pavlova in the

---

24 William John Talbot of Mount Talbot (1859–1923), married in 1897 to Julia Elizabeth Mary Molyneux. Talbot was related to the Talbot-Crosbie family of Ardfert while his wife was related to the knights of Kerry.   25 Mark Bence-Jones, *Twilight of the ascendancy* (London, 1998), p. 45.

lead.[26] His London club was the New University at 57 St James Street, popular for meeting Irish friends including the Wingfields, Brabazons, Kenmares, Cronin-Coltsmanns and Villiers Stuarts, all of whom usually took or had a London town house. Aside from this Irish coterie, Markham had the same circle of English acquaintances for much of his life, many of them from his Oxford days, some of whom had their own country estates. While Markham's acquaintances in Ireland were from the same narrow social circle as himself, his English friends were from a much broader social group, with strong links to the worlds of finance, industry and the law. The most prominent of these was Vernon John Watney of the famous brewing family and later MP for East Surrey, who was married to Lady Margaret Wallop, daughter of the fifth earl of Portsmouth. In 1901, the Watneys bought the estate of Cornbury Park, Charlbury, Oxfordshire, where Markham would often stay over the following three decades. It was through Watney's influence that Markham was appointed to the board of Tomkins, White & Courage. Other close friends included Sir Arthur Thring, who attended Oxford with Markham, and Sir Henry Erle Richards, who was appointed legal advisor to the governor general's council in India in 1904. It was during Richards' tenure in India that Markham took the opportunity to visit the British Raj, using characters from Kiplings's *The Jungle book* to bring the Indian sub-continent to life in his letters home to his young daughter.[27]

What the Callinafercy visitor book and Markham's travels reveal is the narrow social circle in which he and the Kerry gentry moved. Visitors and visits were repeatedly from or to the same group of country houses and revolved around family connections and close friendships. Each country house was of course different and each formed part of a distinct social clique but undoubtedly the same pattern was repeated elsewhere. The one divergence was participation in a much broader English social circle. This ironically was due to Markham's own decision to pursue a professional qualification in response to the effects of the Land War of the 1880s, which saw his Kerry rental income collapse.

The outbreak of the First World War marked a profound break in these annual perambulations. Markham received his mobilization orders on 5 August 1914 and would not return to Callinafercy, except for short periods on leave, until April 1918. For most of 1915 and 1916, he was stationed at Aghada on the eastern side of Cork harbour, with the 3rd Reserve Battalion of the Royal Munster Fusiliers, training men for the front. Although he made acquaintances among Cork county society, the constant possibility of being stationed elsewhere meant that the relaxed atmosphere that had once marked military duties was

26 Diary of MRLM, 8 May 1912 (MHL, LMP).   27 MRLM to May Leeson Marshall, 21 Dec. 1905 (MHL, LMP), 'I left Bombay on Sat & went through Mowgli's country on Sunday. It is just as we expected. The Wainganga is getting low & a big black rock that might be the Peace Rock was just showing ... Hathi still roamed there & there were lots of tiger & pig'.

gone. Life was no longer centred around the mess piano in the evening but around the orderly room. Markham remained at Aghada until October 1917, when the battalion was moved to Ballincollig and then to Fort Stamford in Plymouth.

Serving in the war was regarded as a necessary duty to king and empire, with an expectation that county society would resume its pre-war life after it ended. Few expected it to last as long as it did. Furthermore, despite the shadow of home rule and rising political tensions, no one could have envisaged how Ireland would transform as the war progressed. The 1916 Rising prompted a remarkable growth in Sinn Féin support in Kerry, which, when allied to the threat of conscription, aroused strong nationalist sentiment. Four Sinn Féin MPs were elected for Kerry in the 1918 general election, in a prelude to the outbreak of the War of Independence in early 1919. A growing sense that events were drifting towards some form of confrontation saw some Kerry families depart. Despairing of the plight of southern unionism, James Crosbie sold Ballyheigue Castle in 1918, albeit to his sister, while Daniel Cronin-Coltsmann, also fearing the rise of Sinn Féin, sold Flesk Castle to Markham's friend Jack MacGillycuddy. Ballyard in Tralee was sold to a publican by the Fitzgeralds, who moved to London, while Rose Trent Stoughton decided to dispose of Ballyhorgan outside Ballyduff (which was burnt before the sale was concluded). Despite the departures of these families and increased anxieties about Ireland's future, county society had revived after the war ended. Tennis and croquet parties resumed in 1919, as did bringing guests on sight-seeing excursions around Kerry. Ballymullen barracks in Tralee remained a functioning camp, and there were visits by military officers to Callinafercy, with return invitations to lunches and dinners. True to her political beliefs, Markham's sister Edith Gordon entertained nationalists and republicans such as Albina Broderick, sister of the earl of Midleton, at Ard na Sidhe.[28] In November 1919, Markham went to Clydagh shooting, but, no longer able to ignore the risk of being raided, he handed in his guns to the RIC barracks in Killorglin on his return.[29] Deference had not entirely waned however, as he still received a Christmas present of a turkey and six geese from grateful neighbours, noting that 'in spite of [the] wave of socialism, the old people as nice as ever'.[30]

It is not the purpose of this article to explore in detail what happened the country houses of Kerry during the War of Independence and the Civil War. The focus here is limited to a brief examination of how county society was disrupted during this period. Markham's diaries for 1918 and 1919 mention raids looking for arms on RIC barracks and country houses, and other minor troubling incidents.[31] His 1920 diary, however, reflects a dramatic escalation in

[28] Bureau of Military History, WS 1413 (Tadhg Kennedy), p. 35. [29] Diary of MRLM, 5 Dec. 1919 (MHL, LMP). [30] Ibid., 24 Dec. 1919 (MHL, LMP). [31] T. Ryle Dwyer, *Tans, terror, and troubles: Kerry's real fighting story, 1913–1923* (Cork, 2004), p. 153. Also see Tom

intimidation and violence across Kerry. Old disputes from the 1880s resurfaced and a new phase of land agitation broke out, but this time tinged with republicanism and characterized by the press and Markham as 'Bolshevism', a term generally equated with the expropriation of land.[32] Attending petty sessions as magistrate became increasingly hazardous and the number of cases heard gradually declined as litigants began to use the Sinn Féin courts. Markham recorded that the grand jury of 1920 would probably be the last to be held in Kerry.[33] It certainly was one of the last public events that saw county society assemble as of old, including members such as Sir Arthur Vicars, who would be murdered in 1921, and Charles Warden of Derryquin, who would be burned out in 1922. One gets a strong sense of growing unease in Markham's letters, alongside a determination to continue on as normal where possible. As such there was the obligatory trip to Hollybrooke followed by the General Synod in Dublin in May 1920, while an invitation from Lord Bandon resulted in a fishing excursion to Castle Bernard a month later. Red Cross meetings in Killarney included tea with the Kenmares, where Markham met the famous war correspondent Maurice Baring, who entertained the audience with stories about revolutionary Russia. Here he also met Maurice Bourgeois, correspondent of *Le Matin*, who gave interesting insights on George Bernard Shaw and John Millington Synge. As county families continued their social rounds, the authority of the crown in Kerry was effectively neutralized by the IRA. The response by the RIC, now augmented by the Black and Tans and Auxiliaries, resulted in an escalation in violence, leading to reprisal and counter-reprisal. The Hillville ambush on 1 November 1920 outside Killorglin vividly brought this home, when local IRA companies ambushed a RIC bicycle patrol and killed two Black and Tans.[34] Markham wrote to his daughter:

> Two police murdered at Killorglin and the inevitable reprisals … when we got to Hillville, a pool of blood that nearly made me sick, a horrible sight I shall never forget.[35]

The general escalation in violence had a major impact on the number of guests coming to Callinafercy in 1921 and 1922, comparable to how numbers dwindled during the war years. From nineteen guests in 1919, the number dropped to a low of seven in 1921.

Doyle, *The Civil War in Kerry* (Dublin, 2008), p. 97.   **32** Diary of MRLM, 22 Jan. 1920 (MHL, LMP). See also Terence Dooley, *Burning the big house: the story of the Irish country house in a time of war and revolution* (New Haven and London, 2022), p. 201.   **33** Diary of MRLM, 18 July 1920 (MHL, LMP).   **34** MLRM to May Leeson Marshall, 3 Nov. 1920 (MHL, LMP).   **35** MRLM to his daughter May, 3 Nov. 1921 (MHL, LMP).

Table 10.1 Number of overnight visits to Callinafercy 1912–39[36]

Year	Overnight visits	Year	Overnight visits
1912	30	1926	24
1913	27	1927	23
1914	25	1928	22
1915	7	1929	27
1916	3	1930	27
1917	0	1931	28
1918	4	1932	22
1919	19	1933	7*
1920	19	1934	5*
1921	7	1935	17
1922	11	1936	17
1923	18	1937	7*
1924	22	1938	11
1925	22	1939	5
Total number of visits			456

* Markham was in ill health during these years, which saw reduced visitors.

A more dramatic change is evident when one looks at the length of time guests stayed. In 1919, nineteen guests stayed a total of 166 days; in 1921 seven guests stayed a total of only nineteen days.

Table 10.2 Number of days that guests stayed at Callinafercy 1912–39

Year	Days	Year	Days
1912	153	1926	237
1913	185	1927	183
1914	225	1928	121
1915	61	1929	144
1916	29	1930	79
1917	0	1931	232
1918	15	1932	185
1919	166	1933	34
1920	70	1934	20
1921	19	1935	159
1922	36	1936	279
1923	211	1937	110
1924	121	1938	82
1925	145	1939	19
Grand Total			3,320

36 Callinafercy Visitors Book, 1912–39 (MHL, LMP).

This decline in the number of visitors reflects both a basic breakdown of law and order and repeated disruptions of the train and road networks through strike action and sabotage. For instance, Markham's cousins Noel and Sylvia Power cancelled a trip fearing that the 1920 'munition strike' (when railway workers placed an embargo on the transportation of British military forces and munitions) would see them stranded in Kerry. Another frequent visitor, Ethel Smyth, was aboard a train when it was attacked at Headford by the IRA; this would become an all-too-common experience for rail travellers over the next two years.[37] Attempted and actual murder of friends was another major deterrent. In January 1921, Alice King, a close friend of the family and daughter of the local rector, was shot dead by the IRA in Mallow.[38] That April, Sir Arthur Vicars was shot dead at Kilmorna, allegedly for spying.[39] As IRA activity increased, the gentle social routine of friendly house visits was replaced by a more menacing period of hostile incursions, threats and burnings. Country houses became targets for arson, and theft of arms, ammunition, motor cars, food supplies and clothing.[40] Callinafercy was not immune to these threats. On 10 May 1921, after a day overseeing men working on the embankments, and just as Markham was about to retire to bed, a maid rushed in warning that 'there are men all round the house'.[41] Markham recounts the episode in detail in his diary:

> I went to [the] servant's door. Two masked and long coated men came in. 'We want your bicycles and motor'. Saw at once it was an 'official' job & not violence which was a relief. Men went to front door and let in another. I asked him if he was an officer and what they wanted. He said, 'yes, car and bicycles. Have you any?' I said 'yes'. He, 'show it me'. I did, took him to office where it was. It was wheeled off ... Jones came to say one of them wanted to speak to me. He said courteously, 'sorry to have to upset you Major, but we must obey orders', to which [Meriel] and I replied, 'we understand, thank you for not flourishing pistols'. They seemed strangers, were quiet and courteous but firm.[42]

Similar IRA raids occurred at other country houses such as at Muckross, Churchtown and Caragh Lake. The Hon. Elizabeth Cuffe, who lived with Edith Gordon at Ard na Sidhe, was somewhat more fortunate than Markham in that the IRA only took her car battery (to help blow up Caragh bridge) and not her well-known Rolls Royce, which even the IRA must have considered too conspicuous. Edith Gordon noted rather sarcastically that 'it had taken sixty men, armed to the teeth to obtain a battery from two defenceless women'.[43] The

37 Diary of MRLM, 26 Oct. 1920 (MHL, LMP).   38 Eunan O'Halpin and Daithí Ó Corráin, *The dead of the Irish Revolution* (London, 2020), p. 285.   39 Conor Joy, 'The killing of Sir Arthur Vicars, April 1921: an exceptional case?', *Journal of the Archaeological and Historical Society*, series 2, 16 (2016), p. 165.   40 Dooley, *Burning the big house*, p. 140.   41 Diary of MRLM, 10 May 1921 (MHL, LMP).   42 Ibid.   43 Gordon, *Winds of time*, p. 181.

fact that Markham noted these raids and nocturnal visits in his diaries indicates how keen he was to keep a record of friends and neighbours during the worsening situation. It also reveals how the hardy few were determined to keep up morale, exchange news, and share experiences. He was acutely aware how vulnerable they all were, writing to his daughter, 'one does so dread the beginning of the end … but we will try & save the place please God'.[44] Country houses were regarded as legitimate targets in a growing cycle of violence, regardless of how benign or well-regarded an individual family might be. In one of the last atrocities of the War of Independence, the Ballymacandy Ambush between Milltown and Castlemaine on 1 June 1921 resulted in the death of five RIC officers, including the local sergeant, who Markham knew well. In its aftermath, he received a note to say Callinafercy 'would be burned to the ground' if there were any reprisals.[45] Fortunately, in this instance, there were none. Tom O'Connor, the IRA officer who led the ambush, later claimed that Markham persuaded the military authorities not to retaliate.[46] Hints suggest the family knew exactly who was involved in raids or who was 'on the run'. Edith Gordon writes that members of her indoor staff were in Cumann na nBan and that many of her farm workers were in the IRA.[47] Markham's role as a trustee for maintaining the sea embankments around Callinafercy meant he remained a familiar character locally. His habit of attending the funerals of neighbours (on average eight a year), visiting the sick and needy, attending fairs and markets and a perception that he was approachable ensured he was well informed. Elizabeth Bowen remarks how 'rumours of the republicans' movements preceded them: [such] guests were not unexpected'.[48] Markham's diaries show he was updated regularly on trenches being cut across roads and movements of military convoys, but he is careful never to mention names, and entries are often just matter of fact:

> Heard some soldiers on way to early train to Glenbeigh station attacked & their arms taken. 3 or 4 wounded, a large [IRA] party held up same train at next station Dooks & searched it probably as a precaution in case Glenbeigh attack failed. Shows some planning also.[49]

The War of Independence witnessed the destruction of important country houses in north Kerry such as Ballyheigue Castle, Ballyhorgan, Kilmorna and Tanavalla, effectively decimating that closely knit group. While the truce of July 1921 offered a reprieve from the violence, many families took this opportunity to depart. Oakpark in Tralee, where Markham was a regular overnight guest, was

[44] MRLM to May Leeson Marshall, 25 May 1921 (MHL, LMP). [45] Diary of MRLM, 8 June 1921 (MHL, LMP). See also Owen Shea, *Ballymacandy: the story of a Kerry ambush* (Dublin, 2021), which recounts the ambush in detail. [46] C.K.H. O'Malley and Tim Horgan (eds), *The men will talk to me: Kerry interviews by Ernie O'Malley* (Cork, 2012), p. 138. [47] Gordon, *The winds of time*, p. 200. [48] Elizabeth Bowen, *Bowen's Court* (Dublin, 1998 ed.), p. 441. [49] Diary of MRLM, 27 Apr. 1921 (MHL, LMP).

put up for sale by the Collis-Sandes family. Similarly, Gordon Leahy sold Carriglea outside Killarney and moved to Devon, but not before being given the opportunity to buy back some of his stolen furniture.[50] Arthur de Moleyns and his family departed Rossbeigh, while the Hoods attempted to sell Dromore Castle. What is perhaps surprising is how this hiatus in hostilities saw others return. In a welcome boost to county society, Ross McGillycuddy and his family felt confident enough to resume residence at The Reeks. The purchase of Dunloe by an American barrister, Howard Harrington, who had Kerry roots, was another welcome addition. The election of a new Church of Ireland bishop in September 1921 saw the remaining gentry reassemble in Tralee, while Markham resumed his weekly circuit of visits to those who had persevered. Tennis parties were held again, even if they were more muted affairs; that August, Elizabeth Cuffe's Rolls Royce reappeared at Callinafercy, the 'first car at the door for many months'.[51] Despite signs of normality returning, Kerry remained largely off limits for most visitors given that intimidation continued to permeate everyday life. Events such as the kidnapping of Arthur Blennerhassett of Ballyseedy in an attempt to force him to sign away part of his demesne were hardly likely to encourage visitors.[52] In October 1921, Markham's mother died at the age of eighty-two, and few relatives braved the risk of violence to be at her funeral. Reactions to her death typified ambivalent attitudes to the country house: over a hundred neighbours attended, with local young men carrying her coffin in relays from the house to the avenue gates. Markham was moved to comment that it was 'an old-fashioned mark of respect one hardly thought of these times'.[53]

While treaty negotiations got underway in London, any sense of rural protection vanished as the RIC were gradually evacuated from remaining small barracks to major towns like Killarney and Tralee. At Rattoo Abbey, Ella Browne was repeatedly raided after her police protection was removed.[54] Arthur Blennerhassett complained that 'the Royal Irish Constabulary were removed from Kerry and my arms having been surrendered previously ... my family and I were left at Ballyseedy utterly unprotected'.[55] Markham, reflecting the views of most of his peers, was hopeful that the Anglo-Irish Treaty would see:

> moderation ... come out on top, all farming & business class for it ... also, all who were called southern unionists, though they may not like it, still are going to throw in their lot with their country & be as loyal to the new state of things as they tried to be to the old.[56]

---

[50] Diary of MRLM, 9 Aug. 1923 (MHL, LMP). [51] Diary of MRLM, 30 Aug. 1921 (MHL, LMP). [52] Diary of MRLM, 2 Sept. 1924 (MHL, LMP). MRLM recounts this episode in his 1924 diary after visiting Ballyseedy. [53] Ibid., 28 Oct. 1921 (MHL, LMP). [54] Ella Browne (NAI, Irish Grants Committee, CO 762/60/18). [55] Quoted in Dooley, *Burning the big house*, p. 141. [56] Diary of MRLM, 1 Jan. 1922 (MHL, LMP).

Tragically, such a hope went unfulfilled, and Kerry became a vicious battleground between the anti-treatyites and the National Army during the Civil War. Within days of hostilities breaking out, raids on country houses recommenced: The McGillycuddy's motor car was taken, as were those belonging to the Harringtons, Lord Kenmare and the Vincents of Muckross. An attempt was made to commandeer Markham's remaining horse 'Tommy', but on this occasion the local IRA captain countermanded the order.[57] However, the impending arrival of Free State troops in Kerry and the withdrawal of anti-treatyites to more mountainous inaccessible areas resulted in Callinafercy being raided again. The earlier reprieve for 'Tommy' was revoked and he was taken. Nearby Kilcoleman Abbey was raided by armed men looking for guns, and while they were civil towards Sir William Godfrey and his wife, they still ransacked the house.[58] Country house owners had no choice but to provide food and lodgings for these on the run. At Callinafercy, Markham was forced to host anti-treatyites on various dates throughout August 1922. He attempted to understand their actions: 'they remind one of one's own men, patient, uncomplaining, very sorry for them, though it is hard to understand how they can believe that their course of action is in the interest of their country'.[59] A sign of these troubled times was an entry in the visitors' book for 24 August 1922 very different from earlier ones: '22 armed men in threes or fours – did not leave their names'.[60] A diary entry however the following year makes it clear that Markham knew their identities: 'Heard Boyle … had come in with his wife with permission of his commandant. He was one of the party who were here in August'.[61] It was through these uninvited guests that Markham and his household learned that Michael Collins had been shot.[62] Although no damage was done to Callinafercy, not all country-house owners had such benign experiences. Markham writes how Elizabeth Cuffe 'had [a] horrible visit from [National] troops in "civvies" posing as republicans. Officer began at whiskey bottle at breakfast 6:30am, returned in evening demanded beds & supper. "I will do what I like & sleep where I like." Very offensive in every way.'[63] Aside from such undesirable guests, county families were now almost completely isolated; Edith Gordon wrote 'for weeks we saw no one, went nowhere, heard nothing, did nothing worth recording'.[64]

As the National Army gradually gained control over north and mid-Kerry, attacks on country houses spread southwards, and Askive, Derreen, Derryquin

---

57 Ibid., 25 July 1922, 'On getting home heard my pony had been selected but the local men said enough had been suffered by me in motor & bikes.' This was due to the influence of local IRA Captain John Heffernan, whose family worked at Callinafercy.   **58** Diary of MRLM, 12 Aug. 1922 (MHL, LMP).   **59** Ibid., 24 Aug. 1922 (MHL, LMP).   **60** Callinafercy Visitors Book, 8–24 Aug. 1922 (MHL, LMP).   **61** Diary of MRLM, 23 Apr. 1923 (MLH, LMP).   **62** Ibid., 24 Aug. 1922 (MHL, LMP).   **63** Ibid., 23 Mar. 1923 (MHL, LMP). See Gavin Foster, 'The Civil War in Kerry in history and memory' in Maurice J. Bric (ed.), *Kerry history and society: interdisciplinary essays on the history of an Irish county* (Dublin, 2020), p. 479.   **64** Gordon, *Winds of time*, p. 218.

10.7 The IRA demand issued 8 August 1922 some weeks after 'Tommy' had been taken. 'Sir, Bearer requires the use of pony or horse & trap for a few hours today. Please let him have same immediately. Signed J. O'Flynn O/C.' In his response, Markham wrote, 'Sir, my horse was taken from me 3 weeks ago & never returned. It's not right that I should be deprived of my only means of getting about, yours, MRLM' (The Leeson Marshall Papers, Muckross House Archive Library).

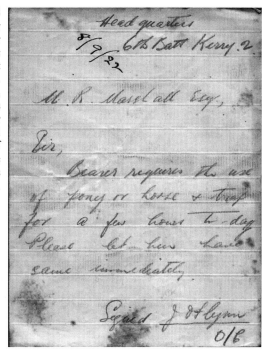

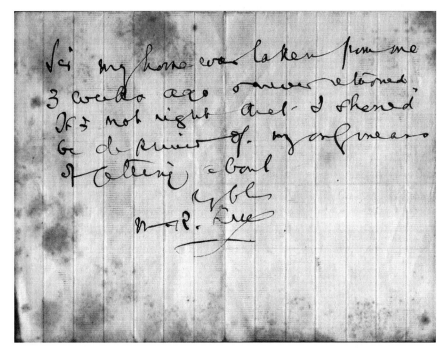

and Rossdohan were looted and destroyed. Against this background, Markham took the view that there was little that could be done should Callinafercy itself be targeted. In late March 1923, he was tipped off that the house was at risk and suitcases were packed in case arsonists arrived: 'the "girls" have had their boxes packed for the last fortnight & Kathleen, returning from early mass on Sunday, wanted hers brought down to the back door'.[65] A series of night-time military sweeps saw local young men taken into custody by the National Army including some of Markham's own farmhands. He intervened with the army officer in charge in Killorglin to release them, and although unsuccessful, this intervention did not go unnoticed and may explain why Callinafercy escaped the torch. Another reason, which has already been alluded to, was Markham's relationship with his neighbours, which was defined by numerous instances of assistance and support. Markham's daughter May, a qualified nurse and physiotherapist, managed to get a local man, Daniel Clifford, admitted into the Mater Hospital for an urgent operation when she returned to Dublin in January 1923. Markham wrote: 'you have done him well & justified our position here as ex-landowners should do. One only wishes one could guide them more'.[66] This shows how some country house owners continued to engage with their neighbours despite their beleaguered status. Another supplicant was Kate McKenna, who was an active member of Cumann na mBan, and who kept a 'safe house' for the local IRA. Kate's military pension file gives detailed information on how she supported 'the cause' by nursing the wounded, washing their clothes, carrying arms and hiding ammunition.[67] In the final weeks of the Civil War, Markham wrote to his daughter:

> Kate McKenna was up yesterday & asked Herself to find out how she could become a maternity nurse. It would be a great thing for her to get her some means of livelihood & a great thing for the whole family. Could you find out for us what course is necessary & what hospital would take her & if free or at what cost?[68]

Aside from individual cases such as these, at least ten or eleven families depended directly on Markham for their livelihoods, aside from those he indirectly supported through charity. The importance of Callinafercy and indeed of many Kerry country houses to the local economy and local community was probably a significant factor in their survival.[69]

What is most remarkable throughout this period is how, despite the burnings, the attacks, the looting, the intimidation, the unwanted and unwelcome visitors,

---

65 MRLM to May Leeson Marshall, 28 Mar. 1923 (MHL, LMP).   **66** Ibid., 23 Jan. 1923 (MHL, LMP).   **67** IRA pension claim form, Catherine MacKenna, Callinafercy, 23 Apr. 1942 (Military Archives, MSP34REF59953).   **68** MRLM to May Leeson Marshall, 18 May 1923 (MHL, LMP).   **69** See Dooley, *Burning the big house*, pp 370–3, which touches on the important economic role of the country house.

and the almost complete isolation, ordinary everyday life was maintained where possible. The routines of the agricultural year, the planting of crops and posting orders for flower and vegetable seeds all continued (even if these remained undelivered). Threshing the oats each October continued to be a major community get-together, with the customary dinner for the workers afterwards, 'A grand day for threshing, 25 men & boys. Cold corned beef for dinner good – very little porter.'[70] The harvest thanksgiving was also held every year during the Troubles albeit the main topic at the 1922 service was the bomb dropped by an aeroplane near Milltown. Despite roads being trenched, bridges demolished and intermittent post, diocesan committee meetings and local vestries were still held and provided a welcome distraction as did fundraising events for the Red Cross and ex-servicemen. Families continued to visit each other discreetly – albeit either walking or cycling – and 'having tea' remained the most important form of social interaction. There were even occasional fishing expeditions and the odd game of tennis. This determination to live life indicates a hope that things might improve.

Callinafercy survived the Civil War intact. Nevertheless, the 'Troubles' marked a profound break in the rhythm of how county society functioned. The destruction of fifteen country houses in Kerry between 1920 and 1923 and the departure of many 'old families' saw former patterns of visits and social gatherings fragment or disappear forever. Visitors from outside the county simply stopped coming, and local families were forced to rely on and support each other. It was undoubtedly a traumatic time. Edith Gordon wrote, 'the Magills, two girls living alone, were attacked, shots fired for over an hour round the house, and their cattle driven off'.[71] The fear the Magills and others suffered, while hinted at, was rarely written down. The uncertainty of when or if an arson attack would come was surely frightening. Yet despite this ever-present menace, and witnessing their entire social world implode around them, it is remarkable how many families not only clung on but tried to maintain a semblance of normality. Each family negotiated this period as best they could, and the Leeson Marshalls' determination to stay, together with their relationship with their neighbours, offers an insight – not perhaps so much into why houses were burnt – but into why so many were not.

It was by no means a foregone conclusion that independence would mark the end of the country house, as was the case elsewhere in Europe, where revolution or regime change usually marked the end of the country house. Indeed, what is striking in Kerry is how surviving families quickly attempted to resume pre-conflict social norms. After thirteen months effectively isolated at Callinafercy, Markham and his wife escaped to London in June 1923 to the welcome embrace of friends, clubs, shops and metropolitan society. A highlight was a reunion of ex-Royal Munster Fusilier officers, but there were also gatherings with various

70 Diary of MRLM, 19 Oct. 1922 (MHL, LMP).   71 Gordon, *Winds of time*, p. 197.

10.8 Wedding of May Leeson Marshall to George Ruth, July 1924, which saw the Kerry gentry reassemble for the first time in a decade (private collection).

Kerry émigrés, including Doris Collis-Sandes of Oakpark and Charles Warden of Derryquin, who gave a first-hand account of his harrowing experiences to Markham. Back in Kerry, Edith Gordon hosted her first tennis party in July 1923, followed by similar get-togethers at Churchtown and The Reeks. Markham and his wife Meriel hosted a tennis party of seventeen that August, retrieving their silverware from the bank for the first time since 1914. As soon as Kerry reopened to visitors they were inundated with guests, one of whom, Louise Hamilton Cox, stayed fifty-two days, to make up for an absence of four years. An indication of how Kerry county society quickly regrouped was the marriage in July 1924 of Markham's daughter May to George Ruth, who was descended from minor Wexford gentry. This saw all surviving county families reassemble, including some who had left *avant le déluge*.[72] In a somewhat remarkable volte-face, revealing yet again the nuanced relationship between country house owners and their neighbours, Markham employed local ex-IRA men to police the grounds to deter uninvited wedding guests:

72 'Before the flood', paraphrasing Louis XV of France, who apparently said *'Après moi, le déluge'*.

My 'police' found a tramp sneaking in woods & ran him out to their great satisfaction. They were Mick Jandy (ex-gun man!), Jack, Thady & Bill Harmon, Kerin (ex IRA) – all well dressed in navy blue.[73]

After the tumult of the previous ten years, those families who remained formed a tight network who mutually supported each other. This included the Blennerhassetts, Butlers, Godfreys, Hoods, Kenmares, Leslies, Magills, McGillycuddys, Merediths, O'Connells, Powers and Vincents. In an encouraging sign, Lord Lansdowne rebuilt Derreen and resumed his yearly visits, while the Blands returned to live at Drimina in 1925. The one main difference is that unlike before the war, county society now regrouped around Killarney. Tralee, which had lost its barracks and accompanying social life, and seen the departure of many of its families, became less important, although it retained its role as the diocesan centre. From 1923, Cecil Leslie of Tarbert became a regular visitor to Callinafercy, as did Ella Brown of Rattoo, indicating how north Kerry society – or what was left of it – now re-orientated southwards. Ella Brown provided much-needed amusement, such as when she came to tea on one occasion with a newly purchased Oxfordshire ram sitting in the back seat of her motor car.[74] She was also secretary to the Kerry branch of the All-Ireland Donkey Society.[75] Olwen Purdue notes that landed families in Northern Ireland after 1921 continued to patronize local arts, remained active in the Church of Ireland, supported charitable causes and sat on the committees of clubs and societies.[76] So too did their counterparts in the south. Their political and economic role may have expired but a public role continued. Social patterns reconfigured around parish 'sales of work', charity bazaars, flower shows, British Legion meetings and fundraising for the Nurses' Pension Fund and the Jubilee Nurse. Markham remained on the Killarney district fisheries board of conservators, as did his neighbour Sir John Godfrey. These functions may not have been as high-profile as before, but they gave remaining families a certain *raison d'être* and provided an outlet for that ingrained sense of civic duty.

Throughout 1924 and 1925, increasing numbers of visitors began to return to Kerry and sightseeing recommenced, including the obligatory visits to Muckross and the Gap of Dunloe, although golf excursions and bathing were now interspersed with nostalgic visits to burnt-out ruins. Markham resumed shooting at Clydagh and received invites from other shoots, particularly those hosted by Lord Kerry (now a Free State senator) at Sheen Falls near Kenmare. Elizabeth Cuffe hosted Lady Dartrey and the duchess of Devonshire (a Fitzmaurice of Derreen) at Caragh, both of whom came to tea at Callinafercy.

73 Diary of MRLM, 30 July 1924 (MHL, LMP). 74 Diary of MRLM, 24 Aug. 1937 (MHL, LMP). 75 *The Liberator* (Tralee), 27 Oct. 1931. 76 Olwen Purdue, 'Big house society in Northern Ireland, 1921–1969' in Terence Dooley and Christopher Ridgway (eds), *The Irish country house: its past, present and future* (Dublin, 2011), p. 146.

Some families attempted to integrate into the new political order, using their homes to entertain a much wider social circle than heretofore. In 1926, The McGillycuddy won a seat on the county council before being appointed to the Senate two years later. A supporter of Cumann na nGaedheal, he entertained a wide selection of guests, including local Kerry TDs such as Fionan Lynch and John Marcus O'Sullivan, and senators such as Oliver St John Gogarty, Dr William O'Sullivan from Killarney, and Samuel Lombard Brown, a Dublin barrister, who Markham would meet on visits to The Reeks. By contrast, visitors to Kenmare House remained very much 'old family', such as Lady Linlithgow, Lady Mayo and Olive Wingfield, whom Markham knew from visits to Powerscourt. Although always important, the Church of Ireland increasingly became a lynchpin of identity for those that remained. This saw more interaction with middle-class Protestants and wealthy mercantile families who served as laymen in the church, occasionally bolstered by ex-colonial retirees. Most of these were not landed in the traditional sense and owed their positions to commercial or professional success. Nonetheless, they were increasingly admitted to gatherings, previously the preserve of the 'old families'. It is also interesting to note that visitors from a much wider circle of country houses now came to stay at Callinafercy. Undoubtedly this was because it was one of the few houses that continued to provide old-style hospitality. Guests who made their first appearance during the 1920s included Otway Wheeler-Cuffe of Lyrath and his wife Charlotte, who was particularly interested in Kerry gardens. Markham wrote in March 1926: 'On Tuesday, Otway Cuffe & his wife, driven by their friend Mrs Price who has a nice Morris Cowley, arrived. They took Meriel to the Gap, Reeks & O'Connells next day & both of us to Killarney on Thursday. They were excellent guests.'[77] One also sees the social milieu gradually expand to include people from academia, albeit these visitors were often only one generation removed from the country house. In 1932, Dr John Joly and Professor Henry H. Dixon were invited to a garden party at Callinafercy and would become regular visitors in the years ahead. Joly was a physicist and professor of geology at Trinity College Dublin, famous for developing radiotherapy, while Dixon was professor of botany, also at Trinity. The 1920s therefore saw a revival of country house society, marked by a fusion of old and new social patterns. This reveals the determination by those families who remained in Kerry to reconstitute an acceptable and sustainable social framework.

Just as county society gradually reconfigured, modern technology made visiting more pleasurable. In 1931, Gertrude Scott, in gratitude for numerous holidays spent at Callinafercy over thirty years, bought Markham a new Pye wireless, which was installed in the dining room.[78] Visits were soon timed to

---

[77] MRLM to May Leeson Marshall, 5 Mar. 1926 (MHL, LMP). [78] Diary of MRLM, 29 Apr. 1931 (MHL, LMP), 'To Caragh with Mary, tea with Lill Cuffe, called Cliffords to see &

coincide with the Rugby Four Nations, Wimbledon, the Grand National and the Derby. The wireless allowed Markham and Meriel to reconnect with the wider empire, and very soon royal events and religious services became a reason for an invitation. The silver jubilee in 1935 saw Markham, family and household listen to the celebratory service from St Paul's Cathedral followed by the king's broadcast to his subjects. The abdication speech of Edward VIII in December 1936 was also a major talking point. Markham's sister Mary caustically remarked, 'I think we are well out of our late king. We have heard so much about him & his "goings on" lately that I think he is much better retired.'[79] The wireless allowed the country house to resume its relationship with familiar loyalties, albeit over the airwaves; an identity that was divided between the local and the distant in a dualism that lasted well into the 1960s.

By now, Markham was in many respects the last grand seigneur of Kerry, whose life had spanned the Land War, the land acts, revolution and finally independence. His death on 13 December 1939, a few weeks short of his eightieth birthday, was genuinely regretted by many. His correspondence is a window into the vanished world of the Kerry gentry. It reveals a rich and varied social calendar before 1914 where visits and visiting were essential ingredients of how country houses functioned. It was a lifestyle that revolved around a set pattern dictated by the time of the day and the season of the year.[80] It was an exclusive, insular world, drawn almost completely from landed society, yet one also grounded in place and locality. As the war abroad merged almost seamlessly into a war at home that lasted until 1923, this rhythm of life was temporarily shattered. Country houses, seen as intrinsic to what Bowen called the 'aesthetic of living', were destroyed, and many friends and families forced to flee, amid an orgy of looting and intimidation.[81] Those who persevered had to deal with a very different type of visitor, whose motives were never certain. Yet, the Troubles in themselves did not mark the end of county society. Families such as the Leeson Marshalls adapted to their new circumstances, regrouping around the church, and embraced a new and gradually more inclusive type of guest. Where possible they resumed the vestiges of their previous lifestyle, with old loyalties bolstered through the wireless and other means. Visits and visiting resumed in a manner not dissimilar to before 1914, and to a degree concealed the partial dismemberment of county society and the glaring absences of important families.

The late 1920s marked the apogee of traditional country house society in Kerry as the realities of independence and a much impoverished State began to have effect. The 1930s and beyond saw remaining county society fragment, as rising taxes, declining incomes, the Economic War and a lack of opportunities took their toll. Tourism and agriculture provided a mainstay for some, but the

---

hear their new Pye wireless, Gertrude Scott having donated us a set.'   79 Mary Godfrey to Mary Constance Edwards, 9 Jan. 1937 (Godfrey Papers, private collection).   80 O'Sullivan, *I heard the wild birds sing*, p. 89.   81 Jacqueline Genet (ed.), *The big house in Ireland: reality*

next generation were inclined to seek their fortunes elsewhere; Sir William Godfrey, for example, set up an agricultural machinery company in Kent in 1933. Muckross was bequeathed to the state in 1932 as it was too costly to maintain. Rattoo Abbey was sold in 1944 and Ella Browne died in a Tralee nursing home. Flesk Castle was dismantled in 1946 and Glanleam sold in 1953. Kilcoleman was sold in 1960, Waterville in 1963 and Ballyseedy in 1967. The Reeks went in 1985 and Dromore in 1994. It was a slow but definitive retreat. Markham's daughter, May Ruth, poignantly referred to herself as a member of 'a disappearing race'. She wrote that if a scientist of the future had to add the Anglo-Irish to the sum of races that have inhabited this planet: 'he probably will have to classify it as "extinct", & in that case, I think he will add "a pity"'.[82] She further remarked: 'on the other hand, the denigration of a whole race is as stupid as it is popular'.[83] May's visitors book stopped in 1977, she died in 1988 and Callinafercy itself was finally sold in 2020. Currently only four country houses in Kerry remain in the hands of the families who built them.

and representation (Dingle, 1991), p. 160.   **82** Incomplete draft introduction to a book on the Leeson Marshalls by May Ruth, *c.*1960 (MHL, LMP).   **83** Ibid.

Visitations: friendlies

CHRISTOPHER RIDGWAY

This final chapter is the counterpart to chapter one that reviewed unwelcome and unfriendly arrivals at country houses, and is a reminder that such places have also commanded respect, interest and affection. However this is a generalization that needs qualifying in respect of times and places where big houses were viewed in terms of class or colonial oppression. If the earlier chapter suggested jeopardy, this review of friendly visitations reveals an encouraging story as to the fate of the country house today. The literature on this topic is extensive and there is little need to rehearse this narrative, but this chapter will try to outline one or two less considered perspectives.

Early tourists and visitors to British country houses included familiar figures such as Celia Fiennes and Daniel Defoe, and continued through the eighteenth century with the likes of Thomas Pennant, Horace Walpole and John Manners. These intrepid travellers were motivated by a spirit of curiosity and their writings usually displayed an architectural, chorographical, genealogical or antiquarian emphasis. Country houses were not always the main focus of attention. Many featured either as buildings worthy of note or because their families were significant.[1] In addition to published works there were countless individuals who left manuscript accounts of their travels. As a rule those who travelled to houses were part of an exclusive social circuit, and came prepared with invitations or had, at the very least, the right connections and respectability for gaining entry to parkland and/or house.[2] This emerging body of literature was supplemented by a long tradition of topographical artists too, such as Jan Siberechts, Peter Tillemans and William Marlow; some artists such as Leonard Knyff, the Buck brothers and Paul Sandby oversaw engraved editions of their work that reached ever wider audiences. The rise of such illustrated volumes, as well as numerous architectural publications, was a way of visualizing houses and their landscapes, presenting them to a wider public, both feeding as well as generating a growing interest in them as cultural entities but also as destinations to visit.[3]

[1] The literature is extensive. Most recently, see Jocelyn Anderson, *Touring and publicising England's country houses in the long eighteenth century* (London, 2018); earlier studies include Esther Moir, *The discovery of Britain: the English tourists, 1540–1840* (London, 1964); Adrian Tinniswood, *The polite tourist: four centuries of country house visiting* (London, 1998); Ian Ousby, *The Englishman's England* (Cambridge, 1990). [2] An especially useful volume is Robin Gard (ed.), *The observant traveller: diaries of travel in England, Wales and Scotland in the county record offices of England and Wales* (London, 1989). [3] John Harris, *The artist and the country house, a history of country house and garden view painting in Britain 1540–1870* (London, 1985);

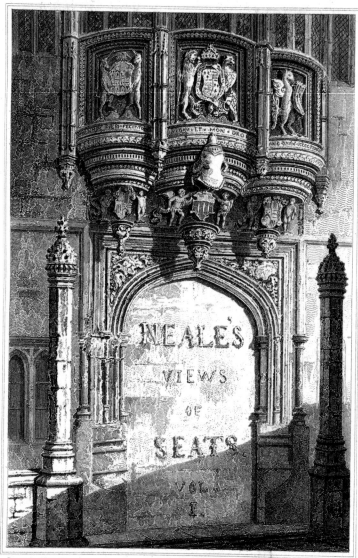

11.1 The title page to the first volume of John Preston Neale's *Views of the seats of noblemen and gentlemen of England, Wales, Scotland and Ireland*, 1818, depicting the doorway at Hengrave Hall, Suffolk (private collection).

By the nineteenth century, various kinds of visitor and publication were beginning to prevail. One kind of visitor produced architectural surveys, such as John Preston Neale, whose *Views of the seats of noblemen and gentlemen of England, Wales, Scotland and Ireland* first appeared in 1818, before a second series was published; in all, Neale illustrated more than 700 houses. Each entry was accompanied by an engraved view with architectural description and a degree of family information.[4] A second class of specialist visitor was the professional genealogist typified by the figure of Sir Bernard Burke, whose father had founded the directory commonly known as *Burke's peerage*. Of Irish descent, Burke junior was a barrister and a herald, and is principally remembered for his *Visitation of the seats and arms of the noblemen and gentlemen of Great Britain*. Consciously invoking the old custom for heralds 'to make Visitations ... amongst the various nobles and landed proprietors', a practice that had fallen into abeyance in the seventeenth century, Burke justified his enterprise as a way of updating 'heraldic and genealogical information', and took it upon himself to address the deficiencies in Neale's earlier work, which he felt had been aimed more at pleasing the eye than the mind. Burke filled two volumes with short entries on hundreds of residences and their owners, but only a small selection of houses were illustrated with 'picturesque views'.[5] These and similar publications, with their encyclopaedic pretensions, were aimed not only at elite audiences who would find their ancestry explained as part of a select genealogical club, but also at a growing audience of country house visitors: some of whom were inevitably armchair travellers, while others were keen to visit for real.

Later in the nineteenth century a third type of visitor included scholars and art historians such as Gustav Waagen,[6] George Scharff[7] and a little later, Tancred Borenius.[8] These figures recorded and evaluated the great collections in country houses, and advised owners. This period also saw the growth of periodicals such as the *Art Journal*, established in 1849, and the *Athenaeum*, founded in 1828; later in the century the latter ran a series of in-depth articles on the private art

and his later, *The artist and the country house, from the fifteenth century to the present day*, exh. cat. (London, 1995).   4 J.P. Neale, *Views of the seats of noblemen and gentlemen of England, Wales, Scotland and Ireland*, first series, 6 vols (London, 1819–24); second series, 5 vols (London, 1824–29).   5 John Bernard Burke, *A visitation of the seats and arms of the noblemen and gentlemen of Great Britain*, 2 vols (London, 1852), pp i–iv.   6 Waagen was one of a number of Continental visitors to English country houses in the nineteenth century; his three-volume *Works of art and artists in England* (1838) was superseded by his *Art treasures in Great Britain*, 4 vols (London, 1854–7). See Giles Waterfield and Florian Illies, 'Waagen in Engand', *Jarbuch der Berliner Museen*, 37.Bd (1995), pp 47–59. Towards the end of the century Adolph Michaelis performed what Waagen had done for painting with sculpture collections in houses, *Ancient marbles in Great Britain* (Cambridge, 1882).   7 See Philip Cottrell, 'A course of wandering picture hunting: George Scharf's survey of English country house collections, 1856–57' in Terence Dooley and Christopher Ridgway (eds), *Country house collections, their lives and after lives* (Dublin, 2021), pp 81–101.   8 Borenius was a Finland-born art historian, who went to London in 1909, where he lectured at University College London; he was later a consultant at Sotheby's, helped found *Apollo* magazine, was editor of the *Burlington Magazine* and acted as art adviser to many country houses; see his entry in the *ODNB*.

11.2 The arrival of Queen Victoria at Castle Howard railway station in August 1850, from the *Illustrated London News* (Castle Howard Collection).

collections in England, emphasizing how these assemblies of treasures were of national importance and on a par with collections in museums and galleries.[9] Among these mass-circulation publications none was more significant than *Country Life* magazine, founded in 1897, which quickly adopted the format of weekly articles on houses, sometime running to two or three instalments.[10] The rise of photography meant that high quality illustrations became the norm, although the photographers and their equipment were not aways welcome. Thus at Audley End, Essex, in 1926, Mrs Ruck did not appreciate how *Country Life* photographer A.E. Henson rearranged her interiors; 'it was worse than burglars', she is said to have complained.[11]

In miniature this particular episode reflects the double-edged nature of such wide publicity: while owners were mostly content for their houses to become well-known and praised for their architecture, collections and landscapes, this often came at the expense of seclusion. The gradual shift from a nation whose houses were closed with families protective of their privacy, to a land in which

[9] For example, no. XXV in the series was a five-part assessment of the collection at Castle Howard, which ran from September to October 1876. [10] John Cornforth, *The search for a style:* Country Life *and architecture, 1899–1935* (London, 1988); Roy Strong, Country Life, *1897–1997: the English arcadia* (London, 1996). [11] Michael Hall, *The English country house: from the archives of* Country Life, *1897–1939* (London, 1994), pp 9–13.

Visitations: friendlies 251

11.3 The gaslit display, 'God Save the Queen' in the great hall at Castle Howard, from the *Illustrated London News*, August 1850 (Castle Howard Collection).

many opened their doors to the paying public began in earnest in the middle decades of the nineteenth century.[12] One episode from Castle Howard in 1850 might typify this momentous transformation.

In August 1850 the seventh earl of Carlisle hosted Queen Victoria and Prince Albert at Castle Howard as the royal couple journeyed north to Balmoral; this was a private visit, at the personal invitation of the earl, who was a confidante of Victoria and Albert. Thus it was not accompanied by the levels of ceremonial

---

12 Peter Mandler, *The fall and rise of the stately home* (London, 1997), pp 71–106, for the opening of houses in the nineteenth century; pp 225–63 for later phases.

pomp and fanfare that characterized her public visitations to other houses and towns. Nevertheless, a large party travelled to Yorkshire, including her family, equerries and other officials. The royals arrived by train at the Castle Howard station, opened five years earlier on the York–Scarborough line; this was something of a first for guests, and a harbinger of things to come.

Although a select group of Yorkshire society joined the dinner in the evening, the visit was quiet and relaxed, not that it didn't cause Carlisle some trepidation after all the expense and panic of preparing for his distinguished guests: there were the familiar concerns that all would go well, and the monarch would be comfortable and suitably entertained. There were tours of the house, with Prince Albert interrogating his host about the collections, a tour of the grounds, a visit to the mausoleum, a ceremonial tree-planting and a cricket match. The highlight was the installation of special gas lighting in the great hall, a ring of burners mounted around the balcony beneath the dome, with 2,000 separate tubes to create fifteen illuminated letters that spelt out 'God Save the Queen'.[13]

After two days the royal party set off for Scotland and Castle Howard began to relax. For Carlisle the visit had passed off successfully, and the gaslight was a triumph. But he and his family had to endure the foibles of the monarch – her notorious wish for windows to be thrown open and fires dampened down, and her customary lateness for receptions. At one point she became lost in the house and was rescued by Carlisle, who, reflecting on the visit, concluded of his guest, 'she has not the way of putting a room quite at its ease'.[14]

Over the following days the house party broke up, and Carlisle set off for Balmoral, swapping his role as royal host for that of royal guest. As he departed he was aware of a throng of visitors arriving at Castle Howard. This was a large party from Pudsey, West Yorkshire, who had arrived by excursion train. Until his elevation to the House of Lords Carlisle had been MP for West Yorkshire for many years, and was always keen to oblige his former constituents, especially by permitting visits to Castle Howard. Carlisle rather quaintly recorded how he left Castle Howard 'in possession of a cheap train' that numbered 2,200 visitors.[15] Although fewer than the 15,000 people who had thronged the grounds to see the queen a few days earlier, their mass entry into the house caused pandemonium: a pane of glass on the door into the great hall was broken and women fainted in the melée. Castle Howard was completely ill-prepared for such a huge crush of visitors, and even by today's standards, 2,000-plus visitors to any house in a single day is exceptional. In September 1850 there was just one housekeeper and a steward on hand to deal with this mass of people, and supervise the tour of the

---

13 Seventh earl of Carlisle, journal, Aug.–Sept. 1850 (CHA J19/8/24); papers relating to the royal visit (CHA, J19/21); correspondence of the seventh earl of Carlisle (CHA, J19/1/49), Aug.–Sept. 1850; estate correspondence (CHA, F5/3, Bundle 2, 1848–51); also the *Illustrated London News*, 31 Aug. 1850 and 7 Sept. 1850.   14 Journal entry 28 Aug. 1850 (CHA, J19/8/24).   15 Ibid., 2 Sept. 1850.

REGULATIONS
FOR VIEWING
WOBURN ABBEY.

The days for viewing WOBURN ABBEY are altered from Mondays to Fridays, from Eleven till Four between Lady Day and Michaelmas, and from Eleven till Three between Michaelmas and Lady Day.

Persons desirous of viewing it to apply to MR. BENNETT, at the Park Farm Office, on Fridays, between Ten and Three in Summer, and between Ten and Two in Winter, for Two TICKETS, (one for the Abbey and one for the Gardens) and to enter their names and residences in a book kept there, and also in a book kept in the waiting-room at the Abbey.

The TICKETS to be dated on the day they are issued, and to serve only for that day.

A TICKET will not admit more than six persons.

Persons having TICKETS to present them at the Abbey, and wait in the WAITING-ROOM till the person appointed to go round with them is ready to do so.

Persons having with them Sticks, Whips, Parasols, or Umbrellas to leave them whilst viewing the Abbey, in the waiting-room.

The TICKET for the Gardens to be delivered, on entering them, to the Gardener.

No persons will be allowed to take with them any collation or refreshments, to take in the Abbey, the Gardens, or the Park.

11.4 Regulations for visiting Woburn Abbey, late nineteenth century (Castle Howard Collection).

house. There was a ring of truth in Carlisle's observation: these people had taken over the house.

After this episode recriminations flew back and forth. His mother was enraged at the confusion, as was Carlisle when he learnt of the true extent of the debacle. The resident agent, John Henderson, was blamed in part for poor organization, as was the railway company, and in turn the organizers from Pudsey. What resulted was the realization that something more organized was needed for tours inside the house, a system for governing admission of visitors. The sixth countess instructed Henderson to write to Chatsworth and other houses to see what rules they had in place, and within a few years the bigger houses in England were beginning to devise and print regulations to guide entry and behaviour.[16]

The royal visit and the public rumpus just a few days later mark two extremes of the visiting spectrum, and the moment also denotes a social shift. Traditionally, in the eighteenth and early nineteenth centuries, big houses were open to a handful of individuals with the correct pedigrees or letters of introduction. The rise of mass transportation brought about by the railways (and in due course, even more by the motor car) meant that excursion trains allowed large groups to visit such places as the seaside, the Great Exhibition, famous beauty spots or country houses. The duke of Wellington had feared that such mass mobility would lead to a breakdown of law and order, and if he had witnessed the Pudsey excursion he would have felt vindicated in his argument against the railways. But for all its chaotic organization that September day represented the future of the modern visitor industry. In terms of numbers, and as a cross-section of society (leaving aside behaviour), it was far more typical of the audiences that would come to dominate country house visiting in the twentieth century and today. If anything the royal visit was the exception, a one-off, a private episode between the house of Howard and house of Saxe-Coburg and Gotha. Nowadays it is the thousands of ordinary visitors to country houses who sustain them, and give them meaning as places for enjoyment; they may be paying visitors but in parting with their money tourists are contributing to their upkeep.

The nineteenth century saw the birth of mass tourism as leisure time grew for large sections of the population: tickets, house regulations, postcards and guidebooks would all become part of a commercial enterprise as more houses opened their doors to the paying public. Instead of a private dinner, mass catering was available in cafeterias; no longer were personal tokens of gratitude exchanged, but gifts would be available to purchase in the shop.

In the twentieth century there emerged a new breed of country house champion – professional writers and architectural historians such as Christopher Hussey, James Lees Milne, John Cornforth and others, many of whom would contribute to *Country Life* or other journals, write guidebooks for specific properties or publish monographs. They were amphibious figures: on the one hand they earned their living by the pen and acting as officials and experts in the heritage world; at the same time they moved comfortably in patrician circles they considered themselves a part of. For the most part they were welcomed as equals, as advocates of an elite way of life, who would not attack notions of wealth and

---

16 For recriminations over the visit, see the letter from the sixth countess to the seventh earl, 5 Sept. 1850 (CHA, J19/1/48/99); letters from the earl to John Henderson, 5 and 7 Sept. 1850 (CHA, F5/3, Bundle 2); also letter of apology from the York and North Midland Railway Company, 5 Sept. 1850 (CHA, F5/1); for visiting regulations for Woburn,

property. Their research visits became social occasions that often included privileged access to family records.[17]

These figures were all champions for, and defenders of, the country house, even if they had reservations about the architectural merit of individual buildings, or the cultural credentials of certain families. But they were not always uniformly welcome. Lees Milne's diaries record his visits to countless houses at the beginning of the Lord Lothian scheme whereby owners could gift their houses to the National Trust. In the eyes of some, Lees Milne was a saviour; others viewed him as an officious upstart. At Longleat House, Wiltshire, Lees Milne was dismissed by the marquess of Bath, and shown down the steps lined by liveried footmen while one servant wheeled round his bicycle. At Charlecote Park, Warwickshire, the door was shut in his face; and at Petworth, Sussex, Lord Leconfield refused any hospitality, directing him to a tea-room over the road that was shut. Other owners, like Lord Berwick at Attingham Park, Shropshire, were more receptive and welcoming. These episodes point to the flipside of this subject: for every guest, there might be an unfriendly host – begrudging, snobbish, rude, dismissive, lax in their obligations – who would leave a sour impression on their visitors. For Lees Milne revenge was indeed sweet in the descriptions he left in his diaries; thus Leconfield was a 'pompous old ass with a blue face and bulbous eyes'; many a house was described as hideous or ruined by later alterations, and such was his dislike of Wool House in Kent he declared acidly, 'A horrible property. I hope it gets bombed.' These diaries point to how beyond the polite veneer of civilized greeting and farewell, guests might leave an unwelcome and permanent legacy in the form of memoirs, diaries or even in fiction. Lees Milne's diaries are still in print more than forty years after they first appeared. For all their waspish qualities, and he was not immune from snobbery himself, the diaries continue to be read as one of the strongest arguments for the preservation of country houses, especially as their survival depended on a move from the private to the public realm.[18] One particular register of this shift is the birth of dedicated heritage organizations, such as the National Trust, English Heritage and, most especially, Historic Houses, founded as the Historic Houses Association in 1973; today it represents nearly 1,500 properties, lobbying government in the interests of private owners and helping to promote access to a multitude of houses and gardens.

Tourism infrastructure would see the growth of railway and coach operations, helpful timetables and gazetteers with opening hours and other essential information; the rise of travel companies was bolstered by marketing drives

Chatsworth, and Blenheim see (CHA, F7/31). 17 See, for example, John Cornforth, 'Christopher and Betty Hussey's visiting albums, 1936–70', I: 'Country house enthusiasms', II: 'Whig vitality', *Country Life*, 175 (26 Jan., 2 Feb. 1984), pp 197–200, 274–7; Lees Milne's diaries are as much about high society as they are about country houses. 18 Diary entries for Charlecote, Saturday 18 July 1942, Lees Milne, *Ancestral voices*, p. 80; Longleat, Michael Bloch, *James Lees-Milne: the life* (London, 2009), p. 100; Petworth, Thursday 19 July 1945,

11.5 *Historic houses and castles in Great Britain open to the public*, the 1954 issue, which was the precursor to *Hudson's historic houses and gardens* (private collection).

across towns and regions, until country house visiting became a staple of the UK economy, supported by such annual publications as *Hudson's historic houses and gardens*.[19] Ever more intrepid excursions with multiple destinations meant that, in the words of soon-to-be-murdered Miss Temple on her three-week coach

Prophesying peace, p. 215.   **19** Christopher Ridgway, 'Time travellers' guide', *Hudson's historic houses and gardens, museums and heritage sites*, thirtieth-anniversary edition (2017), pp 96–101.

tour, in Agatha Christie's Miss Marple mystery *Nemesis*: 'Going over houses is always tiring ... The most tiring thing in the world.'[20] Her words are a reminder that not only is cultural tourism an enormously popular pastime, but also that murder is a staple of country house fiction, where plots revolve around hosts and guests who are either victims or killers. Beneath the protocols of country house sociability there might lie a lethal streak, and the murder victim could be said to be a type of visitor who never leaves the premises.

Fortunately most visitors do not meet their end while touring properties, but by parting with their money for admission they are, in effect, buying into the country house ethos. Their tour of the house and grounds is unlikely to include any intimate exchange with the owner, let alone the offer of a private dinner, party or bed for the night. Nevertheless these paying guests are essential, if not always welcome, in raising vital revenues: little wonder that many houses today elevate regular visitors to the status of 'Friends' or 'Members', rewarding their loyalty with discounted and premium offers, which might include dinner or sleeping in the house – but at a price. This enormous tranche of the public are indeed stalwart friends of country houses, but that relationship is principally transactional and not sociable. Visitors are especially welcome with their secondary spend on teas, scones, guidebooks and merchandise in the gift shop, farm shop or garden centre. Equally, they might be tiresome arrivals – demanding, impolite, unappreciative, disrespectful. But this irritation is usually tolerated, if not alleviated, because they have paid the admission price and will leave at closing time. There is no doubt the millions of visitors to British country houses today count as a formidable cohort of friends and allies, often caring passionately for their local country house, and evincing fiercely proprietorial feelings. No longer recipients of exclusive invitations, they are mass supporters of a slice of national heritage; their interest lies with not simply the physical fabric of these houses but, vicariously, in a vanishing way of life, fuelled by nostalgia and curiosity. Few visitors have not entertained at some point, no matter how fleetingly, the fantasy of belonging to such a milieu, whether as owner or privileged guest.

Today's visitors to country houses come from far and wide, such is the global stretch of heritage tourism. In the past it was customary for houses to provide comments books in which the public would be invited to write down their reactions; these have been largely superseded by more ubiquitous commentaries on social media, which highlight the volume and impact of the public visitor as opposed to private guest. They are the first port of call for marketing departments, and sometimes owners, who scrutinize them for favourable and unfavourable remarks, as a way of evaluating their own performance. Critical comments might suggest a thankless visitor, or they might point to an unwelcome offer on the part of the attraction that left the visitor dissatisfied.

20 Agatha Christie, *Nemesis* (1971; London, 2002), p. 96.

Sometimes it can be hard to distinguish between the friendly and the unfriendly; disagreeable comments might not necessarily indicate a disgruntled visitor but someone who cares enough to proffer advice.

The anonymity of the internet permits a level of candour few private guests would dare to articulate, and at their most helpful these responses create a kind of dialogue, as the property corrects failings or responds to suggestions for improvement; at their worst they are reservoirs of intemperate spleen. The interplay between comment and response also signals something of a shift in the balance of power. Houses must meet the expectations of their visitors, and accommodate particular wishes or new trends; thus the onus falls back onto the traditional obligations of hospitality: a guest feels at ease because of the welcome by his or her host. This is as true for the commercial visitor as the private one.

At the opposite end of the spectrum are the highly bespoke, family guestbooks, usually leather-bound, and characterized by a mass of individual signatures, in various inks, and perhaps accompanied by sketches or rhymes. These volumes still exist in the private quarters of a house but they record a tiny minority of invited guests compared to the many who visit as tourists. Real visitors are also supplemented by enormous numbers of virtual visitors: these are voyagers who never have to leave home but can invite themselves across a digital threshold and, depending on the sophistication of the website in question, have multiple experiences of a house. In their thousands and millions, their impact on the fabric of a place is minimal. Owners do not have to worry about excessive numbers cramping and damaging the site, there is no danger of repeating the debacle of 1850 at Castle Howard; in this respect they are abundantly welcome, especially as every hit on a website can translate into valuable marketing data; with each click these armchair visitors signal repeat visits of one kind or another.

The rise of the virtual visitor points to a number of things. Firstly, that country houses have always existed in the mind as much as for real, and some of the most celebrated fictional depictions of houses and their families celebrate this powerful sense of attraction, most famously Evelyn Waugh's *Brideshead revisited*, published in 1945. The novel is essentially a love affair with a building, and the very title of the novel articulates the repeated comings and goings, whether these be physical or mental journeys in peacetime or during war. Imaginary visits via the internet today, or by such analogue means as reading guidebooks and fiction, or looking at paintings, prints and photographs, are not limited by time or space – these can happen anywhere and at any time. Visitors have no need to consult opening hours (something especially convenient for those overseas in different time zones), nor do they need any invitation; they are self-defined and independent, responsible for their own itinerary and mobility: they are, in effect, self-invited guests.

The volume and limitless potential of virtual visitors points to a second feature, confirming how the isolationist view of country houses has further

11.6 The front cover to the Penguin paperback edition of Evelyn Waugh's *Brideshead revisited*, from the 1950s, depicting the house in wartime (private collection).

dissolved as they move ever more from a private preserve for the elite to somewhere that attracts a much broader demographic. What was once the abode of the few has become the destination for many. Some houses can afford to shut their doors entirely but a good number have repositioned their relationship with the world. Consequently the balance between owner and visitor has been recalibrated, not least of all in terms of visitors who enjoy wandering around what they perceive as private, or formerly private, space; interiors that belong, or belonged, to someone else. Private or elite space has acquired a new public identity, shaped by social curiosity, the wider expectations of leisure and tourism, and lifestyle aspirations emulating what people have seen. Public reactions to the experience of country house visiting mean that the profile and reputation of houses now circulate well beyond the pages of any guestbook. Whereas before private guests would not dream of putting their expressions of thanks and enjoyment into print – these were reserved exclusively for guestbooks or thank-you letters – today more and more people would not consider their visit complete without recording it on Tripadvisor, Twitter or Instagram.

The country house can welcome a multitude of visitors, whether private guests or paying tourists, and for the most part they are warmly appreciated. There is little doubt that houses filled with the latter category, whether enjoying themselves as daily visitors or attending a special event, are fulfilling the basic purpose of these buildings as spaces for congregation and sociability. By spending time and money visitors bring houses to life and underpin their economic viability. Few would gainsay this positive influence although the frequent arrival of large numbers is not without consequences, some of which are beginning to be recognized in a new and troubling light. Because country houses are fundamentally in the country, at some remove from urban environments and not always well served by public transportation, they rely almost entirely on people arriving by car. This means an increasingly unwelcome reliance on fossil fuels, and thus the house-opening operation is responsible for a large carbon footprint (leaving aside the additional demands of heating and powering these large buildings). Society as a whole has to learn to alleviate or reverse these trends, otherwise not only is the microcosm of the country house endangered, so too is the macrocosm of the planet. The challenge ahead is how to make those friends of the country house become more friendly to the environment.

On the whole friends and enemies are easily distinguished, and they can either be accommodated or repelled; the former may bring pleasure and prosperity, the latter may cause hurt ranging from petty injury to destruction. However there is one final category of 'visitor', arguably the worst kind – the absentee. This may sound a paradox but a house with no visitors, and no occupants, is the saddest place of all, and risks becoming entombed in its emptiness. A house with no coming or going may sound like a recluse's paradise, when in fact the opposite is the case. Not only is it empty of inhabitants and lacking the dynamics of human interaction, but it is also devoid of purpose, without any social and cultural value, neglected, at risk of decay, and prey to destruction from the most insidious arrival – the vandal. Understandably insurance companies are most concerned about empty buildings, which pose a different kind of risk to ones filled with inhabitants and guests. William Sherman was right when he declared that homes abandoned by their owners had ceased to be cared for, and therefore forfeited the right to any protection.[21]

In Eastern Europe houses requisitioned under communist rule after 1945 that were not re-purposed as institutions were left empty in a state of decay, such as Czernina Gorna, Boguszyce, Kluczowa, Kraskow and Sulislawice in Silesia.[22] Over time, inevitably, authorities in these countries faced the same pressures as countries that cherished their old buildings, namely a growing bill to repair and conserve. As state coffers ran dry the means and the will (often lukewarm in the first place) to step in and preserve disappeared altogether, and the cycles of dereliction worsened.

Vacant buildings may be the result of flight, death, bankruptcy, confiscation or other reasons. Once empty they are magnets for abuse. Their abandonment in the eyes of some gives licence to vandalize and wreck; and once begun the momentum of this destruction is hard to arrest. More insidiously their neglect points to a cultural indifference, and with each episode of degradation the *raison d'être* for preserving a structure diminishes until it reaches a point of no return.

21 Ridgway, 'Visitations: foes' in this volume, p. 28.   22 Marcus Binney et al., *Silesia, the land of dying country houses*, pp 63, 68, 80, 81, 167.

Visitations: friendlies

11.7 Bloxholm Hall, Lincolnshire, in a state of dereliction in 1963 (Historic England).

These buildings are deemed unworthy of care or attention, dilapidation invites further deterioration from continued elemental decay (wind and rain especially), from pests, from wreckers and arsonists, and ultimately from the arrival of demolition contractors, the modern day descendants of Captain Baynes at Holdenby, and Jean-Francois Hippolyte at Sceaux.[23]

This narrative of abandonment and lack has been pan-European in the twentieth century; but away from contested lands and cultures such as Eastern Europe or Ireland, Britain has also witnessed astonishing levels of ruination and loss. The state of Whitley Abbey, Warwickshire, was a cause for despair in 1927; the ruins of Bulwell Wood Hall in Nottinghamshire were destroyed by vandals in 1937; Shireburn, Yorkshire, was empty and damaged in 1955; a decade later Seaton House, Aberdeenshire, was torched while partially unoccupied; and Corby Hall, Sunderland, was abandoned in 1974, vandalized and then demolished two years later. These are but a handful of examples of houses that suffered while unoccupied.[24] This litany of unloved buildings reached a sorry climax with the seminal *Destruction of the country house* exhibition in 1974,

23 Ridgway, 'Visitations: foes' in this volume, pp 20, 26. 24 Whitley Abbey, *Coventry Evening Telegraph*, Friday 25 Oct. 1929, p. 6; Bulwell Hall, *Nottingham Journal*, 7 May 1937; Shireburn, *Clitheroe Advertiser*, 4 Nov. 1955; Seaton House, *Aberdeen Press and Journal*,

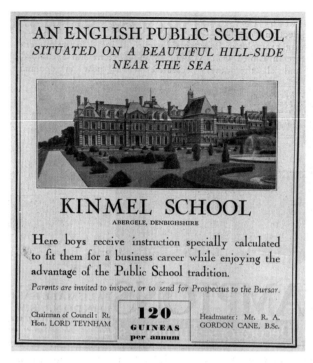

11.8 Kinmel Hall, north Wales, William Eden Nesfield's enormous house of the 1840s has seen a succession of occupants and visitors in the twentieth century; advertisement from Kinmel School, 1932 (*Illustrated London News*/Mary Evans).

chronicling houses that had been destroyed, burned, demolished or vandalized.[25] Indeed the exhibition spawned a new genre of architectural history, with a spate of volumes recording 'lost' or 'vanished' houses in particular counties or localities[26] – as well as a number of powerful publications by SAVE Britain's Heritage, the organization founded in the aftermath of the *Destruction* exhibition.[27] While far from isolated examples, two high-profile houses prompt concern today. First, Kinmel Hall in north Wales, rebuilt by W.E. Nesfield after a fire of 1841 destroyed a previous house on the site: the house has passed from the Hughes family, through two schools, a spa and a conference centre, with a

24 May 1963; Corby Hall, *Newcastle Journal*, 14 July 1992. 25 Roy Strong, Marcus Binney and John Harris, *The destruction of the country house, 1875–1975* (London, 1974); for a more up-to-date record of the number of houses lost in the twentieth century see, lostheritage.org.uk. 26 Among the many such publications are, W.M. Roberts, *Lost country houses of Suffolk* (Woodbridge, 2010); Tom Williamson et al., *Lost country houses of Norfolk* (Woodbridge, 2015); Terence R. Leach and Robert Pacey, *Lost Lincolnshire houses*, 6 vols (Gainsborough and Burgh le Marsh, 1990–2010); Rosemary Lauder, *Vanished houses of North Devon* (Tiverton, 1981) and idem, *Vanished houses of South Devon* (Bideford, 1997); in addition there are similar publications on houses in Leicestershire, Nottinghamshire, Kent, Yorkshire, Durham, Northumberland, Staffordshire and Derbyshire; as well as for regions of Scotland. See also Desmond Fitzgerald et al., *Vanishing country houses of Ireland* (Dublin, 1988). 27 Titles issued by SAVE include Sophie Andreae et al., *Tomorrow's ruins, country houses at risk* (London, 1978), and *Silent mansions, more country houses at risk* (London, 1981); Marcus Dean and Mary Miers, *Scotland's endangered houses* (London, 1990); Thomas Lloyd, *The lost*

Visitations: friendlies

11.9 Mavisbank House, Midlothian, boarded up and closed to visitors (© Chris Lewis, Mavisbank Trust).

further fire in 1975, and today it lies vacant and vandalized. Similarly Mavisbank House outside Edinburgh remains a national disgrace as it moulders away.[28]

That is why new owners, even with no familial or local connection to an old house, are so welcome if they acquire these wrecks and restore them. In Ireland there have been cheering success stories: the Mallaghan family transformed Carton House, County Kildare, which is now flooded with hotel guests and golfers; wealthy individuals like Michael Flatley have rescued houses such as Castle Hyde, County Cork, spending millions saving the building and turning it into a residence for family and guests with an echo of its glamorous interwar life; Johnstown Castle, County Wexford, passed from the Grogan family and became an agricultural college in the twentieth century, but today the site is in the hands of the Irish Heritage Trust, who are reviving both house and grounds as a visitor attraction. In Britain spectacular revivals have included Apethorpe House, Northamptonshire, which was compulsorily purchased by English Heritage in 2004, subsequently restored and sold ten years later to a new owner who expressed a desire to turn the house into a cultural centre. Most recently Hopwood DePree has set about recovering and restoring the derelict Hopwood Hall, near Manchester, his long-lost ancestral home.[29]

houses of Wales (London, 1986); much is summarized in Marcus Binney, *SAVE Britain's Heritage, thirty years of campaigning* (London 2005); see also, Kenneth Powell, 'Houses in search of an owner', *Country Life*, 181 (1 Oct. 1987), pp 174–7.   28 For Kinmel see Elaine Boxhall, *Kinmel characters: a history of Kinmel Hall* (Abergele, 1990); Mark Girouard, 'Kinmel, Denbighshire', *Country Life*, 146 (4 and 11 Sept. 1969), pp 542–5, 614–17; 'A Welsh house in danger', *Country Life*, 160 (21 Oct. 1976), p. 1117. For Mavisbank, see Ian Gow, 'Mavisbank, Midlothian', *Country Life*, 181 (20 Aug. 1987), pp 70–3; Marcus Binney, 'Scottish houses at risk', *Country Life*, 183 (26 Jan. 1989), pp 100–3; 'What to do with Mavisbank', *Country Life*, 188 (30 June 1994), p. 89.   29 Christopher Ridgway, 'Triumph or

11.10 Johnstown Castle, County Wexford, revived under the auspices of the Irish Heritage Trust (The Irish Heritage Trust).

It is clear that houses can withstand all manner of visitation and occupancy. They can be reclaimed and re-inhabited; in the aftermath of extreme events they can be repaired and rebuilt, or even acquire a new life as a managed ruin. Any house can be revived and refashioned: it might be returned to a residence, adapted as an office, school, hotel or other uses; it might equally be transformed into a visitor attraction or cultural centre. The model of recovery chosen will determine degrees of public access, but these very acts of revival give a building fresh purpose, and affirm the resilience of both brick and mortar as well as the resolve of owners or occupants, who continue to receive people and fulfil the *raison d'être* of such buildings. The knock at the door need not bring trepidation and fear but instead prompt the age-old custom of welcoming visitors across the threshold.

travesty? Carton House, Co. Kildare', *Country Life*, 203 (18 Feb. 2009), pp 42–7; Terence Dooley, 'It was like a scene from the ball in *Gone with the Wind*: social life at Castle Hyde, 1931–38' in Terence Dooley and Christopher Ridgway (eds), *The Irish country house: its past, present and future* (Dublin, 2011), pp 150–65, and Terence Dooley, *Castle Hyde: the changing fortunes of an Irish country house* (Dublin, 2017); Liam Gaul, *Johnstown Castle, a history* (Cheltenham, 2014); Kathryn A. Morrison et al. (eds), *Apethorpe: the story of an English country house* (London, 2016); Hopwood DePree, *Downton shabby: one American's ultimate DIY adventure restoring his family's English castle* (New York, 2022).

Contributors

FRAN BAKER has been archivist and librarian at Chatsworth in Derbyshire since 2018. She previously worked for many years at the John Rylands Library, University of Manchester, and her published MPhil was on Elizabeth Gaskell. She has also published widely on Gaskell, literary archives and manuscripts, and archival correspondence in the digital age.

KERRY BRISTOL is a senior lecturer at the University of Leeds, where she has taught various aspects of country house studies since 1999. Her research interests encompass the history, historiography and methodologies of British and Irish architecture and material culture between $c.1600$ and $c.1840$. She is currently researching and writing a book on everyday life in the eighteenth century at Nostell Priory, West Yorkshire.

PHILIP CARSTAIRS is currently engaged in post-doctoral research at the University of Leicester to further the work he started on his PhD dissertation on nineteenth-century charity and soup kitchens.

JOHN COLEMAN has published articles on Knole and its collections while living and working there as National Trust property manager/curator 1995–8. Other publications include articles on the Irish patrons of Sir Joshua Reynolds, the Sligo estate of the 1st earl of Shelburne and his son Hon. Thomas Fitzmaurice, and the military career of Sir Charles Coote, earl of Bellamont.

PETER COLLINGE is visiting research fellow at Keele University. His research focuses on social and economic issues in the eighteenth and nineteenth centuries. He is the co-editor of *Providing for the poor: the old Poor Law 1750–1834* (Chicago, 2022). He has published widely on Georgian businesswomen, the old Poor Law and on health, leisure and tourism.

OLIVER COX is head of academic partnerships at the Victoria & Albert Museum, London.

IAN D'ALTON is the author of *Protestant society and politics in Cork, 1812–1844* (Cork, 1980) and was co-editor of *Protestant and Irish: the minority's search for place in independent Ireland* (Cork, 2019). He has been an honorary senior research fellow in the School of Irish Studies, University of Liverpool; and a visiting fellow at Sidney Sussex College, Cambridge.

TERENCE DOOLEY is Head of Department of History at Maynooth University, as well as Director of CSHIHE.

SHAUN EVANS is lecturer in early modern and Welsh history at Bangor University and Director of the Institute for the Study of Welsh Estates. His research focuses on the history of landed estates and country houses in Wales, *c.*1500–1900, with a particular emphasis on tenant-landowner relations, estate landscapes, and Welsh gentry culture.

JOHN KNIGHTLY is a historian whose area of interest is the social world of the Kerry landed gentry during the nineteenth and early twentieth centuries. His PhD looked at the Godfrey family of Kilcoleman Abbey, Milltown, Co. Kerry, and he has recently completed an extensive assessment of the Leeson Marshall Papers, one of the few Kerry country house collections to remain intact, now deposited in Muckross House Archive Library.

CHRISTOPHER RIDGWAY is curator at Castle Howard, adjunct professor in the Department of History at Maynooth University, and chair of the Yorkshire Country House Partnership. His publications include (co-edited with Terence Dooley), *The Irish country house: its past, present and future* (Dublin, 2011) and most recently *Country house collections; their lives and after lives* (Dublin, 2021).

Index

by Eileen O'Neill.
Entries in **bold** refer to images.

abandoned houses, 260–3, **261**, **263**
Abbeylands, County Antrim, 49
Abbotsford, Scottish Borders, 60
Aberconway, Christabel, Lady, 169
Aberuchill Castle, Perthshire, 49
Abington, Frances (*née* Barton), 122, 128
Achnacarry Castle, 24
Adam, Robert (architect), 87, 88, 92, 93, 152; *Ruins of the palace of the Emperor Diocletian at Spalatro*, 88; *Works in architecture of Robert and James Adam, The*, 88
Addington, John Hubbard, 1st Baron, 112
Addington, Lady, 112
Aghadoe House, County Kerry, 223
Albert Edward, Prince of Wales, 126, 127–8, 183
Albert, Prince Consort, 67, 251–2
Aldborough Hall, Yorkshire, 47
Aldenburg-Bentinck, Count, 40
Alexandra, Princess of Wales, 126, 128, 183
All Saints Church, Northampton, 79
Allenby, General Edmund, 32
Alnwick Castle, Northumberland, 113, 174
American Civil War (1861–5), 27–30
Anderson, Jocelyn, 81, 139
Anglesey, Lady, 108
Anglo-Irish Treaty, 237
Ankerwycke, 113
Annual Historic Houses Conference, 10
Apethorpe House, Northamptonshire, 263
Archaeologia Britannica, 202
Architectural History, 157
architectural styles, 140–4, 204–5; baroque, 52, **56**, 81, 92, 142, 143; baroque style, 52, **56**, 81, 92, 142, 143; castellated, 143, 205; Elizabethan Revival, 94; neoclassical, 11, 95, 142–3, 189; Palladian, 11, 142–3; porticos, 143, 144
Ard na Sidhe Hill, County Kerry, 224, **224**, 232, 235

Aristocrats, The (robbers), 44
Arlington House, Washington DC, 28, **29**
Arnold, Dana, 138, 139
arson, 46, 48–9, 235, 241
Art Journal, 249
Art Treasures Exhibition, 59–60
Ashridge House, Hertfordshire, 112
Astor, William Waldorf, 129
Athenaeum, 249–50
Atholl, James Murray, 2nd duke of, 23
Attingham Park, Shropshire, 152, 255
Audley End, Essex, 250
Axwell Park, Durham, 108

Baccelli, Giannetta, 122, 123, 128
Bachygraig, Tremeirchion, 205, 213
Baginton Hall, Warwickshire, 47
Bagshot Park, Surrey, 85
Bainbridge, Elsie, 169
Ballinagroun, County Kerry, 223
Ballyard, County Kerry, 232
Ballyfin, Queen's County (Laois), 177
Ballyheigue Castle, County Kerry, 232, 236
Ballyhorgan, County Kerry, 232, 236
Ballyseedy, County Kerry, 237, 246
Banting, John (artist), 132
Banville, John, 187; *Snow*, 192
Baring, Maurice, 233
Barker, Juliet, 61
Barnard, Tom, 168
Barnsley Park, Gloucestershire, 166
Baron Hill, Anglesea, 204, 205, 213
Barton Hall, Suffolk, 99
Basing House, Hampshire, 15, 16–18, **17**, 21
Bass family, 110–11
Bass, Michael, 111
Bayham Abbey, 143
Baynes, Captain Adam, 20, 21, 26, 261
Beaufort Castle, Scotland, 24
Beaufort, County Kerry, 222–3, **224**

267

Bedford, Hastings Russell, 12th duke of, 172–3
Bedford House, *see* Château Rosendal
Bedhampton Manor, Hampshire, 167
Begbrook House, Bristol, 49
Beit Collection, 123n24
Belgium, châteaux occupied, 35–8
Bell, Henry (architect), 79
Bellister Castle, Northumberland, 47
Belton House, Lincolnshire, 32
Belvoir Castle, Rutland, 46, 47, 82
Bence-Jones, Gillian, 188
Bence-Jones, Mark, 230
Bentley Park, Suffolk, 166, 169
Bentley Priory, Middlesex, 41
Bentley, Richard, 119–20
Berkhamsted Castle, 113
Berkley Castle, Gloucestershire, 145
Berlin, Isaiah, 192, 193
Berth-lwyd, Llanidloes, 214
Berwick, Noel Hill, 1st Baron, 152
Bess of Hardwick, 52
Bethune family, 38
Betjeman, John, 186
Bianchi, Francesco, 123
Bin Salem bin Kalfasi, Ali (Wali of Gazi), 195
Bishop's Palace, Farnham, Surrey, 140, 145
Blair Castle, 23
Blayney, Arthur, 203
Blenheim Palace, Oxfordshire, 41, 114, 139, 140, 142, 174
Blennerhassett, Arthur, 237
Bletchley Park, Buckinghamshire, 41
Blodwell Hall, Shropshire, 214
Bloxholm Hall, Lincolnshire, 261
Bodelwyddan, Denbighshire, 200
Bodfach, Montgomeryshire, 203
Bodiam Castle, Sussex, 20, 153
Bodidris, Denbighshire, 204
Bodysgallen, Llandudno, 216
Bolton Abbey, Yorkshire, 61
Bolton Hall, Yorkshire, 152
Bonham Carter, Charlotte, 169
Borenius, Tancred, 249
Boston Symphony Orchestra, 184
Bouchier, Thomas, archbishop of Canterbury, 116, 120
boundaries, permeability of, 9–10, 12, 115
Bourdieu, Pierre, 73

Bourgeois, Maurice, 233
Bowen, Elizabeth, 177, 178, 185, 190, 191, 192, 193–4; country houses, observations on, 221, 225, 245; *last September, The*, 187–8, 192; *world of love, A*, 181, 191, 195
Bowen's Court, County Cork, 177, 180, 185, 190, 192, 193–4
Bowes-Lyon, Lady Mary, 190–1
Bowood House, Wiltshire, 173
Brady, John, *Guide to Knole*, 121, 124–5
Bray, William, 85, 155, 156
Bridgeman, John, *History and topographical guide to Knole*, 124
Briggs, M.S., *architect in history, The*, 157
Britannia illustrata, 117
British Library, 76, 77, 96
British Museum, 76, 77
British Newspaper Archive, 96
Broadlands, Hampshire, 141
Broderick, Albina, 232
Brontë, Branwell, 60
Brontë, Charlotte; Gaskell's biography of, 10, 60–1, 62, 70, 71–2, 74; *Jane Eyre*, 62, 71; pseudonym, 68, 72
Brontë, Revd Patrick, 61–2, 64, 71, 72, 73
Brontë sisters, 68
Broughton, Flintshire, 202, 203, 205
Brown, Lancelot (Capability), 86, 158, 173, 215
Browne, Ella, 237, 243, 246
Brownlow, John Cust, 1st Earl, 112
Bruen family, 178–9
Bryant, Julius, 138
Brynkinallt, Wrexham, 205
Brynodol, Gwynedd, 203
Buck brothers (artists), 247
Buckingham and Chandos, dukes of, 104
Buckingham and Chandos, Richard Temple-Nugent-Brydges-Chandos-Grenville, 1st duke of, 10, 100–1
Bulwell Wood Hall, Nottinghamshire, 261
Bulwer-Lytton, Edward, 64, 66; *Not so bad as we seem*, 67
Bunbury, Sir Charles, 99
Bunbury, Lady Sarah, 122
Bunny Hall, Nottinghamshire, 80
Burghley House, Lincolnshire, 48, 93–4, 95
Burghley, William Cecil, 1st Baron, 93
burglary/robbery, 44–5

Index

Burke, Sir Bernard, 249; *Visitation of the seats and arms of the noblemen and gentlemen of Great Britain*, 249
Burke, Edmund, 95, 119, 123–4; Knole, impressions of, 123–4, 125, 136; *Philosophical enquiry into our ideas of the sublime and beautiful*, 123, 124; *Reflections on the revolution*, 124
Burney, Fanny, 10, 119, 121, 122, 123
Burton, Michael Bass, first Baron, 111
Burton Park, Petworth, 166
Buscot Park, Oxfordshire, **167**, 168
Butler, Lauren, 73
Bychton, Flintshire, 201, 204
Byng, John (later Viscount Torrington), 92, 138, 139, 141, 143, 144, 145; access, views on, 149–50, 155; barriers to access, 152–3, 154–5; Leeds Castle visit, 146–7
Byng, General Sir Julian, 32
Byrne, Letitia, **119**
Byron, Robert, 168

Caister Hall Farm, Norfolk, 44
Callinafercy House, County Kerry, 11–12, 220–1, 222, **222**, **224**; guests, 229, 233, **234**, 235, 242, 243, 244–5; IRA raids, 235–6, 238; pastimes, 227; post-First World War, 232; sale of, 246; staff, 227; visitors' book, 12, 222, 225, 231, **234**, 238
Cameron, Alan, 180, 192
Cameron, Donald, 24
Campaign for the Protection of Rural England, 171–2
Campden House, Gloucestershire, 19
Caragh Lake, County Kerry, 223, 224, 235
Carlisle, George Howard, 7th earl of, 251–2
Carlisle, George Howard, 6th earl of, 44
Carlow, Lady, 141, 147, 148
Carr, John (architect), 82, 87, 90, 144
Carracci, Annibale, 120
Carreglwyd, Anglesey, 203
Carriglea, County Kerry, 237
Carrington, Noel, 163
Carter's Corner Place, Sussex, 161–2
Carton House, County Kildare, 263
Carysfort, Lady, 180–1
Cassia House, Cheshire, 168
Castle Bellingham, County Louth, 229

Castle Bernard, County Cork, 193, 229, 233
Castle Freke, County Cork, 47
Castle Howard, Yorkshire, 41, 42, 44, 142, 252–4; Queen Victoria's visit, **250**, 251–2, **251**
Castle Hyde, County Cork, 177–8, 184, 187, 190, 222, 263
Castle Leslie, *see* Glaslough
Castle Menzies, Perthshire, 21, **22**
Castletown demesne, 13
Catholic clergy/hierarchy, 186
Cazenove, Henry, 112
Ceannacroc, Inverness-shire, 166
Centre for the Study of Historic Irish Houses and Estates (CSHIHE), 10
Chambers, Sir William, 85–6
Chapman, Edward (publisher), 67
charity: paternalistic, 111–14; poor people, perception of, 107; rural charity, 10, 96; *see also* poverty/the poor; soup kitchens
Charlecote Park, Warwickshire, 95n126, 255
Charles I, King, **19**, 20, 118, 212
Charlotte, Queen, 121, 137, 156
Charlton Park, Wiltshire, 44
Château d'Amboise, 26
Château de Beaurepaire, 38
Château de Bist, 38
Château de Blois, 25–6
Château de Durbay, 35–6
Château de la For, 36
Château de la Motte aux Bois, 31–2, **31**
Château de Meudon, 26, **26**
Château de Milemont, 36
Château de Pierpont, 38
Château de Rosendal, 39
Château de Tillier, 36
Château de Zellaer, 36, **36**
Château d'Ingelmunster, 35
Château du Boussu, 36
Château Fraineuse, 39–40
Château Franc, 38
Château Gheluvelt, 36–7
Château Hooghe, 37–8, **37**
Château Marke, 38
Château Nerom, 36
Château Neville, 38
Château Roucourt, 38
Château Sceaux, Paris, **25**, 26
Château Vizille, Grenoble, 26–7

Chatsworth House, Derbyshire, **56**, 139, **154**; access to, 153, 155; admission fees, 150; Emperor Fountain, 55–6; estate community, 73; excursion trips to, 54; gardens, 56; Gaskell's visit to, 10, 52, 55–6, 62–4, 73; Great Conservatory, **58**; library, 62, 64–6, **65**, 72; opening hours, 145, 147; perception of, 92, 145; Sketch Gallery, 58; visitors' books, 55; visitor's ticket, 55–6, **55**
Chepstow Castle, 152
Chesnut, Mary, 30
Chetwynd-Stapylton, Lady Barbara, 229
Cheverny, Comte de, 25–6
Chillingham Castle, Northumberland, 46
Chippendale, Thomas, 87
Chirk Castle, Denbighshire, 204, 205, **215**
Choiseul, Duc de, 26
Church of Ireland, 229, 233, 237, 243, 244
Churchill, Consuelo, 114
Churchill, Pamela, 181
Churchill, Winston, 174
Churchtown, County Kerry, 222, **224**, 235, 242
Clandon Park, Surrey, 33, 49–50, **50**
Clarke, Stephen, 138, 153
Clavering, C.J., 108
Clayton Grange, Lancashire, 43, **43**
Clifton Hall, Nattingham, 82
Clifton, Mississippi, 28–9
Clonmeen, County Cork, 178
Clopton Hall, Northhamptonshire, 59
Clough, Richard, 205, 213
Clumber Park, Nottinghamshire, 83, 147
Clutterbuck, Robert, 155
Clydagh, County Kerry, 230, 232, 243
Cobham Hall, Kent, 44
Code Napoleon, 27
Coed-llai, Flintshire, 200
Coetmor, Snowdonia, 216
Coggeshall House, Essex, 44
Colley, Linda, 198
Collins, Michael, 238
Collis-Sandes, Doris, 242
Colman, Henry, 150
Colwick Hall, Nottingham, 42
Commonwealth Graves Commission Cemetery, 39

Conisbrough Castle, Yorkshire, 153
Connaught, Prince Arthur, duke of, 181, 191
Convamore, County Cork, 183
Conwy Castle, 18
Cook, Thomas, 52
Cooleville, County Tipperary, 134, 177
Coolfadda, County Cork, 229
Cooper, Reginald, 166
Coote, Sir Algernon and Lady, 177
Cope, Arabella Diana, 122–3, 128
Corby Castle, Cumbria, 23
Corby Hall, Sunderland, 261
Cornbury Park, Oxfordshire, 231
Cornforth, John, 163, 169, 254
Corsham Court, Wiltshire, 145, 168
Corsygedol, Snowdonia, 203, 204, 209
Cotes, Samuel (miniaturist), 77
Cothay Manor, Somerset, 166, 167
Country Life, 11, 135, 158, 250, 254; Hussey's articles, 162, 166, 171, 175
Cowen, William (artist), **56**
Cox, Louise Hamilton, 229, 242
Craig Castle, Aberdeenshire, 42
Cranfield, Lady Frances, 120
Cranmer, Thomas, archbishop of Canterbury, 118
Cresswell Baker, A.J., 108
Cresswell Hall, Northumberland, 108
Crohen, Barbara (*née* Bray), 165
Cromwell, Oliver, 17, 18
Cromwell, Thomas, 15
Cronin-Coltsmann, Daniel, 232
Croome Park, Worcestershire, 140
Crosbie, James, 232
Crosswood, Cardiganshire, 165
Cruickshank, Dan, 144
Cuffe, Hon. Elizabeth, 235, 237, 238, 243
Culdees Castle, Perthshire, 47
Cullen House, Banff, 23–4
Cumberland, Prince William Augustus, duke of, 23–4, 75
Curraghmore, County Waterford, 183, 184
Curzon, Sir Nathaniel, 21, 93
Cwm Bychan, Merioneth, 207–10, **210**, 211, 213

Dalhousie Castle, Scotland, 148
Dane End, Hertfordshire, 168
Danmore, Hampshire, 168
Darling, Elisabeth, 163–4

Index

Darnley, John Bligh, 4th earl of, 44
Davies, Peter, 202, 203
Davitt, Michael, 181
Dayes, Edward (artist), 94
Dayrell, Revd John, 100
de Beauffort, Comte, 36
de Bruyn, Theodore (artist), 85
de Freyne, Lord and Lady, 230
De La Warr, George West, 5th earl, 126
de Moleyns, Arthur, 237
de Montblanc, Comte, 35
de Narbonne, Marquis, 27
de Nino, Duchess, 138
de Paris, Comte, 104, 105
de Stael, Madame, 27
de Stuer, Gustav, 39
de Talleyrand, Charles, 27
Dearn, Thomas (architect), 143
Deerhurst, George William Coventry, Viscount, 140
Defoe, Daniel, 75, 81, 92, 247
DePree, Hopwood, 263
Derby, Charlotte de la Tremouille, countess of, 18
Derby, Elizabeth Smith-Stanley, countess of, 122, 128
Derby, James Stanley, 7th earl of, 18
Derby Mercury, 146, 148
Dering, Sir Edward and Lady, 108
Derreen, County Kerry, 238, 243
Derryquin, County Kerry, 230, 233, 238, 242
Destruction of the country house exhibition, 261–2
Devonshire, Edward William Spencer Cavendish, 10th duke of, 181
Devonshire, Georgiana Cavendish, duchess of, 68, 92, 122
Devonshire House, 67, 128
Devonshire, William Cavendish, 1st duke of, 52
Devonshire, William Cavendish, 7th duke of, 62, 72
Devonshire, William Spencer Cavendish, 6th duke of, 10, 52, **54**, 55, 57; Gaskell, Elizabeth and, 62–4, **63**, 69–70, **70**; *handbook of Chatsworth and Hardwick, The*, 66; Haworth, visit to, 61, 62, 64; library, 64–6, **65**; literary patronage, 64, 66; theatre and, 66–7

Dickens, Charles, 64, 65, 66–7, 68, 73; *Bleak House*, 114; *Household Words*, 67
Digby, George Wingfield, 134
Disbrowe, Major General, 20
Disraeli, Benjamin, *Sybil*, 43
Dixon, Henry H., 244
Dodgson, George Haydock, 107
Doneraile Court, County Cork, 186
Donington Hall, Leicestershire, 32–3, 33
Donne, John, 9
Dooks Golf Club, County Kerry, 227
Dorland Hall, London, 164
Dorset, Charles Sackville, 6th earl of, 118, 121
Dorset, Edward Sackville, 4th earl of, 118
Dorset, John Frederick Sackville, 3rd duke of, 121–3
Dorset, Thomas Sackville, 1st earl of, 118
double identity, 11, 139
Downing, Flintshire, 205, 215–16, 218
Downton Castle, Shropshire, 145
Drishane, County Cork, 188
Dromana House, County Waterford, 229
Dromoland Castle, County Clare, 179, 187, 192–3, 194, 195
Dromore Castle, County Kerry, 230, 237, 246
Dromquinna, County Kerry, **224**, 230
Druid's Lodge, Anglesey, 108
Drumlanrig Castle, Scotland, 23
Dryden, John, 118
Dumbleton Hall, Worcestershire, 166
Duncombe Park, York, 154
Dunham Massey, Cheshire, 33, 143
Dunloe, County Kerry, 237
Dunsany Castle, County Meath, 185, 229
d'Ursal, Comte, 35–6
Dutton, Ralph, 167, 169

Eacrett, Henry, 184
Earnshill, Somerset, 169
Eastern Europe, requisitioned houses, 260
Eastnor Castle, Herefordshire, 143
Eaton Hall, Cheshire, 41, 43
Eden, Anthony, 181
Edgeworth, Maria, 187
Edward VII, King, 111, 183
Edward VIII, King, 245
Edwards, Ralph, 134
Egerton, Sir Thomas, 15

Egginton Hall, Derbyshire, 41
Elcho, David Wemyss, Lord, 23
Eliot, George (Mary Ann Evans), 62, 66, 68
Elizabeth I, Queen, 15–16, 118
Eltham Hall, 167
Elves, Captain Robert, 77
Emerson, Ralph Waldo, 113
Emes, William, 215
emigrés, 27
Emo Court, Queen's County (Laois), 178, 183, 186, 189–90, 191; visitors' book, **182**, 184, 187, 194
English Civil War, 16–21, 30; Basing House and, 16–18; estates, damage/destruction of, 20; fines levied by Parliament, 20–1; Lathom Hall and, 18; Royalist houses, fate of, 18–19
English Heritage, 12, 255, 263
Enville, Staffordshire, 145
Erddig, Wrexham, 202, 204, 209
Escrick Park, Yorkshire, 33–4
Essenhigh-Corke, Charles (artist), 128, 129
Evans, Evan (antiquarian), 202
Evans, Paul, 202
Exeter, William Thomas Brownlow Cecil, 5th marquess of, 48
Exhibition of British industrial art in relation to the home, 164
Eyton, Kenrick, 202
Eyton, Thomas, 200
Eywood House, Herefordshire, 162

Fabricant, Carole, 78
Faenol Fawr (Vaynol), Denbighshire, 200, 214
Fairfax, Sir Thomas, 18, 20
Faringdon, Gavin, 168
Fawley Bottom, Buckinghamshire, 169
Field, The, 47
Fiennes, Celia, 247
Findlater, James Ogilvy, 5th earl of, 23–4
fire, 46–8, 235, 241
First World War (1914–18), 11, 31–41, 42; Belgian châteaux occupied, 35–8; convalescent homes, 33–4, 36; German High Command, 34–5, 39–40; Germany, houses requisitioned, 34–5; POW camps, 32–3, **33**; Supreme War Council of the Allies, 40; Western Front, 39; Zeppelin raids, 42

FitzClarence, George and Aubrey, 183
Flatley, Michael, 263
Flesk Castle, County Kerry, 232, 246
Fletcher, C.W., 134
Floors Castle, Scotland, 44
Flower, Robin, 186
Foddy, Martha, 101, 103
Foley, Tom and Helen, 168
Fonmon Castle, Wales, 168
Fonthill Abbey, Wiltshire, 146
Forde, Henry Charles, 229
Foreman, Amanda, 122
Foremarke Hall, Derbyshire, 143
Forrest, Theodosius, 10, 76–7, **84**, **86**, **89**, 92, **93**
Forrest's tours, 76, 77
Foster, Lady Elizabeth, 122
Foster, Richard, 108
Fouquet, Nicholas, 26
French Revolution, 24–7, 30, 124, 143
Frenchpark, County Roscommon, 230
Fuller, James Franklin (architect), 221–2
Furzebrook House, Dorset, 168

Gainsborough, Thomas, 116, 122, 123, 128
gamekeepers, 43–4
Gandon, James (architect), 78, 82, 88, 189
Garrick, David, 122
Garthewin, Wales, 216
Gaskell, Elizabeth, 10, 52–3, **53**, 57–60, 67; anonymity and, 67–8; autograph album, 69; Charlotte Brontë's letter to, 70–1; Chatsworth, visit to, 10, 52, 55–6, 62–4, 73; duke of Devonshire and, 62–4, **63**, 69–70, **70**; Haworth, depiction of, 60–1; *life of Charlotte Brontë, The*, 10, 60–1, 62, 70, 71–2, 74; *Mary Barton*, 66, 67, 69; *North and south*, 66; *Ruth*, 67; *Wives and daughters*, 59
Gaskell, Marianne, 57, 69
Gaskell, Meta, 52, 57–9, 60, 63–4
Gastrell, Revd Francis, 140
gate lodge buildings, 11, **106**, 141, 143, **151**
George IV, King, 181, 188
George V, King, 32, 183
Germain, Lady Elizabeth, 120
ghosts, 46
Giardini, Felice, 122
Gibbs, James (architect), 90

Index

Gilmour, Michael, 193
Gilpin, William, 94, 215
Girouard, Mark, 139
Glanleam, County Kerry, 226, 246
Glaslough, County Monaghan, 179, 184, 185, 186, 187, **188**, 194
Glenart, County Wicklow, 180–1
Glencairn, County Waterford, 229
Glendinning, Victoria, 180
Glengarry, Aeneas, 22
Glenthromie Lodge, Scotland, 166
Gloucester Lodge, Windsor, 83
Glover, Stephen, *Peak guide*, 64
Glyndŵr, Owain, 211, 217
Glynllifon, Caernarfon, 209
Godfrey, Sir John, 220, 243
Godfrey, Sir William, 238, 246
Gogarty, Oliver St John, 185, 187, 244
Goldsmith, Oliver, 122
Goodwood House, Sussex, 44
Gordine Hare, Dora (sculptor), 168
Gordon Castle, Scotland, 22
Gordon, Cosmo Gordon, 3rd duke of, 21–2
Gordon, Edith (*nee* Leeson Marshall), 223–4, 227, 230, 235, 238, 241, 242; *winds of time, The*, 224
Gordon of Glenbucket, 22
Gordon, Lord William, 122
Gorhambury House, Hertfordshire, 100, 180
Gow, Ian, 148
Gowers Report, 157, 174
Grant, Duncan (artist), 132
Grant, Johnson, 145
Grant, Ulysses, 29
Green, Charles, 30
Gregynog, Montgomeryshire, 203, 204
Grehan family, 178
Gresham, Sir Thomas, 213
Griffith, John, 203
Griffith, Moses, 205, 206, 210, **215**
Griffith, Thomas, 200
Griffiths, Hugh, 203
Grimston, James Grimston, 3rd Viscount, 100
Grose, Francis (antiquarian), 76–7, 80, 80n31
guests, 177–9, 181; arranging and curating, 191–4; cataloguing and classifying, 187–8; 'fast' guests, 193; framing and displaying, 188–91; hunting and shooting parties, 192–3; royal, 181, 183–4; tennis parties, 193; 'The Perfect Guest', 178; 'The Perfect Pest', 179; *see also* visitors
Guild of Literature and Art, 64, 66, 73
Gwaenynog, Denbigh, 203, 216
Gwydir Castle, Conwy, 204, 205, 206
Gwyer, Cecil, 162

Haddon Hall, Derbyshire, 94, 174
Hagley, Worcestershire, 152–3
Haig, Field Marshal Douglas, 38
Hailsham, Douglas Hogg, 1st Viscount, 161
Haley, Sir William, 172
Hall Barn Manor, Beaconsfield, 112
Hamilton, Eva H., **228**, 229
Hamilton, Letitia, 229
Hammond, Colonel, 17
Hampshire, Stuart, 193
Hampton, Wade, 28
Hanbury, Thomas, 155
Hanmer, Wrexham, 205
Hanson Grange, Derbyshire, 155
Harcourt, Mr and Mrs, 113
Hardwick Hall, Derbyshire, 95, 153, 174
Hardy, Thomas, 62
Hare, Hon. Richard Gilbert, 168
Harefield, Middlesex, 15
Harewood House, Yorkshire, **86**, 87–8, 95, 141
Harlech Castle, 211
Harrington, Howard, 237, 238
Harris, John, 44
Hartsheath, Flintshire, 200
Hatfield House, Hertfordshire, 41, 95, 129, 167, 174
Hatton, Sir Christopher, 20, 21
Hawkstone Inn, 149
Hawkstone Park, Shropshire, 148–9
Haworth, Yorkshire, 10, 60–1, 71
Hayman, Francis, 84, 85
Headfort House, County Meath, 183, 186, 194, 225
Hearst, William Randolph, 190
Heaton Park, Lancashire, 43–4
Heaton, Rose Henniker, 178
Heidt, Revd, 30
Helsington Hall, Yorkshire, 166
Henderson, John, 253

Hengrave Hall, Suffolk, **248**
Henry III, King, 113
Henry VII, King, 116, 118, 211
Henry VIII, King, 118
Henson, A.E. (photographer), 250
Heritage Lottery Fund, 10, 135
Herstmonceux Place, Sussex, 162
Hervey, William (diarist), 100, 101, 104
Hever Castle, Kent, 118
Hicks, Sir Baptist, 19
Highfield House, Yorkshire, 47
Hill, Captain Charles, 60
Hill, Oliver, FRIBA, 164, 165
Hinton Ampner, Hampshire, 167, 169
Hippolyte, Jean-Francois, 26, 261
Historic Buildings Council, 173
Historic Houses Association, 255
Historic houses and castles in Great Britain open to the public, **256**
Hodson, Audrey, 229
Hodson, Eddy, 229
Hodson, Meriel (*later* Leeson Marshall), 220, 229
Hodson, Sir George, 220
Hoghton, Sir Henry, 23
Hoghton Tower, Lancashire, 23
Holbein, Hans, 85
Holdenby House, Northamptonshire, 19–20, **19**, 21, 26, 261
Holkham Hall, Norfolk, 169, **170**
Holland House, London, 42
Hollybrooke, County Wicklow, 220, 229, 233
Holmes, Burton, 191
Holmes, Oliver Wendell, 186
Holywell House, St Albans, 100
Holywell Manor, Hertfordshire, 167
Hone, Joseph, 194
Hone, Nathaniel, 76–7
Hood family, 237, 243
Hoppner, John (artist), 128
Hopwood Hall, Manchester, 263
Horner, David, 169
hospitals/convalescent homes, 33–4, **34**, 41
hosts, 180–1
Howarth, R.W.B., 173
Howe, Richard Curzon-Howe, 1st earl, 111
Howe, Baroness Sophia Charlotte, 140
Howitt, William, *Visits to remarkable places*, 59
Hudson, Edward, 162, 163, 169, 175

Hudson's historic houses and gardens, 256
Huis Doorn, Netherlands, 40, **40**
Humphreys, Melvin, 199
Humphry, Ozias (artist), 124
Hunt, Leigh, 64
hunting/shooting parties, 192–3, 230
Hussey, Christopher, 11, 157–75, **160**, 254; 'Adventures in country houses' (lecture), 173–4; albums, 165–6, 169; architectural criticism and, 163–4; country house movement, 157–9, 168; *Country Life* articles, 166, 171, 175; early life, 161–2; *English country houses open to the public*, 171; family background, 161; Georgian houses, history of, 169; Holkham notebook entries, 169, **170**; perception of, 163–4; *Picturesque, The: studies in a point of view*, 169; radio appearances, 172; scriptwriting, 172; study, 157, **158**; *Tait McKenzie: sculptor of youth*, 160n3; Uppark, article on, 171; visits to country houses, 160–1, 164–9, 172–3; working library, 157
Hussey, Edward, 161
Hussey, Elizabeth (*née* Kerr-Smiley), 157, 165
Hussey, Mary Ann (*née* Herbert), 161
Hussey, Samuel, 223
Hussey, Major William Clive, 161
Hutton Hall, Cumberland, 23
Hyde, Robert, 200

Ilam Hall, Staffordshire, 148
Illustrated London News, 48, 107, **126**, 127, **250**, **251**, **262**
Ince Castle, Cornwall, 168
Inchiquin, Edward Donough O'Brien, 14th Baron, 192–3, 195
Infant Custody Act (1839), 68
Ingleby, John, 205
Irish Civil War, 12, 49, 232, 238, 240–1
Irish Heritage Trust, 263, **264**
Irish Republican Army (IRA), 12, 233, 235, 238, 240
Isted, Mr, 155

Jackson, Colonel, 43
Jacobite Risings (1715, 1745), 21–3, 30
James, Henry, *turn of the screw, The*, 46

Index 275

James I, King, 118, 121
James II, King, 121
James, M.R., 46
James, Samuel and Mary, 226
Jarrett, Christian, 176
Jeffreys, George, 212
Jenkins, Geraint H., 199
Jenkins, Philip, 199
Jenkinson, David, 27
Jermyn family, 19
John Rylands Research Institute and Library, 63, 73
Johnson, Samuel, 122, 144
Johnston gang, 44
Johnston, Jennifer, *Gates, The*, 191
Johnstown Castle, County Wexford, 263, **264**
Joly, John, 244
Jones, Elizabeth Inglis, 165
Jones, John, 212
Jones, Richard, 227, 235
Juniper Hall, Mickleham, Surrey, 27

Kames, Henry Home, Lord, 95
Katheryn of Berain, 205
Kay-Shuttleworth, Sir James, 71
Keats, John, *The Eve of St Agnes*, **117**, 118
Kedleston, Derbyshire, 10, 21, 92–3, **93**, 95, 139, 144, **146**; North Lodge, 150, **151**, 152; opening hours, 145–6
Kedleston Inn, 146
Kelmarsh, Northamptonshire, 155
Kenmare House, County Kerry, 223, **224**, 226, 244
Kenmare, Valentine Browne, 5th earl of, 223, 233, 238
Kennedy, John F., 181
Kennedy, Kathleen (Kick), 181
Kentish Gazette, 107
Kenwood House, Hampstead, 140
Kenyon, Lloyd, 202
Kenyon, Roger, 202
Keppel, Alice, 128
Kerr-Smiley, Elizabeth, 165
Kerr-Smiley, Peter, 168
Kilcoleman Abbey, County Kerry, 220, 222, **224**, 229, 238, 246
Kilkenny Castle, 183
Killin, Scotland, 153
Kilmorna, County Kerry, 235, 236
Kinder Scout, Derbyshire, 44

King, Alice, 235
Kingston, George King, 3rd earl of, 181, 183, 188–9
Kinmel Hall, Wales, 262–3, **262**
Kip, Jan, 117
Knole, Kent, 10, 116–36, **119**, **133**; art collection, 116, 120, 121–2, 128–9, 136; Burke's impressions of, 123–4, 125, 136; Cartoon Gallery, 122; concerts at, 122; depictions of, 117–18; fabric/furniture repairs, 134; furniture, 116, 119–20, 121, 129–30, 136; game of croquet, **126**; gardens, 116; Gothic chapel, 125; grand tour acquisitions, 120, 121; guidebooks to, 121, 124–5, 129, 134; Henry VIII, appropriation by, 118; 'Inspired by Knole' project, 135; King's Room, 117–18, **117**, 121; Leicester Gallery, **131**, 136; Long Gallery, **125**; music room, **132**; musical parties, 123; National Trust and, 117, 119, 129, 130, 133, 134, 135; Poet's Parlour, 118; portraits, sale of, 128; Retainer's Gallery, 136; royal visitors, 116, 118, 121, 126–7, 128; Sackville family, 10, 117–18, 126; sheet music collection, 122; Spangle Bedroom, 136; state rooms, 121; Venetian Ambassador's Room, 121, 134, **135**, 136; visitors, 119, 121, 123–4, 127, 134; visitors' book, 128; Walpole's impressions of, 119–20
Knole Settee, 129–30, **131**, 136
Knyff, Leonard (artist), 117, 125, 247
Koster, Renske, 139, 142, 149

La Grange, Baroness Ernest de, **31**; *Open house in Flanders*, 31–2
labourers, 97–8, 114
Lakeview, County Kerry, 223, **224**
Lambay Island, 166, 167
Lancut, Cracow, 35
land acts, 220, 245
Land War, 231, 245
landscapes, 215–17; trees, 12–13, 216–17; woodlands, 217
Lane Fox, Marcia and Joe, 169
Langrishe family, 183
Lansdowne, Henry Petty-Fitzmaurice, 5th marquess of, 243

Lascelles, Edwin, 87
Lathom Hall, Lancashire, 18
Laughlin, Henry, 184, 190
Lauzun, Duc de, 26
Lavery, Sir John, 186
Lawley, Irene, 33
Lawson, Lady, 112
Le Corbusier (architect), 163, 164
Le Notre, Andre, 26
Leahy, Gordon, 237
Leasowes, The, Shropshire, 147, 153
Leconfield, Charles Wyndham, 3rd Baron, 255
Lee, Mary, 28
Lee, Robert E., 28
Leeds Castle, 146–7
Lees Court, Kent, 20
Lees-Milne, James (diarist), 119, 133–4, 168, 254, 255
Leeson Marshall family, 11–12
Leeson Marshall, Mabel (*née* Godfrey), 220
Leeson Marshall, Major Markham Richard, 220, **221**, 222–3, **223**, **228**; death, 245; death of his mother, 237; First World War, 231–2; friends, 231; income, 221; India, visit to, 231; IRA raids and, 235–6, 238, **239**; marriage of his daughter, 242–3, **242**; neighbours, relationship with, 232, 236, 237, 240; shooting parties, 230, 232, 243; social circuit, 223–5, 229–31, 233
Leeson Marshall, May (*later* Ruth), 220, 240, 242, **242**
Leeson Marshall, Meriel (*née* Hodson), 220, 221, 227, **228**, 229, 235, 242
Leeson Marshall, Zeena (*née* Power), 220, 237
Leeson, Richard, 220
Leeswood, Flintshire, 200, 216
Leez Priory, Essex, 15
Lefebvre, Georges, 30
Legh, Thomas, 15
Lehmann, Rosamond, 193, 194
Leighton Hall, Lancashire, 25n31
Lenton Lodge, Nottingham, 143
Lesdiguieres family, 26
Leslie, Cecil, 243
Leslie, Sir John and Lady, 179, 185, 186, 191
letters of introduction, 153–4

Leven's Hall, Cumbria, 153
Leveson, Sir Richard, 20
Lewes, G.H., 66; *Ranthorpe*, 67
Lewis, Sarah, *Woman's mission*, 71
Lhuyd, Edward, 202
Lilies, The, Buckinghamshire, 112
Lilleshall, Shropshire, 20
Lillingstone Lovell Manor, 166, 167
Lindsey, Lord and Lady, 48
Linley, Elizabeth, 122, 128
Linley, Thomas, 122, 128
Lismore Castle, County Waterford, 181, 229
Littlewood House, Worcestershire, 167
Llanidan, Anglesey, 216
Llanmaes House, Vale of Glamorgan, 168
Llanrhaeadr, Powys, 205
Lleweni, Denbighshire, 204, 213, 218
Lloyd, Bell, 203
Lloyd, Sir Edward, 214, 217
Lloyd, John (Faenol Fawr), 200
Lloyd, John (Wigfair), 211
Lloyd, Revd John, 202, 207, 211
Lloyd, Robert, *Cit's country box, The*, 148
Llwyd, Dai, 208, 211
Llwyd, Evan, 207, 208, 209
Llwyd, Humphrey, 205
Llwydiarth, Powys, 211, 213
Llys Dulas, Wales, 218
Locatelli, Giovanni Battista (sculptor), 123
Londonderry, Lady, 191–2
Longfield, Richard, 179
Longford Castle, Wiltshire, 18, 169
Longleat, Wiltshire, 94, 172, 174, 255
Longnor Hall, Shropshire, 43
Longueville, County Cork, 179
Lothian, Philip Kerr, 11th marquis of, 168, 255
Louis XVI, King, 123
Lovatt, Simon Fraser, Lord, 24
Lowther Castle, Cumbria, 23, 41, 50, 143
Lowthian, Richard, 21
Lude House, Scotland, 23
Lumley Castle, 147
Luton Hoo, 111, 172
Lutyens, Edwin, 129, 166
Lyme Park, Cheshire, 154

MacArthur, Rosie, 138
Macclesfield, earl of, 149

Index

MacGillycuddy, Anthony, **223**
MacGillycuddy, Jack, 223, 232
McGillycuddy, Ross, 237
McGillycuddy, The, 222, 223, 244
McGuinness, William Bingham (artist), **228**, 229
McKenna, Kate, 240
Mackley, Alan, 149
McNeill, James, 186
Maes-y-Garnedd, Merioneth, 212
Maesmynan, Denbighshire, 211
Magill, Nora and Elizabeth, 222, 241
Magill, Stephen James, 222
Mallaghan family, 263
Mandler, Peter, 52, 129, 139, 162
Mann, Horace, 120
March, Lord and Lady, 44
Marjoribanks, Edward, 161–2
Marl, Conwy, 214–15
Marlow, William, 247
Martini, Giovanni Paolo, 123
Mary, Queen, 118, 183
Mason, William, 82
Matrimonial Causes Act, 69
Mavisbank House, Midlothian, 263, **263**
Menabilly, Cornwall, 19
Mentmore Towers, Buckinghamshire, 41
Menzies, Sir Robert, 21
Merdon Manor, Hampshire, 167, 169
Merton, Wales, 204
Middleton, Francis Willoughby, third Baron, 81
Mill House, Astwick, Bedfordshire, 168
Millais, Sir John Everett, *Eve of St Agnes, The*, **117**, 118
Miller, William, *Tunbridge Wells and its neighbourhood*, 119
Milligan, Alice, 186
Millwood Plantation, South Carolina, 28
Milton Abbey, Dorset, 15, **16**
Mitchelstown Castle, County Cork, 188–9
Moir, Esther, 138, 142
Montague, John, 190
moral economy, 98, 107, 112
Mordaunt Crook, Joseph, 157
More, Sir Thomas, *Utopia*, 118, 157
Morgan, J.P., 128
Morgan, Prys, 198
Moritz, Carl Philip, 148
Morris, John, 149

Morton, John, Cardinal, 118
Mostyn Hall, Flintshire, 201, 204, 205, **206**, 211, 218
Mostyn, Sir Pyers, 218
Mostyn, Thomas, 202
motor cars, 226, 254
Mount Stewart, County Down, 192
Mount Talbot, County Roscommon, 230
Mowl, Tim, and Earnshaw, Brian, 141
Muckross, County Kerry, **224**, 226, 235, 238, 243, 246
Murdoch, Iris, 185, **185**
Murray, George, 23
Murray, Gilbert, 39
Murray, John, 163
Murray, Hon. Sarah, 150, 153; *Companion, and useful guide*, 144
Musters, John, 42
Myddelton, John, 203, 216
Myddleton, Sir Thomas, 205
Mytton, John, 202

Nanytclywyd, Denbighshire, 204
Nash, Edward and Constance, 222–3
Nash, Joseph, 136; *Mansions of England in the olden times*, 117, 125, 126
National Trust, 49–50, 161, 174, 255; Country Houses Scheme, 117n3, 168, 255; Knole and, 117, 119, 129, 130, 133, 134, 135; Scotney Castle and, 159, 174, 175
National Trust Historic Houses and Collections, 136
Naworth Castle, Cumbria, 47, **48**
Neale, John Preston, *Views of seats*, 22, 117, 126, **248**, 249
Nerquis Hall, Flintshire, 200
Nesfield, William Eden, 262, **262**
New Hall, Worcestershire, 167
New House, Hampshire, 167
Newcastle, Henry Pelham-Clinton, 4th duke of, 42
Newcastle, Thomas Pelham-Clinton, 3rd duke of, 83
Newdigate, Lady Sophia, 75, 78n14
Newgate prison, **45**
Newham Paddock, Warwickshire, 43
Nichols, Arthur, 61
Nicholson, Harold, 133, 135
Nimmo, Lady Jane, 22

Norfolk, Edward Howard, 9th duke of, 83, 147
Norton, Caroline, 57, 59, 68–9; *English laws for women in the nineteenth century*, 69
Norton, Fletcher, 68
Norton, George Chapple, 68
Nostell Priory, Yorkshire, 15
Nottingham, 80–1, 82
Nottingham Castle, 42, 82
Nottingham County Hall, 82
Nuthall Temple, Nottinghamshire, 82

Oakpark, County Carlow, 178–9, 180
Oakpark, County Kerry, 236–7, 242
O'Connell, Sir Morgan Ross, 223
Oddington House, Gloucestershire, 168
Okeover Hall, Staffordshire, 23, 155
O'Neill, Con, 193
Onslow, Violet, Countess of, 33
Orlands, County Antrim, 49
Ormonde, James Butler, 3rd marquess of, 183
Orton, Arthur, 45, **45**
Ousby, Ian, 138, 139, 142
Owen, Sir John, 205
Owlpen Old Manor, Gloucestershire, 164–5, 166, 167, 168
owners, encounters with, 153–6

Paine, James (architect), 83, 85–6; *Plans, elevations and sections, of noblemen and gentlemen's houses*, 85, 93
Paine, Thomas, *rights of Man, The*, 24
Pantglas, Caernarfonshire, 217
Panton, Paul, 202, 203
Papworth, John (architect), 141
Park, The, Weston, 109
Parker, Pamela Corpron, 69
Parkins, Sir Thomas, 80
Parmentier, Jacques (artist), 85
paternalism, 111–14
Paulet family, 15, 16
Pavlova, Anna, 230–1
Paxton, Sir Joseph, 54, 56, 58, **58**, 59, 66, 72–3
Paxton, Sarah, 54, 59
Peak District, 76, 91–2, 95
Pell, Lieutenant General, 18
Penbedw, Flintshire, 216
Pengwern, Flintshire, 200, 217

Pennant, Thomas, 147, 247; Anglesey, country houses in, 203; 'antient' designation, 204, 219; architectural styles, 204–5; collieries, 218; country houses, ownership changes, 213–15; derelict mansions, 214–15; Downing estate, 205, 215–16, 218; estate landscapes, 215–17; estate management, 217; family background, 201–2, 209; *History of the parishes of Whiteford and Holywell*, 201, 203, 205, 217, 218; industrialization, 218; legends, 211; Montgomeryshire journeys, 203; North Wales, country houses in, 200, 204; *plas*, 196, 197, 198, 200–6; *plas*, cultural character of, 199–200; *plas*, portrayal of, 204–6, 219; *plastai*, significance of, 208, 209; questionnaire composed by, 202; squirearchal network, access to, 202; *Tour in Wales*, 11, 196–219, **197**, **212**; *Tour in Wales*, influence of, 219; tribal patriarchs, 209–11; *uchelwriaeth* (gentility), 203, 208; *uchelwyr* (gentry), 199, 201, 208, 209, 213; Welsh identity, ancestry and, 209
Penrhyn, Richard Pennant, 1st Baron, 218
Penryhn Castle, Wales, 41, 204, 205, 218
Penshurst Place, Kent, 48–9, 172, 174
Pentrehobyn, Flintshire, 200, 204
Pepita (dancer), 127, 128
Perier, Claude, 26–7
Perry, Captain, 44
Peterson, Linda H., 71–2
Petworth, Sussex, 187, 255
Peveril Castle, Derbyshire, 91
Pevsner, Nikolaus; *Buildings of England* series, 80n34, 172; Reith Lectures for the BBC, 172
Phillips, Mary, 96, 113
Piper, John (artist), 132, **133**
Plas Gwyn, Anglesey, 203
Plas Newydd, Anglesea, 108, 204, 205, 217, 218
Plas Teg, Flintshire, 200, 204, 205
Pless Castle, Silesia, 34
Pless, Hans Heinrich Hochberg, prince of, 34
Plumptre, Revd James, 92, 141, 145, 147, 148, 153, 155

Index

poachers, 43–4
Pole, Archbishop Cardinal, 118
political/civil protests, 42–3
Pond, Cornelia Jones, 30
Poor Law Amendment Act (1834), 97
Poor Laws, 97, 99
Pope, Alexander, 140
Portarlington, Earls of, 178, 184, 189–90
Portarlington, Henry Dawson-Damer, 3rd earl of, 189–90
Portland, William Cavendish-Bentinck, 3rd duke of, 83
Postgate, Raymond, 168
Potocki, Alfred, 35
Potocki family, 35
Potterton, Homan, 177
poverty/the poor; deservingness of the poor, 112; famine and, 99, 100, 105; perception of the poor, 107; rural poverty, 97–8; *see also* soup kitchens
POW camps, 32–3, **33**, 41
Powderham Castle, Devon, 47
Powell, Stocks, 184
Power, Noel and Sylvia, 235
Power, Robert Henry, 229
Powerscourt, County Wicklow, 50
Powis Castle, 174, 204, 205
Powys, Caroline Lybbe, 75, 153
Poynton Hall, Cheshire, 153
Presaddfed, Anglesey, 210
pretenders, 45
Price, Uvedale, 215
primogeniture, 27
Pryce family, 210–11
Pryor family, 108–9
Pulteney, General Sir William, 31
Purdue, Olwen, 243
Putnam, George, 191

Quarterly Review, 163
Queensberry, James Douglas, 2nd duke of, 23

Raby Castle, County Durham, 155
railways, 52, 225, **250**, 252, 254
Rake Manor, Surrey, 168
Rangemore Hall, Staffordshire, **109**, 110–11, **110**
Rasmussen, Steen Eiler, *Experiencing architecture*, 157

Rattoo Abbey, County Kerry, 237, 243, 246
Rawthorne, Colonel, 18
Ray, I., 134
Rayners, Buckinghamshire, 101
Redbraes, Berwickshire, 22
Reeks, The, County Kerry, 222, 237, 242, 244, 246
Rees, Goronwy, 193–4
Reform Bill riots (1831), 42
Renishaw Hall, Derbyshire, 169
Repton, Humphrey, 215; *Sketches and hints on landscape gardening*, **151**, 152
Revelstoke, Rupert Baring, 4th Baron, 166
Reynolds, Joshua, 44, 88, 116, 120, 121–2, 128–9
Rhual, Flintshire, 200
Rich, Richard, 15
Richards, Sir Henry Erle, 231
Ritchie, Charles, 193
Robert, Hubert, *Demolition of the Château of Meudon*, 26, **26**
Roberts, Peter, 199
Robertson, Charlotte, 23
Robinson, Lennox, 187; *Big House, The*, 177, 179, 186
Roche Abbey, Yorkshire, 86
Rockingham, Mary Watson-Wentworth, marchioness of, 90
Rodd, Peter and Nancy, 168
Rodin, Auguste, 129
Ronnes, Hannecke, 138, 142, 149
Rooker, Michael Angelo, 126
Rosalie Mansion, Natchez, 29
Rose, Lady, 101
Rose, Sir Philip, 112
Rosée, Baroness, 36
Ross, Walter, 148
Rossbeigh, County Kerry, 237
Rossdohan, County Kerry, 240
Rosse, Countess of, 180
Rosselli, Agrippino, 123
Rothschild family, 111
Roxburghe, Duke of, 44
Royal Academy, 77, 78, 85, 122, 130
Royal Irish Constabulary (RIC), 232, 233, 236, 237
Royal Oak Foundation, 135
Royal School of Needlework, 134
Rufford Abbey, Nottinghamshire, 82
Rumford, Count, 100

Ruskin, John, *stones of Venice, The*, 157
Ruth, George, 242, **242**
Ruth, May (*née* Leeson Marshall), **242**, 246

Sackville family, 10, 117–18, 121–3, 126, 127, 132, 136
Sackville, Charles Sackville-West, 4th Baron, 132, 133
Sackville, Edward Sackville-West, 5th Baron, 130, 134; *see also* Sackville-West, Eddy
Sackville, Lionel Bertrand Sackville-West, 6th Baron, 135
Sackville, Lionel Sackville-West, 2nd Baron, 127
Sackville, Lionel Sackville-West, 3rd Baron, 127, 128
Sackville, Mary and Elizabeth, 123, 126
Sackville, Mortimer Sackville-West, first Baron, 127
Sackville, Robert Bertrand Sackville-West, 7th Baron, 117
Sackville, Sir Thomas, 118
Sackville-West, Anne (*née* Bigelow), 132
Sackville-West, Major General Sir Charles, 132
Sackville-West, Eddy, 119, 132, 136, 177, 178; *Ruin*, 130, 132
Sackville-West, Elizabeth, 126
Sackville-West, Henry, 127
Sackville-West, Victoria, 127–8, 129
Sackville-West, Vita, 116, 119, 129, 130, 132; *Edwardians, The*, 129; *English country houses*, 157; guidebook to Knole, 134; *Knole and the Sackvilles*, 130; Sissinghurst and, 134–5
St Bernard's House, Edinburgh, 148
St Donat's Castle, Wales, 190
Salusbury family, 213, 214
Sandbeck Park, Yorkshire, 85, 86, 143
Sandby, Paul (artist), 75, 86, 88, 117, 125, 247
Sandby, Thomas (architect), 10, 75–95; Bunny Hall, 80; Burghley Hall, admiration for, 93–4, 95; Chatsworth House, assessment of, 92; Devil's Hole, assessment of, 91; Harewood House, 86, 87–8; Kedleston Hall, views on, 92–3; Royal Academy lectures, 78; Thoresby Hall, 10, 82–3; 'Tour into Derbyshire, A', 76, 77–95; Wentworth Woodhouse, 10, **76**, 89–91, **89**, 95; Wollaton Hall, 81, 82, 95; Worksop Manor, 83–5, **84**, 95
Savile, Sir George, 82
Saville, Sir Charles, 82
Scarsdale, Nathaniel Curzon, 1st Baron, 93
Scattergood, John, 92, 155
Sceaux, Paris, 26, 261
Scharff, George, 249
Scotney Castle, 11, 157, **160**, 175; archives, 159, **159**, 161; article in *Country Life*, 162; inherited by Hussey, 159–60; National Trust and, 159, 174, 175; study, 157, **158**
Scott, George Gilbert (architect), 143
Scott, Gertrude, 229, 244
Scott, John Murray, 129
Scott, Lady, 60
Scott, Sir Peter, 186
Scott, Sir Walter, 60
Seaton Delaval, Northumberland, 50
Seaton House, Aberdeenshire, 261
Second World War (1939–45), 41–2
Seeley, J., *Stowe: a description of the house and gardens*, 102
Sequestration Ordinance (1643), 20–1
servants; encounters with, 153–6; tips and, 137, 150
Shakespeare's New Place, 140
Sheehan, Canon Patrick, 186
Sheen Falls, County Kerry, 243
Sheridan, Richard Brinsley, 68, 122
Sherman, William, 28, 30, 260
Shillinglee, Surrey, 44
Shirburn Castle, Oxfordshire, 149
Shireburn, Yorkshire, 261
Siberechts, Jan, 247
Sidney, Sir Philip, 174
Sillahertane, County Kerry, **224**, 226, 230
Simpson, Wallis and Ernest, 132
Sissinghurst, Kent, 134–5
Sitwell, Osbert, 169
Sizergh Hall, Westmoreland, 153
slavery, 218
Sledmere, Yorkshire, 173
Sligo, Howe Peter Browne, 2nd marquess of, 46
Smith, George (publisher), 60
Smith-Dorrien, Lady, 134

Index 281

Smyth, Ethel, 235
Smythson, Robert (architect), 81
Soane, Sir John, 147–8, 158
Society of Artists of Great Britain (SAGB), 77, 78, 85
Society for the Protection of Ancient Buildings, 168
Somerville family, 188
Sondes, Sir George, 20
soup kitchens, 10, 96–7, 99–100; Axwell Park, 108; Cresswell Hall, 108; Druid's Lodge, 108; location of, **109**; payment and, 113; Plas Newydd House, 108; Rangemore Hall, **109**, 110–11, **110**; Rayners, 101; soup recipes, 99, 100, 114; Stowe House, 96, 100–5; Surrenden House, 108; Thornton Hall, 108, **109**; Trentham Hall, 96, 105–7, **109**; urban, 113; in villages, 111, 112; Weston Manor, 108–9, **109**, 113; Whitburn Hall, 108; White House, 108
Spencer, Lady Georgiana, 100
Spencer, Nathaniel, *complete English traveller, The*, 91
Stackpole Court, Pembrokeshire, 168
Staffordshire Advertiser, 148–9
Staffordshire Gazette, 96
Stamford, Lady, 33
Standsted Hall, Essex, 167
Staunton Harold, Leicestershire, 144
Stevens, Ann, 146
Stinsford House, Dorset, 44
Stobart, Jon, 198, 219
Stoke Edith Park, Hereford, 168, 169
Stoke Rochford, Lincolnshire, 166
Stone, Marcus, *Stealing the keys*, 130
Stoughton, Rose Trent, 232
Stowe House, Buckinghamshire, 96, 100–5, 139; Boycott Pavilions, 101; Dairy Court, **102**, 103; duke's birthday celebrations, 104; gardens, 140; soup kitchen, 96, 101, **102**, 103–4; supper for poor children, 104; tenants' ball, 104; west wing, **102**; Yuletide, the poor and, 100–1
Stowe parish, 100, 105
Strachey, Nino, 136
Strafford, Thomas Wentworth, 1st Earl, 89, 147
Stratford-upon-Avon, 140

Strawberry Hill, Twickenham, 120–1, 137–8, 139, 140
Stroud, Dorothy, 157–8, **159**, 161
Stuart, Charles Edward (Young Pretender), 21–3
Stuart, Lady Louisa, 141
Sudeley Castle, Gloucestershire, 167
suffragettes, 48–9
Sullivan, Richard, 83, 145, 146
Summerson, John, 193
Surget family, 28–9
Surrenden House, Kent, 108
Sutherland, George Granville Sutherland-Leveson-Gower, 2nd duke of, 96
Sutherland, Graham, 136
Sweet, Rosemary, 149

Tait McKenzie, R. (sculptor), 160, **160**, 160n3
Talbot, William John and Julia, 230
Talman, William (architect), 92
Tanavalla, County Kerry, 236
Tapton Colliery, 54, 55
Teck, Francis von Hohenstein, duke of, 183
Temple Newsam, Yorkshire, 43, 154
Tennyson, Alfred, Baron, *In memoriam*, 71
Thackeray, William, *Vanity fair*, 65–6
Thanet, John Tufton, 2nd earl of, 20
Thelwall, Sir Eubule, 213
Thompson, F.M.L., 177
Thoresby Hall, Nottinghamshire, 10, 82–3, 147
Thornton Hall, Buckinghamshire, 108, **109**
Thring, Sir Arthur, 231
Tichborne Park, Hampshire, 45
Tides Reach Hotel, Devon, 167
Tillemans, Peter, 247
Tinniswood, Adrian, 138, 140, 225
Torksey, Lincolnshire, 19
tourism, 245–6, 254; Covid pandemic and, 13; domestic tourism, 75, 138; heritage tourism, 256–8; infrastructure, 255–6
Tower, Mold, Flintshire, 200, 211, **212**
Tregonwell, John, 15, **16**
Trent Park, Middlesex, 41
Trentham Bible Class, 105
Trentham Hall, Poor's Lodge, 96, 105–7, **106**, **109**
Trevor, Sir John, 205

Trevor, William, 194
Trollope, Anthony, *Castle Richmond*, 188–9
Troubles, the, 224, 241, 245
Tudor England, 15–16
Turner, Joseph (architect), 204–5
Tyler, William (sculptor-architect), 77, 79, 85

Uffington House, Lincolnshire, 48
Uppark House, Sussex, 49, 171, 174
urban sprawl, effects of, 13

Valewood Farm, Surrey, 164, 167
Van Dyck, Anthony, 85, 120
van Heemstra, Baroness, 40
van Steen, Countess, 36
Vaughan, William, 203
Vevay House, Bray, County Wicklow, 187, 194
Vicars, Sir Arthur, 235
viceregal court, 230
Vickery, Amanda, 150
Victoria and Albert Museum, 134
Victoria, Queen, 67, 127, **250**, 251–2, *251*
Villiers Stuart, Mary (*née* Power), 229
Vincks family, 37–8
Virginia Water, 75
visitors; access, opening hours and, 145–7, **253**; admittance, refusal of, 137, 138, 141, 143, 149–50, 154–5, 255; attitudes towards, 137–8, 140, 253–4, 255; barriers to admission, 147–50; behaviour of, 140; carbon footprint and, 260; interiors, impact of, 144; misinformation and, 148–9; needs of, 153; physical barriers/impediments, 150–3; regulations for visits, **253**; servants, tips to, 137, 150; social media and, 259; as source of revenue, 257; specialist visitors, 249; virtual visitors, 258–9; *see also* guests
visitors' books, 11, 55, 128, 181, 187, 258; Callinafercy House, 12, 222, 225, 231, 234, 238; Emo Court, **182**, 184, 187, 194; Glaslough, 179, 184, 185, 187, 188, 194; Oakpark, 178–9, 180
Vitruvius Britannicus, 78, 82, 87
von Bodt, Johann (architect), 89
von Richthofen, Manfred (Red Baron), 38

Waagen, Gustav, 154, 249
Waldegrave, Lady, 140
Waldegrave, Maria, Countess, 83
Wales, 152; *gwerin* community, 199; historical and cultural revival, 198–9; national consciousness, 11; *plas/plastai* (country houses), 196, 197, 198, 199–206, 219; *uchelwriaeth* (gentility), 203, 208; *uchelwyr* (gentry), 199, 201, 208, 209, 213; Welsh genealogy, 209–10; Ystrad Alun, 200
Wallace Collection, 129
Walpole, Horace, 10, 94, 119–20, 123; *Description of Strawberry Hill*, 120, 137; Strawberry Hill and, 140; visitors, attitude towards, 137
War of Independence, 11–12, 49, 232, 233, 235–7
War of the Roses, 211
Warden, Charles, 230, 233, 242
Warnaffe, Monsieur, 35
Warner, Francis, 188
Warwick Castle, 46, 155
Warwick, Daisy Greville, countess of, 128
Warwick Hall, Cumbria, 23
Waterford, John Beresford, 5th marquess of, 183, 184
Waters, Sarah, *little stranger, The*, 46
Waterville, County Kerry, 226, 246
Watney, Lady Margaret (*née* Wallop), 231
Watney, Vernon John, 231
Waugh, Evelyn, *Brideshead revisited*, 258, **259**
Webster, Sir Godfrey, 153
Welbeck Abbey, Nottinghamshire, 83, 147
Wellington, Gerald Wellesley, 7th duke of, 174–5
Wentworth Castle, Yorkshire, 88–9, 90, 91, 147
Wentworth Woodhouse, 10, **76**, 89–91, **89**, 95, 154
Weret family, 38
West, Mary Cornwallis (princess of Pless), 34–5
Westminster Review, 71
Weston Manor, Hertfordshire, 108–1, **109**, 113
Wheeler-Cuffe, Otway and Charlotte, 244
Whitburn Hall, Durham, 108
White House, Wrekenton, 108

Index

White Lion, Nottingham, 80
Whitley Abbey, Warwickshire, 261
Wigfair, St Asaph, 211
Wilhelm II, Kaiser, 40, **40**
Wilhelmina, Queen, 40
Willersley Castle, Derbyshire, 145
William III, King, 23, 121
Williams, John, 200
Williams, Revd Richard, 200, 202
Williams, Sir William, 214
Williams-Ellis, Clough, *England and the octopus*, 157
Williamson, Lady, 108
Willis, H.N., 124
Wilson, Frank, 186, 188, **188**
Wilson, Richard, 149
Wimpole Hall, Cambridgeshire, 154–5, 169
Winchelsea, George William Finch-Hatton, 10th earl of, 107
Winchester, John Paulet, 5th marquess of, 16–17
Windsor Great Park, 75
Winterton, Edward Turnour, 6th Earl, 44
Witley Court, Worcestershire, 50
Woburn Abbey, Bedfordshire, 172–3, **253**
Wollaton Hall, Nottingham, 81, 82, 95, **142**, 143, 155
Woodward, George, 143

Wool House, Kent, 255
Woolf, Virginia, 119, 130, 132, 190; *Orlando*, 130
Woolfe, John, 82
Worksop Manor, Nottinghamshire, 83–5, **84**, 95, 147, 153
Worksop Priory, Nottinghamshire, 83
Wren, Sir Christopher, 79
Wrest Park, Bedfordshire, 173
Wroxton Abbey, Oxfordshire, 149
Wyatt, Samuel (architect), 205
Wyattville, Sir Jeffry (architect), 52
Wyndham Land Act, 220
Wynn, Sir John, 205–6
Wynn, Sir Watkin Williams, 213
Wynne, Elizabeth (*later* Betsy Fremantle) (diarist), 101, 104
Wynne, John, 200
Wynne, William, 200, 209, **212**
Wynnstay, Wales, 204, 205, 216

Yeats, Willam Butler, 186
York female prison, 143–4, **144**
Yorke, Philip, 75, 83, 92, 202, 209
Young, Arthur, 75, 84, 90, 150, 153

Zetland, Lawrence Dundas, 1st marquess of, 43